T0290624

The Museum Manager's Compendium

The Museum Manager's Compendium

101 Essential Tools and Resources

John W. Jacobsen

with Victor A. Becker, Duane Kocik, and Jeanie Stahl

ROWMAN & LITTLEFIELD
Lanham • Boulder • New York • London

Published by Rowman & Littlefield
A wholly owned subsidiary of The Rowman & Littlefield Publishing Group, Inc.
4501 Forbes Boulevard, Suite 200, Lanham, Maryland 20706
www.rowman.com

Unit A, Whitacre Mews, 26-34 Stannary Street, London SE11 4AB

Copyright © 2017 by John W. Jacobsen. All rights reserved. This book and its 101 resources are protected by copyright. In some cases, work by others is further protected by the original authors and is used here with their permission. Nothing in this book may be reproduced for public or commercial use without the author's permission. However, everything in this book may be copied or adapted for internal use within a museum or museum service organization.

Reprint Acknowledgments

In addition to the sections written by the author and contributing authors, some sections are based on work done earlier by some White Oak associates as part of museum planning commissions.

Adaptation permissions have been given by Mary Jane Dodge (Marketing), Chuck Howarth (Discovery Centers), Bill Peters (Governance), Mark B. Peterson (Quality Visitor Experience), Richard Rabinowitz (Collection Use), Mac West (the Museum Experience), and Crystal Willie (Collection Policy).

The following have given reprint permissions for their published work: ANSI for the ISO (ISO Museum Categories), Minda Borun (Family Learning), David Ellis (Branding), John Falk and Lynn Dierking (The Museum Experience, Identity, Where to Excel, 95% Solution), George Hein (Theories of Knowledge and Learning), Morris Hargreaves McIntyre (Culture Segments), Westat (NSF AISL Evaluation Framework), and Pelle Persson (Use of KPIs). The Logic Model is from the W. K. Kellogg Foundation, Logic Model Development Guide (2004), and is used with their permission. The listing of types of museums and financial data are used with the permission of the American Alliance of Museums. The Association of Science-Technology Centers has permitted the use of their data. The Museum Theory of Action, the Categories of Potential Museum Impacts, the Audience and Supporter Map, and other tables developed by the White Oak Institute are used with their permission, although they are free for all to use.

All rights reserved. No part of this book may be reproduced in any form or by any electronic or mechanical means, including information storage and retrieval systems, without written permission from the publisher, except by a reviewer who may quote passages in a review.

British Library Cataloguing in Publication Information Available

Library of Congress Cataloging-in-Publication Data

Names: Jacobsen, John W., author.
Title: The museum manager's compendium : 101 essential tools and resources /
   John W. Jacobsen.
Description: Lanham : ROWMAN & LITTLEFIELD, 2017. | Includes bibliographical
   references and index.
Identifiers: LCCN 2016058823 (print) | LCCN 2017002340 (ebook) | ISBN
   9781442271371 (cloth) | ISBN 9781442271395 (ebook)
Subjects: LCSH: Museums—Management. | Museums—Planning.
Classification: LCC AM121 .J33 2017 (print) | LCC AM121 (ebook) | DDC
   069/.068—dc23
LC record available at https://lccn.loc.gov/2016058823

♾™ The paper used in this publication meets the minimum requirements of American National Standard for Information Sciences—Permanence of Paper for Printed Library Materials, ANSI/NISO Z39.48-1992.

Printed in the United States of America

ACCESS TO MIIP 1.0 AND THE MUSEUM THEORY OF ACTION

MIIP 1.0, an Excel database of 1,025 potential museum indicators of impact and performance drawn from fifty-one expert sources, was developed under the author's management by the White Oak Institute, a nonprofit museum research initiative. MIIP 1.0 and the Museum Theory of Action diagram are available to all for free independent of this book's publication. To access copies, go to http://www.whiteoakassoc.com/library.html.

The MIIP database is read-only so that the original version remains intact online; however, you can rename and save the file with your initials and go to work adapting it to your needs offline.

While access to MIIP 1.0 is free, you do not get any rights to the indicators, especially not commercial rights. You may need to obtain rights to use some of the indicators if you want to publish any source's collection of indicators. You should contact the sources directly.

This book is dedicated to White Oak's many clients and associates. Over four fruitful decades of collaboration, you researched and implemented innovative museum forms, community services, public components, analysis tools, and planning formats.

To our associates, you were always the best museum professionals we could find to add expertise to our planning teams. To our museum clients, you were visionary leaders, inspiring the best from our teams.

Both of you contributed the heart and soul of the resources in this book. All of us share our love of museums and gratitude for the great gift of riding the Museum Boom together. Thank you!

Contents

List of Tables

Acknowledgments

The Museum Manager's Compendium: 101 Essential Tools and Resources draws from White Oak Associates' analysis, planning, and production work over four decades in the museum field. One of the joys of our projects has been collaborating with clients, associates, and colleagues. This collection of essential decision and planning resources is intellectually indebted to them.

The contributing authors provided important tools among the 101 resources, and I am first grateful to Victor A. Becker, Duane Kocik, and Jeanie Stahl for the sections they wrote and for their perspectives on the book as a whole. They are credited in their sections at the end of each introduction. Victor, White Oak's director of program development, wrote all the sections on his specialty—museum architecture, building, and site. Jeanie, vice president of White Oak, wrote all sections relating to museum finance, attendance, and market analysis and co-wrote operations sections with Duane, another longtime associate, who handled museum staffing and budgets. For decades, Jeanie, Victor, and Duane have provided their expertise and sound judgment to White Oak's planning, and I am beholden to their dedication and quality standards. Thank you for your active involvement in writing and shaping this book and for passing along your expertise to the future—and thank you for the friendship and support.

This book is indebted to many other White Oak associates who developed parts of our master plans that evolved over the years into many of these 101 tools and resources. Sections based on their planning work include those by Dave Chittenden (Education), Mary Jane Dodge (Marketing), Chuck Howarth (Discovery Centers), Bill Peters (Governance), Mark B. Peterson (Quality Visitor Experience), Richard Rabinowitz (Collection Use), Mac West (the Museum Experience), and Crystal Willie (Collection Policy).

In our wonderfully collaborative field, many collegial friendships have shaped my thinking. Some colleagues' ideas appear directly in this book, including Minda Borun (Family Learning), David Ellis (Branding), John Falk and Lynn Dierking (The Museum Experience, Identity), George Hein (Theories of Knowledge and Learning), Pelle Persson (Use of Key Performance Indicators), and Roy Shafer and Mary Sellers (Core Ideology).

Other articulate museum writers and thinkers have influenced my thinking and informed White Oak's museum analysis and planning. I have learned from all who write and speak out thoughtfully about museum purposes and values, and I am particularly grateful to those who have personally commented on my evolving thinking. White Oak's other team members and clients have also shaped this framework over decades and over hundreds of museum analysis and planning projects. One of the many pleasures of this work is to collaborate with great minds and museum leaders, including all those mentioned above plus Tom Aageson, Phil Aldrich, Joe Ansel, Ted Ansbacher, Ron Baillie, Gail Becker, Ford Bell, Jaime Bell, Larry Bell, Kate Bennett, Chuck Bentz, Andre Bilodeau, Ann Bitter, Bill Booth, Carol Bossert, Lois Brynes, Lou Casagrande, Kim Cavendish, Chris Chadbourne, Lisa Collins, Rich Conti, Mickey Culver, Tim Curnen, Mike Day, Al DeSena, Anne D. Emerson, Claude Faubert, Mike Fawcett, Chad Floyd, Ron Forman, John Fraser, Sarah George, Peter Giles, Norm Glouberman, Sheila Grinell, Elaine Gurian, Jo Haas, Alf Hatton, Marilyn Hoyt, Kim Hunter, James Hyder, Bob Janes, Linda K. Johnson, Lynda Kaplan, Phil Katz, Jeff Kennedy, Jeff Kirsch, Al Klyberg, Emlyn Koster, Eli Kuslansky, Peter Kuttner, Wayne LaBar, Ed Lantz, Betsy Leichliter, Peter Linett, Greg MacGillivray, John Mackay, Mary Maher, Art Manask, Ian McLennan, Toby Mensforth, Beth Merritt, Ann Mintz, Joe Moore, George Moynihan, David Mugar, Mary Ellen Munley, Al Najar, Tengku Nasariah, Freda Nicholson, Wit Ostrenko, Berred Ouellette, Jim Peterson, Wendy Pollock, Gigi Priebe, Fern Proulx, Barbara Punt, Christine Reich, Janet Rice Elman, Steve Rich, Jim Richerson, Laura B. Roberts, Brent Robinson, Steve Rosen, Christine Ruffo, Madlyn Runburg, Bob Russell, Moshe Safdie, Jean Saint-Cyr, Dennis Schatz, Kate Schureman, Carol

Scott, Marsha Semmel, Beverly Sheppard, Eric Siegel, Nina Simon, Mary Davis Smart, George Smith, Jack Spoehr, Mark St. John, Peter Sterling, Martin Storksdieck, Sarah Sutton, Charlie Trautmann, Bonnie VanDorn, Jeanne Vergeront, Sandy Welch, Tim Willis, Dennis Wint, Joseph Wisne, and Elizabeth Wylie.

I caught my love for museums from four museum mentors who may be gone but certainly are not forgotten: Roger Nichols, the director of the Museum of Science and my boss during one of the Museum's most vibrant and successful eras; Roy Shafer, the museum director who went on to coach museums to develop their "conceptual frameworks"; Alan Friedman, the committed museum educator who led by the example of his principled character and brilliance; and Stephen Weil, whose writings underlie all contemporary assumptions about museums and their value and whose thinking weaves throughout this book.

Thank you, colleagues—your guidance and insight were very helpful. Thanks also to Charles Harmon, Kathleen O'Brien, and Elaine McGarraugh for their editorial and publication support.

Special acknowledgments go to Karen Hefler of White Oak Associates for her painstaking dedication to producing the manuscript and its tables and worksheets, to Rebecca Robison for her patient assembly of these materials, and to my partner in everything, Jeanie Stahl, for her guidance and support.

Preface

WHY THIS BOOK? WHY NOW?

What have we learned over the past half a century? What resources has the museum field developed to help you, as a fellow museum manager, make and implement decisions? How do you get hold of those resources?

In the past 50 years, the museum field has more than doubled internationally, increased per capita visits, formed museum associations, founded affinity groups, published shelves of books, launched museum studies programs, established standards, convened conferences at all scales and geographies, and accumulated volumes of data. We have advanced museums.

Yet we have to document, communicate, and share those advances before the museum field can share widely used metrics and standards as do more mature professions. We need to manage museums informed by what we have learned over the past half a century and inspired by what we can add to the future.

This book, The *Museum Manager's Compendium: 101 Essential Resources and Tools*, begins to address that lack. The 101 sections present definitions, processes, menus, samples, and categories in major areas of museum management. Collectively, they reflect the literature and contributions of some of the field's best thinkers as well as the authors' decades of experience developing and using these field-tested resources.

The U.S. Museum Boom, from the early 1980s to 2008, was an explosion of new forms of museums fueled by the investment of billions of dollars in museum expansions and new facilities. For the museum planners, architects, designers, and managers lucky enough to ride the wave, it was like being a painter in Paris during the Belle Époque or a writer in Boston in the 1840s.

Add to this activity and cash flow the collaborative nature of museum colleagues, and we had the perfect conditions for rapid evolution and creative progress. Museum professionals collaborated globally during the Museum Boom, exchanging ideas and sharing innovations. Together, we invented advances for museums that moved the field forward: new services, new audiences, and new methods; new materials and new standards; new ways of thinking and evaluating; new choices; new impacts and new benefits; and, of course, new kinds of museums.

This book has the collected and distilled resources that our team at White Oak Associates developed over decades of projects with scores of talents and experts internationally.

HOW TO USE THIS BOOK

How does your museum make decisions? Strategically or opportunistically? Thoughtfully or intuitively? Informed by data or by road savvy? And how do *you* make decisions?

The *Museum Manager's Compendium* will help you and your museum make and implement decisions. The book contains 101 resources covering many aspects of museum practice, organized alphabetically so that you can find them easily. The index and the list of tables are also helpful, along with the cross-references in the text. The 101 resources include the following:

Descriptions, briefings, and theories
Menus of the main options in key areas
Diagrams and planning templates
Bibliography for citations and references
Implementation processes
Planning worksheets
Checklists and reminders
Floor plans and adjacency diagrams
Data tables and statistical charts
Calculations, formulas, and key performance indicators
Categories and frameworks
Policy drafts
Concepts and strategies
Definitions
Budgets and financial reports
Decision templates
Examples from sample museums
Ways of thinking about complex issues

This is a reference book to use, not a narrative to read cover to cover. You can adapt the text and images to your museum's context (search and replace "museum" and "XX"). Italic text is addressed to you as helpful hints, use instructions, cross-references, and authorship. Some sections can be read as briefings on a topic. For example, if you want Falk and Dierking's Museum Experience Model, you will find it in "33. Education: Learning Theory" with their diagram, a page or two of explanation, and two blank worksheets for you to think about your visitors' personal and sociocultural contexts. Or if you need to write a request for proposals to select an exhibit designer, you can adapt the steps outlined in "1. Architect Search Process" and add selected specifications from "98. Visitor Experience: Concepts." Or you can browse through the 101 sections for new ideas and insights. You can adapt any diagrams or text for internal use to share with board members, partners, contractors, and staff.

With the exception of the sections covering definitions, most resources start with an introduction that summarizes what is in the resource and how to use it. Some sections end with open planning worksheets for you to try out different scenarios. All citation references are in "15. Bibliography for Museums."

Several sections are menus of possible choices that a museum might consider. The descriptions and outlines can be adapted to insert into preliminary concept designs and cost estimates. Others are processes that can be adapted into scopes of work for staff and contractors.

Most of these descriptions are written in "future positive," that is, that your museum will have [the following text]. These blocks of text in future positive are meant to be inserted into a plan for the future, describing what the future museum will be like after it is finished and open to the public. Consider the following example of a planning plank that you might adapt into your museum's future programming plan:

"Each Family Sunday will be cosponsored by a different community organization (the police, the Elks, the local hospitals, etc.) in return for getting their messages out and the chance to do some fund-raising."

If the gist of this seems right, you should ask the following questions as you adapt it:

1. Should we call it "Family Sunday"?
2. Do we have Elks? And are there better, more local examples?
3. Does our museum policy permit others to raise money on-site?
4. How do we make sure their message aligns with the museum's brand?
5. Is the verb tense right? Instead of *will*, should we use *could* or *might*?

Of course, this book is not complete. Neither the 101 sections nor the individual menus claim to be comprehensive. The systems of categories, on the other hand, are intended to cover their full territory; while you may imagine a new category, chances are good that it will fall underneath or within one of the larger fields.

HOW CAN THIS BOOK HELP ME?

You can use *The Museum Manager's Compendium* in many ways:

- As a frequent reference book to consult when facing decisions or planning for the future
- As a source of images, choices, and diagrams to use in presentations and discussions
- As a crib book to extract text when drafting internal proposals and plans
- As a primer when welcoming new partners and board members
- As a quick study and refresher of key aspects of museum practice
- As an orientation to new staff
- As a source of examples and templates of common museum reports
- As a source of answers to strategic planning questions, such as these:
    - What is the big picture of the museum field as a whole?
    - How do we find out what our community needs are?
    - How do we relate to our audiences and supporters?
    - Why do we exist? Which purposes are most important?
    - What observable and measurable impacts should result from our actions?
    - What do we have? What are our holdings and strengths?
    - How should we think about, use, and care for collections?
    - What components might interest potential funders?
    - How should we approach architecture?
    - Do we have resources that could be generating greater returns in impact or income?
    - What long-term infrastructure do we need to operate efficiently and effectively?
    - How can we think about programming the museum? What are our daily, weekly, monthly, and yearly offerings?
    - How do we select the best programs to feature?
    - Can we get more use from some of our spaces and resources?
    - How might we organize our staff? What benefits might we offer?
    - How do we budget?
    - What should we charge to whom and for what?
    - What is our peak capacity? How many cars is that?
    - How do we strategize marketing and membership?
    - What benefits do audiences want?
    - How do we evidence changes in our impact, performance, and value?
    - What is our market? What are its size and character?
    - What is our potential attendance?
    - How are we doing compared to our peers?
    - What public spaces do we have? How easy is it to change their content?
    - How do we organize and schedule a capital project?
    - What are typical capital project implementation phases and benchmarks?
    - How do we plan an operationally effective and efficient building?
    - How do we tell architects what we want?
    - How do we budget a project? What categories of costs should we consider?

BACKGROUND

This book is the conclusion of a logical sequence for this museum professional, who was lucky enough to be aboard for the Museum Boom. Many years and steps led to this book:

1. Almost 50 years of experience with hundreds of museum analysis and master planning commissions in many disciplines and sizes helped me understand what was different and what was common among diverse museums. This experience also deepened my love of museums for their rich variety and honorable values.
2. In 2009, I challenged museum managers and museum evaluators to work together to find a way to evaluate museums as whole institutions in "A Research Vision for Museums," my address at the annual CARE luncheon of the American Association of Museums, later published in *Curator* (Jacobsen, 2010b).
3. In 2014, I wrote "The Community Service Museum: Owning Up to Our Multiple Missions." This academic article made the case that many museums were contributing additional values beyond their stated missions and were operating as multimission museums. It was published in the peer-reviewed *Journal of Museum Management and Curatorship* (Jacobsen, 2014).
4. In 2016, I brought together years of researching indicators and their use with my study of evaluation frameworks in *Measuring Museum Impact and Performance: Theory and Practice*, published by Rowman & Littlefield. This book developed a taxonomy

of impacts, a glossary of terms, and a shared museum theory of action, along with ways museums can use them to self-evaluate (Jacobsen, 2016).

5. In 2017, with the help of colleagues, I assembled *The Museum Manager's Compendium: 101 Essential Resources and Tools*, the book you are reading. This process filtered our almost five decades of learning through the aspirations and frameworks developed in the sequence of publications into a consistent view of museum management aligned to the taxonomy, glossary, and theory of action (Jacobsen, 2017).

CAVEATS AND CAUTIONS

This book and its 101 resources are protected by copyright. In some cases, work by others is further protected by the original authors and is used here with their permission. Nothing in this book may be reproduced for public or commercial use without the author's permission. However, everything in this book may be copied or adapted for *internal* use within a museum or museum service organization.

The numbers used in the tables are only to illustrate the mathematics and formulas among the columns. *Do not use* these numbers in your assumptions; rather, research and develop your own numbers, particularly dollar and population numbers, which will change from these samples. Some tables reflect judgment calls; those are for illustration only and are not to be applied to your context and time. These are sample judgment calls, and the authors make no assertion that they are the right call for your museum.

These sample frameworks and templates are intended to be adapted by individual museums and modified to their contexts, as policies and procedures may vary based on state laws, museum size and sector, organizational culture, and other factors. The frameworks in this book should not be considered legal or accounting advice and do not reflect state laws and regulations. Any use of these frameworks should be reviewed by legal and/or accounting counsel for compliance with local laws and regulations.

Some resources were developed for or are particularly apt for science-oriented museums, such as science centers, natural history museums, zoos, and some children's museums. In most cases, these discipline references can be adapted to history, art, and culture museums.

CONCLUSION

You hold the distillation of half a century of museum experience. I hope it is helpful in making and implementing your decisions as a museum manager and in strategic planning. However, we need to continue advancing the museum field. As you read and use this book, your job is to improve and add to these resources, with humility and respect for the work of your colleagues in the past.

Now, step back from the fray for a moment to imagine your ideal museum. Look to the future. What will success look like in 10 years? This book helps you make key policy choices about where you want to go. Once you know that, you can lead the way out of the fray.

See "15. Bibliography for Museums" for citation references.

Introduction

Museums provide services to their communities, audiences and supporters. Museum sage and writer Stephen Weil (2002) observed that "museums can provide forms of public service that are all but infinite in their variety."

The Guggenheim Museum in Bilbao, Spain, attracts tourists. The British Museum cares for civilization's treasures. The Texas State History Museum tells their story. The Yad Vashem Holocaust History Museum (Jerusalem, Israel) establishes a global symbol. The Monterey Bay Aquarium protects the ocean. The Museum of Art and History (Santa Cruz, California) gathers the community. The Lawrence Hall of Science (Berkeley, California) develops curriculum materials, and the District Six Museum (Cape Town, South Africa) preserves heritage.

Of course, all these museums also do more. They provide visitor experiences, they create jobs, they inspire innovation, they offer respite and beauty, they preserve memories and objects, and they communicate regional identity. Each of these museums has a business model—the people, agencies, and organizations that pay the museum the money needed to provide these services.

The Museum Manager's Compendium: 101 Essential Tools and Resources embraces the idea that a museum is more than just its galleries and that it serves far more people than just its gallery visitors. Museums have many impacts and benefits for many people and organizations. Museums are community service resources full of values. This is the book's foundational assumption.

Additional assumptions about museum theories and definitions underlie the 101 resources that are the substance of this book. While all of these assumptions are based on museum practice and come from museum managers and planners and most of them are familiar to seasoned museum managers, some are innovations that deserve an introduction. Understanding these underlying assumptions will clarify the resources and make them more useful as tools. The following potentially unfamiliar concepts are woven through the 101 resources and discussed in this introduction:

- The Professional Aspiration: The Need for Improvement
- What Is a Museum? What's It For?
- Community Needs as the Foundation for Purposes and Planning
- Stakeholders: Community, Audiences, and Supporters
- The Museum Theory of Action
- Museums Create Public, Private, Personal, and Institutional Values
- Many Museums Are Servants of Four Masters
- Museums Share a Theory of Action
- Public Spaces Should Be Planned for Programming
- The Importance of Shared Definitions and Language

THE PROFESSIONAL ASPIRATION: THE NEED FOR IMPROVEMENT

All nonprofits are facing pressure to account for their impact, as outlined in a 2010 Harvard Business School working paper on the limits of nonprofits:

> The world of nonprofit organizations, philanthropy, and social enterprise has been preoccupied with two powerful mantras in recent years. Since the early 1990s, the refrain of "accountability" has been ascendant, with demands from funders, taxpayers, and concerned citizens and clients for nonprofits to be more transparent about their fundraising and spending, how they are governed, and what they have achieved with the resources entrusted to them. A more recent manifestation of this discourse has centered on the mantra of "impact" or demonstrating results in addressing complex social problems such as poverty and inequality. (Ebrahim & Rangan, 2010)

Museums already use data operationally. Staff annual objectives, attendance forecasts, and the number of grant proposals are examples of common tactical uses of data, and museum managers have dashboards of indicators and metrics that matter to them so that they can make operational adjustments. The next step is to use data strategically in forward planning to prove and improve value.

The Cultural Data Project's (now DataArts) 2013 analysis by Sarah Lee and Peter Linett of the use of data in the cultural sector, which includes museums, performing arts, and other cultural nonprofits, found that

> we face an abundance of data about the cultural sphere. But it is not yet clear that the cultural sector is making effective and strategic use of all of this data. The field seems to be approaching an inflection point, where the long-term health, sustainability, and effectiveness of cultural organizations depend critically on investment in and collective action around enhancing the field's capacity for using data strategically and thoughtfully to inform decision-making. (Lee & Linett, 2013)

Lee and Linett (2013) also found that the cultural sector needs to address "the lack of a strong organizational vision for how data can be used to inform internal planning and decision-making, as well as the lack of examples of such vision from the field" (pp. 1–2).

Because we have so many impacts, audiences, and supporters; because every museum is unique; and because each museum pursues its different missions differently, the global field of museums has no easy metric to measure impact and performance. Our richness and complexity challenge any simplistic assessment of a museum's value and impact, such as attendance or collection size.

To address this complexity, we need to adopt a framework for thinking about and monitoring the museum field's complex mixture of outcomes, audiences, and supporters, necessarily aligned with how the rest of the world thinks about value and ideally aligned with museum counting and accounting systems and with shared data definitions.

In short, we need to further professionalize the museum field.

WHAT IS A MUSEUM? WHAT'S IT FOR?

We also need to establish the conceptual framework for museums, beginning with our concepts and assumptions about what museums are, why they exist, and for whom. This book builds on the International Council of Museums' definition of nonprofit museums (see "55. Museum Definitions") and on four concepts that museums in North America, the United Kingdom, and the Eurozone might agree with, though the implications may not be clear:

1. Stephen Weil's introduction to John Cotton Dana's selected writings from the 1920s quoted Dana's maxim that museums should find what the community needs and fit the museum to those needs (Peniston, 1999). Weil's own theory of museums bases a museum's worth on the good it has accomplished, and the museum's resources are the means to that end. The performance evaluation is then of the museum's effectiveness at achieving its purposes and of the efficiency of its resource use (Weil, 2002, 2005).
2. John Falk and Lynn Dierking, in describing their Contextual Model of Learning, place emphasis on museums' unique business model of free-choice learning that meets personal and sociocultural needs in physical contexts (Falk & Dierking, 2000; see also Falk & Dierking, 2012; Sheppard & Falk, 2006). Free choice means that museums are in a competitive marketplace controlled by the consumers. No one has to visit. No one has to give museums money. This is a fundamental difference in our business model from schools and other formal educational institutions. We have to attract and benefit our audiences and supporters.
3. George Hein builds a wide mission on John Dewey's progressive education that is sharable by all museums: the mission of building a better and more democratic society (Hein, 2006).

These conceptual foundations have implications for today's museum leaders:

- Dana's Implication: Museums are responsible for offering their communities services that address their needs and aspirations.
- Weil's Implication: Museums should use their resources (means) to achieve their purposes (ends) and be evaluated on how effectively and efficiently they do that (performance).
- Dierking and Falk's Implication: Museums operate in a competitive, free-choice marketplace by offering physical and social services valued by their audiences and supporters.
- Hein's Implication: Museums aspire to make the world better and more democratic, such as advancing community development and social good.

Synthesized, these concepts underlie museum economic theory: the community funds the museum to use its resources to provide effective services back to the community. The museum provides these services efficiently and, instead of privatizing its net revenues, contributes to community development and social good.

COMMUNITY NEEDS AS THE FOUNDATION FOR PURPOSES AND PLANNING

Successful museum planning is founded on addressing significant community needs and aspirations. Museums grow and adapt in response to providing services to families, professionals, students, teachers, businesses, foundations, agencies, and other sponsoring investors. Assessing what the community needs and where it wants to go is a key element of strategic planning.

A museum can conduct a series of community needs assessments with key stakeholders, supporters, current and future donors, board members, community leaders, political officials, business leaders, educators at both the secondary and the postsecondary levels, students, museum members, casual museum visitors, nonusers, museum partners, and vendors. The objective is to assess the needs and aspirations of those who live, work, and play in the community, state, and region that the museum serves. The museum should use diverse methodologies to collect diverse perspectives on the community's needs and opportunities (see table I.1).

Once the museum's community's needs, aspirations, capacities, profile, and direction are understood, the museum can suit its purposes to those needs, to paraphrase John Cotton Dana. Once the needs are translated into purposes, the museum uses its resources to deliver activities that help address the community's needs. For example, if a community needs to bridge cultural divides, then the museum could adopt a purpose of strengthening community connections, to be achieved, in part, by an active schedule of cross-cultural community events.

Table I.1   Sources of Community and Institutional Needs

Research Methodology/Source

External Input

Literature Review of regional visioning and analysis documents
Community Needs Interviews with civic leaders and spokespeople
Surveys and Visitor Studies
World Cafes, Interest Group Meetings and Open Houses
Brainstorming Sessions with Content Experts
Market Analysis: Demographic and Psychographic Market Profile
Best Practices in Peer Museums

Internal Input

Museum Performance Assessment and Recommendations
Operating Data Trend Analysis
Space Use Analysis and Recommendations
User/Non-User Focus Groups
Leadership Policy Guidance Workshop(s)
SWOT Exercise Results
Staff Project and Wish Lists
Database of Needed Upgrades and Capital Projects

STAKEHOLDERS: COMMUNITY, AUDIENCES, AND SUPPORTERS

Stakeholders is an umbrella term covering all external people and organizations that relate to the museum. It includes individuals, such as visitors, organizations, and the community at large. It includes people who support the museum as well as parties that could oppose the museum. Under this umbrella term are community, audience, and supporters, and these categories provide a framework for researching, thinking about, and making decisions.

Community is the big-picture, inclusive term, used broadly in many ways and often pluralized; it is roughly synonymous with the museum's markets, cultural context, authorizing environment, city, neighborhood, and so on. Audiences are those who attend the museum's exhibits and programs and are also known as visitors, users, learners, guests, program participants, customers, and so on. Supporters provide the museum with its support revenues and in-kind services and are distinguished by source of funds (public and private) and by kind of support (volunteer, partner, collector, and funder). The framework also recognizes nonusers.

The museum's external environment—its communities, audiences, and supporters—is diagrammed in table I.2.

Table I.2   The Community and Its Audiences and Supporters

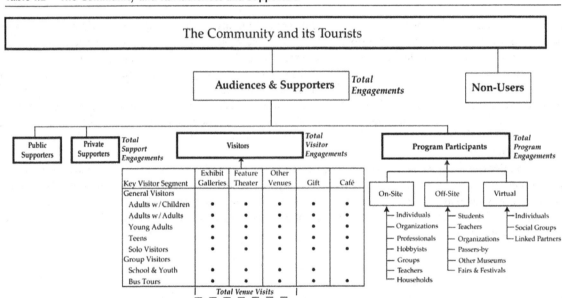

Source: White Oak Institute.

THE MUSEUM THEORY OF ACTION

A review of established nonprofit and museum evaluation frameworks in Measuring Museum Impact and Performance finds that they overlap (Jacobsen, 2016). Analysis of the overlap informed the development of the museum theory of action, with seven steps: (1) intentional purposes, (2) guiding principles, (3) resources, (4) activities, (5) operating and evaluation data, (6) key performance indicators, and (7) perceived benefits. The narrative version of this numbered sequence is as follows: The museum, in service to its community, decides on its intentional purposes and desired impacts. Then, guided by its principles, the museum uses its resources to operate activities for its community and its audiences and supporters that result in valued impacts and benefits. Engagements with these activities generate operating and evaluation data that can be incorporated into key performance indicators that monitor the museum's effectiveness and efficiency. This theory of action is diagrammed in table I.3.

The museum theory of action can organize all this book's tools and resources into its several steps, as shown in the accompanying text boxes. This categorizing aligns the resources with museum practice and helps museum managers find the most useful resources based on where they are along the action sequence.

Table I.3   The Museum Theory of Action

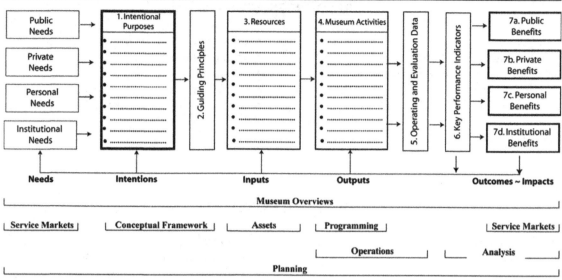

Source: White Oak Institute.

OVERVIEWS (ENTIRE MUSEUM THEORY OF ACTION)

- Museum definitions and field counts
- Categories (types) of museums
- Categories of potential museum impact
- Community needs and museums
- Museum theory of action
- Conceptual diagrams and frameworks

THE STAKEHOLDERS (BEGINNING AND END OF THE MUSEUM THEORY OF ACTION)

- Community needs and benefits
- Visitors and program participants
- Supporters: funders, partners, volunteers, and collectors
- Market analysis
- Servant of four masters
- Earned and support revenues

INTENTIONAL PURPOSES AND GUIDING PRINCIPLES (STEPS 1 AND 2)

- Purposes and impacts
- Multiple-mission museums
- Museum impacts and benefits
- Intentional purposes
- Guiding principles
- Museum learning theory

RESOURCES (STEP 3)

- Collections
- Site, architecture, and facilities
- Sustainable design/alternative energy sources
- Architectural program
- Public learning spaces: categories
- Key concepts
- Education concepts

- Community concepts
- Venture capture rates
- Public spaces: menu of options
- Support facilities
- Support systems, technology, and networks
- Capital assets

ACTIVITIES (STEP 4)

- Content development
- Visitor programming
- Theater programming
- Programming: menu of options
- K–12 education strategy
- Programming: Delta approaches

- Multimode operation
- Key qualities of visits to museums
- The museum and visitor experience concepts
- Education concepts
- Community and audience concepts

OPERATIONS (STEP 5)

- Governance
- Chief executive officer profile and budget
- Financial management
- Operating budgets
- Earned revenue: business lines
- Operating data standards
- Ticket prices

- Facility and security
- Human resources
- Insurance
- Audience and visitor services
- Capacity calculations
- Marketing
- Membership

ANALYSIS (STEP 6)

- Institutional evaluation concepts
- Community needs assessments
- Market demographic and population analysis
- Audience research
- Exhibit evaluation filters

- Best practices research
- Selecting key performance indicators
- Attendance potential estimates
- Peer performance assessments
- Space use analysis

PLANNING (FEEDBACK FROM STEP 7 BACK TO STEP 1)

- Capital project: planning principles
- Planning frameworks and diagrams
- Concept and strategic master plans
- Implementation phases, schedules, and tasks

- Architectural planning
- Site selection
- Museum capital budgets
- Capital project: first steps

MUSEUMS CREATE PUBLIC, PRIVATE, PERSONAL, AND INSTITUTIONAL VALUES

At least three scholarly journals have devoted issues to museum public value and economic factors: the *Journal of Museum Management and Curatorship* 24(3), September 2009; the *Journal of Museum Education* 35(3), Summer 2010, and 35(3), Fall 2010; and *The Exhibitionist* 31(2), Fall 2012.

The September 2009 special issue of *Museum Management and Curatorship* 24(3) on museum value includes Carol A. Scott's "Exploring the Evidence Base for Museum Value." Scott's later book *Museums and Public Value: Creating Sustainable Futures* (Scott, 2013) organizes 11 articles, and her introduction covers many perspectives on museum value. While there are previous efforts to establish frameworks for museum evaluation (D. Anderson, 1997; Baldwin, 2011; Friedman, 2007; Sheppard & Falk, 2006), the data infrastructure to support such frameworks has not been in place until recently. Achieving this goal is now possible because of increased transparency of museum operating data (G. Anderson, 2004; Stein, 2009); the growing body of evaluation findings and evidence posted on http://www.visitorstudies.org and http://informalscience.org and new national data compilations of museum operating data, such as the online database of the Association of Children's Museums, DataArts, Guidestar's collection of IRS 990 data forms, and other online museum data.

This book expands the public value discussion to include private and personal values on an equal conceptual footing, leaving to others the debate about whether one kind of value or impact is more worthy than another.

Weil (2002) states that a museum's value lies in what impacts it delivers. One way to evaluate a museum on its impacts is to look at how others value those impacts through their exchanges of time, effort and money. While we cannot measure total impact and hence total value, we can seek indicators of changes in that value by looking at changes in these exchanges.

In order to analyze how thoughtful museum professionals globally have been thinking about impacts and performance, the White Oak Institute collected 51 systems of museum indicators of impact and performance (MIIP) into an aggregated database (MIIP 1.0) of 1,025 indicators.

MIIP 1.0 was developed by the White Oak Institute and is available for free to everyone, along with the museum theory of action diagrams. To download copies, go to the website listed on page v.

Analysis of the MIIP 1.0 database found 14 categories of potential museum impacts. These categories of potential museum contributions and benefits fall under four impact sectors and include seven categories of public impacts (broadening participation, preserving heritage, strengthening social capital, enhancing public knowledge, serving education, advancing social change, and communicating public identity and image), two private impacts (contributing to the economy and delivering corporate community services), three personal impacts (enabling personal growth, offering personal respite, and welcoming personal leisure), and two institutional impacts (helping museum operations and building museum capital).

Table I.4   Categories of Potential Museum Impacts.

		# of MIIP indicators
Public Impacts		
A	Broadening participation	85
B	Preserving heritage	47
C	Strengthening social capital	76
D	Enhancing public knowledge	43
E	Serving education	56
F	Advancing social change	40
G	Communicating public identity & image	27
Private Impacts		
H	Contributing to the economy	85
I	Delivering corporate community services	9
Personal Impacts		
J	Enabling personal growth	147
K	Offering personal respite	4
L	Welcoming personal leisure	11
Institutional Impacts		
M	Helping museum operations	308
N	Building museum capital	87
Total indicators in the MIIP 1.0 database		1,025

Source: White Oak Institute.

MANY MUSEUMS ARE SERVANTS OF FOUR MASTERS

Embedded into their community's cultural, educational, and economic ecosystems, today's museums compete in the marketplace to survive, perchance to grow. Museums pursue multiple purposes for multiple audiences and supporters. For example, museums can have both learning and tourism impacts, for both school and tourist audiences, supported by paying visitors, government agencies, private foundations, and corporate sponsors.

The four categories that make up the museum's audiences and supporters—visitors, program participants, public supporters, and private supporters—are also the museum's sources of potential revenue. A museum with regular revenues from all four service market sectors must be a servant of four masters, as illustrated in table I.5.

Table I.5   Servant of Four Masters

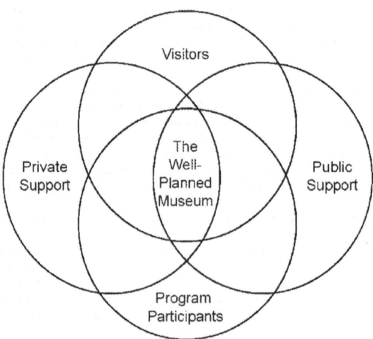

In the Servant of Four Masters diagram, the horizontal axis is support revenue, and the vertical axis is earned revenue. This diagram illustrates the need to find the sweet spot: a museum plan that provides enough benefits efficiently to enough sectors to sustain operations.

Becoming intentional about providing our audiences and supporters the benefits that meet their needs may improve impact and performance in those areas, and it may give the museum greater opportunities to further its intentions. Counting all a museum's impacts and benefits totals a more complete picture of the museum's contributions without taking sides about the relative worthiness of any category of potential museum impact. We need equally rational ways to measure learning outcomes as well as societal and economic impacts, even though some may feel that one is more worthy than the others. To conserve the prestige and value long enjoyed by museums but now facing stiff competition, we need to deliver value to our audiences and supporters and count every benefit we provide.

PUBLIC SPACES SHOULD BE PLANNED FOR PROGRAMMING

The museum's building has capitalized platforms for changing content. Just like performing arts complexes, museums might think of their building as a container of a variety of public spaces with a range of built-in equipment capable of hosting changing exhibits and programs. These capabilities and spaces should complement other museum facilities in the community.

Changing programming that is up to date and connected to community is fundamental to a community museum's operating vitality. As a result, the implementation of a capital project should focus on providing the institution with adaptable resources that can be used in many ways over the next decades. The capital project needs to include an opening set of programs in all learning spaces, but these should not be thought of as permanent.

Some museum planners argue for undifferentiated, neutral exhibit and program spaces provided by the architecture, delegating the creation and differentiation of the spaces' character to the exhibit design process. While this approach seems to promise the most flexibility, in practice these flexible galleries often remain in their opening configurations because the cost of creating new arrangements of walls and systems is often prohibitive. On the other hand, differentiating galleries architecturally allows for both light and dark spaces, both intimate and grand spaces, creating a variety that keeps the experience fresh for the visitors.

Several resources consider a museum's long-term public spaces (aka physical components) as part of the museum's resources. The physical components are organized according to table I.6.

Table I.6   Potential Museum Components (Public Spaces)

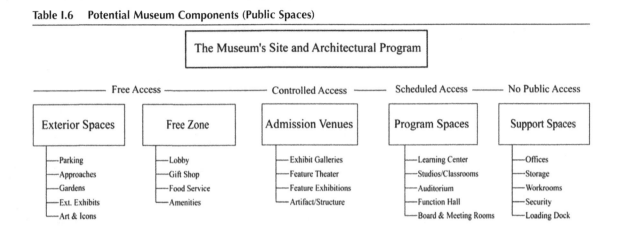

THE IMPORTANCE OF SHARED DEFINITIONS AND LANGUAGE

The museum field has not aligned data definitions and collection because alignment is difficult: (1) someone has to establish the fieldwide standards, and no association has yet been willing to take on the job, as each already has its definitions and many years of data based on those definitions; (2) each association and museum needs to compare its current definitions to the new standards and decide whether the effort and disruption is worth the effort; and (3) every museum must see worthwhile benefits from shifting to shared data standards and from taking the effort to report their data.

In response to these resistance points, this book establishes definitions and assumptions to be shared. Because the lack of shared language and definitions is one of the museum field's main obstacles (Lee & Linett, 2013), the family of terms and definitions is based on the field's most tested and accepted definitions where available. These definitions are strongest when specific, such as site visitor, but we also need more inclusive terms, such as program participants, and as yet unreported terms, such as dwell time. Good shared data will help museums show evidence of their impact and improve their value.

The umbrella term museum engagements collects attendance at all the museum's activities—gallery attendance, lecture series attendance, volunteer shifts, board meetings, interactions with partners, outreach participations, and so on—into one number. A physical museum engagement is defined as one person-trip to a museum site or to a museum-sponsored program off-site by a person not employed or contracted by the museum to be there. The person-trip is a measure of effort spent by the person (time and often money are also spent). Virtual museum engagements involve much less effort but still require time.

People also come to museums to participate in programs (for a partial listing, see "72. Programming: Menu of Options"). A museum can hold its programs on-site, off-site, and virtually—the last two are also called outreach. While one of the goals of outreach is to reduce audience effort, there is still some effort to attend an off-site program, so each program participation is counted as one per person-trip, even if it is off-site. If a ceramics workshop has six sessions on different days and a program participant attends all of them, that counts as six museum engagements.

Any museum engagement that is not a visit is a program participation. By this definition, board meetings, volunteer shifts, meetings with grant officers, and event rentals are programs, and the individuals attending them are program participants.

On-site attendance includes both visitors and program participants counted by person-trips to the museum's site. The motivation to make the trip is the distinction between visitors and program participants—did they come primarily for a visit or a program?—and usually shows up in the museum's transaction records—did they buy an admission ticket or pay for a program or get a pass to attend a meeting? Many exhibit gallery admissions get programs included for free, some school groups add fee-based programs to their base admission, and some patrons buy combination tickets. These multiple venue visits do not increase on-site attendance, as they do not increase the number of person-trips.

In addition to their earned revenues from visitors and program participants, museums typically receive support revenues and in-kind donations from funders, partners, volunteers, and collectors.

CONCLUSION

The resources and tools in this book use these terms, theories, and assumptions. Collectively, they provide a coherent way to think about museums—what they are for and how they work. The framework is intended to be globally inclusive of those museums that meet the definition (see "55. Museum Definitions"). Specifically, the tools are here to help you and your museum plan strategically and make and implement decisions. Adapt them to your needs. Use them often as needs arise in managing your museum. This introduction helps you understand the resources' shared assumptions, just as the preface explains their background and how to use them.

See "15. Bibliography for Museums" for citation references and further information.

Section 1

Architect Search Process

INTRODUCTION

The process for selecting an architect assumes that staff and consultants will do background work and periodically bring policy decisions to a museum-selected Architectural Search Committee.

In addition to using this section as an outline of the process for selecting an architect, you can adapt the process to select other creative talents and production firms.

This section is by contributing author Victor A. Becker.

ARCHITECT SEARCH PROCESS

Goal

The search for the architect should be guided by the objectives the museum has defined for the building: to develop an operationally successful museum building that will also contribute to the cultural and architectural quality of the neighborhood and region and work within the logistical, budgetary, and schedule parameters of the project.

Qualified Museum Architect

The exacting demands of the site and situation (e.g., tightness requiring intricate stacking and routing of museum functions) and aspects of the project that have extremely detailed requirements (e.g., café kitchen, planetarium, large-screen theater, and animal care facility) require a lead architect experienced in museum design. Specifically, the lead architect should have in-house experience with new museums in a range of disciplines (science, history, or art) and a range of sizes, from at least 50,000 square feet to 100,000 square feet and up. Museums are increasingly technical spaces, especially with the Delta approach to changing spaces, and the lead architectural firm must bring to the table successful experience with museum programs, and the relevant principal should lead this team.

On a practical and political level, the process is about selecting an architectural team, not just a lead architectural firm. The architectural team should include locally based architects in a supportive role. The team will also need a number of specific talents, including theater specialists, acousticians, and information technology infrastructure engineers. In short, the search is not just for a lead design architect but rather for a team whose members are responsive to the particular needs of the site and project.

Open Process

The process of selecting an architect for a prominent public building needs to be open, sensitive to the political environment, and squeaky clean—the last thing any project needs is some investigative reporter uncovering improprieties in the spending of taxpayer or donor dollars. For this reason, the architect selection process needs to be guided by an architectural search committee, chaired by a board member, and comprised of representatives of the museum, the neighborhood or city and other committed and potential donors. At least two volunteer experts should be included: an individual with recognized aesthetic judgment and familiarity with contemporary architecture, such as a dean of the school of architecture, and an individual experienced with contracting architects and constructing buildings. The board should appoint this ad hoc committee of 6 to 10 people, and a staff person should keep a record of their meetings and correspondence.

Architectural Search Consultant

The Architectural Search Committee will need staff and a consultant to do their work, as they are volunteers who can only review materials, do interviews, and make the selection but will not be able to write requests for qualifications (RFQs) and requests for proposals (RFPs), handle inquiries from prospective architects, and negotiate the contract. Typically, an architectural search consultant is engaged to run this process.

Summary of Search Process

The following multistep selection process produces a short list of top designers who have track records of creating successful museum buildings. An architectural search consultant can facilitate the process.

1. Form the museum's ad hoc Architectural Search Committee.
2. Develop a full list of qualified museum architects, inviting suggestions from many affected and interested constituencies.
3. Send that list an initial solicitation letter (RFQ).
4. Review the RFQ responses (Search Committee).
5. Develop a short list of four to eight architectural teams (Search Committee).
6. Verify that funding is in place and available to spend on the early design phases by an architect selected by this process. Sending out RFPs when the funding is not yet secured is disrespectful of the proposers' good-faith investment of their time and expenses, unless disclosed in the RFP.
7. Send the short list more detailed information and a formal RFP.
8. Compare their proposals.
9. Do extensive background research on them and with their previous clients.
10. Interview the top teams (Search Committee).
11. Make a final selection (Search Committee).
12. Negotiate and sign with the finalist (Museum).
13. Announce selection (Museum).
14. Search and select an owner's rep or construction manager (Museum).
15. Authorize the architects to proceed on their early phases of work: review of the museum's architectural program (or collaborate with the museum to create one) and begin concept design phase (Board).
16. Form the museum's ad hoc Building Committee, involving some members of the Search Committee (Board).
17. Search and select the general contractor (Building Committee).

RFQ Process

The RFQ should contain sufficient background material to allow architects to form appropriate teams and respond to a realistic program. In addition to response logistics, the RFQ should include summaries of the architectural program, some adjacency diagrams, the site analysis and constraints, and a description of the museum's components, all led by a vision statement that encapsulates the mission, values, and key concepts for the project.

The RFQ should be distributed to a list of qualified museum architects. The RFQ should also be posted on professional notice boards in the architectural community; the selection process should not be hidden from any architect, and all firms are welcome to submit qualifications in the first round. For most large projects, the initial RFQ is likely to get fifty or more responses.

Design Competitions

A design competition is not an effective way to achieve the main goal of an operationally successful museum, and it cannot address the budget and site issues. It is important that the process select an architect on the basis of experience, museum references, portfolio reviews, and interviews rather than selecting a winning entry to a design competition. Design competitions emphasize the exterior appearance of the building without detailing its interior and are often won by the most attractive illustration of a building rather than by the most attractive and functional building.

Further, a design competition also reveals little of the architect's collaborative nature, the strength and appropriateness of the rest of their team, their abilities to work within budget, and numerous other factors.

Section 2

Architectural Considerations

INTRODUCTION

The development of the architectural program, the selection of the site, and the exploration of adjacency diagrams focus primarily on definition of the spaces and their size and relationship to each other and to the site. This process and its products now need to be put into context: What are we doing this for?

The physical home of any museum will be a significant presence in any neighborhood and any region. It will be perceived in myriad ways, but a number of approaches stand out, as discussed in this section.

You can use this section as a checklist of the considerations your museum and its architect can look for during the evolving overall layout and design parti. *See also "Building: Design Criteria and Operational Characteristics."*

This section is written by contributing author Victor A. Becker.

ARCHITECTURAL CONSIDERATIONS

Gross Circulation Considerations
Levels Desired/Required

Most museums will benefit greatly from locating their exhibits, programs, and amenities on a single functional level. A high degree of ease of circulation for the visitor is accompanied by the elimination of the need for expensive elevators, escalators, accessibility ramps, fire stair towers, and similar vertical circulation.

If there are constraints that limit the area of the site that the building itself may occupy or if the desire for exterior program elements requires a building footprint smaller than that optimal for the building's architectural program, the resulting multistory building will require additional creativity in its design to ensure that all floors are equally accessible, attractive, visible, and important to the visitor's experience.

The visitor's awareness of additional floors of potential experience can be enhanced by entering the building at its middle floor instead of at its lowest floor. Escalators, multistory lobbies and atria, views within the building, and similar architectural devices for making the entire facility tangibly visible can also educate visitors to the multiplicity of opportunities open to them.

Pedestrian Access and Vehicular Parking Considerations

The main visitor drop-off area should accommodate both cars and buses carrying school groups and tourists. The facility may also benefit from a single main entrance and a single lobby that provides an entrance experience for arriving guests.

A service area for light vehicle deliveries should be located out of sight, possibly utilizing a separate access and providing temporary parking for small delivery vehicles.

The service area should also provide a loading dock for more substantial service and maintenance vehicles, accommodating full-size tractor-trailer trucks. Access to this area by large trucks should be easily negotiated and, if possible, hidden from all visitor entrances.

Some part of the service area may contain facilities that accommodate broadcast media vehicles (e.g., TV vans) and special event equipment (e.g., generators).

Group Entrance

The group entrance is a separate entrance into the facility for school groups or other groups that reduces potential traffic problems in the main entrance. It is often the gateway to a common area where groups can be oriented at the start of their experience and/or debriefed at the end of their experience.

The Free Zone

The free zone is that part of the site and building that the public can enjoy without charge at any time the facility is open. For the museum visitor, the free zone offers a lobby containing the information booth, ticketing counters, a membership area, a café or other food vending space, a museum store, a number of free programs and activities, and various visitor amenities.

The free zone ends at the controlled-access gateways into the paid-admission areas. The free zone can also provide a more flexible access to a learning center that offers a wide variety of programs and events that are at times open and free of charge while at other times restricted by admission charge or by invitation.

Equally important is the role the free zone plays in providing a wayfinding device for its users. It can become an identifiable transition space for visitors as they explore the museum moving from the café and museum store to the ticketing process to the exhibit areas, the theaters, the learning center, or elsewhere in the facility.

It is important to note that the free zone may well include more than one level and may be developed in a variety of ways, offering, for example, a site for an overlook on an upper level that takes advantage of one or more views of the other floor(s) of the museum, the exterior program areas that surround it, or views of the region beyond.

Paid or Controlled Zone

The paid or controlled zone is any part of the facility that requires controlled admission, such as obtaining a ticket or passing through a turnstile in order to participate in the activity. The paid zone is usually carefully contained with as few entrances requiring staff to take tickets or scan IDs as possible.

Building as Spatial Experience

- The interior lobby and program areas are often tall: sometimes clear ceiling heights are 20 feet or more for exhibits and 50 feet or more of clear interior space for a giant-screen theater. The resulting volumes of space add enormously to the visitor experience. The interior spaces are many and varied. The visitor experiences them sequentially, one at a time, continually adjusting to their different sizes and natures. This spatial "exercise" enhances significantly the various processes of exploring, absorbing information, making connections with both mind and hand, and reflecting on the exhibit or program experience.

Building as Experience

- The museum and its surroundings need to be an integrated experience that is replete with choices of routes and destinations for visitors. In addition to choices within the sequences of entrance and exit spaces (e.g.,

the café and museum store), visitors will have choices of major venues from a main lobby as well as choices of exhibit areas, perhaps organized around an exhibit hub. While security and efficient ticket-taking are obviously important to the operation of the museum, it is equally important that the visitor's experience be self-directed.

- The museum's exhibit areas, theaters, and/or themed program labs or classrooms are to be designed as environments for learning, specifically for interactive concept exploration. While the exhibit and theater designers will be responsible for many aspects of this, the architecture is expected to create the context for these learning spaces by providing them with character, flexibility, and built-in systems appropriate to the long-term learning needs of each space.
- Planners and architects must design with a high level of flexibility for future uses and users—the Delta museum—heeding, for example, the observations of Stewart Brand in his book *How Buildings Learn* (Brand, 1994).

Building as Functional Spaces on Program

The building design will reflect the owner's desired program and its later detail in the *Room Book*[1] with regard to size, function, infrastructure, and adjacency.

Building as Expandable Space

- Most architectural programs are planned to fit within a very specific budget formulated at a particular time for exacting reasons. Based on the assumed success of the vision of the original facility, future capital investment is likely to expand functions and add program components that will require space into which to expand. Additional exhibit halls, theaters, classrooms, and program spaces are among the likely possible expansions. Also possible is the development of a preschool or a charter school within the museum's scope of management.
- The identification and facilitation by the architect of future expansion zones within the design as it develops will help ensure the feasibility and cost-effectiveness of future additions of space to the facility.

Building as Sustainable System

- As a public, educational facility, the museum should project an image of responsible citizenship. The building and site offer an opportunity to embody the principles of sustainability through the utilization and articulation of "green" technologies. The project should meet high "green" building standards, as articulated in the standards of the Leadership in Energy and Environmental Design (LEED) program created by the U.S. Green Building Council.
- The interpretation of sustainable energy systems and resources may be incorporated into the design of the site features and the building. Significant features on the

exterior of the building could interpret these technologies to all visitors and passersby.

See "15. Bibliography for Museums" for citation references.

NOTE

1.   A *Room Book* is a document that provides the basis for understanding a museum's expectations of each room in the program. It provides a coordinated description of the character of its spaces and their functional objectives and adjacencies, the technical requirements of program areas and the equipment and systems needed to make the facility effective, and a definition of the various scopes of base building, premises enhancement, scenario shell expectations, exhibit utility interfaces, owner-provided items, and similar categories of interrelated work. It defines the museum's expectations of the architectural process and is, in practice, a binding extension of the contract between owner and architect. It will also provide the various exhibit design teams, media specialists, equipment providers, and other specialized vendors with a single, comprehensive guideline to the museum's intentions and preferences with regard to its facilities.

Section 3

Architectural Design Phases

INTRODUCTION

The architectural design phases are the recognized steps in the architectural process of turning an architectural program into a completed set of building plans.

You can use the process and sequence in this section to schedule a capital project involving construction. This process is also embedded in the full project task list in "Implementation Phases, Schedules, Milestones, and Tasks."

This section is written by contributing author Victor A. Becker.

ARCHITECTURAL DESIGN PHASES

Concept Phase

This first phase of design begins with the architect collaborating with the museum to define the general goals and specific requirements for the project. Working with the architectural program and *Room Book*[1] created by the museum, the architect creates a design concept—also called the *parti*—that organizes the required spaces placed on a specific site. The final product of this phase is a set of very diagrammatic sketches of each floor of the building illustrating the intended adjacencies of the net areas, ignoring wall thicknesses, structural systems, and MEP spaces.

Schematic Phase (SD)

This phase develops the design concept into a set of design drawings that begin to address spatial relationships, scale, and form with attention to zoning and code requirements. Several iterations of the design concept may be required to meet the demands of site, program, circulation, and budget. The final products of this phase are a site plan, floor plans, sections, one or more exterior elevations, and other images of the facility.

Design Development (DD)

This phase focuses on making the schematic design workable in terms of structure; mechanical, electrical, and plumbing; and architectural detail. Specifics of dimensions, materials, locations of doors and windows, color scheme, and elevations of all important areas of the building appear in a set of documents to be reviewed and—if satisfactory—approved by the museum.

Construction Documents (CD)

After approval by the museum, the DD documents are detailed further with material choices and construction specifications. The final CD documents will be sufficiently detailed to be used for the competitive bidding that results in choosing a general building contractor.

NOTE

1.   A *Room Book* is a document that provides the basis for understanding a museum's expectations of each room in the program. It provides a coordinated description of the character of its spaces and their functional objectives and adjacencies, the technical requirements of program areas and the equipment and systems needed to make the facility effective, and a definition of the various scopes of base building, premises enhancement, scenario shell expectations, exhibit utility interfaces, owner-provided items, and similar categories of interrelated work. It defines the museum's expectations of the architectural process and is, in practice, a binding extension of the contract between owner and architect. It will also provide the various exhibit design teams, media specialists, equipment providers, and other specialized vendors with a single, comprehensive guideline to the museum's intentions and preferences with regard to its facilities.

Section 4

Architectural Functional Adjacencies

INTRODUCTION

While the architectural program suggests how individual spaces should be grouped by function—and, by inference, by adjacency—it does not allow the museum or architect team to see the interrelationships between groups of spaces that signal a well-functioning museum. Something more visual is required for the museum team to communicate its needs to the architect—without falling into the trap of being amateur architects.

Adjacency diagrams—also known as "bubble diagrams"—can fill this need. They are comparatively simple two-dimensional sketches that illustrate how the various spaces in a facility relate to each other. They can be used at the very beginning of the visualization process to explore broad concepts of space as well as to detail the interrelationships within a group of spaces with a common function. There may be several of these diagrams for an envisioned facility describing the adjacencies required for the visiting public, the special event invitees, exhibit components, the movement of cash, the removal of trash, and so on.

This section is written by contributing author Victor A. Becker.

ARCHITECTURAL FUNCTIONAL ADJACENCIES

Parti Adjacency Diagrams

Space and the relationships between spaces can be very difficult to express in words but lend themselves very well to a diagrammatic expression of an idea of how a museum or a piece of it may function. These diagrams represent each major space of the architectural program as a circle on the page—a "bubble"—that demonstrates its relationship to the other spaces. It is useful for the bubbles to relate to the net area called out in the architectural program because it is easier to find good locations for the smaller support spaces than it is to establish the fundamental relationship(s) between the larger ones.

The three adjacency diagrams shown in tables 4.1 to 4.3 are derived from the same architectural program and illustrate how the core spaces of the museum can be manipulated to create very tangibly different visitor experiences. Looking at each of these diagrams provides an intuitive sense of how different a visit to each organization of the "same" spaces might be like.

Table 4.1   Sample Adjacency Sketch A

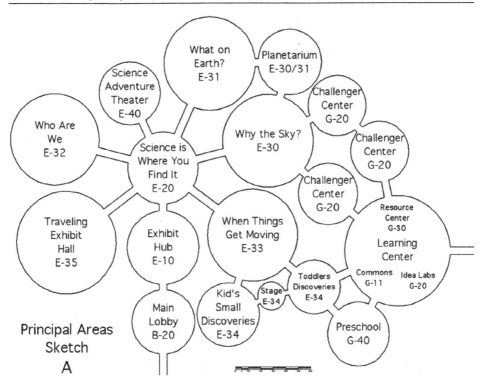

Table 4.2   Sample Adjacency Sketch B

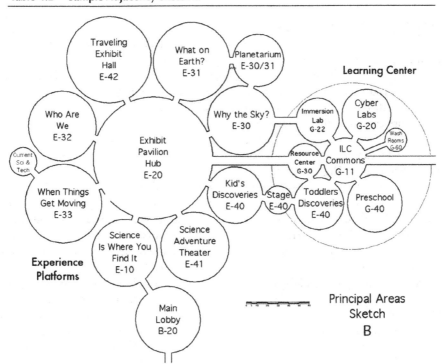

Table 4.3   Sample Adjacency Sketch C

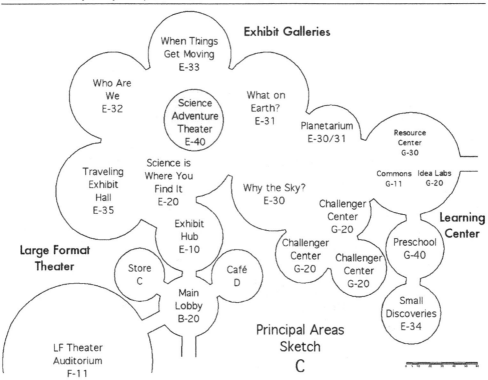

FUNCTION ADJACENCY DIAGRAMS

Adjacency diagrams can also help focus on a single function of the museum, providing a detailed view of the relationships between all the individual spaces associated with that function.

It is important to remember that these diagrams are not designs or architecture. They are communication devices first to help the museum team develop its understanding of specific spatial aspects of the museum and second to help communicate that understanding to the architect team. This means that the first priority of each diagram is clarity; there is no need for consistency between diagrams or resolution of conflicting priorities. That is the architect's job: to synthesize all the spaces and their desirable adjacencies into a coherent whole in real space.

The three adjacency diagrams shown in tables 4.4 to 4.6—all derived from the same architectural program—describe the adjacencies inherent in three of the many groups of spaces in a particular museum.

Note that in these sketches. an effort has been made to diagrammatically reflect the likely heights required for the spaces.

Also note that "connections" do not represent corridors or actual distances; they too are diagrammatic, indicating only which spaces need to be accessible to each other and which ones do not. Rendering the sketch as an isometric drawing can add visual interest to the sketch but has no impact on the nature of the adjacencies.

SITE ADJACENCIES

Adjacency diagrams (see table 4.7) can also be used to explore ways in which to fit ambitious architectural programs onto challenging sites. The process is identical, and the acknowledgment of the diagrammatic nature of the exercise is just as important because the final product can look temptingly like architecture.

A site adjacency diagram (or several) created by the museum team serves as an important piece of the planning; it is the first confirmation that the fit between the architectural program and the chosen site is a sound one.

Table 4.4   Sample Free Zone Adjacency Diagram

Table 4.5   Sample Education Center Adjacency Diagram

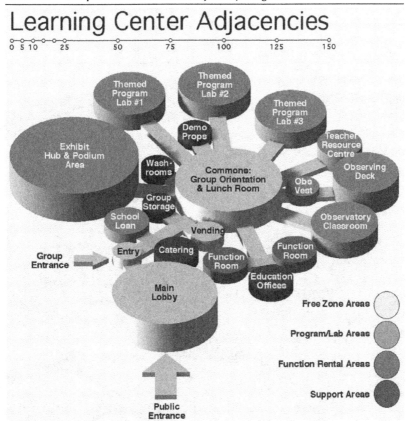

Table 4.6   Support Spaces Adjacencies Diagram

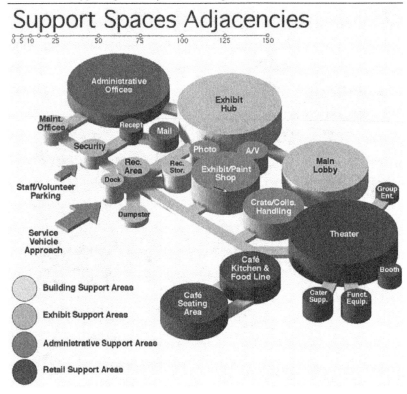

Table 4.7   Sample Site Adjacency Diagram

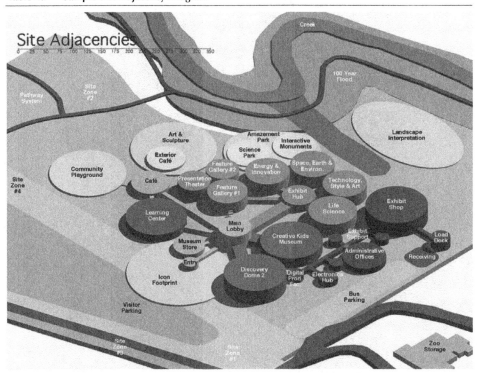

Section 5

Architectural Planning

INTRODUCTION

It does not matter how the complex process of creating a new (or substantially renovated) museum facility starts. It might be inspired by a clear vision of a community need for more experiences of art, history, science, or all of the above. It might be the availability of a site well situated to draw visitors and program participants. It might be the need to accommodate growing attendance at an existing facility.

What *does* matter—and matters greatly—is that the process integrates all the aspects of planning that are required: vision, museum planning, site selection, architectural design, exhibit design, budget management, construction management, and personnel management. Many of those ingredients are explored in other parts of this book; this section focuses on the architectural process of getting from the idea phase to the beginning of the construction phase.

It is highly recommended that museums devote a great deal of effort to vision and planning before looking for a site or an architect. This section is organized around that principle.

This section outlines a process for developing your museum's specifications for what spaces you want from a capital project involving architecture.

This section is written by contributing author Victor A. Becker.

ARCHITECTURAL PLANNING

Among the many results of the early processes should be the building budget, which includes both the hard costs of actual construction and the soft costs of planning, architecture and engineering, permits, staff and resource relocation, additional staff, cost estimation, construction management, bridge loans, and escalation—everything that is not directly related to the construction itself. Soft costs are typically about one-quarter to one-third of the entire building budget.

When the typical cost per square foot of construction for a particular kind of building in a particular region is applied to the anticipated construction portion of the project budget, a total number of gross square feet (GSF) that the museum can afford to build emerges. Be sure to compare to other museums or to factor for higher spaces and museum-specific infrastructure.

This GSF number represents the entire interior area of the facility contained within its entire outer skin (not just for its footprint[1]), no matter what the function of any of the space may be. In addition to the exhibits, theaters, program spaces, support spaces, and storage areas, it includes wall thicknesses, vertical structure, chases, voids, and other unusable "hidden" spaces. Elevators are usually included as the area of the shaft and its walls on one floor only; a staircase is usually included as the total of the areas it occupies on every floor.

This single GSF number initiates the process that follows.

DETERMINING TOTAL BUILDING SIZE

The architectural program is the definitive list of required program spaces within the facility with their specific net area[2] (and sometimes their clear ceiling height[3]) usually organized primarily by their function and secondarily by their adjacency.[4] It does not include the circulation[5] (except for lobby spaces), code-required restrooms (with the exception of family restrooms, baby changing rooms, or similar visitor amenities), stairs or elevators, MEP spaces,[6] ducts, chases, or structure. This architectural program document is usually presented as a set of "instructions" to the architect, determining the scale, program functionality, and operational nature of the finished building. The architectural program may also be one of the first collaborative products of the earliest phase of the architectural design process.

The first step in the development of the architectural program is a stab at estimating the gross-up ratio (also referred to as the gross-up, gross-up factor, or net-to-gross factor). The gross-up factor is the multiplier that determines the amount of GSF that will be needed to outfit the net-square-foot requirements of an architectural program[7] into a fully functional building.

Estimating the likely gross-up ratio at the very early stages of the process can be quite difficult because there is little actual design information to base it on. Often, a "placeholder" ratio of 1.50 is assumed until more is known about the design. At this phase in the visualizing of the building, it is important to appreciate that the gross area needed to make the building functional may be substantial.

Later in the process, the architect will be able to begin to refine this crude guess at a gross-up ratio into a real number based on the actual design.

The placeholder ratio should be increased if the vision of the facility or the nature of the site suggests a multistory building; the gross-up ratio will be larger because of the necessity of stairwells and elevators, which will add circulation and other nonprogram space to the building.

If, on the other hand, the site is relatively flat and sufficiently large, the placeholder gross-up ratio can be reduced.

Determining Total Net Area

Dividing the affordable GSF by the gross-up ratio yields the number of net square feet (NSF) available for all aspects of the visitor experience, including support, dedicated storage, and all other net areas (see table 5.1).

Table 5.1   Calculating Affordable Net Square Feet

$$\frac{(\text{Capital Budget})\ (\%\ \text{for Building Construction})}{\$/\text{GSF}} = \text{GSF}$$

$$\frac{\text{GSF}}{\text{Gross-Up}} = \text{NSF}$$

Space Allocation: Step 1

The first pass at the actual architectural program is the "executive" allocation of space by function. It is recommended that this "simple" first breakdown be done to ensure that the space allocations align with the museum's priorities. It is counterproductive, for example, to imagine a botanical garden that consumes 25 percent of the available program space if it will likely service only 10 percent of the visitor dwell time or 10 percent of the museum's earned income.

In addition to specifying NSF for each function, it is useful to think also in terms of the percentage of the total building net area that function represents.

The typical breakdown of functional space categories that begin to define the nature of a specific museum-to-be follows:

- **Entrance Spaces:** Including entrance vestibule, main lobby, admission areas, cash rooms, orientation areas, icons, baby stroller storage area, coatroom or locker area, and local storage area for crowd control equipment and orientation materials.
- **Retail Spaces:** Including café or other food-vending arrangements for the museum visitors, catering space for rental function guests, museum store, and spaces either dedicated or usable as function rental space.
- **Exhibit Spaces:** Including all museum galleries, exhibit halls, orientation spaces, and their support spaces. While the core visitor experience in the exhibit areas may be highly preorganized, there is general agreement in the field that casually self-directed experiences are preferred by the majority of visitors. In most museums, the specific spaces will range widely in size, nature, and character. To organize the exhibit experiences, some museums have developed a central exhibit hub in which there is opportunity for the visitor to be oriented to the exhibit choices, reflect on an experience just completed, or simply take a breather before the next exploration. The hub is clearly within the controlled or paid zone[8] of the museum and quite distinct from the main lobby.
- **Theater Spaces:** May include large-screen theater, dome theaters, multipurpose auditoriums, planetariums, demonstration stages, and so on. Usually, these are separately ticketed venues with clearly established schedules and stand-alone experiences. Some theaters, such as small planetariums and demo stages, allow visitors to come and go as they wish.
- **Program Spaces:** Classrooms, laboratories, workshops, and similar areas and their support spaces that provide directed programs on specific topics. Usually, the programs in these spaces require some kind of ticket or registration for admission. Some kinds of libraries and resource centers are included in the mix of program spaces. Often, the program spaces are collected into a "program center" or "learning center," but they are also sometimes distributed throughout the exhibit areas to allow docents to talk in a semiprivate space to interested groups during their exploration.
- **Collections Spaces:** Spaces devoted to the care, maintenance, and storage of collections artifacts when they are not employed in exhibits or demonstrations.
- **Administrative Spaces:** Generally not part of most museum visitor experiences, these spaces include workspace and support for the staff and volunteers, meeting rooms, planning and design studios, and so on.
- **Facility Management Spaces:** Include janitor closets, a facility maintenance shop, offices for security and maintenance staffs, loading dock(s) and receiving areas, and so on. If the museum offers frequent traveling exhibits, there may be a shipping crate storage area.

A specific museum may, of course, not have all of these features or may have other features unique to its location or genesis.

Another way to visualize a complete museum is to organize the desired net spaces according to the nature of their access by visitors. Table 5.2 shows the typical museum component spaces listed above but organized according to a spectrum of access, running from completely free access, open to anyone, to completely nonpublic spaces.

The first point of decision making is, therefore, to identify the major components envisioned in the new facility. The next is to make an "executive" allocation of the total available (i.e., affordable) NSF to those features. This stab in the dark is essentially a balancing act, tweaking the numbers until the balance feels right. This may be approached by dividing up the available space through a "sense" of the amount of space required. This sense may be the result of museum spaces previously experienced or by identifying known nonmuseum spaces (e.g., gyms and lobbies) that help visualize how large, for example, a space of 3,000 NSF actually is. An illustration of step 1 of the executive space allocation is shown in

table 5.3; the numbers are simply illustrations of what a mid-size multidisciplinary museum might contain.

The executive allocation may also be approached by thinking conceptually about how space ought to be "spent" to serve each component function of the overall vision of the museum. Instead of starting with NSF, this exercise focuses on what percentage of the overall building is to be allotted to each function. A typical result of that approach is shown in table 5.4.

Space Allocation: Step 2

The next iteration of this process is to craft a program summary that is more specific about the spaces to be included in the museum with a more refined guess at the size of each component. It is arguably less important at this point to worry about the accuracy of the size guesses than it to be sure that every important function is included. Again, it is a balancing act of tweaking numbers up and down to achieve the sense of the total facility within the established space "budget." An example of this level of executive space allocation is shown in table 5.5.

Table 5.2   Potential Museum Components (Public Spaces)

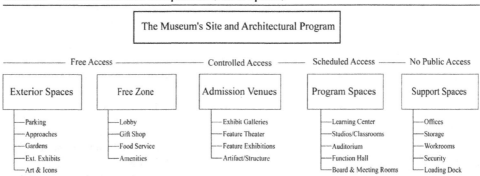

Table 5.3   Sample Executive Allocation of Space by Area

Space Categories	NSF	Net %
Entrance spaces	4,000	6.7%
Retail and function spaces	4,500	7.5%
Exhibit spaces	28,000	46.6%
Theater spaces	7,500	12.5%
Program spaces	7,500	12.5%
Administrative spaces	4,000	6.7%
Facility management spaces	2,000	3.3%
Total net area	60,000	100.0%
Gross-up (1.50)	30,000	GSF
Total gross area	60,000	GSF

Table 5.4   Sample Executive Allocation of Space by Percentage

Space Categories	NSF	Net %
Entrance spaces	3,600	6.0%
Retail and function spaces	4,500	7.5%
Exhibit spaces	27,000	45.0%
Theater spaces	7,200	12.0%
Program spaces	9,000	15.0%
Collections management spaces	2,400	4.0%
Administrative spaces	4,200	7.0%
Facility management spaces	2,100	3.5%
Total net area	60,000	100.0%
Gross-up (1.50)	30,000	GSF
Total gross area	90,000	GSF

Table 5.5   Sample Executive Allocation of Space by Component

Entrance spaces	NSF	Net %
Museum Lobby and Admissions Spaces	3,000	5.0%
Lobby Amenities	1,000	1.7%
Subtotal	4,000	6.7%
Retail & Function Spaces		
Café/Catering Spaces	2,400	4.0%
Museum Store	1,250	2.1%
Function Rental Spaces	800	1.3%
Subtotal	4,450	7.4%
Exhibit Spaces		
Exhibit Galleries	20,000	33.4%
Traveling Exhibit Galleries	5,000	8.3%
Exhibit Support Spaces	3,000	5.0%
Subtotal	28,000	46.7%
Theater Spaces		
Feature Theater	3,600	6.0%
Multipurpose Theater	2,000	3.3%
Theater Support Spaces	1,500	2.5%
Subtotal	7,100	11.8%
Program Spaces		
Classrooms	3,500	5.8%
Laboratories	2,400	4.0%
Program Support Spaces	1,500	2.5%
Subtotal	7,400	12.3%
Collections Management Spaces		
Collections Management Spaces	350	0.6%
Collections Storage Spaces	2,000	3.3%
Subtotal	2,350	3.9%
Administrative Spaces		
Reception Area	250	0.4%
Office Landscape	1,000	1.7%
Enclosed Offices	2,000	3.3%
Office Support Spaces	1,000	1.7%
Subtotal	4,250	7.1%
Facility Support Spaces		
Facility Administration Offices	250	0.4%
Facility Maintenance Shop	1,250	2.1%
Loading Dock	750	1.3%
Receiving Spaces	200	0.3%
Subtotal	2,450	4.1%
Total Net Area	60,000	100.0%
Gross-up (1.50)	30,000	GSF
Total Gross Area	90,000	GSF

Space Allocation: Step 3

Once an architectural outline of the museum is developed, greater detail is required to ensure that the envisioned components are workable and efficient in the real world of operations. Each needs to be thoroughly thought through in terms of specific spaces with specific net areas. In addition, the overall program requires some sort of identification system to ensure that all the planners are talking about the same specific space. The numbering system can be any that clarifies the hierarchy of spaces and identifies subcomponents (even when their size may not yet be determined).

Again, it is more important to identify every discreet space required than to worry about being "accurate" in the net areas;

Table 5.6   Architectural Program Sample Detail #1: Entrance Areas

		NSF	Clear Height
B.	Entrance areas		
B-10	General public entrance		
	B-11 Public entrance vestibule	in gross	10
	B-12 Group entrance vestibule	in gross	10
B-20	Main lobby and ticketing area (free zone)		
	B-21 Main lobby	3,200	TBD
	B-22 Lobby icon area		
	B-23 Information booth		
	B-24 Ticket and membership areas		
	B-25 Admissions office and cash room	240	10
B-30	Free zone amenities		
	B-31 Public lockers	200	10
	B-32 Public coatroom	450	10
	B-33 Washrooms	in gross	10
	B-34 Family washroom/first-aid room	60	10
	B-35 Lobby storage	50	10
	Subtotal	4,200	•

Table 5.7   Architectural Program Sample Detail #2: Feature Theater

		NSF	Clear Height
F.	Discovery dome		
F-10	Theater lobby and support spaces		
	F-11 Theater lobby	1,000	15
	F-12 Concession stand		
	F-13 Theater lobby storage	100	10
	F-14 Theater exit lobby	in gross	10
	F-15 Theater area washrooms	in gross	10
F-20	Discovery dome		
	F-21 Sound/light lock entry	200	10
	F-22 Theater	6,400	TBD
	F-22.1 Seating and presentation stage area		
	F-22.2 Signature dome capabilities demo		
	F-22.3 3D studios (3D glasses)		
	F-23 Theater technology studio/ projection booth	400	10
	F-24 Sound/light lock exit	100	10
F-30	Theater support spaces		
	F-31 Ushers' room	150	10
	F-32 Dome server room	150	10
	F-33 Theater management office (three staff)	240	10
	Subtotal	8,740	•

the architectural team will apply its expertise in evaluating the net areas once it is on board.

The excerpts presented in tables 5.6 and 5.7 from an architectural program illustrate a typical organization of the thinking about space.

Table 5.8   Sample Space Allocation Comparison: Family Museums

Spaces	Museum (program)	Peer A (actual)	Peer B (prog)	Peer C (actual)	Peer D (actual)	Peer E (actual)	Average of Peers
Net Sq. Ft.	94,895	131,745	96,000	82,368	101,442	149,129	102,889
Gross Sq. Ft.	133,518	203,041	144,000	120,190	136,788	205,280	151,005
Entry Spaces	4.6%	9.2%	4.5%	3.7%	3.1%	4.6%	5.0%
Retail Spaces	**3.1%**	11.1%	7.8%	6.3%	6.4%	5.2%	7.4%
Exhibit Spaces	45.5%	38.8%	50.2%	51.4%	52.4%	52.3%	49.0%
Theater Space	**16.8%**	10.0%	13.8%	15.6%	13.6%	14.4%	13.5%
Program Spaces	**5.3%**	16.1%	8.4%	8.2%	5.6%	8.6%	9.4%
Administrative Spaces	**23.7%**	7.0%	7.2%	5.5%	6.6%	7.6%	6.8%
Facility Support	**1.0%**	7.9%	8.1%	9.3%	12.3%	7.3%	8.9%

A sample of a complete architectural program for an actual, large facility is included in "18. Building: Sample Program."

Space Allocation: Step 4

When the development of an architectural program is nearly done, a good exercise to verify its validity is a program comparison with other museums' programs (see table 5.8). The comparison museums are chosen for their similarity in market size and/or purpose.

There is no "ideal" size for any museum, and the comparisons illustrated are not intended to "measure" the museum's spaces against either an ideal or an average but, instead, to help illustrate what is—and is not—worthy of more scrutiny or investigation.

To provide a fair method for examining these data, all subsequent comparisons of institutions are expressed in terms of the percentage of a building's total net space that is devoted to each of the functions listed. While this method may be a bit skewed when facilities of extremely different gross sizes are compared, the desired end products of this process are more qualitative than quantitative in nature.

Note that the numbers cited in table 5.8 for the museum's peers are based on actual museums. Besides offering real numbers for comparison, the numbers also vividly express the variations in space allocations between institutions. Presumably, every museum had a clear basis for determining the proper space allocation for the priorities of its purposes.

Any specific number in bold text in the comparisons indicates that there is something worth investigating about the number, usually because there is a significant variance between the museum and the average of the peer institutions that bears some examination.

Space Allocation: Step 5

To complete the architectural program, another look at the amount of GSF is needed to outfit the allocated NSF area. A refining of the placeholder gross-up ratio may now be possible with the allocation of spaces complete.

Like the previous steps in the prearchitectural planning, this one applies subjective observations to adjust the gross-up ratio up or down by looking at the following kinds of implications of the allocated spaces in the architectural program:

- Does the program call for a great number of small-scale spaces? If so, that implies that a large number of corridors and other circulation spaces will be needed to access them. This would push the gross-up ratio higher.
- Does the program have comparatively fewer, relatively large spaces? If so, that implies that there is less need for circulation space and that the gross-up ratio could be reduced.
- Is there a great variety of clear ceiling heights in spaces in the program that are not likely to be adjacent? If so, the cost efficiency of a low number of roof planes is likely to result in much "wasted" space above the spaces with low ceiling height. This is likely to raise the gross-up factor.
- Is there an exhibit hub that provides efficient, organized access to all the exhibit spaces, or does each gallery require its own unique circulation? The hub approach is likely to reduce the circulation required and, in turn, the gross-up factor.
- What is the relationship of the building size to the available buildable site size? The tighter the fit, the more likelihood of multiple stories and a higher gross-up ratio.

Many similar questions may arise from the visualization of the architectural program and projecting it onto the site. To illustrate the impact of this refinement of the gross-up ratio, the sample building illustrated in earlier tables could be almost 10,000 GSF smaller if it were an efficient program on an accommodating site. It could also be more than 10,000 GSF larger if the program were inefficient and/or the site were challenging. This 10,000 GSF could translate into a $5 million or more decrease or increase in the building cost.

Space Allocation: Future Steps

It is important to think of the architectural program as an evolving document that guides the continuous process of designing the building and the exhibits and amenities contained within it. As more becomes known through research, design, and development of the visitor experience, the architectural program needs to be continuously updated to facilitate the next stages of design. Beside its value to the architectural team, it is one of the most important guidelines for the exhibit design team, which usually begins its work a year or more after the architectural team begins its work.

NOTES

1.   The footprint is that part of the site area occupied by the ground floor of the building. It does not include any area on any additional floor levels.

2.   The net area (also referred to as net program area) is the area—expressed in net square feet (NSF)—of those spaces within a facility that present or support the exhibits, theaters, programs, and all other visitor activities in the museum. The net area includes both public and nonpublic spaces as required by the museum's activities but usually does not include interior spaces required to make the building function, such as electrical rooms.

3.   The clear ceiling height is the height of a space from the top of the finished floor to the bottom of the lowest ceiling element (e.g., horizontal structure, ducts, conduits, and lighting fixtures).

4.   Adjacency is the functional need for specific spaces to be physically close—even adjacent—to other specific spaces in order to achieve the practical goals of the museum.

5.   Circulation is that part of the facility required to direct visitors and program participants from one activity space to another. Circulation space can be utilized to orient visitors and program participants to the physical layout of the facility, to introduce exhibit themes, or to interpret other aspects of the visitor experience.

6.   The MEP spaces are those spaces dedicated to the operation of the building's support systems: mechanical (heating, ventilating, and air-conditioning) rooms, electrical rooms, and plumbing support spaces.

7.   If a theoretical building had 100 GSF in which all 100 square feet were usable for the visitor experience, it would have a gross-up ratio of 1.00 (100/100 = 1.00). A building with 100 GSF in which only 50 square feet were usable for the visitor experience would have a gross-up ratio of 2.00 (100/50 = 2.0). A large, institutional building design with a gross-up of 1.35 is about as efficient as a facility can be. Any large building design with a gross-up ratio over 1.65 is probably very inefficient and needs rethinking and redesigning.

8.   The controlled or paid zone is any the part of the facility that requires passing a control point, which may require paying a fee or obtaining a ticket in order to participate in the activity. The paid zone is usually carefully contained with as few entrances requiring staff to take tickets or to scan IDs as possible.

Section 6

Architectural *Room Book*

INTRODUCTION

It is important that all the planning done before the architects begin work be organized in a way that facilitates the process of familiarizing the architectural team with the museum's values, thinking, and planning. The architectural *Room Book* is an excellent device for this purpose. It provides the basis for understanding the museum's expectations of the character of all spaces related to the visitor experience, describing their functional objectives and adjacencies.

It details the technical requirements of program spaces and the equipment and systems needed to make the facility effective and efficient. It outlines the requirements of the built-in capacities needed to support a changing experience for the visitor. It clarifies the buildingwide services and systems that connect and integrate the building's components into a coordinated whole.

It also defines the various budgets and responsibilities of the architectural processes: base building, premises enhancement, scenario shell expectations, exhibit utility interfaces, owner-provided items, and similar categories of interrelated work.

As the level of detail grows in the planning stage and in the architectural design stages, the *Room Book* level of detail parallels that growth. It represents the museum's growing set of requirements and preferences.

This section is written by contributing author Victor A. Becker.

ARCHITECTURAL ROOM BOOK

Room Book: Sample Table of Contents

The table of contents from an actual *Room Book* shown in table 6.1 illustrates the depth of detail the document can reach. Although much of this is determined before the architect begins work, the content will continue to expand and grow in technical detail as the architectural design phases occur.

Sample Specification Template

As the architecture progresses through the design phases, the importance of "Part Four: Space Specifications" steadily grows in importance. As the level of detail in the design increases, the need for answers to increasingly detailed question increases as well. The sample specification template shown in table 6.2 offers a model that can be tailored to a museum's specific needs.

Sample Space Specification

To illustrate the kinds of information that the specifications furnish to all the teams involved, table 6.3 provides specifications for one space in the building that the *Room Book* table of contents describes.

Table 6.1   Sample *Room Book* Table of Contents

Part One: Introduction
- Introduction: Objectives, Process, Scope; Acknowledgments

Part Two: Concepts
- Conceptual Framework: Vision, Learning, Planning, and Programs
- Overview of the Visitor's Experience: Target Visitors and Components of the Visitor's Experience
- Physical Perspectives: Objectives, Site, Gross Circulation, and Spatial Adjacencies
- Overall Design Criteria: Safety, Security, Building Integrity, Design Aesthetics, Design for Learning/Visitors, Sustainable Design, Adaptability, Digital Connectivity, Expandability, Fixed Budget and Inclusive Scope
- Outline Architectural Program
- Future Program and Facility Expansion
- Scope of Work: Base Building, Owner Provided, Building/Exhibit Interface Allowances

Part Three: Spaces and Adjacencies
- The Exterior of the Building: Identity in the Community, A Community Gathering Place, Infrastructure Requirements, and Security
- The Icons: Potential Icon Locations, Icon Nature, and Icon Matrix
- The Entrance Area: Control of Access, Elements of Lobby/Free Zone, Gateways and Dispersed Exhibits
- The Museum Store: Role of the Museum Store in the Museum Experience, Appearance, Access, and Involving a Retail Planner
- The Café and Food Areas: Role of the Café in the Museum Experience, Appearance, Access, Special Events in the Museum, Catering in the Museum, and Involving a Restaurant Planner
- The Exhibit Areas: Gallery and Theater Spaces, Basic Circulation, Dispersed Exhibits, Special Events in the Exhibit Areas, Camp-Ins, Differentiating Experience Platforms, Making Transitions between Exhibits Areas
- The Standard Exhibit Infrastructure and Special Exhibit Areas
- The Giant Screen Theater: Economic and Operational Considerations, Public Theater Areas, Non-Public Theater Support Areas, Lighting Requirements, and Additional Connectivity
- The Learning Center: Summary of Public and School Programs, Learning Center Areas, and Adjacencies
- The Program Support Areas: On-Site Program Support, Off-Site Program Support, and Adjacencies
- The Administrative Area: Standard Office Infrastructure
- The Building Support Areas
- The Future Phase Areas: Phasing Process

Part Four: Space Specifications
- Specifications: The Exterior Areas
- Specifications: The Entrance Areas
- Specifications: The Store Areas
- Specifications: The Café/Food Areas
- Specifications: The Exhibit Spaces
- Specifications: The Giant-Screen Theater
- Specifications: The Learning Center
- Specifications: The Program Support Areas
- Specifications: The Administrative Areas
- Specifications: The Building Support Areas
- Specifications: The Potential Phase 2 Spaces

Part Five: Appendices
- Appendix A: Organizing Museum Space: Learning Spaces as Physical Context
- Appendix B: Bibliography for Collections Environments #1: Planning
- Appendix C: Bibliography for Collections Environments #2: Light
- Appendix D: Bibliography for Collections Environments #3: Temperature and Relative Humidity

Table 6.2   Sample Specification Template

Museum Space Name and Code
Functional Criteria
Nature of Space:
Current Function:
Future Function:
Future User:
Maximum Capacity:
Net Area:
Clear Ceiling Height:
Net Volume:
Location Criteria
Interior Access:
Access to Exterior:
Critical Adjacencies:
Desirable Adjacencies:
Desirable Floor Level:
Qualitative Criteria
Access Natural Light:
Description of Mood:
Description of Image:
Special Shape:
Interior Columns:
Other Remarks:
Technical Criteria
Floor Loading:
Wall Loading:
Ceiling Loading
Door Size or Type:
Window Size or Type:
Floor Finish:
Wall Finish:
Ceiling Finish:
Acoustic Requirements:
Electrical Requirements:
Humidity Requirements:
HVAC Requirements:
Plumbing and Drainage:
Fire Protection:
Lighting Requirements:
Security Requirements:
Special Code Requirements:
Maintenance Requirements:
Vibration Requirements:
Waste Requirements:
Other Requirements:
Communications and Data
Telephone:
Public Telephone:
Data Connection:
Signage:
Paging:
Intercom:
Other Requirements:
Furnishings and Equipment
Fixed Equipment:
Fixed Furnishings:
Fixed A/V Systems:
Owner Equipped (NIC):
Owner Furnished (NIC):
Other Requirements:

Table 6.3   Sample Space Specifications

E-11 Exhibit hub/circulation spine Functional Criteria

Function description	Provides an exhibit area circulation space with entrances to all galleries and with opportunities for exhibits or artifacts hanging overhead. Provides a respite area, a way-finding space in which visitors can relax, discuss, and reflect before heading to their next experience. Provides the environment for the visitor input stations that, in conjunction with the e-concierge system, offer an exhibit introduction to the overall experiences and opportunities available in the museum's exhibit area. Provides an area for queues to the planetarium.
Description of user	Visitors and staff; function rentals; cocktail parties; formal dinners
Maximum capacity	100
Net area	3,000 NSF
Clear ceiling height	15 feet
Net volume	45,000 NCF
Location Criteria	
Access	Only from main lobby free zone
Access to exterior	None
Critical adjacencies	All core gallery spaces (E-21 through E-33) Gallery zone function catering support (E-12) Gallery zone function equipment room (E-13) Gallery zone washrooms (E-14)
Desirable adjacencies	Gateway to all halls of fame (E-41 through E-43) Gateway to the national feature exhibit gallery (E-51) Gateway to the planetarium (E-61)
Floor level	Level 2
Qualitative Criteria	
Access natural light	Very desirable
Description of mood	Light, friendly, orienting
Description of space	The exhibit hub/circulation spine offers a rich environment that features an intriguing architectural space with bridges and enclosures. It offers a panorama of maps, migrating birds, views of the river, and stations at which visitors can contribute a record of their personal and family memories. The experience provided in the exhibit hub is the first of many learning spaces; it primes the entire family for their active participation in all that the museum has to offer. It is the central hub around which all the learning spaces are physically organized.
Special shape	In addition to the flow of visitors to and from exhibits, the exhibit hub also provides space for the ever-shifting queues for the planetarium. It is hoped that the surrounding circulation and adjacencies to the exhibit spaces can enhance the visitors' experience even while they are waiting in line. A circulation design is required that allows these waiting visitors to be protected from the swirl of other visitors experiencing exhibits but still provides them with an interesting view of the exhibit hub.
Interior columns	Possible if integrated into the scenario shell.
Other remarks	The exhibit hub, perhaps the sole access to the galleries, needs to be sized to accommodate the transporting of large exhibit elements. If alternative means of access are available, then ceiling heights, floor loading requirements, and turning radius considerations can be changed as best fits the specific environment needed for the hub. It is critical to note that the exhibit hub experience is probably both the first and the last experience in the exhibit area: All visitors will pass through it on their way into and out of the area.
Technical Criteria	
Floor loading	Standard exhibit infrastructure
Wall loading	Standard exhibit infrastructure
Ceiling loading	Standard exhibit infrastructure
Floor Finish	May feature a complex graphic that incorporates the river with a map of the city and surrounding counties (see Exhibit Master Plan Storyboard). Must be able to be cleaned easily, quickly, and frequently. Must be able to accommodate power and signal access.
Wall finish	May feature a continuation of the graphic on the floor into the vertical plane in which artifacts, photographs, specimens, and views outside the building are coordinated into a kaleidoscopic experience.
Ceiling finish	Open to multiple lighting positions below dark structure and utilities.
Acoustic requirements	While the noises of entering and exiting visitors need to be controlled, there remains a need for this space to feel "live" and exciting.
Electrical requirements	A flexible power supply system in the floor and lower walls of the entire space is particularly important for this iconic space.
Plumbing/drainage	Standard exhibit infrastructure
Lighting Requirements	Standard exhibit infrastructure
Communications and Data	
Data connection	Standard exhibit infrastructure
Signage	In addition to the exhibit requirements, significant numbers of way-finding, identification, donor, and sponsor signs are likely.
Paging	Standard exhibit infrastructure
Furnishings and Equipment	
Owner equipment (NIC)	All exhibit components

Section 7

Architectural Standards and Green Resources

This section is assembled by contributing author Victor A. Becker.

GENERAL ARCHITECTURAL REFERENCES

- Architectural Graphic Standards, by Charles Ramsey and Harold Sleeper, presented by the American Institute of Architects and published by John Wiley & Sons. A compendium of facts and standards that offers information about the objects and spaces that make up our world and the way they are represented in architectural drawings and specifications. Currently, it is in its twelfth edition, but any available edition will have the kinds of information a museum planner needs.
- Defining the Architect's Basic Services, American Institute of Architects. PDF version can be found on Internet by searching for "aiap026834." A two-page breakdown of the basic architectural design phases and their deliverables and expectations of the architectural process.
- *Design for Accessibility—A Cultural Administrator's Handbook*, National Assembly of State Arts Agencies. A handbook that addresses several key points:
  - Cultural programs must be fully accessible and inclusive to every individual, including citizens with disabilities and older adults.
  - Cultural Service organizations need to set an example for their constituents by making their facilities, meetings, Web sites, print materials and activities fully accessible and inclusive to everyone.
  - The assurance of equal opportunity for all people to participate in the humanities and the arts should be a fundamental starting point.

GREEN RESOURCES

- American Alliance of Museums, The Sustainable Museum, *Museum*, 53 (2014).

CURRENT SUSTAINABILITY STANDARDS

A variety of standards and metrics prescribe and measure the sustainability of buildings and sites, from construction and renovation processes through operations and maintenance; to some degree, they also relate to the interpretation of sites. The programs described here are used in the United States to varying degrees of popularity, adoption, adherence, and achievability. They also cover a spectrum from highly technical and practical to aspirational. With the exception of the Sustainable Sites Initiative and Arts: Earth Partnership, none were developed to suit the unique needs of cultural institutions such as museums, yet all have been adopted over the past decade by hundreds of museums, historic sites, and similar institutions.

The following summaries are adapted from the Summit on Sustainability Standards handouts. For more detailed listings, view the complete report at http://aam-us.org/resources/professional-networks/pic-green-network.

Living Building Challenge Project (https://living-future.org/lbc): A green building certification program that defines the most advanced measure of sustainability in the built environment possible today and acts to diminish the gap between current limits and ideal solutions.

Sustainable Sites Initiative (http://www.sustainablesites.org): Provides a comprehensive rating system for sustainable design, construction, and maintenance of built landscapes.

Energy Star and Portfolio Manager, U.S. Environmental Protection Agency (https://www.energystar.gov): A voluntary program that helps businesses and individuals save money and protect the climate through superior energy efficiency.

Leadership in Energy and Environmental Design (LEED), U.S. Green Building Council (http://www.usgbc.org/leed): A green building tool that addresses the entire building life cycle by recognizing best-in-class building strategies.

Green Building Initiative, **Green Globes** (http://www.thegbi.org): A green building guidance and assessment program that offers a practical and affordable way to advance the environmental performance and sustainability of a wide variety of building types.

Green Exhibit Checklist (http://www.exhibitseed.org): A tool to evaluate the environment sustainability of exhibits and inspire exhibit teams to plan exhibits with environmental considerations in mind.

Sustainable Operations Tool Kit, AAM PIC Green (http://www.AAM-us.org/resources/resource-library/FRM/): A resource in development that focuses on solutions for greening day-to-day museum operations.

Green Business Certification for Cultural Institutions, Arts: Earth Partnership (http://artsearthpartnership.org): An official green business certification for cultural facilities, theaters, museums, dance studios, art galleries, performing arts companies, concert venues, and individual artists.

See "15. Bibliography for Museums" for citation references and further information.

Section 8

Attendance Potential Estimates

INTRODUCTION

Accurate attendance potential estimates for future on-site visitation are obviously critical to museum sustainability. Overestimating can result in financial shortfalls and low morale. Underestimating may compromise the visitor experience, strain staff and other resources, and increase operating costs as more visitors and participants utilize the facility than anticipated.

The forecast is called an *attendance potential estimate*, especially when forecasting for new museums, as it reflects the attendance and operating potentials of a museum in comparison to existing, mature museums similar to what the museum wants to become. These comparables have a longer track record and are often more stable entities than new or newly expanded museums.

An attendance potential estimate is not an attendance forecast based on assessing the appeal of a particular design; rather, it is an informed judgment of how many people a museum could serve if it were designed to be as appealing as a list of comparable museums.

Attendance potential estimates cannot be done in a void; rather, they must be considered as only one aspect of an integrated economic model. For example, attendance is related to the amount of capital invested, the marketing expenditures, the quality of the exhibits, the programming strategies, the appeal of destination feature theater films and temporary exhibits, and the ticket pricing. Changes to any of the main operating and capital assumptions are likely to change the attendance potential estimate. Major changes in the economic, tourist, and competitive environment, as well as the weather, can also affect attendance.

It is very difficult to accurately predict on-site attendance, as there are so many factors that affect it. It is a subjective exercise, not a scientific one. When asked about forecasting museum attendance, a well-known forecaster whose expertise is in projecting the winning and losing odds for professional football teams in the United States stated that, in regard to museum attendance forecasting, there are far too many variables to be able to project with any level of sustained accuracy. Nevertheless, with that caveat, one still has to find a way to identify reasonable and justifiable parameters to plan within.

If the estimate is for a new or expanding museum, a museum should first estimate attendance for a future stable or normalized year of operations, which is typically three to four years after opening. A stable year is one in which attendance is driven more by programming and marketing choices than by the excitement surrounding the opening years of a new museum. If a museum follows industry norms with a strong marketing campaign, opening-year attendance will be higher, though there are always exceptions. Years 2 and 3 might decline slightly with attendance stabilizing in year 4. Of course, a large and successful traveling exhibit or blockbuster giant-screen film can boost attendance if programmed in year 2 or 3. Expanding museums that have limited funds for and/or unsuccessful marketing launch campaigns may not have the big boosts of years 1 and 2. There are instances where attendance increased in years 2 and 3 after the opening year.

This section is written by contributing author Jeanie Stahl.

ATTENDANCE POTENTIAL ESTIMATES

Methodologies

The attendance potential estimate relates only to on-site visitation. It is a subset of total engagements, which includes off-site program participants, distance learning, and those accessing a museum's website and online social media. Annual attendance is the number of physical person-trips or site visits to the museum in a year. It includes people visiting multiple times a year. It counts a person who buys a combination ticket to two venues (e.g., a theater and exhibit galleries) as one site visit, increasing the attendance count by one, not two. It includes admission visitors, program participants and those attending function rentals, special events, and other on-site activities. Even volunteers and board members could be counted, although that attendance is not often counted by museums in their reported attendance, and so it would make it more difficult to compare data to other museums.

Since the attendance potential estimate is ultimately a subjective choice, it is best to apply several methodologies that converge on a range of figures, as shown in table 8.1.

Table 8.1 Attendance Potential Estimate Methodologies

1. Analysis based on attendance at peer museums
2. Analysis based on market segment populations
3. Analysis based on historical ticketed attendance at an existing museum going back five to ten years and broken out by:
    a. Ticket category and venue for ticketed admissions, noting anomalies in each year, such as blockbuster exhibits or films
    b. On-site paid programs
    c. Function rentals
    d. Special events
    e. Any other on-site attendance that is tracked
4. Analysis based on attendance at other local and regional museums and attractions

Considerations

Each of the methodologies and analysis should be informed by the findings from "27. Community Needs Assessments: Process" and "49. Market Demographic and Population Analysis." Considerations should include, among others, the following:

- Opportunities and challenges of the market that may affect museum performance
- Current and projected demographics of the resident population base
- Analysis of school populations and future enrollment
- A review of the number of area tourists and their characteristics
- The level of competition in the area
- The health of the local economy, overall trends, and development projects in the pipeline
- The assumed future size, components, budget, and quality of a planned future museum

The market analysis illuminates the factors that will affect the performance of a museum in a positive or negative way. The overarching question is, What are the anomalies of the museum? What will make the museum outperform or underperform in comparison to other museums? The following are examples of factors to be considered:

- Is the museum's community wealthier and more educated than average (indicators for potential visitation for many types of museums)?
- Does the museum have a large traveling exhibit space, an event venue, or a destination theater that would boost attendance?
- What is the size and related projected average dwell time at the museum compared to other museums?
- Is there a lot or a little competition in the museum's market?
- Does the museum's community have a larger- or a smaller-than-average tourist population?
- Will the museum have higher- or lower-than-average ticket prices?
- What are the psychographic characteristics of the resident market? Are they museumgoers?
- Will there be adjacent and adequate parking at the museum?

- Is the museum appealing, accessible, welcoming, popular, and relevant?

STUDY MUSEUM ATTENDANCE POTENTIAL ANALYSIS

The numbers used in the tables in this section are only to illustrate the mathematics and formulas among the columns. *Do not use* these numbers in your assumptions; rather, research and develop your own numbers, particularly dollar and population numbers, which will change from these samples. Some tables reflect judgment calls; those are for illustration only and are not to be applied to your context and time. These are sample judgment calls, and the authors make no assertion that they are the right call for your museum.

In this section, you can use the phrase *Study Museum* to refer to your museum as compared to the peer museums. The data presented are for a hypothetical museum.

Methodology 1: Analysis Based on Attendance at Peer Museums

Many experts in the museum field believe that, along with other comparative statistics, there is a correlation between exhibit hall size and attendance. The data behind this is that facilities of a given size—exhibit halls and components (e.g., a giant-screen theater)—generally attract the same number of people regardless of resident market size.

In general, comparing attendance figures for museums of somewhat similar population bases can be useful for a broad overview but obviously does not explain anomalies among attendance figures. For example, a museum may have a relatively large attendance because it does not charge admission, because it has an unusually large tourist population, or because it had a blockbuster traveling exhibit in that year. Some museums are more adept at marketing than others or have less or more competition in their area. Others may have better exhibits or visitor services. It is important to consider many aspects of each museum's performance.

Here are the steps for this methodology:

1. *Choose peer museums* as part of developing the attendance potential estimate (see also the definition

in "66. Peer Performance Assessments"). It will be difficult to find museums that have similarities in all qualities and categories. Sometimes, it is useful to include some outliers in the group to bracket high or low parameters:

- Similar-sized facility
- Similar-sized exhibit galleries
- Similar venues (e.g., feature destination theater, planetarium, or traveling exhibit space)
- Similar-sized resident population
- Similar population identifiers (e.g., metropolitan or micropolitan statistical area)

2. *Collect data on peer museums* through either primary or secondary sources. Ideally, collect three to five years of attendance data to mitigate differences due to anomalies in one year. Some museums form networks that share data on an ongoing basis. For secondary sources, many of the museum associations collect attendance and operating data, as do other organizations, such as DataArts. (See 66. "Peer Performance Assessments" for a detailed list.)

3. *Verify the data* regardless of the source of the data. Association surveys often define attendance differently. It is important to read what the definitions are so that the data are comparable. The data entered by the museums sometimes have errors. If something looks out of whack, it is important to research why.

4. *Create tables of data for the peer museums*, including key performance indicators (KPIs), for each museum. A critical KPI is the attendance-to-population ratio, which is a standard way to analyze attendance. The ratio is calculated as on-site attendance divided by the population (e.g., the metropolitan statistical area [MSA] in the United States or the census metropolitan area in Canada or whatever parameter one is using). It is not called a "capture ratio" of the resident population, as it does not account for tourists and day-trippers.

5. *Calculate the median and average, high, and low figures* for the peer museums. Do not include your museum.

6. *Enter base data for the Study Museum*, excluding attendance. See how the Study Museum compares to the peer data. Note anomalies.

7. *Enter first attendance potential estimate* by entering a percentage ratio for the Study Museum. The ratio should take into account the opportunities and challenges of your market and anomalies or unusual operating characteristics of the Study Museum.

8. *Analyze the fit of the Study Museum's attendance potential estimate* among its peers. Make adjustments as needed.

9. *Analyze the attendance potential number* against the other methodologies.

10. *If attendance is adjusted*, reenter data to the table of peer museums and see whether it appears reasonable and justifiable.

Generally, the larger the market population, the lower the attendance ratio, as there is more competition in larger markets. Conversely, the smaller the market, the higher the ratio. Midsize to large museums in very small markets, such as those with destination theaters and high tourist populations, can have ratios of over 100 percent of their metropolitan area. Museums that are free usually have higher-than-average attendance ratios.

The metropolitan area is often defined as the primary market when compared to other museums and attractions, as data are accessible and defined similarly for cities of a certain size. Smaller cities may have a micropolitan statistical area. Very small or rural towns will not have a specifically defined population area beyond the local population, and it is more difficult to compare to other museums.

A larger population area is the designated market area (DMA) (see 49. "Market Demographics and Population Analysis"), which is the reach of a network television station. It includes the MSA within its geographic boundaries. The DMA geographic borders have been a standard way of looking at greater metropolitan markets, but with the fractured television market and the large number of channels and alternatives to network TV (e.g., Netflix, Hulu, and YouTube), this way of defining a market is increasingly outmoded. The counties in the secondary ring surrounding a city may still generally align with the original DMA county lines. We are in a time of transition.

Table 8.2 presents data comparing museum facility size, attendance, population, and associated ratios. In this scenario, an existing museum is planning an expansion. Its facility size will increase by a factor of 1.2. The MSA population base is expected to increase by 15 percent, and the school population it serves is projected to increase by only 2.8 percent. Its current attendance-to-population ratio is slightly below the average for the peer museums and slightly above the median. Even though, typically, as population size increases the ratio declines, the future ratio for the Study Museum is expected to increase. The Study Museum is adding new exhibit space and renovating several existing exhibit galleries. It also is increasing its traveling exhibition space so that it will be able to host very large blockbuster traveling exhibits.

Note that the data and the KPIs shown are only a selection of the data that will be collected from the peer museums, as collected data will also include operating expenses, number of memberships, staffing costs, number of staff, and more. The data in table 8.2 focus on attendance data and facility size but assumes that the other data for the peer museums have been taken into consideration. Sometimes, the same data are shown

Table 8.2 Sample Study Museum and Peer Museums: Population and Associated Ratios

Museum	Total Indoor Facility Sq. Footage	Total Indoor Exhibit Sq. Footage	On-site Attendance	MSA Population	On-site Attd to MSA Ratio	DMA Population (includes MSA)	On-site Attd to DMA Ratio	On-site School Attendance	Ratio School On-site Attd to MSA Population
A	205,000	50,000	292,830	2,184,231	13%	3,764,085	8%	40,106	1.8%
B	93,000	30,000	426,060	3,144,201	14%	3,142,776	14%	60,204	1.9%
C	172,000	86,000	382,686	2,728,517	14%	2,918,811	13%	81,606	3.0%
D	194,200	114,000	344,713	2,065,925	17%	3,837,645	9%	28,776	1.4%
CURRENT MUSEUM	300,000	72,000	550,000	2,700,000	20%	4,200,000	13%	71,000	2.6%
E	370,000	45,000	507,792	2,353,414	22%	2,841,900	18%	68,384	2.9%
F	400,000	75,000	798,608	3,317,492	24%	4,548,658	18%	137,401	4.1%
G	172,000	61,000	992,687	3,500,178	28%	4,875,028	20%	57,766	1.7%
H	250,000	147,000	872,083	2,252,449	39%	3,168,345	18%	74,790	3.3%
Excludes current museum:									
AVERAGE	232,025	76,000	577,182	2,693,301	21%	3,637,156	15%	68,629	2.5%
MEDIAN	199,600	68,000	466,926	2,540,966	19%	3,466,215	16%	64,294	2.4%
FUTURE EXPANDED	365,000	102,000	730,000	3,100,000	24%	4,900,000	15%	73,000	2.4%
High for Peers	400,000	147,000	992,687	3,500,178	38.7%	4,875,028	20.0%	137,401	4.1%
Low for Peers	93,000	30,000	292,830	2,065,925	13.4%	2,841,900	8.0%	28,776	1.4%

Source: Data are derived from various years of ASTC Science Center Statistics, Copyright © Association of Science-Technology Centers, Washington, D.C., http://www.astc.org.

in each table, as it is useful to see the base data next to the KPI related to those data.

Table 8.3 presents data comparing museum facility, exhibit and traveling exhibit square footage, on-site attendance, gate admissions attendance, and associated ratios. Gate admissions attendance, sometimes called paid visitors, includes paid and free visitors and members attending for free with their prepaid membership.

The Study Museum's exhibit gallery square footage will increase by 1.4 and its traveling exhibition square footage by 1.5, thus adding 25,000 square feet of general exhibit space and an additional 5,000 square feet of traveling exhibition

Table 8.3 Sample Study Museum and Peer Museums: Size and Attendance Ratios

Museum	On-site Attendance	Total Indoor Facility Sq. Footage	Attendance / Facility SF Ratio	On-site Gate Admissions Attendance	Traveling Exh. Sq. Foot	Total Indoor Exhibit Sq. Footage	Admission Attend. / Exh SF Ratio	Admission Attend. % of On-site Attend.
A	292,830	205,000	1.4	255,214	7,000	50,000	5.1	87%
B	426,060	93,000	4.6	336,955	2,400	30,000	11.2	79%
C	382,686	172,000	2.2	357,212	7,000	86,000	4.2	93%
D	344,713	194,200	1.8	201,132	12,000	114,000	1.8	58%
CURRENT MUSEUM	550,000	300,000	1.8	335,000	10,000	72,000	4.7	61%
E	507,792	370,000	1.4	447,686	n/av	45,000	9.9	88%
F	798,608	400,000	2.0	753,211	12,000	75,000	10.0	94%
G	992,687	172,000	5.8	946,608	16,000	61,000	15.5	95%
H	872,083	250,000	3.5	836,604	7,000	147,000	5.7	96%
Excludes current museum:								
AVERAGE	577,182	232,025	2.8	516,828	9,057	76,000	6.8	86%
MEDIAN	466,926	199,600	2.1	402,449	7,000	68,000	5.9	91%
FUTURE EXPANDED	730,000	365,000	2.0	440,000	15,000	102,000	4.3	60%
High for Peers	992,687	400,000	5.8	946,608	16,000	147,000	15.5	96%
Low for Peers	292,830	93,000	1.4	201,132	2,400	30,000	1.8	58%

Source: Data are derived from various years of ASTC Science Center Statistics, Copyright © Association of Science-Technology Centers, Washington, D.C., http://www.astc.org.

space. The current museum has a large portion of its attendance from nongate admissions, as indicated in the far right column showing paid admissions as a percentage of on-site attendance. This needs to be taken into consideration when comparing to the peer museums, each of which has a much higher percentage of attendance from gate admissions. The potential issue would be overestimating admissions for the Study Museum and, as a result, overestimating admissions revenue and related ancillary revenue.

The ratio of attendance to facility square feet and the ratio of paid admissions to exhibit square feet indicate whether the museum is crowded, This ratio includes admissions to all venues, such as a destination feature theater. As a result, those museums that have a feature theater will normally have a higher ratio. Ratios under 5 percent for gate admissions to exhibit square footage in, for example, science centers indicate that the exhibit galleries are not crowded and that there is room to increase exhibit attendance without compromising the visitor experience. It may also indicate that a museum's exhibits are not that appealing and may be in need of renovation or complete overhaul. The important point is to research anomalies. If the Study Museum's data and ratios are out of line, the reasons need to be researched and justified if they are to remain.

In summary, this method leads to an attendance potential estimate of 730,000 based on an MSA-to-attendance ratio of 24 percent and a DMA-to-attendance ratio of 15 percent.

The DMA ratio is in line with the median and average for the peer museums, as is the school attendance ratio. The MSA ratio is higher than the average or median for its peers. There are several reasons that justify the higher ratio. The total facility and exhibit square footage and the traveling exhibit square footage are larger than the average and median for the peer museums. The exhibit square footage is the third highest among the peer museums and the traveling exhibit gallery the second largest. Data not shown are that the Study Museum has a very large tourist population. Some mitigating factors are that the Study Museum has a lot of competition in the area. It is in a warm climate and has significant competition from outdoor attractions and activities. The population is older than average.

The projected DMA-to-attendance ratio of 15 percent for the Study Museum is in line with the average and median for the peer museums. The MSA-to-attendance ratio is higher but is lower than two of its peers and takes into account the large number of nonadmissions attendance. Gate admissions projected for the Study Museum are between the average and median and ranks it fifth highest.

The ratio of visits per square foot for the Study Museum is a little low, indicating that there is room in the building and the exhibit halls to grow attendance. At the same time, it raises the question of whether the future museum's exhibit galleries are sized correctly.

Table 8.4   Template: Study Museum and Peer Museums: Size and Attendance Ratios

Museum	Total Indoor Facility Sq. Footage	Total Indoor Exhibit Sq. Footage	On-site Attendance	MSA Population	On-site Attd to MSA Ratio	DMA Population (includes MSA)	On-site Attd to DMA Ratio	On-site School Attendance	Ratio School On-site Attd to MSA Population
A									
B									
C									
D									
CURRENT MUSEUM									
E									
F									
G									
H									
Excludes current museum: AVERAGE MEDIAN									
FUTURE EXPANDED									
High for Peers Low for Peers									

Methodology 2: Analysis Based on Market Segment Populations

This methodology looks at capture ratios for each market segment. Generally, the primary market (geographically closest to the museum site) will have the highest capture ratio. The secondary market ratio is often approximately one-quarter of the primary market, though it varies depending on the geographical distance of the market as well as other factors. The tourist capture ratio is usually 5 percent or less of the tourist population. Of course, there are always anomalies. For example, the capture ratio of the tourist market will be less if the tourist population is extremely large and there is a lot of competition in the area. Museums in New York City will generally have a smaller capture ratio of the tourist population than a museum in a small to midsize city.

Developing capture ratios for the Study Museum is based on the following:

- Knowledge of the museum field and capture ratios by type of museum

- Knowledge of museum field capture ratios for each of the market segments
- Factoring for opportunities and challenges in the market
- Factoring for anomalies of the Study Museum, such as free admission, an unusually large traveling exhibit gallery, and much more

Table 8.5 presents attendance potential estimates and capture ratios for the hypothetical Study Museum.

Table 8.5   Sample Stable-Year Attendance Potential Estimate by Market Segment

Market Segment	Population 20XX	Capture	Attendance	Share
Primary (MSA)	3,100,000	15.0%	465,000	61.2%
Secondary (DMA less MSA)	1,800,000	3.0%	54,000	7.1%
School	284,000	23.0%	65,320	8.6%
Tourist (Overnight)	7,000,000	2.5%	175,000	23.0%
Total/Cumulative	12,184,000	6.2%	**759,320**	100.0%

	Current Yr 20XX Data	-15.0%	Future Stable Year	+15%
On-Site Attendance	550,000	645,150	**759,000**	872,850
Attendance Increase over 20XX		95,150	209,000	322,850
Attendance Increase over 20XX		17.3%	38.0%	58.7%
MSA Population	2,700,000		3,100,000	
MSA Ratio	20%	21%	24%	28%
School Share			8.6%	
Resident Share			68.4%	
Tourist Share			23.0%	

Methodology 3: Analysis Based on Historical Attendance at the Study Museum

Table 8.6 looks at five years of historical attendance data at the Study Museum. This methodology takes into account the highs and lows of what an existing museum has done in the past as a way of understanding what a future expanded museum might do in an average or stable year.

Each year notes whether there was a traveling exhibit. In one case, there was a blockbuster traveling exhibit. Estimated future attendance, after an expansion is completed, is compared to the average of the five years of data. The future stable year is expected to have a nonblockbuster traveling exhibit. The average for the current Study Museum excludes data for year 1, which had a blockbuster traveling exhibit.

Table 8.6   Sample Stable-Year Attendance Potential by Historical Data

	Current Museum						Future Expansion Estimate		
	Base Yr 1	FY 2	FY 3	FY 4	FY 5	AVG no	Stable Yr	Increase from	
Traveling Exhibit?	yes, BB	yes	small	yes	yes	FY 1	yes	Average	
Gate Attendance									
Paid General Public Attendance	200,000	145,000	120,000	190,000	160,000	153,750	tbd		
Members	110,000	100,000	88,000	90,000	90,000	92,000	tbd		
Groups with Chaperones	88,000	80,000	65,000	80,000	75,000	75,000	tbd		
Free/Complimentary	14,000	10,000	15,000	13,000	12,000	12,500	tbd		
Total Gate Attendance	412,000	335,000	288,000	373,000	337,000	333,250	415,000	81,750	25%
Education Programs	28,000	25,000	28,000	30,000	35,000	29,500	40,000	10,500	36%
Other On-site	221,000	190,000	225,000	185,000	205,000	201,250	220,000	18,750	9%
Total Other On-site Attendance	249,000	215,000	253,000	215,000	240,000	230,750	305,000	74,250	32%
Total On-site Attendance	661,000	550,000	541,000	588,000	577,000	564,000	720,000	156,000	28%

Table 8.7   Sample Stable-Year Attendance Potential Compared to Historical Data

COMPARISON OF METHODOLOGIES 1, 2, AND 3

Once attendance potential estimates have been developed for the Study Museum using each methodology, the results are compared. In some cases, the resulting ratios can be averaged, though that is not necessarily the best approach. Another method is to factor each method for relative validity for a variety of reasons. In all cases, the analyst needs to be able to justify why the Study Museum might have attendance higher or lower than its peers or regional museums and attractions.

Table 8.8 presents the attendance potential estimates for the future expanded Study Museum for each of the three previous methodologies. In this example, the approaches are averaged to come up with a final attendance potential figure. Once that number is determined, an attendance range should be developed. The range could be as little as ±10 percent to as high as ±20 percent. Existing museums with a track record could use the ±10 percent range. New museums and expansions should use the ±15 percent or ±20 percent range. For planning purposes, the lower attendance number might be used for revenue budgeting and the higher number to help analyze whether the planned museum is sized appropriately.

The final figure, whether the average of the methods or another figure, should be entered into the table of peer museums to check whether the attendance ratio looks reasonable and is justifiable.

Methodology 4: Analysis Based on Attendance at Local and Regional Museums and Attractions

Knowing the attendance at local and regional museums and attractions will help determine the upper and lower boundaries

Table 8.8   Sample Stable-Year Attendance Potential Comparison by Methodology

MSA Population 3,100,000	Attendance Potential Estimate	MSA Attendance Ratio
Method 1: Comparison to peers	730,000	23.5%
Method 2: Market segment capture ratios	759,000	24.5%
Method 3: Historical attendance	720,000	23.2%
Average	744,500	24.0%
Plus 15%	856,175	27.6%
Less 15%	632,825	20.4%

of performance for your museum. It is good for broad parameters but is less precise than the other methods. It is used to double-check the attendance potential estimate to see where it falls among the region's museums and attractions and whether it appears reasonable. If it does not appear reasonable, then the attendance potential estimate should be revised, unless the variance is justifiable.

Often, the attendance ranking of museums and attractions in an area fall within the same rankings by type of entity, though there are always anomalies. Free parks, beaches, casinos, and annual festivals may have the highest attendance in a region. Reasonably sized zoos and aquariums usually have higher attendance than a children's museum or a history museum or a historic dwelling. In larger cities, large science centers and art museums often have the highest attendance. Since attendance can vary significantly from year to year, it is best to collect data for several years and research whether there were any anomalies, such as blockbuster exhibitions or inclement weather, that affected attendance.

Table 8.9 Sample Local and Regional Museums and Attractions

Current MSA population	2,700,000	
Future metropolitan population	3,100,000	Attendance
Attraction	Year XX	Ratio
Amusement park	4,000,000	148%
Zoo	1,000,000	37%
Aquarium	750,000	28%
Future museum stable year	744,500	24%
Current museum average	564,000	21%
Children's museum	200,000	7%
Art museum	90,000	3%
History museum	80,000	3%

Table 8.10 presents median attendance by discipline as published in the American Alliance of Museum's 2009 Museum Financial Information. Living Collections includes zoos, arboretum/botanic gardens, and nature centers. Before fiscal year 2006, those disciplines were broken out, and zoos in fiscal years 2003, 2004, and 2005 had the highest median attendance, which was ±440,000 in each of those years.

Table 8.10 Median Museum Attendance by Discipline

Attendance by Discipline Median	FY2003	FY2004	FY2005	FY2006	FY2007	FY2008	#Respondents At Least 1 Yr
Zoo	438,989	438,540	440,502	now in Living Collections			
Science/Technology Center/Museum	296,388	174,695	244,589	379,970	400,663	357,103	25
Living Collections	-	-	-	196,572	214,421	208,574	14
Children's/Youth Museum	66,510	72,000	78,500	128,142	132,271	130,870	15
General Museum	46,846	50,632	43,500	51,542	53,214	58,500	65
Nat'l History/Anthropology Museum	67,929	61,503	62,803	58,306	58,607	58,176	28
Art Museum	54,831	58,705	59,822	44,555	42,745	44,878	142
Specialized Museum	20,000	18,443	20,000	21,000	25,251	22,000	64
Historic House/Site	18,000	16,392	16,000	11,000	11,644	11,700	75
History Museum/Historical Soc.	11,607	10,500	10,750	8,550	9,000	10,000	159
ALL DISCIPLINES	**34,215**	**34,000**	**33,446**	**27,500**	**26,696**	**26,500**	**587**

Source: American Association of Museums, 2009 Museum Financial Information, p. 43.

UPDATING THE ATTENDANCE POTENTIAL ESTIMATE

Attendance potential estimates are developed years before a new museum or expansion opens. The estimate is based on a set of assumptions (e.g., size, components, capital budget, and population projections), and as those assumptions change over time, the attendance potential estimate must be updated.

Section 9

Audience Research and Evaluation Methodologies

INTRODUCTION

Audience research is a management tool that helps inform but not dictate decisions. Using methodologies such as mall intercepts, telephone surveys, Web surveys, focus groups, visitor panels, and other forms of audience research, the museum can come to a better understanding about which of its creative ideas are of greatest appeal and how it should position its experiences for each of its audiences.

Improving the product in the eyes of the audience, both as a learning resource and as a compelling visitor experience, is the most critical research process for an institution dependent on earned revenue from its audience. The process involves understanding the audience and customers, who they are, how they evaluate and understand the museum's programs and services, and the dynamics by which they interact with those programs and services. The following methodologies are among those available (for a summary, see table 9.1; for comparison, table 9.2, and sequencing, see table 9.3):

Table 9.1   Audience Research and Evaluation Methodologies

Focus groups
Intercept interviews
Online surveys
Telemarketing surveys
Visitor advisory groups
Invited visitors
Geodemographic profile
Psychographic profile
Attitude, awareness, and usage study
Visitor analysis
Appeal studies (draw)
Visitor satisfaction and learning surveys (fulfillment)

AUDIENCE RESEARCH AND EVALUATION METHODOLOGIES

- **Focus Groups:** Focus group sessions will be held with key components of the audience segments (visitor cohort groups) currently attending museums as well as segments not currently attending but that we hope to attract in the future. Visitor cohort groups might include the following:
  o   Families with children ages 4 to 7 in the primary and secondary areas
  o   Families with children ages 8 to 15 in the primary and secondary areas
  o   Older adult residents in the primary and secondary areas
  o   Young adult residents in the primary and secondary areas
  o   Tourists: family, business, and group tours
  o   Schoolteachers and their students

Each focus group will be drawn from specific key visitor segments as defined by the cohort definition analysis. These sessions should be utilized primarily to discern the public's reaction to proposed plans and creative ideas. Generally, these sessions are utilized to gather only qualitative information only that is not analyzed in a statistical fashion.

- **Intercept Interviews:** Clipboard interviews with passersby in other museums, shopping malls, airports, and places where future visitors tend to congregate.
- **Online Surveys:** Individuals are invited to fill out an online questionnaire and, if they agree to participate, are given access codes and e-mail reminders until the survey period is completed. Participants can be enlisted in malls and other public spaces (with permission) or by phone or mail. Automated survey sites such as SurveyMonkey.com facilitate responding and tabulating.
- **Telemarketing Surveys:** Outgoing calls by marketing agencies prepared with a questionnaire script. These calls can be made to a representative sample that matches the market profile, which is the least expensive process, or to a more targeted selection. The latter case, which may target people who might visit the museum (there are segments of the overall market who are not potential visitors) is based on a screening instrument, which, in effect, consists of the initial questions asked by the telemarketer. If respondents do not qualify for the target, then the telephone call is terminated. Telemarketing is a methodology that is appropriate for only certain types of information, as it is not possible to use visual materials, and the telemarketer cannot confirm that the responses are accurate. While telemarketing is relatively inexpensive, many households are getting fed up with telemarketing to the point that the people who respond to telemarketing tend toward senior citizens and stay-at-homes who have time on their hands.
- **Visitor Advisory Groups:** Comprised of volunteers in certain key visitor segments, visitor advisory groups can be convened from time to time to react to ideas in development. Advisory groups might include teachers, travel agents, parents of young children, and others who are familiar with the behavior of a particular segment.
- **Invited Visitors:** Before opening, once the museum is safe for invited guests, people can be invited to look at the exhibits as they are being installed and react to questions posed by researchers who will accompany them. Invited visitors will be helpful during shakedown and previews and, after opening, in summative evaluations of the opening scenarios. The invited visitors will be observed by researchers who will stop and ask questions from time to time and ask them to fill out a questionnaire before departure. In some instances, invited visitors will be asked for follow-up research by telephone.
- **Geodemographic Profile:** Utilizing existing software programs, profiles of visitors by ZIP code residence can be developed. The information can be utilized to measure the effectiveness of ongoing advertising and promotion programs and help plan future efforts. Additionally, this information is frequently useful when preparing fundraising proposals and other external documents.
- **Psychographic Profile:** By capturing the addresses (street address and ZIP code) of a significant sample of the museum visitors, a psychographic analysis of museum visitors can be conducted utilizing cluster analysis methods. Once a profile has been developed, it can be utilized to determine areas within the established market where people would be likely to have a higher-than-average propensity to visit the museum. In addition to providing the museum with lifestyle profiles of its audience, the data can be especially effective for highly targeted marketing efforts, such as direct-mail campaigns, social media, and cable television advertising.
- **Attitude, Awareness, and Usage Study:** This study would be conducted by telephone shortly after opening and every few years thereafter by contacting a cross section of the population of the primary and secondary market areas. Questionnaires will be designed to gain a broad market assessment as to the attitude of residents toward the museum and their awareness of the museum and its programs and to measure how frequently people utilize (or believe they utilize) the facility. The study should also compare the museum to other major attractions in the region. Typically, such a study has a significantly large sample to allow statistical analysis of the data. Such a study can be of great use in establishing baseline attitudinal data on the museum and comparing it to similar attractions in the region. Such information can help the museum decide which messages to emphasize during a campaign and identify any major weaknesses to be addressed. By compiling the results of such questioning, approximations can be made as to the effectiveness of promotional and advertising efforts. What percentage of the audience did advertising attract? How does this compare to the expenditure? Although such an analysis is far from perfect, it does allow for some degree of cost-effectiveness to be determined and also provides a basis for comparative analysis of efforts over time.
- **Visitor Analysis:** These can be tagged onto the other studies listed above or done separately. The museum should develop a battery of demographic information that is collected on a regular basis. It should include questions such as the following:
  o   How many people in your party?
  o   What are their ages?
  o   Are you visiting with family? friends? other?
  o   What mode of transportation is used to visit?
  o   Where do they live (city, state, ZIP code)?
  o   What is the level of educational attainment (adults)?
  o   What is the annual household income?

Tracking such information over time can help develop a deeper profile of the key visitor segments by season. This is important because this profile can change dramatically over the course of a year. Understanding these changes can help develop an optimal marketing plan. Additionally, changes in this profile over time can be tracked and used to modify marketing efforts.

Table 9.2 Audience Research: Methodology Matrix

Research Task	Quantitative		Qualitative		
	Intercept or Web Surveys	Telephone Surveys	Focus Groups	Advisory Groups	Invited Visitors
1. Key visitor segment definition analysis	√		√		
2. Concept testing with key visitor segment			√	√	
3. Name and identity research	√		√		
4. Formative evaluation	√		√	√	
5. Base awareness survey		√			
6. Design support research			√		
7. Prototype testing	√				√
8. Pricing and positioning study			√		
9. Shop testing					√
10. Shakedown and previews				√	√
11. Summative/opening evaluation	√		√	√	√

- Appeal Studies (Draw): Are the museum and its currently featured programs sufficiently appealing to draw visitors? Whenever the museum opens a new major program or exhibit and supports the opening with media and promotion, it is always valuable to conduct research to determine how these efforts impacted the gate. This can be done through questionnaires administered to a random sample of the museum's audience that ask questions such as the following: What motivated you to visit today?
  o Did you hear about [special attraction] before you came to the museum? Where?
  o How many were in your party?
  o Who made the decision to visit?
  o When was the decision made?

By compiling the results of such questioning, approximations can be made as to the effectiveness of promotional and advertising efforts. What percentage of the audience did advertising attract? How does this compare to the expenditure?

- Visitor Satisfaction and Learning Surveys (Fulfillment): Once marketing and promotion have drawn visitors through the door, a different set of questions is needed to determine whether they enjoyed themselves and learned something and whether the experience matched or exceeded their expectations. Sometimes, catchy titles and heavy marketing investment can draw crowds (appeal), but thin experiences after such marketing hype can lose friends and supporters quickly (fulfillment). A few standardized questions should be developed to measure fulfillment and satisfaction both directly and indirectly so that relative levels can be monitored as conditions change. For example, visitor satisfaction tends to decline as crowd levels increase, and satisfaction surveys are useful ways of determining an optimum capacity. A key part of satisfaction in museums is getting something valuable out of the experience, and surveys that assess whether visitors are learning are useful to both program developers and sponsoring investors.

SEQUENCE OF RESEARCH: DEVELOPMENT OF A NEW VISITOR EXPERIENCE STUDY

Table 9.3 Audience Research: Phased Sequence

	Phase Budget Source	Budget
1. Key visitor segments definition analysis	Planning	
2. Concept testing with key visitor segments	Planning	
3. Name and identity research	Marketing	
4. Formative evaluation	Program	
5. Design support research	Program	
6. Awareness survey	Marketing	
7. Prototype testing	Program	
8. Pricing and positioning study	Marketing	
9. Shop testing	Program	
10. Shakedown and previews	Program	
11. Summative/opening evaluation	Planning	
Total		

Section 10

Audiences: Nonusers

Benefits

INTRODUCTION

Nonusers are those who do not engage with the museum in any transactional way—they neither attend the galleries nor participate in programs.

Nevertheless, museums can benefit nonusers, as museum researcher Dr. Carol A. Scott found:

> A growing body of literature suggests that the absence of direct use does not preclude attribution of value and that non-use values such as option, future and bequest value are significant dimensions of the total value of culture. (Scott, 2007, p. 5)

NONUSERS: BENEFITS

Option refers to the nonuser's desire to have many options of activities, even if he or she does not use them. *Future* refers to the nonuser's trust that museums will interpret the nonuser's world to the future, and *bequest* refers to the nonuser's sense that he or she or his or her affiliates can give the museum some thing or some story that will be a permanent legacy.

Additionally, Scott found that nonusers, if they were aware of the museum, benefited from its symbolic value in creating a sense of civic identity and that simply existing as a public institution contributed to civic trust (Holden, 2004, as cited in Scott, 2007, p. 5).

See "15. Bibliography for Museums" for citation references.

Section 11

Audiences: Program Participants

INTRODUCTION

Program participants are the other category within audiences, after visitors. In many cases, the programs they are participating in are scheduled, and in many of those cases, the participants have reserved in advance. A series of six ceramics workshops on six Saturday mornings is an example of six programs, as is a corporate function rental with invited guests as the participants. Programs, however, include any nonvisit engagement, and therefore the term has a miscellaneous role, with its inherently fuzzy definitions. Hence, program participants also include attendees at off-site festivals run by the museum, volunteers, and all virtual and outreach engagements.

The following text and tables may be selected and adapted to suit your museum.

PROGRAM PARTICIPANTS

Table 11.2 lists many kinds of programs, with each having many possible topics, formats, and audiences. Programs are a relatively new methodology for museums, and commonly shared frameworks and terms are still evolving.

Table 11.1 Program Participant Segments by Geography

Key Program Segment	Primary Residents	Secondary and Tertiary	Day-Trippers	Overnight Tourists
Regional households				
Collectors, clubs, and hobbyists				
Professional communities				
Businesses and corporations				
Community organizations				
Leaders, advisers, and supporters				
Schools and universities				
Other museums and public venues				

Table 11.2   Potential Programs

Studios and workshops	Evening young adult programs
Citizen (science) programs	Evening empty-nester programs
Summer camps/camp-ins	Museum product production and distribution
Corporate and private function rentals	Tour and travel programs
Kids discovery day care/preschool	Community events
Teacher professional development and institutes	Distance learning programs
Outreach programs	Intern programs
Communications programs	Birthday parties
Academic and business conferences	Online and social media programs
School and youth group programs	Research facility and services
Festivals	Lecture series
Challenges Function rentals	Museum school
Home school programs	On-site charter/magnet school
Restoration workshops	Library branch
Book and affinity clubs	Live broadcast studio
Volunteer programs	Café forums
Collection loans	Governance and advisory meetings
Conservation services and lab	Intellectual property leases
	Virtual programs

Section 12

Audiences: Key Visitor Segments

INTRODUCTION

While it is important to know individual learning stages and needs, our visitors typically come to a museum in some *sociocultural context* or, in plainer English, with friends or as part of a school group or with the family. We need to understand the learning needs of these groupings of visitors or *key visitor segments*. Most museum visits are social experiences, and groups such as families involve multiple ages, interests, and learning styles.

Lev Vygotsky's social constructivism reminds us that learning is also dependent on culture and language and on the people around us. Dr. Paul G. Heltne has observed that a human family moves through a museum in similar ways to a primate family of chimps moving through a forest: both families play, teach, exercise, and learn at the same time. Studies such as the PISEC research in Philadelphia look at the learning dynamics among family members as they move through a museum (for more detail, see "33. Education: Learning Theory" and "35. Education: Strategies").

The six key visitor segments reflect the major visitor groups for museums (see table 12.1). A museum can use this framework to assess how its annual attendance falls into these sociocultural contexts. Five groups are social groups of two or more individuals, and one addresses solo visitors (see also tables 12.2 and 12.3).

Table 12.1   Social Context Framework: Key Visitor Segments

Adults visiting with children	Young adults 18–34 without children
• Small family groups	• Dating couples
• Extended families	• Groups of friends (18 to 34)
• Day-trip and tourist families	• College students
• Preschoolers and caregivers	
Pre-K–12 school and youth groups	Teens 11–18
• Elementary school	• After-school teens
• Middle school	• Groups of friends 13–18
• High school	• Sports activities
• Day care groups	• Science and hobby clubs
• Home schoolers	
Adults 34+ visiting with adults	Solo visitors 18–75+
• Couples without children	• Students on projects
• Empty nesters	• Singles
• Seniors	• Travelers
• Group tours	• Aficionados
• Business conferences	
• Adult tourists	

Table 12.2   Sample Shares of Visitor Segments

	Children's Museum	Science Center with IMAX	History Museum	Art Museum
Adults visiting with children	70%	57%	23%	20%
School and youth groups	25%	23%	35%	17%
Adults (35+) visiting without children	2%	7%	28%	44%
Young adults without children	0%	6%	3%	10%
Teens	1%	3%	1%	1%
Solo adults	0%	1%	8%	6%
Others	2%	2%	2%	2%
Total annual exhibit/gallery visitors	100%	100%	100%	100%

Note: These are specific museums and may not be representative or predictive of other museums in the sector.

Table 12.3   Key Visitor Segments by Geography: Planning Worksheet

Segment	Core Resident Market	Primary Resident Market	Secondary Resident Market	Day-Trippers	Overnight Tourists
Adults with children					
Adults with adults					
School and youth groups					
Teens					
Young adults					
Solo visitors					

✓✓✓ = likely to be the prime segment.
✓✓ = likely to be the secondary segment.
✓ = likely to be minor, but important share.
+ = targeted programs might attract this group.

Section 13

Audiences: Visitors by Category

INTRODUCTION

In addition to categorizing visits by their sociocultural context (see "12. Key Visitor Segments") a few other ways of categorizing visitors are needed for meaningful comparisons and analysis: by residence, by motivation, by identity, by the kind of benefit sought, and by psychographics.

VISITORS BY CATEGORY

Visitors by Location of Residence

Distance from an attraction or museum is one of the key indicators for attendance; the closer you live to a museum, the more likely you are to attend. The foundational way of looking at the market is through geographic zones radiating outward from the museum. After opening, the capture ratio of the resident population in these zones can be quantified and analyzed through ZIP code tracking of visitors. These data can be used to target marketing.

The principal segments identified by this perspective are *core* (optional), *primary, secondary, tertiary (optional) day-trippers, tourists,* and *school students.* See full definitions in "49. Market Demographics and Population Analysis."

Visitors by Motivation

These frameworks help a museum understand why visitors might come by looking at their reasons for visiting, at their personal identity, and at the benefits they get from their visit (see tables 13.1 to 13.4).

See "15. Bibliography for Museums" for citation reference.

Table 13.1   Reasons Why Visitors Come to Museums (by Priority)

1. To have a good time with friends and family
2. To experience something new
3. To learn something new

Table 13.2   Identity-Related Reasons for Visiting

1. The Explorer: I want to see what's new.
2. The Facilitator: I want to see all of us have a good time.
3. The Professional/Hobbyist: I'm into this kind of stuff.
4. The Experience Seeker: I want to feel something.
5. The Spiritual Pilgrim: This is a meaningful journey for me.

Source: Falk (2009) with edits by John Jacobsen.

Table 13.3   Personal Benefits Sought from Museums

1. To have the opportunity to be with people (social interaction)
2. To do something worthwhile
3. To feel comfortable and at ease in one's surroundings
4. To have a challenge of new experiences
5. To learn
6. To participate actively in leisure events

Source: Marilyn Hood Museum News, 1983.

Table 13.4   Culture Segments: Visitor Profiles by Psychographics

Enrichment—mature outlook; traditional minded and interested in heritage, nostalgia, and lifelong learning

Affirmation—aspirational; seek quality time, build self-identity, and look for self-improvement

Essence—sophisticated, discerning, independently minded and spontaneous; very active cultural consumers

Release—time poor, busy, ambitious; struggle to prioritize leisure activities; wistful and need guarantees they're not wasting time or money

Expression—community focused, receptive, confident, value inclusivity, and creatively inclined

Perspective—settled, self-sufficient, focused, content, with fulfilling interests; appreciate being reminded how much they enjoy occasional cultural outings

Stimulation—contemporary minded; social, active, and experimental and like discovery and being the first to know

Entertainment—enjoy mainstream fun, popular acts and events; see mainstream culture as great social and leisure opportunities

Source: Morris Hargreaves McIntyre (2016). To take the test, see http://www.mhminsight.com/culturesegments.

Section 14

Best Practices Research

INTRODUCTION

Fortunately, the museum field is highly collaborative and shares information and procedures on a routine basis. A museum can look to other museums operating in other cities for models that might be adapted for its own use. In particular, research into best practices in such areas as ticketing, exhibitions, marketing, attracting underserved audiences, visitor services, staff morale, and other areas of museum operation should be identified by talking to other museum directors and staff and then researched in-depth by the museum's parallel staff members.

Best practices research is also a good way to constructively engage donors, board members, volunteers, and other stakeholders who travel, visit museums, and come back with suggestions for your museum.

The objective of the "Best Practices Research" section is to outline formal processes that will help your museum gain an awareness of successful museum practices throughout the field, especially practices that can act as a model for the museum. The processes outlined include ways of harnessing volunteers in the research. During the long, early years of a project, sending folks out into the world in search of best practices is a proven way of both advancing planning and maintaining momentum and interest among board members.

BEST PRACTICES RESEARCH

Within the best practices studies, there are four levels of research:

1. Staff identify museums to study
2. Volunteers and staff visit the museums
3. Staff review best practices
4. The museum's future is benchmarked

Each level will determine a different kind of data—external information (site visits and best practices review) versus research that is based on internal information (benchmarking)—and the research will be most effective if all levels are pursued.

BEST PRACTICES RESEARCH PROCESS

1. Identify museums to study
   a. Contact museum directors and staff at conferences and ask their opinions about which museums excel in what areas.
   b. Identify common best practices.
   c. Define areas of museum practice and operation that are to be studied.
   d. Identify models for the museum to use in planning for the future.
2. Site visit reports (by volunteers, often board members)
   a. Train volunteers; orient them to our objectives for the research.
   b. Present hypothetical examples of asking questions and documenting the answers effectively so that the site visit report is as useful as possible for comparing data.
   c. Define which museums or types of museums should be visited. Create a list and map of museums to visit.
   d. Volunteers visit museums.

e. The staff or volunteers file a standardized form report with the following questions answered:
   - ➢ What museum did you visit?
   - ➢ Who visited and is writing this site visit report, and when did the visit take place?
   - ➢ What were the conditions of your visit? (e.g., was the museum crowded, were there school groups there, or was it raining outside?).
   - ➢ What was your experience? What parts did you visit?
   - ➢ How long were you in the building? How long was it from site arrival to departure?
   - ➢ With whom did you speak?
   - ➢ What were you impressed by? What should we consider doing like this museum?
   - ➢ What should we not do like this museum?
   - ➢ How do you think this museum and/or experience can best influence the museum?
   - ➢ Who can our staff speak with at a later time to learn more about the experience or exhibition? (who is in charge of [name experience of exhibition]?).
   - ➢ Photograph or video relevant images.
   - ➢ List collateral materials and other attachments (e.g., brochures, maps, and photos)
   - ➢ What online or mobile experiences influenced your experiences?
   - ➢ Other comments?

3. Best practices review (undertaken by staff in later phases)
   a. Read site visit reports and/or arrange a staff visit.
   b. Add data to summary comparison matrix.
   c. Staff contacts peers at each institution to discuss policies, programs, expertise, and costs:
      - ➢ How will our key indicators compare to theirs? (e.g., number of participants and number of new programs).
      - ➢ Determine their program's start-up and capital costs.
      - ➢ Determine their program's direct operating revenues and expenses; inquire about overhead impact and resources not included in costs.
      - ➢ How are their exhibits, programs, staffing, facility and equipment similar to or different from ours? (e.g., number of staff, number of programs, facilities available, and equipment used).
      - ➢ Have they already dealt with challenges similar to ours? How did they overcome them? (Identify key challenges to discuss.)
      - ➢ What other museums do they consider excellent in this area?
      - ➢ What do these institutions have in common that make them "the best?" (e.g., documented expectations and standards and strategies).
   d. Summarize each museum program investigated on one page.
   e. Compare key indicators, exhibits, staffing, facilities, equipment, and so on.
   f. Identify "best in class" museums for each functional area; identify benchmark indicators.
   g. Discuss approaches to challenges the museum may face.

4. Benchmarking
   a. Compile and annotate documentation. Create comparison chart of key information.
   b. Document how the museum is doing compared to benchmarks.
   c. Identify aspects to be improved and key pieces of information relevant to planning.
   d. Review practices in museums and similar institutions—talk to peer staff to confirm and share literature and documentation.
   e. Develop and revise policies and practices based on best practices identified. Use comparison chart to inform decisions.

Section 15

Bibliography for Museums

Alford, J., & O'Flynn, J. (2009). Making Sense of Public Value: Concepts, Critiques and Emergent Meanings. *International Journal of Public Administration, 32*(3-4), 171-191.

Allen, S. (2004). *Finding Significance*. Port Richmond, CA: Paris Printing.

American Academy of Arts & Sciences. (2010, February). *Humanities Indicators*. Retrieved December 1, 2014, from American Academy of Arts & Sciences : http://www.humanitiesindicators.org/content/document.aspx?i=108

American Alliance of Museums (AAM). (n.d.). *Ethics, Standards and Best Practices: Collections Stewardship*. Retrieved May 28, 2017, from American Alliance of Museums: http://www.aam-us.org/resources/ethics-standards-and-best-practices/collections-stewardship

American Alliance of Museums. (2012). *Mission and Institutional Planning*. Retrieved from aam-us.org: http://aam-us.org/resources/ethics-standards-and-best-practices/characteristics-of-excellence-for u-s-museums/missions-and-planning

American Alliance of Museums. (2012). *Museum Benchmarking Online*. Retrieved February 2012, from American Alliance of Museums: http://www.aam-us.org/mbo

American Alliance of Museums. (2014). The Sustainable Museum. 47.

American Association of Museums (AAM). (1994). Leisure Decisions Influencing African American Use of Museums. Washington, DC: AAM.

American Association of Museums (AAM). (1996). *Museums and Consultants: Maximizing the Collaboration*. Washington, DC: American Association of Museums (AAM).

American Association of Museums (AAM). (2002). *Directory of Historical Organizations in the United States and Canada*. Washington, DC: American Association of Museums (AAM).

American Association of Museums (AAM). (2003). *Slaying the Financial Dragon: Strategies of Museums*. Washington, DC: American Association of Museums (AAM).

American Association of Museums. (1992). *The Audience in Exhibition Development*. Library/Exhibits. American Association of Museums.

American Association of Museums. (1993). *Shaping the Museum: The MAP Institutional Planning Guide*. Wahington, DC: American Association of Museums (AAM).

American Association of Museums. (2000). Building New Audiences. *Audio Cassette*. Washington, DC: American Association of Museums.

American Association of Museums Task Force on Education. (1992). Excellence and Equity: Education and the Public Dimension of Museums. Washington, DC: American Association of Museums.

American Associaton of Museums (AAM). (1984). *Museums for a New Century*. Washington, DC: American Associaiton of Museums (AAM).

American Institute of Architects. (2014). Defining the Architect's Basic Services. In A. I. Architects, *The Architect's Handbook of Professional Practice* (15 ed., pp. 952-975). Hoboken, NJ: John Wiley & Sons.

Americans for the Arts. (2012). *Arts & Economics Prosperity Calculator*. Retrieved from Americans for the Arts: http://www.americansforthearts. org/information_services/research/services/economic_impacts/005.asp

Amherst H. Wilder Foundation. (1986). *Marketing Workbook for Non-Profit Organizations*. St.Paul, MN: Amherst H. Wilder Foundation.

Amherst H. Wilder Foundation. (1986). *Strategic Planning Workbook for Non-Profit Organizations*. St. Paul, MN: Amherst H. Wilder Foundation.

Anderson, D. (1997). *A Common Wealth: Museums in the learning age*. London: DCMS.

Anderson, G. (. (2012). *Reinventing the Museum (Second Edition)*. Lanham, MD: Alta Mira Press.

Anderson, G. (1998). *Museum Mission Statements: Building a Distinct Identity*. Washington, D.C: American Association of Museums.

Anderson, G. (2004). *Reinventing the Museum*. Washington, DC: American Association of Museums (AAM).

Anderson, G., & Adams, R. (1998). *Museum Mission Statements: Building a Distinct Identity*. Washington, DC: American Association of Museums (AAM).

Anderson, M. L. (2004). *Metrics of Success in Art Museums*. Los Angeles: The Getty Leadership Institute, J. Paul Getty Trust.

Anderson, P. (1991). *Before the Blue Print: Science Center Buildings*. Washington, DC: Association of Science-Technology Centers (ASTC).

Andreasen, A. R. (1995). *Marketing Social Changes*. San Francisco, CA: Jossey-Bass Publishing Co. .

Angelica, E. (2001). *Crafting Effective Mission & Vision Statements*. St. Paul, MN: Amherst Wilder Foundation.

Angelica, E. (2001). *The Fieldstone Alliance Guide to Crafting Effective Mission and Vision Statements*. Saint Paul: Fieldstone Alliance.

Archibald, R. R. (2004). *The New Town Square*. Walnut Creek, CA: Alta Mira Press.

Association of Children's Museums, White Oak Institute and Advisory Committee Leaders . (2011). *Key Indicators and Benchmark Calculator*. Developed under an Institute of Museum and Library Services grant under the 21st century Museum Professionals progr.

Association of Children's Museums (ACM). (1997). *Collective Vision: Starting and Sustaining Children's Museums.* Washington, DC: Association of Children's Museums (ACM).

Association of Children's Museums. (2004). *The 21st Century Learner: the Continuum Begins with Early Learning.* ACM.

Association of Children's Museums. (2011). Key Indicators and Benchmark Calculator. *21st Century Museum Professionals Program.*

Association of Science-Technology Centers (ASTC). (1993). *Executive Summary-Vision to Reality: CRITICAL DIMENSIONS IN SCIENCE CENTER DEVELOPMENT.* Washington, DC: Association of Science-Technology Centers (ASTC).

Association of Science-Technology Centers (ASTC). (1997). *Status Report on Science Centers: Vision to Reality.* Washington, DC: Association of Science-Technology Centers (ASTC).

Association of Science-Technology Centers (ASTC). (1998, October 17). Corporate Sponsorships: Fact, Fiction, and Practicalities. Association of Science-Technology Centers (ASTC).

Association of Science-Technology Centers (ASTC). (n.d.). *What Research Says About Learning In Science Museums.* Washington, DC: Association of Science-Technology Centers (ASTC).

Association of Science-Technology Centers (ASTC), Met Life Foundation. (2009). *A Lifetime of Curiosity: Science Centers and Older Adults.* Washington, DC: Association of Science-Technology Centers (ASTC).

ASTC Ancillary Services. (n.d.). *Museum Accounting Guidelines.* Washington, DC: ASTC Ancillary Services.

Backer, D. T. (2002, November). *Partnership as an Artform: What Works and What Doesn't in Nonprofit Arts Partnerships.* Retrieved 09 21, 2016, from California State University Human Interaction Research Institute: http://www.csun.edu/sites/default/files/hiri_b25.pdf

Baldwin, J. H. (October 2011). The Challenge of "Value" Engaging Communities in Why Museums Exist. *A Museum Association of New York | Museumwise White Paper.*

Barry, B. W. (1986). *Strategic Planning Workbook for Nonprofit Organizations.* Amherst H. Wilder Foundation.

Bartels, D. (2013). ASTC CEO Debate 2.

Bateson, M. C. (1994). *Peripheral Visions: Learning Along The Way.* HarperCollins.

Becker, V., Fraser, J., Hyder , J., Jacobsen, J., Lantz, E., Oran, A., et al. (2011). DISCUSS Proceedings Including DIGSS 1.0. In J. Hyder (Ed.), *The DISCUSS Colloquium.* Marblehead: National Science Foundation: ISEAward No. 0946691.

Beinhacker, S. M. (2004). *Generating and Sustaining Nonprofit Earned Income.* San Francisco: Peter Lang Publishing.

Bell, P., Lewenstein, B., Shouse, A. W., & Feder, M. A. (2009). *Learning Science in Informal Environments - People, Places, and Pursuits.* Washington, D.C.: THE NATIONAL ACADEMIES PRESS.

Berger, K., Penna, R. M., & Goldberg, S. H. (2010, 1 May). *The Battle for the Soul of the Nonprofit Sector.* Retrieved October 8, 2014, from Philadelphia Social Innovations Journal: http://www.philasocialinnovations.org/site/

Berger, S. (2003). *Understanding Nonprofit Financial Statements.* Washington, DC: BoardSource.

Bergeron, A., & Tuttle, B. (2013). *Magnetic: The Art and Science of Engagement.* Washington, DC: American Alliance of Museums (AAM) Press.

Berra, Y. (2015, September 23). *usatoday.com.* Retrieved June 14, 2016, from http://ftw.usatoday.com/2015/09/the-50-greatest-yogi-berra-quotes

Birckmayer, J. D., & Weiss, C. H. (August 2000). Theory-Based Evaluation in Practice: What Do We Learn? *Evaluation Review, 24*(4), 407-431.

Bloch, M. (2005, May/June). Forum: Mission as measure: Second thoughts. *Museum News, 84*(3), 37–41, 78–79.

Borrup, T. (2006). *The Creative Community Builder's Handbook.* St. Paul: Fieldstone Alliance.

Borun, M. (1998). *Family Learning in Museums: The PISEC Perspective.* Philadelphia/Camden Informal Science Education Collaborative.

Borun, M., Kelly, B. M., & Rudy, J. (2011). *In Their Own Voices.* The Franklin Institute.

Bradburne, J. M. (2001). A New Strategic Approach to the Museum and its Relationship to Society. *Museum Management and Curatorship,* 75-84.

Brand, S. (1994). *How Buildings Learn.* Willard, OH: Donnelly & Sons.

Brecht, B., & Weill, K. (1954). *The Threepenny Opera Adaptation by Marc Blitzstein.* (K. W. Brecht, Performer)

Brecht, B., Weill, K., & Desmond Ivo Vesey, a. E. (1964). The Threepenny Opera. Grove Press.

Bridal, T. (2004). *Exploring Museum Theatre.* Walnut Creek: Alta Mira Press.

Britain Thinks. (2013). *Public Perceptions of - and Attitudes to - the Purposes of Museums in Society.* London: Britain Thinks for Museums Association.

Brophy, S., & Wylie, E. (2008). *The Green Museum.* Lanham, MD: Alta Mira Press.

Browne, C. (2007). *The Educational Value of Museums. . .* New England Museum Association Annual Conference.

Carbone, L. (2004). *Clued In: How to Keep Customers Coming Back Again and Again.* Upper Saddle River, NJ: Prentice Hall Financial Times.

Carnegie Science Center. (2002). What is the Effect on Attendance When a Science Center Expands? Pittsburgh: Carnegie Science Center.

Carr, D. (2003). *The Promise of Cultural Institutions.* Walnut Creek: Alta Mira Press.

Carr, D. (2006). Mind as Verb. In H. Genoways, *Museum Philosophy for the Twenty-first Century.* AltaMira Press.

Carver, J., & Carver, M. (2006). *Reinventing Your Board: A Step-by-Step Guide to Implementing Policy Governance.* San Francisco: Jossey-Bass.

Chung, J., & Wilkening, S. (2009). Life Stages of the Museum Visitor. Washington, DC: American Association of Museums.

Clewell, B. C., & Fortenberry, N. (Jun 30, 2009, June 30). *Framework for Evaluating Impacts of Broadening Participation Projects.* Retrieved November 4, 2014, from National Science Foundation: http://www.nsf.gov/od/broadeningparticipation/framework-evaluating-impacts-broadening-participation-projects_1101.pdf

Coble, C. (2013). *Strategies that Engage Minds: Empowering North Carolina's Economic Future.* North Carolina Science, Mathematics, and Technology Education Center.

Cohen, R., & Kushner, R. J. (2014). *National Arts Index: 12-year span of 2001-12.* Retrieved December 1, 2014, from Americans for the Arts: http://www.americansforthearts.org/sites/default/files/pdf/information_services/art_index/2014-NAI-Full-Report.pdf

Collins, J. (1994). *Built to Last: Successful Habits of Visionary Companies.* New York: Harper Collins.

Collins, J. (2001). *Good to Great.* New York.

Collins, J. (2001). *Good to Great: Why Some Companies Make the Leap...And Others Don't.* New York: HarperBusiness.

Collins, J. (2005). *Good to Great and the Social Sectors: A Monograph to Accompany Good to Great.* New York: HarperCollins.

Committee on the Evaluation Framework for Successful K-12 STEM Education; Board on Science Education and Board on Testing and Assessment' Division of Behavioral and Social Sciences and Education. (2013). *Monitoring Progress Toward Successful K-12 STEM Education.* Washington, D.C.: THE NATIONAL ACADEMIES PRESS.

Cooperrider, D. L., Whitney, D., & Stavros, J. M. (2008). *Appreciative inquiry handbook: For leaders of change.* Brunswick: Crown Custom publishing, Inc.

Crane, V., Chen, M., Bitgood, S., & Serrrell, B. (February 1, 1994). *Informal Science Learning: What the Research Says About Television, Science Museums, and Community-Based Projects.* Dedham, MA: Research Communications Ltd.

Crutchfied, L. R., & Grant, H. M. (2008). *Forces for Good: The Six Practices of High-Impact Nonprofits.* San Francisco: Jossey-Bass, A Wiley Imprint.

Csikszentmihaly, M. R. (1990). *The Art of Seeing. An Interpretation of the Aesthetic Encounter.* Los Angeles: The J. Paul Getty Museum.

Csikszentmihalyi, M. (1997). *Finding Flow: The Psychology of Engagement with Everyday Life.* New York: Basic Boos/HarperCollins.

CyMAL - Museums Archives and Libraries . (2010). *A Museums Strategy for Wales.* . Wales.

Dana, J. C. (1999). *The New Museum: Selected Writings by John Cotton Dana -Introduction by Stephen E. Weil.* Newark: The Newark Museum Association.

Danilov, V. J. (1991). *Corporate Museums, Galleries and Visitor Centers: A Directory.* New York: Greenwood Press.

Danilov, V. J. (2005). *Women and Museums: A Comprehensive Guide.* New York: Alta Mira Press.

Darragh, J., & Snyder, J. S. (1993). *Museum Design: Planning and Building for Art.* New York: Oxford Press.

Davies, S., Paton, R., & O'Sullivan, T. (2013). The museum values framework: a framework for understanding organizational culture in museums. *Museum Management and Curatorship, 28*(4), 345-361.

Definitions Project. (2006). Retrieved May 5/19/2016, 2016, from Definitions Project: http://www.definitionsproject.com/

De Rojas, M. d. (2006). Experience and Satisfaction of visitors to museums and cultural exhibitions. *International Review on Public and Non Profit Marketing 3(1),* pp. 49-65.

Denzin, N. K. (1970). *The Research Act: A Theoretical Introduction to Sociological Methods.* Chicago: Aldine Publishing Co.

Dierking, L. D., & Falk, J. H. (1995). *Public Institutions for Personal Learning.* Washington, DC: American Association of Museums (AAM).

Dierking, L. D., & Falk, J. H. (2002). *Lessons Without Limit.* Walnut Creek, CA: Alta Mira Press.

Dierking, L. D., & Falk, J. H. (2004, July). Science Education in Principle, In Practice: Perspectives on a Decade of Museum Learning Research. *Science Education, Vol. 88, Supplement 1.* Washington, DC: Association of Science-Technology Centers (ASTC).

Doering, Z. D. (1999). Strangers, guests or clients? Visitor experiences in museums. *Curator: The Museum Journal (42(2),* pp. 74-87.

Doran, G. (1981). There's a S.M.A.R.T. way to write management's goals and objectives. *Management Review, 70*(11), 35-36.

Draper, L. (1987). *Museum Audiences Today: Building Constituencies for the Future.* Los Angeles: Museum Educators of Southern California.

Ebrahim, A., & Rangan, V. (2010, May). *The Limits of Nonprofit: A Contingency Framework for Measuring Social Performance.* Retrieved October 29, 2014, from Harvard Business School: http://www.hbs.edu/faculty/Publication%20Files/10-099.pdf

Eilean, H.-G. (10 Mar 1988). Counting visitors or visitors who count? In R. Lumley, *The Museum Time Machine: Putting Cultures on Display* (p. 211). London: Routledge.

Falk, J. (2009). *Identity and Museum Visitor Experiences.* Walnut Creek: Left Coast Press.

Falk, J. H. (2001). *Free Choice Science Education: How We Learn Science Outside of School.* New York: Teachers College, Columbia University.

Falk, J. H., & Dierking, L. D. (1992). *The Museum Experience.* Washington, D.C.: Left Coast Press, Inc.

Falk, J. H., & Dierking, L. D. (2000). *Learning from museums: Visitor experiences and the making of meaning.* Walnut Creek: AltaMira.

Falk, J. H., & Dierking, L. D. (2010, November-December). The 95 Percent Solution. *American Scientist, 98*(6), 486.

Falk, J. H., & Dierking, L. D. (Dec, 2012). *The Museum Experience Revisited.* Walnut Creek: Left Coast Press Inc.

Falk, J. H., & Dierking, L. D. (December 15, 2012). *Museum Experience Revisited.* Walnut Creek: Left Coast Press.

Falk, J. H., Heimlich, J., & Foutz, S. E. (2009). *Free Choice Learning and the Environment.* Lanham, MD: Alta Mira Press.

Falk, J. H., Randol, S., & Dierking, L. (2008). *The Informal Science Education Landscape: A Preliminary Investigation.* National Science Foundation.

Falk, J. S. (2006). *Thriving in the Knowledge Age: New Business Models for Museums and Other Cultural Institutions.* Lanham, MD: AltaMira Press.

Florida, R. (2002). *The Rise Of The Creative Class: And How It's Transforming Work, Leisure, Community And Everyday Life.* New York: Basic Books.

Fraser, J., Heimlich, J. E., Jacobsen, J., Yocco, V., Sickler, J., Kisiel, J., et al. (2012). Giant screen film and science learning in museums. *Museum Management and Curatorship, 27*(2), 179-195.

Friedman, A. J. (2007, January). The Great Sustainability Challenge: How Visitor Studies Can Save Cultural Institutions in the 21st Century. *Visitor Studies, 10*(1), 3-12.

Friedman, A. J. (2008, March 12). *Framework for Evaluating Impacts of Informal Science Education Projects.* Retrieved November 4, 2014, from informalscience.org: http://informalscience.org/documents/Eval_Framework.pdf

Gardner, H. (1999). *Intelligence Reframed: Multiple Intelligences for the 21st Century.* New York: Basic Books.

Garnett, R. (2001, July 12). *The Impact of Science Centers/Museums on their Surrounding Communities: Summary Report.* Retrieved October 8, 2014, from The Association of Science-Technology Centers (ASTC): http://www.astc.org/resource/case/Impact_Study02.pdf

Gates, B. (2013, January 2013). *Annual Letter.* Retrieved October 21, 2014, from Bill & Melinda Gates Foundation: http://www.gatesfoundation.org/Who-We-Are/Resources-and-Media/Annual-Letters-List/Annual-Letter-2013

Genoways, H. H. (1995). *Museum Philosophy in the 21st Century.* Lanham, MD: Alta Mira Press.

Genoways, H. H., & Ireland, L. M. (2003). *Museum Administration: An Introduction.* Walnut Creek, CA: Alta Mira Press.

George, G., & Sherrell-Leo, C. (2004). *Starting Right: A Basic guide to Museum Planning (2nd Edition).* Lanham, MD: Alta Mira Press.

Gilmore, J. (1999). *The Experience Economy.* Boston: Harbard Business School.

Griffiths, J.-M., & King, D. W. (2008, February 28). *Interconnections: The IMLS National Study on the Use of Libraries, Museums and the Internet.* Retrieved November 11, 2014, from Interconnections: http://www.interconnectionsreport.org/

Grimm, W., & Morris, M. W. (2009). *Planning Successful Museum Building Projects.* Lanham, MD: Alta Mira Press.

Grinell, S. (1993, January/February). Conference Speakers Debate Directions for Science Centers of the Future, Vo. 21, #1. *ASTC Newsletter.*

Grinell, S. (2003). *A Place for Learning Science: Starting a Science Center and Keeping It Running.* Washington, DC: Association of Science-Technology Centers (ASTC).

Grogg, A. H. (1994). *Museums Count: A Report by the American Association of Museums.* Washington, D.C.: American Association of Museums (AAM).

Groves, I. (2005). *Assessing the Economic Impactd of Science Centres on Their Local Communities.* Retrieved from Asia Pacific Network of Science & Technology Centres: http://www.aspacnet.org/apec/research/_pdfs/EconImpact-whole.pdf

Gurian, E. (1996). *Institutional Trauma: Major Changes in Museums and its Effects on Staff.* Washington, DC: American Association of Museums.

Gurian, E. (2005). Free at Last: A Case for Eliminating Admission Charges in Museums. *Museum News, Vol. 84, No. 5 September/October.*

Gurian, E. (2006). *Civilizing the Museum: The Collected Writings of Elaine Gurian.* New York: Routledge.

Gurian, E. H. (2006). *Civilizing The Museum.* New York: Routledge.

Gutwill, J., & Allen, S. (2010). *Facilitating Family Group Inquiry at Science Museum Exhibits.* Chicago: Wiley Periodicals, Inc.

Hartman, F. T. (2000). *Don't Park Your Brain Outside.* New Town Square, PA: Project Management Institute.

Hatton, A. (2012, May 11). The conceptual roots of modern museum management dilemmas. *Museum Management and Curatorship, 27*(2), 129-147.

Hein, G. E. (1998). *Learning in the Museum.* London: Routledge.

Hein, G. E. (1999). *Museums: Places of Learning.* Washington, DC: American Association of Museums.

Hein, G. E. (2006). Museum Education. In S. MacDonald, *A Companion to Museum Studies* (pp. 340-352). Oxford, United Kingdom: Blackwell Publishing.

Hein, G. E. (2012). *Progressive Museum Practice: John Dewey and Democracy.* New York: Left Coast Press.

Hein, G. E., & Alexander, M. (1998). *Museums: Places of Learning.* Washington, DC: American Association of Museums (AAM).

Heritage, M. f. (2009). *Cultural Indicators for New Zealand 2009.* Retrieved November 4, 2014, from Ministry for Culture & Heritage: http://www.mch.govt.nz/files/CulturalIndicatorsReport.pdf

Hill, C. T. (2007). *The Post-Scientific Society.* Retrieved December 29, 2014, from Issues in Science and Technology: http://issues.org/24-1/c_hill/

Hirsch, J. S., & Silverman, L. H. (2000). *Transforming Practice: Selections from the Journal of Museum Education 1992-1999.* Washington, DC: Museum Education Roundtable.

Hirzy, E. C. (1992). *Excellence and equity : education and the public dimension of museums.* Washington, D.C: American Association of Museums.

Hirzy, E. C. (2008). *Excellence and Equity: Education and the Public Dimension of Museums.* American Alliance of Museums.

Holden, J. (2004). *Capturing Cultural Value.* Retrieved 4 2014, November, from Demos: http://www.demos.co.uk/files/CapturingCulturalValue.pdf

Hood, M. G. (1983). Staying Away: Why People Choose Not to Visit Museums. *Museum News, 61*(4).

Hooper-Greenhill, E. (1998). Counting visitors or visitors who count? In R. Lumley, *The Museum-Time Machine.* London: Comedia Routledge.

Howarth, C., & Medrano, M. A. (1997). *Architecture & Exhibition Design.* Washington, DC: Assocation of Science-Technology Centers (ASTC).

Howe, J. (1997). *The Board Members Guide to Strategic Planning.* San Francisco: Jossey-Bass Publishers.

Howe, N., & Straus, W. (2000). *Millenials Rising.* New York: Vintage Books.

Hughes, C. (2002). *Museum Theatre: Communicating with Visitors Through Drama.* Washington, DC: Assocation of Science-Technology Centers (ASTC).

Humphrey, T., & Gutwill, J. P. (2005). *Fostering Active Prolonged Engagement.* San Francisco, CA: Exploratorium APE Team.

ICOM Statutes. (2007, August 24). *Development of the Museum Definition according to ICOM Statutes (2007-1946).* Retrieved November 11, 2014, from International Council of Museums: http://archives.icom.museum/hist_def_eng.html

ICOM, S. (2007). *Museum Definition.* Retrieved November 4, 2014, from ICOM.MUSEUM: http://icom.museum/the-vision/museum-definition/

Institute of Museum and Library Services (IMLS). (2004). *Exhibiting Public Values: Government Funding for Museums in the US.* Washington, DC: Institute of Museum and Library Services (IMLS).

Institute of Museum and Library Services (IMLS). (2005). *Museum Data Collection Report and Analysis.* Washington, DC: Institute of Museum and Library Services (IMLS).

Institute of Museum and Library Services (IMLS). (1998). *True Needs, True Partners: Museums & Schools Transforming Education.* IMLS.

Institute of Museum and Library Services (IMLS). (2008). *Interconnections: The IMLS National Study on the Use of Libraries, Museums and the Internet.* IMLS.

Institute of Museum and Library Services (IMLS). (2009). *Partnership for a Nation of Learners: Joing Forces, Creating Value.* Washington, DC: IMLS.

Institute of Museum and Library Services (IMLS) and Corporation for Public Broadcasting. (June 2009). *Partnership for a Nation of Learners, Joining Forces, Creating Value.*

Institute of Museum and Library Services (IMLS). (July 2009). *Museums, Libraries, and 21st Century Skills (IMLS-2009-NAI-01).* Washington, D.C.: Institute of Museum and Library Services (IMLS).

Institute of Museum and Library Services, I. (2004). *Charting the Landscape, Mapping New Paths: Museums, Libraries, and K-12 Learning.* Washington, DC: Institute of Museum and Library Services (IMLS).

Isaacson, W. (2011). *Steve Jobs.* New York: Simon & Schuster.

ISO. (2016, March 3). This material is adapted from ISO 18461: 2016 with permission of the American National Standareds Institute (ANSI) on behalf of ISO. All. *International Museum Statistics.*

Jackson, M.-R., & Herranz Jrr., J. (2002). *Culture Counts in Communities: A Framework for Measurement.* Washington, DC: The Urban Institute.

Jacobsen, J. (2014). The community service museum: owning up to our multiple missions. *Museum Management and Curatorship, 29*(1), 1-18.

Jacobsen, J. W. (1999). *The Delta Museum Building an Institution for Change.* Marblehead: Forum '99.

Jacobsen, J. W. (2002). *Museums and Learning Stages.* Marblehead, MA: Forum '02.

Jacobsen, J. W. (2004, March/April). Organizing Museum Space: Learning Stages as Physical Context. *ASTC Dimensions,* pp. 12-13.

Jacobsen, J. W. (2006). *Experiential Learning Museums.* Marblehead, MA: Forum '06.

Jacobsen, J. W. (2008, September). Setting GS Digital Specs. *LF Examiner, 11*(8), 1, 8-9.

Jacobsen, J. W. (2009, Spring). From Red Dinosaurs to Green Exhibitions. *Exhibitionist, 28*(1), pp. 6-12.

Jacobsen, J. W. (2009, March). Jacobsen's Long View. *LF Examiner, 12*(3), 1, 14-15, 18-19.

Jacobsen, J. W. (2009, March). Jacobsen's Long View The Future of Institutional Giant-Screen Theaters and Fulldomes. *LF Examiner, 12*(3), pp. 1, 14-15, 18-19.

Jacobsen, J. W. (2010, July). A Research Vision for Museums. *Curator, 53*(3), 281-289.

Jacobsen, J. W. (2010, December). Connecting Digital Museum Theaters. *LF Examiner, 13*(9), 9-11.

Jacobsen, J. W. (2010). Value for Money: How to Think about Earned Revenue. *Hand to Hand, 24*(1), 1- 2, 6-8.

Jacobsen, J. W. (2012, Fall). Book Review: Nonprofit Finance for Hard Times by Susan Raymond, Ph.D. *Exhibitionist, 31*(2), 92-94.

Jacobsen, J. W. (2012, Fall). Book Review: Nonprofit Finance for Hard Times by Susan U. Raymond, Ph.D. *Exhibitionist, 31*(2), pp. 92-94.

Jacobsen, J. W. (2012, Jan. - Feb.). The Elephants in the Galleries. *The Informal Learning Review, 112,* pp. 28, 26-27.

Jacobsen, J. W. (2013, May - June). Follow The Money To Community Success. *The Informal Learning Review*(120), pp. 19-21.

Jacobsen, J. W. (2014). The community service museum: owning up to our multiple missions. *Museum Management and Curatorship, 29*(1), 1-18.

Jacobsen, J. W. (2016). *Measuring Museum Impact and Performance: Theory and Practice.* Rowman and Littlefield.

Jacobsen, J. W. (2017). *The Museum Manager's Compendium: 101 Essential Tools and Resources.* Lanham, MD: Roman & Littlefield.

Jacobsen, J. W., & Richerson, J. (2013, January/February). Peoria's Community Service Museum. *The Informal Learning Review*(118), 15-19.

Jacobsen, J. W., Katz, P., & Stahl, J. (2011). *Museum Census Roadmap for Museums Count, the proposed IMLS National Museum Census.* for the Institute of Museum and Library Services. The White Oak Institute and the American Association of Museums for the Institute of Museum & Library Services.

Jacobsen, J. W., Wisne, J., MacGillivray, S., & West, R. M. (2014, March/April). A New, Additional Format for Changing Visitor Experiences. *Informal Learning Review*(125), 13-16.

Janes, R. (2011, Fall). Museums and the New Reality . *Museums & Social Issues, 6,* 137–146.

Janes, R. R. (2009). *Museums in a Troubled World: Renewal, Irrelevance or Collapse?* Abingdon, Oxon: Routledge.

Janes, R. R. (2013). *Museums and the Paradox of Change, Third Edition.* Abingdon, Oxon: Routledge.

Janes, R. R., & Conaty, G. (2008). *Looking Reality in the Eye: Museums and Social Responsibility.* Calgary: University of Calgary Press.

Jolly, E. J., Campbell, P., & Perlman, L. (2004). *Engagement, capacity and continuity.* Boston: GE Foundation.

Kammen, C. (2003). *On Doing Local History.* Walnut Creek: Alta Mira Press.

Kaplan, R. &. (2001). *The Strategy-focused Organization: How Balanced Scorecard Companies Thrive in the New Business Environment.* Boston: Harvard Business School Publishing Corp.

Katz, P. (2009). Benchmarking & KPI Definitions. In P. &. Katz, *Museum Financial Information 2009* (pp. 15-17). Washington, DC: The AAM Press.

Kellogg, W.K. (2006, February 2). *Logic Model Development Guide.* Retrieved October 21, 2014, from W.K. Kellogg Foundation: http://www.wkkf.org/resource-directory/resource/2006/02/wk-kellogg-foundation-logic-model-development-guide

Kellogg, W.K. Foundation. (2004). *W.K. Kellogg Foundation Logic Model Development Guide.* Retrieved from The Alabama Cooperative Extension System: https://sites.aces.edu/group/commhort/vegetable/Vegetable/logic_model_kellogg.pdf

Kennedy, J. (1997). *User Friendly: Hand-on Exhibits that Work.* Washington, DC: Association of Science-Technology Centers (ASTC).

Kolb, D., Boyatzis, R. E., & Mainemelis, C. (1999). *Experiential Learning Theory: Previous Research and New Directions.* Cleveland: Weatherhead School of Management.

Korn, R. (2007, April). The Case for Holistic Intentionality. *Curator,* 255-264.

Koster, E. E. (2000). Giant Screen Films and Lifelong Learning Complete Symposium Proceedings. Chicago: Giant Screen Theater Association (GSTA).

Koster, E. (n.d.). XX. *Forum XX.*

Koster, E., & Falk, J. H. (2007). Maximizing the external value of museums. *Curator, 50,* 191-6.

Lake Snell Perry & Associates. (2001). *Americans identify a source of information they can really trust.* American Association of Museums.

Langfield, A. (2015, June 1). *Art Museums Find Going Free Comes With a Cost.* Retrieved 2015, from Fortune.com: http://fortune.com/2015/06/01/free-museums/

Lee, N. (2005). *The Mom Factor: What Really Drives Where We Shop, Eat and Play.* Washington, DC: Urban Land Institute.

Lee, S., & Linett, P. (2013, December). *New Data Directions for the Cultural Landscape: Toward a Beter-Informed, Stronger Sector.* Retrieved October 8, 2014, from Cultural Data Project: http://www.culturaldata.org/wp-content/uploads/new-data-directions-for-the-cultural-landscape-a-report-by-slover-linett-audience-research-for-the-cultural-data-project_final.pdf

Legget, J. (2009). Measuring What We Treasure or Treasuring What We Measure? *Museum Management and Curatorship.*

Levy, F. (2010, April 29). *America's Most Livable Cities.* Retrieved December 1, 2014, from Forbes: http://www.forbes.com/2010/04/29/cities-livable-pittsburgh-lifestyle-real-estate-top-ten-jobs-crime-income.html

Lilley, A., & Moore, P. (February 2013). *Counting What Counts: What Big Data can do for the Cultural Sector.* Magic Lantern Productions Ltd.

Lord, B., & Lord, G. (2012). *Manual of Museum Planning: Sustainable Space, Facilities, and Operations.* Lanham: AltaMira Press.

Mackay, J. (n.d.). President (Ret.). *Discovery Place.* Charlotte.

MacMillian Dictionary. (2014). *Focus*. Retrieved November 25, 2014, from MacMillian Dictionary: http://www.macmillandictionary.com/us/thesaurus/american/focus_18

Manask, A. (2002). *Foodservice in Cultural Institutions*. New York: John Wiley & Sons.

McCallie, E., Bell, L., Lohwater, T., Falk, J. H., Lehr, J. L., Lewenstein, B. V., et al. (2009). *Many Experts, Many Audiences: Public Engagement with Science and Informal Science Education. A CAISE Inquiry Group Report*. Washington, D.C: Center for Advancement of Informal Science Education .

McLean, K. (1993). *Planning for People in Museum Exhibits*. Washington, DC: Association Science-Technology Centers (ASTC).

McLean, K., & McEver, C. (2004). *Are We There Yet? Conversations about Best Practices in Science Exhibition Development*. San Francisco, CA: The Exploratorium.

McLean, K., & Pollock, W. (2007). *Visitor Voices in Museum Exhibitions*. Washington, DC: ASTC.

Menger, C. (1976). *Principles of Economics*. New York: New York University Press. Originally published in 1871.

Merritt, E. E. (2008). *National Standards and Best Practices for U.S. Museums*. Washington, D.C.: American Association of Museums.

Merritt, E. E. (2010, December 21). *Museum Financial Information 2009*. United States of America: The AAM Press.

Merritt, E. E., & Katz, P. M. (August 1, 2009). *Museum Financial Information 2009*. American Association of Museums .

Moore, M. (1995). *Creating Public Value: Strategic Management in Government*. Cambridge: Harvard University Press.

Morris Hargreaves McIntyre. (2015, Q4, Vol. 20). People Power. *Attractions Management*, pp. 56-59.

Morrisey, G. L. (1994). *Morrisey on Planning, A Guide to Strategic Thinking: Building Your Planning Foundation*. San Francisco: Jossey-Bass.

Mulgan, G. (2010, Summer). *Measuring Social Value*. Retrieved November 4, 2014, from Stanford Social Innovation Review: http://www.ssireview.org/pdf/2010SU-Feature_Mulgan.pdf

Munely, M. E. (n.d.). *The Human Origins Initiative (HOI) What Does It Mean to Be Human?* MEM & Associates for National Museum of Natural History .

Museum Education Roundtable. (1992). *Patterns in Practice: Selections from the Journal of Museum Education*. Washington, DC: Museum Education Roundtable.

Museum Store Association. (2004). *Museum Retail Industry Report 2004, Museum Store Financial, Operations and Salary Data*. Denver: Museum Store Association.

Museums Association. (2013, July). *Museums Change Lives*. Retrieved November 4, 2014, from Museums Association: http://www.museumsassociation.org/download?id=1001738

Museums Association. (2013). Museums Change Lives - the MA;s Vision for the Impact of Museums.

Museums, A. A. (2013, May 21). *Summit on Sustainability Standards in*. (Various, Performer) Baltimore Convention Center, Baltimore, MD, USA.

Museums, Libraries and Archives Counci . (n.d.). *Inspiring Learning: An Improvement Framework for Museums, Libraries and Archives Toolkit* .

National Assembly of State Arts Agencies (NASAA) . (1994). *Design for Accessibilty: A Cultural Administrator's Handbook*. Retrieved May 28, 2017, from National Endowment for the Arts: https://www.arts.gov/sites/default/files/Design-for-Accessibility.pdf

National Parks Service. (1990). *NPS Museum Handbook, Chapter 4*. Retrieved May 28, 2017, from National Parks Service: https://www.nps.gov/museum/publications/MHI/mushbkI.html

National Science Board. (2012). *Science and Engineering Indicators 2012*. Arlington VA: National Science Foundation (NSB 12-01).

Netherlands Museum Association. (2011, April). *The Social Significance of Museums*. Retrieved from Museum's Vereniging: http://museumvereniging.nl/LinkClick.aspx?fileticket=cAjXpj4iX-Q%3Dtabid=674

Noyce Leadership Institute. (April 18, 2011). *Cohorts 1 and 2 on Community Impact*. Noyce Leadership Institute. Los Altos, CA: The Noyce Foundation.

Oppenheimer, F. (n.d.). Direct Quote. *The Exploratorium*. San Francisco, CA.

Pacific Science Center. (1997). *Collaboration: Critical Criteria for Success*. Washington, DC: ASTC.

Packer, J. (2008). Beyond learning: Exploring visitor's perception of the values and benefits of museum experiences. *Curator: The Museum Journal 51(1)*, 33-54.

Patton, M. (2011). *Developmental Evaluation: Applying Complexity Concepts to Enhance Innovation*. New York: The Guilford Press.

Pekarik, A. D. (1999). Exploring satisfying experiences in museums. *Curator: The Museum Journal 42(2)*, 152-173.

Peniston, W. A. (1999). *The New Museum Selected Writings by John Cotton Dana*. American Alliance of Museums Press.

Perry, D. L. (2012). *What Makes Learning Fun?* Lanham, MD: Alta Mira Press.

Perry, D., Huntwork, D., & St. John, M. (1994). *Investments in informal science education: A framework for evaluation and research*. Inverness: Inverness Research Associates.

Persson, P. (2011, Nov. - Dec.). Rethinking the Science Center Model? *The Informal Learning Review, 11*.

Persson, P. E. (2000). Community Impact of Science Centers: Is There Any? *The Museum Journal*, 9-17.

Persson, P.-E. (2011, Nov. - Dec.). Rethinking the Science Center Model. *The Informal Learning Review*(111), 14-15.

Pitman, B. (1999). *Presence of Mind*. Washington, DC: American Association of Museums (AAM).

Pollock, W. (n.d.). Direct Quote. *Association of Science Technology Centers*. Washington, DC.

Porter, M. E. (1985). *Competitive Advantage: Creating and Sustaining Superior Performance*. New York: Simon and Schuster.

Ramsey, C., & Sleeper, H. (1994). *Architectural Graphic Standards*. New York: Wiley.

Raymond, S. U. (2010). *Nonprofit Finance for Hard Times: Setting the Larger Stage*. Hoboken: John Wiley & Sons.

Reichheld, F. (2003, Dec). *The One Number You Need to Grow*. Retrieved May 21, 2017, from Harvard Business Review: https://hbr.org/2003/12/the-one-number-you-need-to-grow

Roberts, L., Morrissey, K., Silverman, L., & Perry, D. (1996). Listening Outside and Within. *Journal of Museum Education, 21*(3), 67.

Rocco, F. (2013). Temples of Delight. *The Economist*.

Rosenzweig, R., & Thelen, D. (1998). *The Presence of the Past: Popular Uses of History in American Life*. Columbia University Press.

Rosenzweig, R., & Thelen, D. (1998). *The Presence of the Past: Popular Uses of History in American Life*. New York: Columbia University Press.

Rounds, J. (October 2012). The Museum and Its Relationships as a Loosely Coupled System. *Curator: The Museum Journal, 55*(4), 413–434.

Ryan, R. (2007). *Live First, Work Second: Getting Inside the Head of the Next Generation*. Madison, WI: Next Generation Consulting.

Sani, A. B. (2013). *Report 3 - Measuring Museum Impacts*. The Learning Museum Network Project.

Saul, J. (2004). *Benchmarking for Nonprofits: How to Measure, Manage, and Improve Performance.* Saint Paul: Fieldstone Alliance.

Sawyer, K. (2003). *Group Creativity: Music, Theater, Collaboration.* Lawrence Erlbaum Associates.

Sawyer, K. (2007). *Group Genius: The Creative Power of Collaboration.* Cambridge, MA: Basic Books.

Schuster, J. M. (1992). *The Audience for American Museums.* Washington, DC: Seven Lock Press.

Science Centre Economic Impact Study, Q. –T. (2005, February). *Making the Case for Science Centers.* Retrieved November 3, 2014, from Association of Science-Technology Centers: http://www.astc.org/resource/case/EconImpact-whole.pdf

Scott, C. (2007, August). *Advocating the value of museums.* Retrieved November 4, 2014, from INTERCOM: http://www.intercom.museum/documents/CarolScott.pdf

Scott, C. A. (2009). Exploring the evidence base for museum value. *Museum Management and Curatorship, 24*(3), 195-212.

Scott, C. A. (2013). *Museums and Public Value: creating sustainable futures.* London: Ashgate.

Sector, H. C. (n.d.). *Job Descriptions Template.* Retrieved July 15, 2016, from hrcouncil.ca: http://hrcouncil.ca/hr-toolkit/right-people-job-descriptions.cfm

Semmel, M. (2009). How Do We Prove the Value of Museums? *AAM annual meeting.* Philadelphia, PA: Institute of Museum & Library Services.

Serrell, B. (May 15, 2006). *Judging exhibitions: a framework for assessing excellence.* Left Coast Press.

Sheppard , B., & Falk, J. H. (2006). *Thriving in the Knowledge Age: New business models for museums and other cultural institutions.* Lanham, MD: AltaMira Press.

Silverman, L. H. (2010). *The Social Work of Museums.* Milton Park, Abington, Oxon: Routledge.

Simon, N. (2010). *The Participatory Museum.* Santa Cruz: Museum 2.0.

Smithsonian. (2014). *Mission.* Retrieved November 25, 2014, from Smithsonian: http://www.si.edu/About/Mission

SPECTRUM. (2011). *The UK Museum Collections Management Standard-SPECTRUM 4.0.* London: Collections Trust.

St. John, M., Perry, D., & Huntwork, D. (1994). *Investments in Informal Science Education: A Framework for Evaluation and Research.* Inverness Research Associates.

Stahl, J. (2012). ACM's Online Benchmark Calculator and Menu of Key Performance Indicators. *White Oak Institute Bulletin 2*, pp. 1-2.

Stein, R. (2009, November 3). *Transparency and Museums.* Retrieved October 21, 2014, from Indianapolis Museum of Art: http://www.imamuseum.org/blog/2009/11/03/transparency-and-museums/

Sterling, P in personal correspondence with the author. (1999). *25 Indicators of Success .* Children's Museum of Indianapolis.

Stevenson, D. (2013). Reaching a 'Legitimate" Value? A Contingent valuation study of the National Galleries of Scotland. *Museum Management and Curatorship, 28*(4), 377-393.

Stowell, F., & West, D. (1991). *The Appreciative Inquiry Method.* New York: Springer US.

Sumners, C., Reiff, P., & Weber, W. (2008, December). Learning in an immersive digital theater. *Advances in Space Research, 42*(11), 1848-1854.

The Association of Children's Museums and the White Oak Institute for the Institute of Museum and Library Services. (2012). *ACM's Online Benmark Calculator and menu of Key Performance Indicators for the children's museum sector of the museum field.* Marblehead: The White Oak Institute.

The National Science Foundation. (2012, 2013). *Grant Criteria from Grant Solicitation Advancing Informal STEM Learning (AISL) Solicitation NSF 13-608 and NSF 12-560 .* The National Science Foundation.

The White Oak Institute and the American Association of Museums. (2011, March 31). *Museum Census Roadmap.* Retrieved October 21, 2014, from White Oak Associates: http://www.whiteoakassoc.com/pdf/museum_census_roadmap.pdf

The White Oak Institute and the American Association of Museums. (2011). *Review Guide of Existing Museum Surveys.* for the Institute of Museum & Library Services.

U.S. Dept. of Justice, Disability Rights Section. (1998). *1998 AA Compliance Book.* Washington, DC: U.S. Dept. of Justice.

Underhill, P. (1999). *Why We Buy, The Science of Shopping.* New York: Simon & Schuster.

United Nations Educational, Scientific And Cultural Organization (UNESCO) . (2012). *Expert Meeting On The Protection And Promotion Of Museums And Collections.* UNESCO.

Vogel, C. (2011, March 17). The Spirit of Sharing. *New York Times.*

Weil, S. (2002). *Making Museums Matter.* Washington, D.C.: The Smithsonian Institution.

Weil, S. E. (2000). *Beyond Management: Making Museums Matter.* Retrieved 2015, from INTERCOM: International Committee on Management: http://www.intercom.museum/conferences/2000/weil.pdf

Weil, S. E. (2000). Transformed From a Cemetery of Bric-a-Brac. In *Perspectives on Outcome Based Evaluation for Libraries and Museums* (pp. 4-15). Washington, DC: The Institute of Museum and Library Services.

Weil, S. E. (2003, November/December). Beyond Big & Awesome Outcome-Based Evaluation. *Museum News*, pp. 40-45, 52-53.

Weil, S. (January/February 2005). A Success/Failure Matrix for Museums. *Museum News*, 36-40.

Weinberg, M. L., & Lewis, M. S. (2009). The public value approach to strategic management. *Museum Management and Curatorship, 24*(3), 253-269.

Weisburd, C., & Sniad, T. (2005/2006, Winter). *Theory of Action in Practice.* Retrieved October 21, 2014, from Harvard Family Research Project: http://www.hfrp.org/evaluation/the-evaluation-exchange/issue-archive/professional-development/theory-of-action-in-practice

Wilkening, S. (2015, Nov/Dec). By the Numbers. *Museum, 94*(No. 6), 6.

Wisconsin Historical Society - Division of Executive Budget and Finance Department of Administration. (2013). *State of Wisconsin Executive Budget for the Wisconsin Historical Society .*

Yao, C. C. (2006). *Handbook for Small Science Centers.* Lanham, MD: Alta Mira Press.

Yocco, V. S., Heimlich, J. E., Meyer, E., & Edwards, P. (2009). Measuring Public Value: An Instrument and an Art Museum Case Study. *Visitor Studies, 12*(2), 152-163.

Section 16

Branding

Naming Process

- Ad hoc brand identity committee
- Staff
- Interviewer/facilitator/analyst
- Naming agency*
- Brand identity developer*
- Graphic designer*
- Web designer*
- Printer
- Visitor researcher: qualitative focus groups (hired by program budget)
- Visitor researcher: quantitative Web or clipboard survey (hired by marketing and/or naming agency)
- Icon designers (program budget)

* = selected by request for proposal (RFP); may be one or more firms.

PROCESS OF DEVELOPING A WELCOMING, CLEAR, AND SHARED CHARACTER AND IDENTITY

- Find interviewer/analyst
- Write questions
- Set up interviews with ±50 stakeholders
- Review and incorporate existing project research
- Do interviews
- Do focus groups (part of exhibit evaluation)
- Analyze, synthesize, and report
- Management dialogue
- Adopt position statements, brand promises, and key statements; express that identity in a name, byline, and master concept

- RFP selection process for naming agency and brand identity developer
- Develop six alternatives
- Do visitor research/report findings
- Recommend formal name (if needed), public name, and byline
- Adopt names and byline; visualize that name and byline in a logo and corporate identity system (CIS)
- Logo design alternatives
- Select and adopt logo
- Refine and extend logo
- Design CIS style sheet and "camera-ready" (digital files) art; interpret the CIS in corporate materials, campaign materials, and website

See tables 16.1 to 16.3.

Table 16.1   Corporate Identity System: Main Components

	Status	*Future Actions*
Marketing name		
Logo and logotype		
Slogan		
Signature		
Institutional colors and font		
Graphic standards manual		
Mascots		
Media animation		
Audio identifiers		
URLs and social media sites		
Artwork package for media and sponsors		
Approval and enforcement system		

Table 16.2   Brand Management Principles

The brand embodies our guiding principles
Eye catching and memorable
Use the brand everywhere
Keep talking about the brand and what it stands for
Enforce the brand

Source: David Ellis.

Table 16.3 Naming and Identity: Players and Process

	Brand Identity	Staff with or without Help	Interviewer/ Facilitator/ Analyst	RFP Branding Firms				Printer	Visitor Research: Qualitative	Visitor Research: Quantitative	Icon Designer
				Naming Agency	Brand Identity Developer	Graphic Designer	Web Designer				
1. Develop clear identity											
Find interviewer/analyst		√									
Write questions		√	√								
Set up interview		√									
Do interviews			√								
Do focus groups			√						√		
Analyze, synthesize, and report			√							√	
Management dialogue	√	√									
Adopt position statements	√										
2. Express that identity in a name, byline											
RFP selection process		√									
Develop six alternatives				√							
Do visitor research/report findings				√						√	
Recommend name(s) and byline		√		√	√						
Adopt name and byline	√	√									
3. Visualize name and byline											
Logo design alternatives					√						
Select and adopt logo	√	√			√						
Refine and extend logo						√					
Design CIS style sheet						√					
4. Interpret the CIS											
Corporate materials						√		√			
Campaign materials						√		√			
Website							√				
Interactive and artistic icons											√

Section 17

Building

Design Criteria and Operational Characteristics

INTRODUCTION

The following design and operational criteria provide a checklist of fundamental expectations of the design of a new addition or facility. While some will seem obvious, they can often get lost in the design process in the pressure of competing needs and desires, especially as the architectural team adds new members in the construction document phase who may not understand the museum's initial goals for the facility.

This section is written by contributing author Victor A. Becker.

BUILDING DESIGN CRITERIA AND OPERATIONAL CHARACTERISTICS

Safety, Security, and Compliance

The safety of the public and staff in the building and surrounding exterior areas is the highest priority. Both the reality and the perception of safety are critical to the public. To be successful, the site and building must be perceived as clean, healthy, safe, and secure during all open hours.

Full compliance with all applicable code and universal design expectations is assumed; pro-active measures in these areas are encouraged.

Building Integrity

The basic performance of the building will meet high professional standards. The facilities will be:

- Watertight: Roofs, windows, basements, canopies, and similar joints will not leak;
- Operable: The building and site will be designed to minimize operating costs and to be energy-efficient; they will have the effective practical amenities - such as loading docks and freight elevators - for all the museum's operational and programmatic purposes; and
- Maintainable: Windows, surfaces, lighting fixtures and similar building elements will be accessible, replaceable, and able to be easily and cost-effectively maintained.
- While these expectations may seem obvious, it is instructive to note that in a recent casual poll of executive directors of museum facilities, nearly half reported leaks in the roof of their facility sufficiently serious to impact their daily programming.
- While these expectations may seem obvious, it is instructive to note that in a recent casual poll of executive directors of museum facilities, nearly half reported leaks in the roof of their facility sufficiently serious to impact their daily programming.

Net Program Spaces

The program spaces as specified in the architectural program provided by the planning team constitute the museum's fundamental expectations for its facility. The details of these expectations are described in significant detail in the museum's architectural room book.

The first phase of the work of the architectural team will be an in-depth review of these net area expectations, with recommendations for the implementation of adequate support spaces, building systems, parking, vertical circulation, and other elements that together will determine the gross area of the entire building.

Imagery and Design Aesthetics

The museum will be a distinctive, stand-alone facility that integrates its indoor and outdoor spaces. It will capitalize on attractive, fun, inviting and appealing imagery, engaging a broad-based audience.

- Imagery: No aspect of the museum environment will be neutral; instead it will be complex, layered, and full of encouragement experience the programs it contains. Every element of its array of physical characteristics will inspire the visitor to visit again.
- Marketing Appeal: The landscape design and exterior iconic experience will be dramatic, exciting, and fun; it will promise adventure inside. The experience of the interior space will be friendly yet sophisticated; it will be a provocatively designed, artistic expression of the museum's way of thinking and feeling. The architecture and landscape design will express to visitors the appeal of the programs within, encouraging them to enter and participate. Various user-generated additions to the structure itself will influence the tone of the architecture: large banners, flags, graphics, and a variety of signs announcing changing programs and attractions. Even the activities of arriving visitors will affect how the general public perceives the building.
- Design Receptivity and Open Design Standards: The aesthetics of the building and site will be welcoming to later addition of new elements in a diverse range of styles and fashions, such as children's art and community-built sculptures.
- Visual Expression: The visual expression of the museum's program components in the building's internal layout, its range of spaces, and it use of materials and systems will enhance both the overall institution and the visitor experience. The museum's exhibit and theater programs offer many concepts and metaphors that lend themselves to their expression in the physical character of their spaces and boundaries.
- Advance Organizing: The exterior environment and many aspects of the interior spaces must function as "advance organizers," giving visitors a better sense of the experience that awaits them through the nature of their approach to the building entrance and interior free zone. Efficient physical circulation spaces can be combined with attractive, intriguing program elements and selective information devices to help visitors become more receptive to playful learning and discovery as they enter the building and its program zones.

Communicating the Characteristics of the Institution

Table 17.1   Architecture as Expression of Character

Interactivity	Experiences	Exploration
Regionally based	Engagement	Inspirational
Fun	Creativity	Dialogue
Fascination	Inquiry	High quality
Collaboration	Friendliness	Hands-on

Design for Learning

The museum's exhibit areas, theaters, and themed program classrooms will be designed as environments for learning, specifically for interactive concept exploration. Different kinds of learning will happen in different kinds of architectural spaces. The architecture is expected to provide learning spaces with character and built-in systems appropriate to each space's long-term needs.

Exhibit designers will work within the architecture character of each space to further define the exhibit environment for each exhibit component and/or for each exhibit theme or focus. Each exhibit scenario will likely define its own distinct visual language, interpreting the architectural character in one of a wide variety of ways. Neither the opening-day scenario nor subsequent scenarios will have, however, sufficient resources to create daylight where no windows are present, significantly increase the scale of the space, or make an acoustically lively space into a contemplative one.

Note that a single exhibit space is likely to have a number of different learning styles/stages within it. This requires well-considered combinations of architectural features with the best choice of scale, natural light, exterior views, interior views, finishes, acoustic energy, and similar variables.

Making Transitions between Exhibit Areas

Nearly every exhibit area works best when it "tells one story at a time." The story may have several self-standing "chapters" - possibly even many - but they all work together to form a coherent whole.

It is important, however, to also see these stories in real time and three-dimensional space as the visitor experiences them sequentially, one at a time. The transition from one experience to the next requires careful consideration on a more architectural level than individual exhibit designers can usually manage.

The architecture can invigorate the transitions from one exhibit experience to the next by providing some of the following:

- Clear definitions of the transitions between exhibit areas.
- A variety of design styles or languages.
- The establishment of a strong physical point of view of particular areas – especially as the visitor approaches and enters them.
- Sequences of smaller areas creating larger, richer, and more mysterious larger ones.
- Juxtapositions of small areas and large areas to keep each a "fresh" experience.
- "Penetrations" of space that offer the visitor a glimpse of what is to come.
- "Echoes" of space that reminds visitors of where they have already been.

Design for the Visitors

The building and its exterior and interior spaces will be easy to use, easy to move through and comfortable for visitors and staff.

Its rooms will function smoothly both as independent spaces and as an integrated whole with easily understood circulation possibilities. The design of the spaces will derive from their functions, and the design of the building will integrate these interrelationships of spaces with the spatial features of the site.

Some specific areas of functionality:

- Vehicle Access: School busses, delivery vans, special-needs vans, armored vehicles, tour busses, and limousines will be regular visitors, and provisions for sheltered drop-offs and loading docks are important.
- Operational Adjacencies: Program space adjacencies, layout, and design - particularly in the free zone, service areas, theaters, and galleries - will be driven by marketing and operational needs. These adjacencies will be suggested by the museum's planning team to the architectural team initially through adjacency diagrams included in the architectural room book and developed collaboratively in the concept design and schematic design phases of the building design. In addition, the spaces within the building will have:
  - Access to secure, dedicated outdoor areas wherever possible, enabling some programs to be both inside and/or outside.
  - Access to service, maintenance, and deliveries.
  - Access as appropriate to food service areas and catering facilities.
  - Access for moving large exhibits in and out.
  - An easily managed security infrastructure.
- Traffic Flow: The museum will handle large crowds without difficulty; yet not feel empty on a slow day. The design of the circulation will prevent long lines, intersecting traffic flows, and bottlenecks in circulation wherever possible.
- Way-finding: Clear signs and directions create the visitor's sense of orientation. These begin with exterior signs highly visible from the main approaches and continue with site and building entrances that are intuitive. Inside the facility's primary circulation patterns, visitors will always understand where they are and how to get back to the facility's principal landmarks.
- Sensitivity to the Visitor Experience: The circulation pattern will offer visitors a variety of architectural and aesthetic experiences along the way that contribute to the quality of their cumulative experience.
- Acoustic Isolation and Control: In addition to a generally high level of acoustic separation between spaces throughout the building, there is particular need for areas within the building that need to be "quiet and contemplative" to be protected from those that are encouraged to be "loud and invigorating." All interior spaces and activities need to be protected from all exterior noises that distract from the visitor's experience.
- Access: Control of access is important and is independent of a decision about the necessity of security guards at staff or delivery entrances. The control of access varies depend-ing on the nature of the transition from space to space; a variety of approaches may be assembled into a security plan that provides coherent control of access:
  - Outside to inside: keys and alarms
  - Large object route (12' x 12' x 12'): staff present
  - Free zone to any paid program zone: ticket collection point
  - Food & garbage route: sealed off from the public circulation and isolated from all collections spaces
  - Any public zone to any semi-public zone: staff present
  - Any public zone to any non-public zone: staff keys by department
  - Delivery area to inside: intercom/buzzer
  - Visitor elevator/escalator: in paid zone only
  - Freight/staff elevator: staff present (keyed)

Parking and Circulation

On-site parking is usually required both for the general public and for staff. The number of spaces for cars and busses will be determined by the museum or its consultant. Functional amenities such as bus circulation and drop-off areas will also be integrated into the design of the parking and entrance areas.

Expandability

It is highly likely that future expansion of programs and activities will require additional space and support areas. The museum will benefit from addressing this likelihood in the building design process, identifying places where expansion is possible and providing the infrastructure to make those additions easier and more affordable to construct.

The museum's architectural room book may provide a discussion of the possible needs for expansion and the potential constraints on successful implementation.

Low Operating Costs

The entire building and all outdoor programming will be designed to minimize operating costs (utilities, upkeep, janitorial, maintenance, bulb replacement, etc.) and to be energy efficient consistent with the goals of green building technology. Systems and equipment will be specified that require the minimum inventory of replacement parts, particularly in the area of lighting.

Adaptability, Versatility, and Programmability

The museum will be designed to facilitate modifications and program changes, allowing it to evolve with new uses and users over time. Many of its spaces will be multi-functional, requiring easy and smooth transitions. The design of spaces will maximize storage by integrating storage areas into spaces unusable as part of the visitor experience.

Utilities and services will be designed for change throughout the building wherever possible with added empty conduits, raceways, cable troughs, and other dedicated pathways for the future connection and service of new communications and information equipment. A crawl space and/or computer floors under exhibit galleries may be the best compromise of accessibility and cost. The architectural room book may provide a more detailed discussion of the need and possible approaches for adequate access to exhibit utilities.

The ability – preferably local - to control lighting, audio, and other systems will provide opportunity to change the feeling and use of a space very quickly and easily. In addition to centralized and/or automated control of the building systems, some areas - notably the more complex exhibit areas - will require control that is programmable to facilitate multiple operational modes.

Fixed Budget; Inclusive Scope

The program expects considerably more from the building than is normally expected from shopping malls, office buildings and other facilities where the fit-out is typically done by tenants. The museum will specify the character, partitions, utility distribution, and built-in systems that the museum expects in each room as part of the base building budget. Exhibit lighting infrastructure, IT wiring, special floor loading, the addition of crawl spaces, exhibit utility connections and distribution, dimmable controls, addition of vestibules and development of equipment storage areas are among the kinds of requirements that exceed a more standard structure.

If any of these functional requirements are not yet designed at the time of a cost estimate, allowances will be included in the budgeting for their eventual inclusion.

Public Involvement:

"Open architecture" is a good description of the desired relationship between the architecture and its public visitors. It welcomes and encourages public participation.

Sustainable Design/Alternative Energy Sources

The museum will be designed as a "building that teaches." The project will meet high "green" building standards, as articulated in the standards of the Leadership in Energy and Environmental Design (LEED) program created by the U.S. Green Building Council. The facility will be a demonstration of the use of environmentally sensitive design.

The museum facility will meet or exceed state-of-the-art expectations in the following broad categories:

- Sustainable Site: development density, brownfield redevelopment, alternative transportation, bicycle access and/or access to public transit, reduced site disturbance, storm water management, heat island effect, and light pollution reduction.
- Water Efficiency: water efficient landscaping, innovative water technologies, and water use reduction.
- Energy and Atmosphere: optimization of energy performance, renewable energy, additional commissioning, ozone depletion, and green power.
- Materials and Resources: storage and collection of recyclables, construction waste management, resource re-use, recycled content, local/regional materials, rapidly renewable materials, and certified wood.
- Indoor Environmental Quality: carbon dioxide monitoring, ventilation effectiveness, construction indoor air quality management, low-emitting materials, indoor chemical & pollutant source control, controllability of systems, thermal comfort, daylight and views.
- Innovation and Design Process: innovation in design and the utilization of LEED accredited professionals.

Section 18

Building

Sample Program

This section is by contributing author Victor A Becker.

Table 18.1   Building: Sample Program

Room Code			Room Name	Net Square Footage (NSF)	Net Square Meters (NSM)	Height
A.	*Exterior Spaces*					
A-10	Site perimeter					
	A-11		Perimeter curb cuts and signs	Site	Site	Open
	A-12		Sidewalk systems	Site	Site	Open
A-20	Public art envelope					
	A-21		Public art envelope	Site	Site	Open
	A-22		Public art envelope support space	(300)	(28)	Open
A-30	Visitor arrival					
	A-31		Car passenger drop-off area	Site	Site	Open
	A-32		Bus passenger drop-off area	Site	Site	Open
	A-33		Arrivals area structure	(1,500)	(139)	12
	A-34		Car parking (588 spaces + 12 handicapped)	(245,000)	(22,770)	Open
	A-35		Bus parking (12 spaces)	(15,400)	(1,431)	Open
	A-36		Staff and volunteer parking (60 spaces)	(24,000)	(2,230)	Open
A-40	Exterior program areas					
	A-41		Discovery pathways and trails			
		A-41.1	Sculpture and art areas	(15,000)	(1,394)	Open
		A-41.2	Regional pathways and trails	(50,000)	(4,647)	Open
	A-42		Landscape interpretation area			
		A-42.1	Interpretive areas	(20,000)	(1,859)	Open
		A-42.2	Community-built playground	(15,000)	(1,394)	Open
	A-43		Discovery park (access from explore/imagine)			
		A-43.1	Interactive sculptures	(2,000)	(186)	Open
		A-43.2	Outdoor science park	(3,000)	(279)	Open
	A-44		Exterior program support space	(900)	(84)	TBD
A-50	Building service entries					
	A-51		Service vehicle approach	Site	Site	Open
	A-52		Exterior service loading dock (vans, pickups, etc.)	Site	Site	Open
	A-53		Service loading door	Site	Site	Open
	A-54		Exterior exhibits loading dock (tractor-trailers)	Site	Site	Open
	A-55		Exhibits loading door	Site	Site	Open
	A-56		Staff service entrance	Site	Site	Open
A-60	Exterior of building					
	A-61		Exterior building and program signs	Site	Site	•
	A-62		Exterior building lighting	Site	Site	•
B.	*Entrance Areas*			NSF	NSM	Height
B-10	General public entrance					
	B-11		Public entrance vestibule	In gross	In gross	10
	B-12		Group entrance vestibule	In gross	In gross	10

(Continued)

Table 18.1   Building: Sample Program

B-20	Main lobby and ticketing area (free zone)				
	B-21	Main lobby	3,200	297.4	TBD
	B-22	Lobby icon area			
	B-23	Information booth			
	B-24	Ticket and membership areas			
	B-25	Admissions office and cash room	240	22.3	10
		FOH guest services manager			
		Cashiers supervisor			
		Cashiers (12)			
B-30	Free zone amenities				
	B-31	Free zone public lockers (20% PMC)	200	18.6	10
	B-32	Free zone coat room (50% PMC)	450	41.8	10
	B-33	Free zone washrooms	In gross	In gross	10
	B-34	Family washroom/first-aid room	60	5.6	10
	B-35	Free zone public telephone area	In gross	In gross	10
	B-36	Free zone lobby storage	50	4.6	10
		Subtotal	4,200	390.3	•

C.	*Museum Store Areas*		*NSF*	*NSM*	*Height*
C-10	Retail area				
	C-11	Store retail area	2,400	223.0	15
C-20	Support areas				
	C-21	Store manager and staff office (2)	200	18.6	10
		Subtotal	2,600	241.6	•

D.	*Café/Food Areas*		*NSF*	*NSM*	*Height*
D-10	Museum café areas				
	D-11	General café seating area (150 seats at 15 SF)	2,250	209.1	15
	D-12	Outdoor café area (200 at 20 SF)	(4,000)	(372)	Open
D-20	Support areas				
	D-21	Café kitchen/servery	1,200	111.5	10
	D-22	Café food line area	In gross	In gross	15
	D-23	Café manager's office (1)	125	11.6	10
	D-24	Café loading area	200	18.6	
		Subtotal	3,775.0	350.8	•

E.	*Museum Galleries (Venue 1)*		*NSF*	*NSM*	*Height*
E-10	Exhibit hub and podium area				
	E-11	Exhibit hub/circulation spine	4,000	371.7	TBD
	E-12	Gallery function catering support	150	13.9	10
	E-13	Gallery function equipment room	150	13.9	10
	E-14	Gallery zone washrooms	In gross	In gross	10
	E-15	Demo equipment storage	170	15.8	10
E-20	Theme pavilions—wing A				
	E-21	Science/National Museum (connecting galleries)	In gross	In gross	20
	E-22	Energy and Innovation			
		E-22.1 Entrance	500	46.5	20
		E-22.2 Object Theater	800	74.3	20
		E-22.3 Power Play	4,200	390.3	20
		E-22.4 Innovation Skunk Works	1,500	139.4	20
		Subtotal	7,000	650.6	•
	E-23	Earth, Space, and Our Environment			
		E-23.1 Entry: Wonders of the Universe	300	27.9	20
		E-23.2 Observation Ports on Planet Earth	3,500	325.3	20
		E-23.3 EarthWatch Theater	450	41.8	20
		E-23.4 Imagining the Cosmos	250	23.2	20
		E-23.5 Out of This World	1,500	139.4	20
		Subtotal	6,000	557.6	•
E-30	Theme pavilions—wing B				

			NSF	NSM	Height
E-31		The Human Body			
	E-31.1	The Human Body	1,500	139.4	20
	E-31.2	Self-Test Center	2,625	244.0	20
	E-31.3	Health Alert	500	46.5	20
	E-31.4	The Global Family Gallery	375	34.9	20
		Subtotal	5,000	464.7	•
E-32		Technology, Style, and Art			
	E-32.1	Entry: Technology and Icon	500	46.5	20
	E-32.2	Pressure by Design	1,250	116.2	20
	E-32.3	Digital Design Studio (multimodal) (blog)	500	46.5	20
	E-32.4	Media Stage	750	69.7	20
	E-32.5	Experiment Benches	1,500	139.4	20
	E-32.6	Tech Mech Workshop (multimodal)	1,500	139.4	20
		Subtotal	6,000	557.6	•
E-40		Early Learning Discovery Center			
	E-41	Playtown	2,500	232.3	20
	E-42	Mindscapes	1,200	111.5	20
	E-43	Scribble and Messy Arena	1,500	139.4	20
	E-44	Perception Arena	1,200	111.5	20
	E-45	Sound/Music	1,500	139.4	20
	E-46	Artist's Studio	850	79.0	20
	E-47	Theater	1,250	116.2	20
	E-48	Multipurpose Classroom	1,000	92.9	20
		Subtotal	11,000	1,022.3	•
E-50		Feature presentation galleries			
	E-51	Feature Presentation Gallery #1	5,000	464.7	20
	E-52	Feature Presentation Gallery #2	4,000	371.7	20
	E-53	Support Space	200	18.6	10
E-60		Presentation theater			
	E-61	Audience area	1,200	111.5	20
	E-62	Stage space	600	55.8	40
	E-63	Entry/exit sound/light lock(s)	150	13.9	10
	E-64	Control booth and equipment room (1)	250	23.2	10
	E-65	Change room	250	23.2	10
		Subtotal	51,120	4,750.9	•
F.	*Discovery Dome (venue 2)*		NSF	NSM	Height
F-10		Theater lobby and support spaces			
	F-11	Theater area lobby	1,000	92.9	15
	F-12	Concession stand			
	F-13	Theater lobby storage	100	9.3	10
	F-14	Theater exit lobby	In gross	In gross	10
	F-15	Theater area washrooms	In gross	In gross	10
F-20		Discovery Dome			
	F-21	Sound/light lock entry	200	18.6	10
	F-22	theater	6,400	594.8	TBD
		F-22.1 Seating and presentation stage area		0.0	
		F-22.2 Signature capabilities demo		0.0	
		F-22.3 Visualization studios		0.0	
	F-23	Theater technology studio/projection booth	400	37.2	10
	F-24	Sound/light lock exit	100	9.3	10
F-30		Theater support spaces			
	F-31	Ushers' room (3)	150	13.9	10
	F-32	Dome server room	150	13.9	10
	F-33	Theater management office (3)	240	22.3	10
		Theater manager			
		Theater maintenance tech			
		Projectionist office			
		Subtotal	8,740	812.3	•

(Continued)

Table 18.1   Building: Sample Program

G.		Learning and Conference Center (LCC)	NSF	NSM	Height
G-10		Common spaces			
	G-11	The Commons: group orientation and lunchroom	1,000	92.9	15
	G-12	Group storage area	200	18.6	10
	G-13	Function rooms			
	G-14.1	Function room A	300	27.9	15
	G-14.2	Function room B	300	27.9	15
	G-14.3	Function room C	300	27.9	15
G-20		Themed program labs			
	G-21	Themed Program Lab 1	800	74.3	15
	G-22	Themed Program Lab 2	800	74.3	15
	G-23	Chevron Open Minds	900	83.6	10
	G-24	Observatory vestibule and exhibit area	300	27.9	10
	G-25	Observing deck	700	65.1	TBD
	G-26	Observing deck and exterior entrance (exterior)	(800)	(74)	Open
G-30		LCC support spaces			
	G-31	Teacher resource center	400	37.2	10
	G-32	Education offices (3)	300	27.9	10
	G-33	Demo/prop storage	250	23.2	10
	G-34	School loan center	400	37.2	10
	G-35	LCC research chair office (1)	150	13.9	10
	G-36	LCC research chair student spaces (5)	365	33.9	10
	G-37	Catering support	150	13.9	10
	G-38	LCC washrooms	In gross	In gross	10
		Subtotal	7,615	707.7	•

H.		Program Support Areas	NSF	NSM	Height
H-10		Exhibit support			
	H-11	Graphics design studio	300	27.9	10
		Graphic designer (internal)			
	H-12	Exhibit planning room	350	32.5	10
		Project manager			
		Project manager			
		Designer			
	H-13	Live animal room	100	9.3	10
	H-14	Exhibits production workshop (7)			
	H-14.1	Shop	2,500	232.3	20
	H-14.2	Exhibits storage	7,000	650.6	10
	H-14.3	Senior exhibit maintenance tech			
	H-14.4	Exhibit maintenance staff			
	H-15	Advanced learning hub/electronics workshop/headend/AV center			
	H-15.1	IT workshop/storage (4)	700	65.1	10
	H-15.2	IT office (1)	100	9.3	10
	H-15.3	Server complex	200	18.6	10
	H-16	Exhibit operator's office (2)	120	11.2	10
H-20		Theater technical support			
	H-21	Digital production facility	600	55.8	10
		Producer/astronomer			
		Producer			
		Graphic designer (shows)			
		Animator			
	H-22	Theater area staff washroom	In gross	In gross	10
		Subtotal	11,970	1,112.5	•

I.	*Administrative Areas*			*NSF*	*NSM*	*Height*
I-10	Office landscape					
	I-11	Staff entrance from lobby		In gross	In gross	10
	I-12	Office entrance and reception (1)		100	9.3	10
	I-13	Open office (23 cubicles at 64 SF)		1,472	136.8	10
I-20	Enclosed offices					
	I-21	Chief executive officer's office		150	13.9	10
	I-22	Vice president office		120	11.2	10
	I-23	Vice president office		120	11.2	10
	I-24	Vice president office		120	11.2	10
	I-25	Vice president office		120	11.2	10
	I-26	Manager office		100	9.3	10
	I-27	Manager office		100	9.3	10
	I-28	Manager office		100	9.3	10
	I-29	Manager office		100	9.3	10
	I-30	Manager office		100	9.3	10
	I-31	Manager office		100	9.3	10
	I-32	Manager office		100	9.3	10
	I-33	Manager office		100	9.3	10
	I-34	Manager office		100	9.3	10
	I-35	Manager office		100	9.3	10
	I-36	Manager office		100	9.3	10
	I-37	Accounting/HR office		450	41.8	10
	I-38	External relations office		600	55.8	10
I-40	General service areas					
	I-41	Board/conference room		550	51.1	15
	I-42	Meeting room/contractor hotelling spaces (2)		400	37.2	15
	I-43	Volunteer lounge/locker room		400	37.2	15
I-50	Office support spaces					
	I-51	Office mail, equipment, and supply room		300	27.9	10
	I-52	Space office/interim meeting space		100	9.3	10
	I-53	Management information services office		150	13.9	10
	I-54	Administrative washrooms		In gross	In gross	10
			Subtotal	6,252	581.0	•

J.	*Building Support Areas*			*NSF*	*NSM*	*Height*
	Building support spaces					
	J-11	Janitorial and facility support (3)		150	13.9	10
	J-12	Staff washrooms/showers		400	37.2	10
	J-13	Maintenance office landscape		500	46.5	10
		Maintenance engineer				
		Maintenance tech				
		Building controls office				
		Cleaning staff (8)				
	J-14	Building controls room		120	11.2	10
	J-15	Security office (5)		150	13.9	10
	J-16	Retail storage		200	18.6	10
	J-17	Freight elevator		In gross	In gross	n/a
	Loading support areas					
	J-21	Shipping/receiving area		1,000	92.9	20
	J-22	Receiving area storage				
			Subtotal	2,520	234.2	•

K.	*New Spaces*			*NSF*	*NSM*	*Height*
	Digital Visualization Lab					
	K-11	Digital Visualization Lab		2,650	246.3	TBD
			Subtotal	2,650	246.3	•
			Total net area (NSF)	101,442	9,427.7	

(Continued)

Table 18.1   Building: Sample Program

L.		Gross-Up Areas		
	B.	Entrance areas	1,680	156.1
	C.	Museum store areas	1,040	96.7
	D.	Café/food areas	1,245	115.7
	E.	Exhibits Area	15,335	1,425.2
	E.	Discovery Dome (Venue 2)	3,495	324.8
	G.	The LCC and observatory	3,045	283.0
	H.	Program support areas	4,310	400.6
	I.	Administrative areas	3,126	290.5
	J.	Building support areas	1,010	93.9
	K.	New spaces	1,060	98.5
		Total gross floor area (GSF/GSM)	35,346	3,284.9
		Total building area	136,788	12,712.6

Section 19

Capital and Long-Term Assets

INTRODUCTION

In addition to its resources to produce and house its activities, many museums own other resources that support operations. These long-term and capital assets can be categorized as follows:

- Endowment
- Intellectual property
- Leasable land and space
- Intangible assets

The first three are usually managed to provide annual revenue, and the last is responsible for the museum's goodwill, partnerships, community identity, public trust, and in-kind contributions, such as free land use. Only some of these, such as the endowment, are valued and listed on a museum's financial statements as capital assets.

The following text may be adapted to fit your museum's context and needs. There are likely to be additional kinds of capital assets.

CAPITAL AND LONG-TERM ASSETS

Endowment

The mantra among many museum chief executive officers is endowment, endowment, endowment. Cash endowments, invested wisely, can provide income to support operations. The conventional wisdom is that the only sure way to financial security is a large endowment because other forms of revenue are subject to market competition and outside forces. The Great Recession of 2008–2009 took a heavy hit on endowments, challenging this conventional wisdom for a few years.

The board's finance committee will manage the endowment to generate enough revenue to first cover inflation of the principal and then earn more to transfer to the operating budget on a rolling five-year average. For example, if the endowment earns 6 percent on its principal during a year when inflation ran 4 percent, then 2 percent is available to be spent, leaving the balance in the account to increase the principal to parity for next year.

All endowment funds are managed centrally with revenue available for unrestricted use. The museum accepts funds with use restrictions or management specifications only as a last resort and after approval of the finance committee.

Intellectual Property

The museum's intellectual property (IP) includes the following:

- Collection
- Brand identity (e.g., logo)
- Inventions and proprietary software
- Productions (e.g., traveling exhibitions, curricula, virtual experiences, scripts, and media productions)
- Publications (images as well as music and text generated by the museum and its work-for-hire contractors)

The museum will manage and license its IP to generate unrestricted net revenue without placing the value or condition of the IP at risk.

Leasable Land and Space

The museum has land and building space beyond its operational needs as a museum. Given permissions as needed, the museum will manage these assets to generate lease revenues from suitable sublease tenants.

Intangible Assets

The museum has long-term assets that are hard to quantify in either capital value or annual benefit to the museum. However, many of these assets are critical to the museum's survival and operation, even if they do not appear on the balance sheet. The museum's intangible assets include the following (partial list only in random order):

- Nonprofit tax status
- Free land or building
- Other regular in-kind contributions
- Extra government services (e.g., heightened police, ambulance, and fire)
- Community recognition, identity, and reputation
- Expertise
- Partnerships
- Existing business lines and revenues
- Legacy and history in the community
- Location and proximities
- Category claims (i.e., the region's history museum and the most prestigious board)
- The museum's economic impact (while quantifiable, this asset is not liquid)
- Symbolic role
- Community gathering and bridging role

Section 20

Capital Project

Budgets

INTRODUCTION

This section looks at how the fund-raising goal established by the museum should be strategically assigned to the tasks detailed in the museum's capital project *plan*. It looks at the line items covering spending, also called the allocations side (for sources of funding, see "Supporters").

Not everyone will regard all items in the budget as "capital" expenses in the strict definition of the term. Some categories include preopening operating expenses and ongoing cash and endowment funds. However, the total budget attempts to be an estimate of all the expenses needed before opening day, when the operating budgets take over.

You can use this section as a checklist of the kinds of costs you may have to cover during a capital project. Too many projects start their budgeting by adding up items as they think of them: "What will it cost to build a new wing?" "Oh, that figure did not include soft costs?" "Wait, we have to put stuff inside, in addition." "Oh, no, we have to conduct an environmental impact study." And so on. This section offers a better way: a full list of costs faced by at least one museum capital project so that you can think in advance about likely costs. You can choose which costs your museum should budget for.

You can use the "Notes to the Capital Budget" below as a menu of options to adapt to your budget reports. See tables 20.1 to 20.3.

Museum Capital Project Budgets

Table 20.1   Capital and Start-Up/Preopening Budget Categories

Building and site construction
Building-associated soft costs
Museum equipment and systems (FF&E)
Program (exhibits and content)
Project costs and preopening expenses
Museum funds and reserves
Total capital and preopening

Table 20.2   Sample Summary Capital Budget: 20XX$

Building contract	$18,092,960
Building associated	$ 4,439,522
Museum equipment	$ 1,212,000
Indoor program costs	$14,160,000
Project management	$ 4,650,000
Museum funds	$11,845,949
Total	$54,400,431

Table 20.3   Capital Project Organization Chart

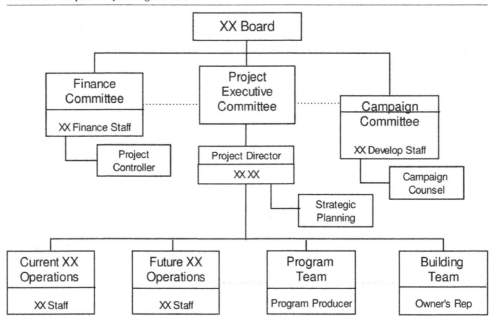

OVERVIEW OF THE CAPITAL AND PREOPENING OPERATING BUDGET

All expenses incurred prior to opening have to fit into one or more of the existing line items. If new categories of expenses are created, then other existing line items must be reduced, as the total capital budget should not be increased without board approval.

From a management viewpoint, this means that each line item needs to carry all costs associated with that area in the broadest definition possible. For example, if $70,000 is allocated for a system, this does not mean that the museum should look for a system with that price tag; rather, the budget needs to cover the cost of a system consultant who might write a request for proposal, expenses associated with staff visiting other facilities that may have candidate systems installed, and change orders to the building cabinetry to accommodate the selected system, delivery, installation and travel costs, staff training, and other related expenses in addition to the system itself, which might end up being only half the budget. Unless the capital budget provides otherwise, any category of expense should include its design, subcontractors, installation, and all other associated expenses.

A corollary to this inclusive coverage will be the dawning realization by managers and designers that the budgets are already tight even though the budget seemed initially a generous figure.

Having stressed the inclusive nature of each line item, it is also important to emphasize the need for flexibility in managing the capital budget. Areas of the capital budget will be delegated to key team members to manage, and they should have the flexibility to adjust assignments and categories within their subtotals as long as the operating economics are not poorly affected. The capital budget has been organized according to a number of management responsibilities, with the key premise that the designer or manager in charge has to operate within a fixed budget. Budget accountability will reside with a gover-

nance group, but responsibility for staying in budgets will be assigned to "task managers" for each row in the capital budget.

This organization and division of the budget by delegable categories of responsibility to task managers is most useful in the early phases. Later, during production and installation, the budget may get reorganized by vendors, by status of completion, or by the museum's evolved chart of accounts.

The museum will not green-light any process or contract until it has raised all those funds in order to avoid wasteful terminations or debt. This is particularly important with construction; museums that entered into debt to finish construction have usually suffered for years.

The museum will run a second campaign after the opening focused primarily on adding to the small initial endowment.

Additionally, the museum needs to account for the cash flow deficits, particularly as some funding commitments may extend beyond the museum's opening, and the museum needs to spend its capital prior to opening.

If Two Budgets Are Needed

Note: In some contexts, two campaigns are needed: one for strictly capital expenses (bricks and mortar) and another for transitional operating support. Ideally, the two are combined into a "capital and preopening operating budget."

The overall project budget contains two components: the capital budget ($XX), which meets the government definition of infrastructure capital, and the transition budget ($XX), which covers the museum's incremental costs over the operating budgets in order to increase levels of operating support, raise the capital funds, and manage and launch the project until opening day. It is important that these transition budget funds are unrestricted and in cash (not in-kind). The overall project budget is $XX million (see table 20.4).

Table 20.4   Capital Budget Outline

	FN	Unit Cost	Amount	Area Total	Department Total
Building contract					
Construction costs					
Building allowances					
Change orders					
Landscaping					
Site preparation					
Signs and graphics					
Equipment systems					
Special lighting					
Kitchen and catering equipment					
Building security equipment					
Building audio system					
Subtotal building					$0
Building associated					
Land					
Relocation					
Design and engineering					
Reimbursable expenses					
Consultants					
Construction support					
Fees, permits, taxes, and titles					
Site survey					
Test borings					
Engineering and environment					
Appraisals and review					
Legal and accounting					
Insurance					
Contingency on building contract					
Subtotal building associated					$0
Museum equipment					
Furniture and fixtures					
MIS network					
Other office systems					
Telephone system					
Visitor service equipment					
Ticketing system					
Audiovisual systems					
Security and cash handling					
Building maintenance equipment					
Grounds maintenance equipment					
Museum van					
Signs					
Museum store					
Retail equipment					
Movable cart					
Decor and environment					
Initial logo stock					
Museum café					
Equipment					
Tables and chairs					
Decor and environment					
Special event catering					
Subtotal equipment					$0
Indoor program costs					
Exhibit pavilions and icons					
Linking galleries					
Exterior exhibits					
Exhibit lighting					
Exhibit program maintenance equipment					

(Continued)

Table 20.4   Capital Budget Outline

Theaters
     Hard costs
     Furnishings and supplies
     Goods/services/other
     Signature show
     Initial programming
Program spaces
     Demonstrations equipment
     Opening programs
     Furnishings and supplies
     Other theater and program costs
Cross-zone scopes
     Visitor research and evaluation
     Exhibit and program master plans
     Content research
     Label copy
     Design support and coordination
     Installation expenses
     Travel and expenses
     Management and coordination
     Owner-furnished items
     Rights and object acquisition
     Program integration with architecture
     Standards manuals
     Program marketing facilities
     Subtotal program $0
Park program costs
     Fantasy forest
     Carnival rides
     River pavilion programs
     Special events equipment
     Outdoor exhibits (park)
     Outdoor program equipment
     Sound playground
     Community build budget
     Playground equipment
     Park sculpture and art
     Subtotal park programs
     Subtotal capital costs $0
Project management
     Organizational costs
     Preopening operating support
     Capital campaign costs
     Marketing launch costs
     Bridging interest costs
     Moving and setup
     Fund-raising campaign
     Planning fees and studies
     Subtotal management $0
Museum funds
     Escalation reserve at 3% per year
     Endowment and project contingency
     Operating cash reserve
     Subtotal funds $0
Total $0

NOTES TO THE CAPITAL BUDGET

1. In-Kind Donations: Many parts of the budget assume some level of donated services and equipment. The museum's concept depends on donations of hardware. The planning team has no good information on what might be donated and what might have to be purchased, but we are assuming that most demonstration technology and student resources will be donated. If this assumption proves false, then the budget should be increased accordingly or the program plan revised to use less sophisticated techniques. When unplanned donations are received, their value should not be deducted from these figures but rather added to both the campaign total and the appropriate budget.

2. Start Date: While the museum has spent money on the project in the past, those are separate funds, and this budget assumes a start date for phase XX of XXQ, 20XX, when XX expenses can start to be charged against the $XXM budget.

3. The capital budget assumes that the site will be prepared by others. The budget, therefore, does not include the landscaping, driveways, site preparation, services, and secure foundation for a building.

Building Contract

4. For details behind the construction estimate, refer to the "Architectural Program." The construction cost estimate of $XX per square foot in 20XX dollars does not include architectural and engineering fees, built-in allowances, site preparation, or other costs detailed elsewhere in the capital budget.

5. Landscaping applies a rule-of-thumb percentage to the total new construction cost.

6. Building-Associated Costs: This collection of costs is often referred to as the "soft costs."

7. Construction Support: At this writing, it is not clear what kind of construction management services the museum will require, which are often determined by the funding sources and the structure of public projects. One solution is to engage an owner's rep, who will essentially be a staff person for the duration of the detailed design and construction period. Another solution is to engage a construction management firm, which undertakes a wider range of supervisory activities, record keeping, and budget control. Cost for these services can vary widely, from an annual consultancy to a complete project management team.

8. Museum Program Interface Specifications: These constitute a budget to cover the development of the *Room Book* and the ongoing review of the architectural design to make sure it conforms to the needs of the museum and its exhibits, theaters, and other programmatic elements. This figure is listed in building-associated costs to emphasize its connection to the capital investment in the building, as some funding sources are limited to bricks and mortar and their associated costs. This specialized individual or firm is responsible for monitoring building functionality and is effectively the liaison between the program team and the architectural and construction teams.

Museum Equipment

9. Information Technology, Telephone, and Ticketing Systems: These systems are converging, and the museum should consider scoping them together with the hope that a centralized system and vendor will provide the best service for the available funds.

10. Promotional facilities include video monitors, kiosks, display vitrines, daily program announcement boards, LED sign systems, and other means of letting people on-site know what is going on and engaging their attention in upcoming programs. Placed throughout the museum to encourage deeper and further use of the museum's other services, poster cases, display vitrines, message boards, and video monitors let guests in the free zone and visitors in the museum galleries know about volunteer opportunities, educational programs, coming events, and upcoming exhibitions.

11. Retail inventory refers to the opening stock that needs to fill the gift shop at its opening. This is one of several examples that are not, strictly speaking, capital funds but rather money that needs to come from somewhere before opening, so it is part of the capital and preopening budget.

Program

12. The exhibit master plan is to be completed by experienced exhibit designers. The document lays out the unifying themes and approaches, with specific concepts and renderings developed for all galleries. The museum's graphic look, based on the museum's logo, is illustrated in visual metaphors throughout the document. The document also specifies the museum's kit of parts, allowing staff to order consistent display units, partitions, and so on.

13. Budgets for the Museum's Exhibits: At the present level of development of the concept, it is not possible to provide more than general guidelines and industry standards: typical square-foot budgets for peer exhibits run around $XX per square foot. However, the types of exhibits planned for the museum rely heavily on sophisticated media and electronics, which will drive this cost up to $XX per square foot. This budget is inclusive of all design fees, fabrication, and installation but not of the staff salaries and related expenses (see table 20.5).

Table 20.5   Museum Galleries: Capital Cost

Museum Galleries	Square Feet	$ per Square Foot	Capital Cost
Exhibit master plan			
Visitor research			
Management costs			
Other above-the-line costs			
Subtotal shared costs			
Gallery A			
Gallery B			
Gallery C			
Subtotal gallery costs			
Totals			

14. Experience platforms and initial scenarios are separately budgeted to reflect the principals of a Delta museum (see table 20.6). The allocations for experience platforms should be invested by the museum in long-term infrastructure, including equipment, mezzanines, background environment, and other aspects of creating a Delta gallery. The initial scenarios, on the other hand, should be commissioned from exhibit designers to play on the experience platforms with the assumption that they will be replaced by a second scenario at some point in the future, leaving the base experience platform intact. The separation between these two layers should be man-aged carefully, as designers of the opening experiences are likely to blur the line in the pressure to get something opened with a limited budget.

15. Experience Platforms: This budget is intended to cover the design, implementation, and installation costs of the long-term program support infrastructure in each of the themed program areas. These elements should be designed to be used in multiple exhibits and educational programs. Examples of long-term infrastructure might include a bank of video monitors, a built-in heliostat, plant support systems, and so on. The per-square-foot costs include design fees.

Table 20.6   Delta Museum Galleries: Capital Cost

Museum Galleries	Experience Platform		Opening Scenario		Total Cost
	Square Feet	$ per Square Foot	Cost	$ per Square Foot	
Exhibit master plan					
Visitor research					
Management costs					
Other above-the-line costs					
Subtotal shared costs					
Gallery A					
Gallery B					
Gallery C					
Subtotal gallery costs					
Totals					

16. Opening Scenarios: This budget is to produce and install the exhibits and programs that will be in each of the themed program areas on opening day. The figure assumes that staff time and in-house resources are already covered by the museum's operating budget, so these amounts are principally for materials and specialized external contracts.

17. Permanent or Long-Term Exhibits: These are areas dedicated to curriculum-integrated exhibits that include simulated environments, naturalistic dioramas, and other exhibits that are not easily changeable and that will be designed, produced, and installed to last 20 years or more. Teachers who learn how to use this resource will depend on returning year after year if their students find it to be an effective and successful program.

18. Iconic Exhibits: These are large-scale, iconic exhibits prominently displayed and integrated into the lobby and other public spaces. This budget is an allowance for the design, preparation, and installation of the exhibits within spaces prepared as part of the architecture.

19. Theater: All costs associated with the feature theater have been derived from XX's report of 20XX and subsequent conversations.

20. Fully Programmable Features: The *fully programmable*, multimode operating capabilities of the museum will be achieved through the integration of building, media,

and exhibit systems brought together into a single unified interface.

21. Digital Information and Story Collection (DISC): This figure covers overseeing development of the museum's collection-quality digital storage servers and acquiring the hardware and the access software along with as many digital files in the collection as the budget allows. DISC should be set up in advance of occupancy in order to build the collection, debug access software, and train staff in its use and care. The use of the DISC will be governed by the museum's Digital Asset Management (DAM) policy that will protect the specific usage rights of each item in the collection; define how staff, researchers, and the public can access each element in the collection; and an acquisition policy for visitor and affiliate input.

22. Exterior Exhibits: This figure is an allowance to cover three broad areas (1) an outdoor play structure that also serves as a symbolic sculptural element, (2) the testimonial and memorial commemoratives and structures that might be incorporated into the park, and (3) orientation and marketing graphics that greet visitors and direct them to the museum's different components and areas.

Table 20.7   Preopening Operating Costs

	FY-4	FY-3	FY-2	FY-1	FY1	TOTAL
Pre-opening Staff and benefits						
Search and employment agencies & costs						
Staff Travel						
Leased Space - storage and office						
Office equipment for new staff (not covered elsewhere)						
Shut down costs - staffing and other						
Printing (copier)						
Postage						
Professional development						
Insurance - New Facility						
Utilities - New Facility						
Maintenance, Engineering % Janitorial - New Facility						
Misc./contingency						
TOTAL	$0	$0	$0	$0	$0	$0

23. Notes to Preopening Operating Costs: During the capital phase, currently scheduled for 20XX through 20XX, funds will be needed to cover planning and production staff, the marketing launch, campaign expenses, general operations, and moving costs. This budget addresses staff and expenses needed to plan and launch the museum during the years prior to public opening, when the operating budgets should take effect. This category addresses the routine needs of a growing team assembled to create the visitor's experience, such as a newsletter, membership drive, informational package, ongoing public relations campaign, training and community outreach programs, and so on. Table 20.7 Preopening Operating Costs assumes that temporary furnished and serviced office space and support will be in the current facility or donated and near the construction site until occupancy.

24. Marketing: Principal marketing expenses will be associated with the launch and the campaign to announce the project broadly in the region through paid advertising, promotions, public relations, collateral preparation and distribution, and numerous other communications techniques to be detailed in the marketing plan. Funds in 20XX will cover the visitor and market research into content, style, and approach that is needed to guide the exhibit and program plan and other operations choices. Early funds are for the marketing plan and the corporate identity system. These funds should result in a new name, a logo, subhead and artwork for a new letterhead, a press release paper, and several other near-term collateral materials.

25. Fund-Raising: As the strategy is for the board to raise the capital personally among a close community of funders, this budget does not include expenses normally associated with running significant capital campaigns, such as fund-raising materials, videos, publications, preparation of grant proposals, maintenance of extensive donor data files, negotiating and contractual expenses, donor recognition events, promotion, and stewardship.

26. Bridging Interest Costs: This figure requires a relatively small budget to cover financing of some pledge payments

that may extend past opening. This figure is too small to accommodate major donations coming in after opening or to manage sophisticated financing or tax credit schemes. The museum planners strongly advise against borrowing money to complete the project with the hope that the loans can be repaid by future fund-raising or by excess revenues generated by earned income; museums that have tried this road have routinely suffered.

27. Planning Fees and Studies: This figure covers ongoing planning and studies at an institutional level, including food service, parking, museum planning counsel, updates to the economic model, and other consultant-based work that will support institutional planning and that is not explicitly covered by the program budget or by the building-related soft costs.

28. Escalation Reserve: This figure addresses inflation issues between cost estimates and final contracting.

29. Operating Support Fund: As some donors to the museum campaign will still be paying off pledges after opening, this amount is included in the budget to offset the difficulty in raising operating funds during the early years from the same donors who have supported the capital project and/or may be still paying off pledges.

30. Net loss from disruption is to cover lost income due to construction disruptions and reductions of available services.

31. Endowment of $XX will be raised as part of the campaign, as part of establishing the museum on a longer-term sustainable economic model. The amount has been calculated so that, at a 5 percent drawdown, the fund should be able to cover 10 percent of the operating budget. In other words, the endowment is roughly two times the annual operating budget. The museum is not sustainable long term until this endowment and the rest of the promised visitor and customer experience are completed.

Section 21

Capital Project

First Steps

INTRODUCTION

The first steps to secure core funding for a capital project are critical and not often understood. Many museums spend years in explorations, relationship building, and false starts before their silent campaign succeeds in identifying the lead funders. There is no formula to secure lead funding, and each museum campaign has unique starting stories. After lead funding is identified, project implementation can rely on traditional phases and systems (for phase numbers, see "45. Implementation Phases, Schedules, Milestones, and Tasks").

The following text and tables are a full menu of roughly sequential tasks that have been part of some or most capital projects in the early years. You should select the tasks relevant to your project and adapt them to suit your museum.

CAPITAL PROJECT: FIRST STEPS

Sequence of Start-Up Analysis and Planning Steps

1. Identify funding commitments for initial planning (phases 2 to 5).
2. Orientation, Study, Review, and Analysis: Review existing materials, including the following:

   a. Community and regional brochures, vision documents, and master plans
   b. External reports, market research, and community needs assessments
   c. Attendance and revenue trends at area attractions
   d. Operating and financial data: past five years
   e. Constituencies currently served: key service markets
   f. Institutional mission and strategic direction

3. Community and Institutional Needs Assessment: Illustrates the current perceptions of the museum and establish the region's needs that might be met through use of the museum's resources. Community needs can help establish a framework for future potential community partnerships with the museum, as partnerships will increase the museum's role in the community. A full needs assessment has the following components:

   a. Conduct a Market Analysis: A look at demographics in relation to key indicators of museum and program use. The market analysis will review the demographics of the museum's primary, secondary, school, and tourist markets and review of the region's current economic and cultural trends, all from the perspective of understanding the needs and opportunities of the new museum's potential audiences.
   b. Community Needs Interviews: A series of specific community organizations during a two-and-a-half-day agenda of face-to-face meetings with key individuals to collect a wide range of data as well as attitudes among community leaders regarding prospects and how the project might best serve the community's needs. The individuals to meet include leadership of the chambers of commerce, research departments at local newspapers and media, community and government leaders, school department officials, tourism groups, local developers, and several other figures who can provide the researchers with specific data, studies, and related master plans. Other community surveys have had 10 or so meetings with 50 to 70 community representatives set up over the two-and-a-half-day period.
   c. Conduct a Gap Analysis and Identification of Opportunities: What learning, leisure, and cultural activities are available in the region? What gaps exist in the region's cultural, educational, and leisure infrastructure? And what services

are already too competitive? In addition to looking at regional listings and individual attraction websites, look at social media attitudes and parent blog comments about the key competitors and list the options and their apparent target audiences, locations, and other factors to identify services that may be underprovided.

d. SWOT (Strengths, Weaknesses, Opportunities, Threats) Exercises and Analysis: Will engage all staff members, volunteers, board members, and other stakeholders from the start in the planning process. Based on several sessions with different groups following a loose format, the output of the flip-chart suggestions will become an institution-wide database of the perceived internal strengths and weaknesses and the external opportunities and threats facing the museum today. The raw data should be entered by the museum into a sortable Excel database (the "Menu of Ideas") categorized by source and kind (S, W, O, or T).

e. Literature Review: A review of other visioning documents, master plans, and regional analysis by the government and regional agencies.

f. Menu of Ideas: Import all comments and meeting notes from the above, regardless of feasibility or desirability at this stage, into an Excel database and code for source. Previous databases have

had more than 400 ideas. Analyze to illuminate pervasive desires and issues and allow leadership to see the alignment between what the community wants (external comments) and what the museum wants (internal) and plan adjustments.

4. Space Use Analysis: Looks at all spaces in the current layout for total size and allocation of square footage among component categories and for the degree of Delta change already supported in each space. Express this quantitative analysis in tables and floor plans, showing every existing space colored by function with its square footage and unique name or code. Make recommendations for adjustments of space assignments, illustrated in color-coded future floor plans, along with functional requirements for new infrastructure to be added to make the spaces more operationally efficient and effective.

5. Conduct a policy guidance workshop that engages leadership in determining policy. What are our purposes? Whom should we serve? What kind of museum do we want? What components and programs? What economic models and capital budgets? Using "dotmocracy" exercises on 20 to 30 policy maps hung on the walls, participants vote on what they want the future museum to be. Policy scales will be used to collect the group's direction about institutional purpose, audiences, values, strategic priorities and future museum components, business models, degree of change desired, and economics like the sample shown in table 21.1.

Table 21.1   Visitor Source

Findings: The votes clustered around the three-quarter mark toward residents.

Alignment: Moderate

Policy Guidance from Museum Leadership: Target an audience mix that is approximately 75% resident and 25% tourist

a. Policy Guidance Documentation: Results of policy scales and policy statements.

6. Develop three alternative models to implement policy direction for the future museum that explore different ways the policy directions can be implemented. Ideas will be drawn from the Menu of Ideas. These alternatives are likely to be in such choices as institutional purposes, type of market, type of facility, and scale of operation and capital as well as components, exhibit approaches, and community programs. Leadership will be involved in developing and then approving the three alternatives:

a. Develop alternative presentation boards for each model as props or survey instruments for use in stakeholder interviews.

b. Interview stakeholders and potential funders to get their reactions to the three alternatives, particularly to their purposes, capital cost, and business models.

c. Summarize findings from interviews.

7. Concept Development Workshop: Review stakeholder interviews and alternative models, synthesize, and recommend priorities to serve as basis for the strategic

master plan. The four-hour workshop with leadership will decide among the alternatives, most likely synthesizing a new planning model from the best parts of the alternatives, pending feasibility investigations.

    a. Concept Development Documentation: A statement of the draft planning model.

8. Visitor and Program Participant Research Studies: Gather data on perceptions of the museum's current and envisioned programs and visitor experience and the museum's image. Methodologies might include focus groups, clipboard interviews, kiosks in the museum, time-and-tracking studies that watch visitors in the exhibit halls, member surveys, and online forums. This is an informative process that checks and evolves the business assumptions with the anticipated audiences and earned revenue sources.

9. Concept Development Plan: Provides detailed, hard planning data for the new facility, including a description of the programmatic themes and venues, a market analysis of the region, projected attendance, capital budgets, and operating budgets. It will be a comprehensive planning document that establishes chapters on all key areas. Each section can be updated and filled in as planning matures. With a short, attractive stand-alone executive summary, the concept development plan is both a reassuring document for donors and a comprehensive planning tool for staff and contractors who need to integrate the implementation of each section with the larger vision.

    a. Adopt the Plan: The steering committee should propose to the full board that the concept development plan be adopted as the next baseline in planning.

10. Receive sufficient pledges and cash flow to authorize work in phases 4 to 6.
11. Authorize Phase 4: Campaign feasibility.
12. Check with a site and/or landscape architect to test (and revise) the feasibility of the plan.
13. Develop a phasing plan and preliminary capital budget for the early phases.
14. Retain fund-raising Counsel to advise the campaign.
15. Retain a public relations firm to help with the campaign phase (from now to groundbreaking) of the museum's public communications.
16. Prepare Fund-Raising Materials: Preliminary and flexible case statements, portfolios, and images of naming opportunities can be effective sales and closing tools. As the project is bound to evolve, use media that are inexpensive to update or discard.
17. Continue a quiet communications campaign to inform regional leadership that this project is moving forward with strength and vision.
18. Assess the museum's abilities to raise capital (capital fund-raising feasibility study) to see if the capital bud-

get is achievable and to involve potential supporters in evaluating the models. Part of that process is to translate or excerpt the concept development plan into a case statement.

19. Prepare management and staff to run the project and to operate the larger institution once it is complete. This is an ongoing professional development process that should be started in a modest way at this time and ramped up during the development years into a fully articulated transition plan. During these next three phases, having an organizational coach on a retainer basis will be useful to help sort out interim organizational charts and human resource opportunities and challenges. This service is a useful adjunct to the next step.
20. Define Organizational Personality Profile: Understand and articulate who the museum is and what it values by doing a facilitated Myers–Briggs type of profile for the current institution. This analysis process, which is based on in-depth online interviews with staff and key leadership, profiles the personality of the institution and identifies its natural strengths and weaknesses. It will also identify what the institution is good at doing on its own and which skills it should search for outside of the corporate culture when undertaking a project of this scale.
21. Attract the support of key leaders to the project (ongoing).
22. Prepare the Board: This may involve trustee training through such processes as the Carver method of board policy governance and the establishment of appropriate subcommittees that can supervise site and architecture, program development, collections policy, the capital fund-raising campaign and financial overview, and other aspects. In a period of expansion, the board should focus on the fundamental policy choices and delegate key operational and strategic choices to the professional staff.
23. Start a site selection process by forming a board-level committee and identifying a real estate expert who can help guide the project toward a commitment to either its current site or an alternate location.
24. Special Format Theater Recommendation: Keeping in mind the objectives and specific requirements, commission an analysis of the economic feasibility of a feature theater and make a format recommendation. This theater study will firm up the number of seats, the economic model, the architectural program requirements, and other considerations that will be important in selecting a vendor and providing direction to the architect. This study should be substantially complete before draft B of the strategic master plan.
25. Verify Program Components: Clarify the theme areas and content of each of the principal program components. For both the institution as a whole and each component, state the purposes and desired impacts and articulate what the visitor experience and community benefits might be like.
26. Schedule of Investment and Naming Opportunities: Links the program concepts with benefit packages and

price tags for potential donors and sponsors. Management, working with campaign counsel, can identify and price the major program components that might lend themselves to naming opportunities.

27. Select the site and start the negotiation process.

28. Authorize Phase 5: Lead gifts and project organization.

29. Secure lead funding of pledge commitments and public funds equal to at least half the campaign. Identifying ongoing support revenues needs to be addressed at the same time as the capital funds are raised. Typically, such support revenues come from city, county, or state budgets; school system fees; endowment income and project grants; and/or contributions from individuals, corporations, and foundations.

30. Capital Budget Cash Flow: Define parameters and cash flow for the preopening capital budget, the inflows of pledges and public funds, and other finance and proposal requests.

31. Prepare a land and architectural briefing package for landlords so that they can understand what the capital project is going to be both conceptually and physically. There may be some sensitivity to the massing of the project with regard to green space and parking requirements, and massing diagrams should be part of this orientation package.

32. Define lease agreement and terms.

33. Start Architectural Search Process: Prepare a scope for architectural services and circulate it to a short list of qualified museum architects. The building team and the executive committee should evaluate the responses, interview a number of finalists, visit their buildings, talk to their previous clients, understand the business offer, and make a selection. There are consultants specializing in advising architectural search processes. See Table 21.2.

34. Develop and Complete the Site Development Plan: All the affected partners need to participate in a centrally conducted site development plan that will establish demising and property lines, pedestrian, car and bus traffic patterns, acceptable view sheds, and other height-related issues that will determine the maximum masses

Table 21.2   Architect and Exhibit Designer Selection Processes: Three Alternatives

Interviews and credential reviews (ideal)
  Best when scope and budgets are not yet clear
  Best when time and efficiency are issues
RFQ/RFP bidding processes (if needed)
  Clear scope and budget known and in hand
  Funding sources expect competitive bidding
  Lots of work: Time is available as are workers
  Can find firms hungry to work for lower cost
  Engages a selection committee
Design competition (not recommended)
  Gets visibility and images quickly
  Big mistakes often follow lack of collaboration

of the various buildings as well as the eventual ownership and programming of the area. Only after there is agreement and preliminary permitting of these choices can each project, including the capital project, start its schematic design.

35. Collaborate on Updating the Building Program and Functional Adjacency Diagrams: The architects, exhibits designers, food service analysts, and museum planners need to work with leadership to develop the functional requirements for the building, starting with the program in the concept development plan.

36. Envision Scenarios: Hold scenario development workshops to discuss the ideas and involve the community in the program development. Outline the thematic areas and then invite suggestions from the audience about possible scenarios that might play within those areas. A robust list of potential scenarios gives the program planners a perspective of the range of activities that might happen in each theme area. The list helps define the experience platforms and specify the most useful equipment and environment for those platforms.

37. The campaign communications plan should include a publicity plan, a speakers bureau with script and presentation materials, a project press kit, and a collateral plan, including a campaign newsletter, video, fund-raising materials, and other communications media.

38. Revisit Governance Structure: As new partners come into the project, the makeup and governance of the museum should be reviewed by legal counsel to accommodate the project and include new funding partners and content providers.

39. Institutional Partnership Framework: Determine a process and structure for partnerships and affiliations between the institution and its community and investment partners. A number of categories at different levels of commitment will help the board set policy about establishing letters of support, standing agreements, memoranda of understanding, and so on with institutional affiliate partners and donors.

40. A food service and function rental study will establish the operating model for the café and the function rentals with potential net revenues. The study will also specify architectural support requirements to achieve the potential revenue. Maximizing the benefit of function rentals and food services in a museum context is best achieved by expert and manageable expectations and integration of museum food specialists, architecture, brand identity, and programming.

41. Authorize Phase 6: Strategic master plan.

42. Commission a comprehensive strategic master plan (see table of contents earlier in this section) that is built on the chapters of the concept development plan and that integrates the results from recent studies and plans and includes the new ideas from project supporters. Detailed line-item departmental budgets will be calculated from

the bottom up, based on a full staffing list and a new organization chart and assumptions about the number of cashiers, educators, and so on. Early in the process, a workshop of museum experts will be held to review plans and assumptions to date and to recommend directions to pursue.

43. Visitor Experience Research: A second round of qualitative visitor research will help the program team understand what types and styles of experiences interest visitors inside each of the major thematic areas. This is a more detailed level of research than the previous visitor concept research, and it explores ideas coming out of the scenario development workshops and helps management assign budgets and space to the different program components.

44. Experience Platform Definitions: Articulate the desired characteristics and support systems for each experience platform. Assign space and budget to each of the public experience platforms. Select the architect and negotiate a contract and authorize them to proceed on their first two phases: architectural program and schematic design.

45. Start a Building Contractor Selection Process: Some projects are selecting their building contractor shortly after the architect is on board in order to have the builders at the table during the early design phases, when the client has the greatest control over the cost of the project. This selection process should also be headed by a board-level committee, facilitated by a consultant. The skills needed for this selection process are significantly different from those needed for the architectural search, although the steps taken are somewhat similar.

46. Commission land surveys and other analysis of the site.

47. Authorize Phase 7: Architectural program.

48. Create the *Room Book* (see "6. Architectural *Room Book*"), which is the owner's direction to the architect about what should be in each space. This document, also known as the architectural program, will be developed by museum operations experts working with the architect to establish physical characteristics, support systems, and architectural characteristics for each space in the project's outline architectural program. This document, which might run more than 300 pages, will be the comprehensive record of what is expected by the owner in each space. Naturally, the document will evolve as the design and contracting proceed.

49. Authorize Phase 8: Schematic design.

50. Architecture: Schematic design and building visuals.

51. Expand Program Design Team: Once the experience platforms are defined, sized, and budgeted, exhibit, theater, and program designers can be selected to start working on the design of the opening scenario on each platform. This overlap of experience platform designers and exhibit designers is an opportunity to get a better fit

between the experience platform and the scenario. Note: Tasks in phases 9 and later are not described. In addition to this sequence of steps, external conditions and specific site considerations will add new steps, unpredictable at this time. Other museum projects have added to their early process: environmental impact studies, site title disputes, public tax referenda, lobbying campaigns, brownfield remediation surveys, and other tasks added in response to community demands and the museum's specific financing strategies. See table 21.2.

Ongoing Processes

1. Develop a Shared Sense of Vision: From board members to project volunteers, the intellectual concepts, character, and soul of the museum need to be discussed regularly and refined in terms of its core business, corporate values, and community service objectives. A broad understanding of why the museum is doing this and what will result should be shared by everyone involved in the project. In time, as staff are added, this discussion about framework will become the institution's corporate culture and brand identity. One method is to read and discuss a series of books that will be influential in your planning.

2. Grant and proposal writing will continue to be an important part of the campaign, and the museum should establish processes and materials to be able to respond quickly with targeted proposals to specific potential donors. Some proposals may require consultants, presentation visuals, and considerable research to formulate; as more proposals get written, a stock of text, images, covers, data, and other materials will be useful.

3. Community Discussions: Engage potential community partners in discussions about the master plan and make adjustments as needed to accommodate partnerships without adversely affecting the economics or the planning to date. Early partnerships will have more flexibility than later ones.

4. React to opportunities presented by the community. Such opportunities should be evaluated against the growing planning framework, perhaps by calling on coaching and consulting services as needed. Opportunities embraced that were not part of the master plan and budget must be followed by adaptations to the plan to integrate the new opportunity.

5. Organize tours of other new museums to educate the board and potential donors and build connections among the project's leadership. Define a museum visit research process for board members and volunteers to share reports on visits to other museums.

6. Define a best practices research process that will include examples of specific museum practices that should be studied carefully by the museum's planners.

7. Maintain an orientation package to give to new project team members. This 20- to 30-page summary should include vision and purposes, values and philosophy, project objectives, component descriptions, summary architectural program, project organization chart and contact list, and master schedule.

During all of this, professional development by staff and training for key board members are important. Staff should attend conferences, read books about planning and developing museums, and talk to colleagues who have been through expansions and other capital projects.

Section 22

Capital Project

Planning Principles

INTRODUCTION

When contemplating a significant capital project such as expanding or building a museum, follow these basic principles to avoid postopening troubles, which in some cases have included museum bankruptcy.

CAPITAL PROJECT: PLANNING PRINCIPLES

- No debt (some bridge loans on the last years of secure pledges are okay if the financing costs are included in the budget). Too many projects authorize groundbreaking before they have raised all the money. Later, when a site is full of workers and equipment, the pressure to borrow money to keep them working is too great. Do not start a contract until all the funds to pay for it are identified. Funds covering either the whole contract or discrete and terminable phases of work should be identified and sequestered in the cash flow.
- Attendance potential calculations must be based on truly comparable museums and are only potentials. Exhibits and programs then have to be designed and marketed to achieve those potentials, and staff must be trained professionals who know how hard it is to achieve the same results as the existing comparable museums. They must have the time, resources, and support to do a tough job. If the budget changes or the funding goals are not met in time, then attendance and other assumptions need to be updated.
- Reserves for rocky times in years 2 and 3 must be included in the capital budget and not spent on cost overruns. Delays, building change orders, escalation, and cash flow issues are the largest sources of overruns. First, they eat up contingencies, then the postopening reserves, and then the exhibits that are supposed to generate the revenues.
- Post–capital operating budgets need more operating support dollars, not less, although the share of earned revenue can be slightly higher. A major shift in the balance of earned to support revenue is untenable unless the staff culture is also changed dramatically (new staff?). Serving visitors is a very different skill from serving donors and government agencies. Both are hard but different.
- The board has to be behind the project financially and have dollars in their own pockets and rich friends. Appointed government boards may not have the capacity to drive a major capital campaign.
- The capital project must be in response to real community needs backed by funders who believe the project will actually address those needs and by implementers who are focused on addressing those needs. Too often, leadership, staff, architects, and designers go off on tangents of their own.
- It is important to recognize that the capital budget is a strategic allocation of funds and not a specific estimate of expenses in each area. Nothing is designed yet, so nothing can be priced, and the overarching management task is to get everyone to design and fabricate within budget.
- The operating sustainability of the institution depends on raising funds that can be spent on the capital budget items as listed. The sources of funds must match the allocation of funds; if other funds are raised for other projects or phases, then either the campaign goal must be raised by the same amount or the gift must be postponed. For example, trying to build more gallery space without increasing the operating support will be damaging, not helpful, to the operating sustainability, as the extra space may cost more to maintain than it will earn in more visitation.
- The project needs to raise unrestricted funds and funding dedicated to each of the specific soft costs in the capital budget in order for the project to move forward. The museum should not seek to open its doors without all this funding in place or pledged, as the funding is necessary for operations and to be able to cover the development of the museum's professional staff, which needs to be on board one to two years before opening. Unrestricted funds are typically needed to cover fund-raising, marketing, staff, overhead, legal, consultants, finance charges, and other soft costs.
- And again, *no debt, no debt, no debt!*

Section 23

Chief Executive Officer Profile and Budget

CHIEF EXECUTIVE OFFICER PROFILE AND BUDGET

"Level 5 leaders channel their ego needs away from themselves and into the larger goal of building a great company. It's not that Level 5 leaders have no ego or self-interest. Indeed, they are incredibly ambitious—but their ambition is first and foremost for the institution, not themselves" (Collins, 2001, p. 21).

See "15. Bibliography for Museums" for citation reference.

Table 23.1   Sample Chief Executive Officer Office Budget and Departmental Profit/Loss Statement

	Total Budget - Revised	Current Year Actual	Total Budget Variance - Revised
Revenue			
Fees-Miscellaneous	-	-	-
Board Meetings	-	-	-
Grants-General	-	-	-
General Donation	-	-	-
Permanent Transfer	-	-	
Net Assets Released - Private	25,000	-	(25,000)
Total Revenue	25,000	-	(25,000)
Expenditures			
Full Time Salaried	529,703	1,415	528,288
FT-AV Labor	-	-	-
Hourly	-	-	-
Hourly-Production	-	-	-
Exhibit Division Labor	-	-	-
PTO	-	-	-
Benefits	141,431	-	141,431
Telephone	-	-	-
Postage	255	(7)	262
Printing and Duplicating	100	-	100
Meeting M S	6,700	-	6,700
Mileage Parking	1,400	10	1,390
Supplies	1,750	125	1,625
Professional Services	15,000	7,138	7,862
Prof Dev, Training, Travel	13,000	-	13,000
Insurance	24,300	-	24,300
Lease Rents	-	-	-
Computer Hardware < $5,000	2,500	-	2,500
Subscrip and Memb	13,734	2,338	11,396
Board Expenses	16,145	-	16,145
Internet Expenses	-	-	-
Outstate Bd Exp	-	-	-
AAM Accreditation	250	-	250
Bd Assoc Mtgs	9,225	-	9,225
Outside Spkg Engag	2,000	-	2,000
Event Supplies	800	-	800
Entertainment	-	-	-
Maint Repair-Hardware	-	-	
Donor Recognition	11,900	-	11,900
Total Expenditures	790,193	11,019	779,173
Net	(765,193)	(11,019)	754,173

Note: This sample is for a $40 million annual budget.

Section 24

Collections

Policies

INTRODUCTION

This section is based on excerpts from a collections policy drafted by Crystal Willie. These selections from existing collections policies do not include all aspects of a collections policy that could be written, such as collections mandate, care, handling, storage, provenance documentation, emergency preparedness, access, records management, insurance, or lines of authority beyond the board (i.e., staff authorities or use of a collections committee).

COLLECTIONS: POLICIES

Example Ethical Standards

As an organization, we commit ourselves to meeting basic museum standards as set out by the museum community and related agencies. Our collections are held in the public trust in perpetuity and thus will not be sold to fund-raise for the organization. Likewise, they will not be considered capital assets or listed as such on our financial statements.

We will adhere to ethical behavior in collection development (e.g., repatriation and human remains), and we will meet municipal, provincial, and federal legislative requirements that have an impact on collecting activities (e.g., illicit materials) and that have an impact on collections management and documentation (e.g., firearms and hazardous materials).

Our organization will not acquire objects in an illegal or unethical manner. We will likewise not acquire objects where legal ownership by the donor or seller or the provenance of the object cannot be substantiated or where there are other reasons to suspect that the object may have been obtained illegally.

Board, staff, and volunteers will declare any existing conflicts of interest in their personal collecting activities. Board, staff, and volunteers will refrain from actively collecting materials of a similar nature to the museum's collections while they are associated with the museum. Under no circumstances should information obtained through association with the museum be used for personal gain.

Categories of Collections

For the purposes of managing the care and use of the collection, we have established collections categories. As each category of collection has different needs and expectations for care, access, use, and record keeping, they may be stored in different areas of the museum. An object should be easily identified as belonging to one of the categories; the object's collections category will be part of its records.

Permanent Collection

These are the objects acquired with an expectation of permanence. Objects in the permanent collection can be loaned to other institutions, exhibited, and studied. They are stored, handled, and cared for with the utmost respect for museum standards for storage and display of collections, especially preventive conservation methods. Establishing and maintaining records for our permanent collection will be considered a high priority.

Study Collection

These are the objects that a curator or scholar has brought together for comparison, such as to study the evolution of an artist's style, the complete line of Coca-Cola products, or the designs of duck decoys. The term implies that the objects are displayed en masse rather than spotlit on individual stands. When in storage, access is typically requested by researchers rather than general visitors.

Education Collection

These are the objects used in place of permanent collection objects to share the story with the public. They are used for learning- and experience-based programs where participants can touch or use the objects. The education collection is constituted of duplicates, damaged items, or objects lacking historical significance. When objects from the permanent collection are transferred to the education collection, this decision is approved by the Collections Committee, and the reasons for the transfer are recorded. Objects can be actively acquired for the education collection if a strategic educational purpose is identified; donors should be made aware that the item is being acquired for the education collection and the nature of this collection and its care and use. Likewise, program participants handling objects from the education collection should be notified that the object is part of an education collection intended for handling. Participants should still be made aware of expectations for respectful handling and care. Objects in the education collection can be loaned to other institutions, exhibited, studied, and used for programs and other hands-on activities.

Archival Collection

These are documents, audio or video materials, photographs, personal documents, and occasionally books and periodicals (especially when associated with personal records) that contain relevant information. These collections are maintained as reference material for research. They are made available to the public for research purposes under circumstances that provide appropriate security, care for the physical integrity of the item, and respecting ethical and legal obligations, in particular regarding privacy, intellectual property, and copyright. They are acquired with an expectation of permanence and managed respecting standards of practice for archival collections.

Digital Collection

The objects include both digitized versions of physical collections and *born digital* files for collections that were created digitally, such as current music releases, NASA space images, and recent photography. A museum's digital asset management system covers its policies, handling software, and secure storage servers for its digital collection.

Acquisition Policy

Priority for acquisition is given to objects that fill a gap in our story line and our planned areas of collections development. In deciding to acquire an object, we will consider the resources required to acquire, assess, document, and preserve the object. We will also consider whether the object does the following:

- Supports the mission
- Fits within the criteria established in Scope of Collections
- Is a priority in alignment with the museum's collections development planning
- Is in good condition and can be adequately cared for using the museum's preventive conservation practices
- Is of a size and nature that it can be adequately stored and exhibited

The Collections Committee will consider objects for collection, and they will be accepted only with approval from the board. While under consideration, we will issue a temporary custody receipt if the object is left at the museum.

We will acquire objects by donation whenever possible. When deemed appropriate by the Collections Committee with approval from the board for costs beyond budgeted allowance, we may acquire objects by purchase.

We will issue tax receipts at a donor's request only after an appraisal to determine fair market value undertaken at the donor's expense. Under no circumstances will a tax receipt be issued for items valued at $1,000 or higher without an independent external appraisal.

All donations are deemed to be unconditional gifts. Gift agreements will be signed by the donor and an authorized museum representative giving us unqualified, legal ownership of the objects with no donor restrictions. When applicable, the gift agreement will also seek to ensure that copyright and other intellectual property rights are assigned to us. In any case, rights that reside outside the museum (e.g., artist's moral rights) will be documented.

Deaccessioning Strategy

As an organization, we approach deaccessioning decisions cautiously, respecting our role in holding collections in the public trust and with consideration for reputational issues and the maintenance of positive relationships within the community. Objects are deaccessioned and disposed of only with approval from the board.

We will consider objects for deaccessioning under any of the following circumstances:

- An object is no longer or has been minimally relevant to the mission and purpose of the museum and does not support the collections development plan or exhibitions, programming, or research activities of the museum.
- An object was acquired illegally or unethically and is being returned to the appropriate authority or party.
- An object has failed to retain its physical integrity or authenticity and cannot be properly preserved, stored, and used.

- An object has been damaged through an accident, disaster, deterioration, or vandalism and can no longer be properly preserved, stored, and used.
- An object is duplicated, redundant, or overrepresented in our collection.
- An object has been lost or stolen and must be deaccessioned for object records to accurately reflect the fact that the object is no longer in the collection.

Priority will be given to ensuring that deaccessioned objects remain in the public domain.

Disposal of deaccessioned objects will be made by one of the following means:

- Donation to another museum or charitable institution.
- Exchange with another museum or charitable institution.
- Sale to another museum or charitable institution.
- Sale at public auction outside the museum's immediate location.
- Objects that are damaged beyond repair or that constitute a health or safety risk can be recycled or destroyed. If they contain hazardous materials, they should be surrendered to an authority or agency qualified to dispose of them. In both of these cases, the object should be destroyed or given up in front of witnesses.

We will not return deaccessioned objects to the donor. Museum board members, staff, and volunteers may not purchase items deaccessioned from the collection, even at public auction.

We will use the funds obtained through the sale of deaccessioned objects at public auction to support collections care and development. We will not sell objects that belong in the collection to raise funds for other purposes.

Loans and Shared Uses of Collections

Museums frequently loan objects to each other for educational, scholarly, or exhibition purposes. In doing so, they negotiate loan agreements that establish, among other things, the term of the loan, conditions under which the object will be kept, and risk management provisions, including insurance. Our collections policy considers incoming objects, outgoing objects, and objects in custody.

Outgoing Loans

We will consider loan requests from similar organizations (such as galleries, heritage institutions, universities, and other museums) that have the capability of meeting museum standard conditions for the care, handling, and documentation of objects.

We will loan objects only if they are in stable condition and will not be harmed by transport or the conditions under which they will be exhibited or stored at the borrowing institution.

Organizations will be considered qualified to borrow objects from us in the following circumstances:

- Loaned objects will be used solely for educational, scholarly, or exhibition purposes.
- The purposes identified by the borrowing institution for the loan do not compromise the mission or reputation of the museum.
- The borrower submits a completed "General Facility Report," as outlined by the AAM.
- The borrower demonstrates that it will provide an exhibit space that has adequate environmental controls and security.
- The borrower demonstrates that the object will be handled only by trained staff members using standard preventive conservation methods.
- The borrower insures the object for the value assigned to that object and submits a certificate of insurance coverage to the museum prior to receiving the objects. The borrower's insurance will cover the object through the transport to and from the museum and while it is in the care of the borrowing organization.
- Any and all use of loaned objects will be credited in writing as being on loan from the museum.
- If granted, permission to the borrowing organization to photograph an object for research, educational, or publicity purposes will be stipulated in the loan agreement.
- A borrowed object remains the property of the museum and may not be claimed, mortgaged, loaned, assigned, used as collateral, or otherwise encumbered by the borrower.
- Objects can be loaned up to a maximum of three years.
- The borrower must return an object on loan from the museum on or before the agreed-on date.
- The borrower notifies the lender immediately in writing of any loss, theft, or damage related to an object.
- The condition of the object will be recorded using a condition report before the object leaves the museum, when it arrives at the borrowing organization, when it leaves the borrowing organization, and again on arrival back at the museum.
- Borrowers are responsible for all costs incurred in the packing and transportation of the object from and to the museum.

Incoming Loans

From time to time, we will borrow objects for exhibit purposes from other institutions. Not surprisingly, these objects will likely be governed by outgoing loan policies similar to our own, outlined above. Regardless of the other institution's policies, our collections policy commits us to do the following:

- Provide agreed-on environmental controls, record keeping, and security throughout the time the objects are on loan to the museum.

- Ensure that only trained staff and volunteers will handle borrowed objects.
- Not accept objects for "permanent" loan to the museum.
- Acquire proper insurance coverage for the length of time loaned objects are on the premises and while they are in transit.
- Assume responsibility for all costs incurred in packing and transporting loaned objects from and to the place of origin.
- Notify the lending organization or individual in writing of any loss, theft, or damage that has occurred to the objects.
- Record the condition of the object using a condition report before the object leaves the lending museum, when it arrives at our museum, when it leaves, and again on arrival back at the lending museum.

Objects in Custody

The museum normally accepts objects into temporary custody only when being considered for acquisition. Such objects are accepted only by authorized staff and when received are recorded using a temporary custody receipt.

Objects found in the collection will be treated as newly accessioned objects, but their unknown provenance will be noted in the object's records; however, objects abandoned at the museum will not be accepted into our collection or care because we cannot substantiate the object's legal ownership or its provenance.

Collection Resources

Collection Storage and Conservation Rooms

The museum will need to follow through with museum-standard responsibilities for maintaining, conserving, and interpreting collections. The American Institute for Conservation has established guidelines for the acquisition and maintenance of historical artifacts; while these guidelines are nonbinding, it is a prudent policy to aim toward eventual accreditation for the museum and to build in the support spaces, policies, corporate culture, staffing, and other collection requirements.

If collection acquisition is elected, then the *architectural program* should include collection storage spaces with strict environment controls and security as well as study and conservation rooms where items from the collection can be looked at by scholars and worked on by conservators.

Section 25

Collections

Categories and Uses

INTRODUCTION

Collections have been central to museums for centuries. Museums without collections are more recent, but even those make provisions for temporary collections and consider their exhibits and dioramas as collections of learning resources.

So much has been written about collections and the scholarship they inspire that this section is more referential and deferential than other sections. Mature collections-based museums will have much more detailed collections policies than outlined here. Tier 3 members of the American Alliance of Museums (AAM) can access more than 1,000 documents and forms used by accredited museums, including collections policies, loan agreements, condition reports, and more. *Nomenclature 4.0* establishes frameworks for collection categories and terms. The AAM's professional committees, such as the registrars and the curators, have established standards, such as the "General Facility Report," which the reader should consult directly. The American Institute for Conservation (AIC) is an independent organization serving those caring for collections, historic sites, and other objects in their stewardship. The AIC has an annual meeting and a peer-reviewed *Journal of the American Institute for Conservation*. The AIC publishes guidelines for collection care. "SPECTRUM The UK Museums Collections Management Standard" contains detailed processes and advice. The ISO 18461: 2016 International Museum Specifications defines key terms, such as *artefact* and *digital object*.

COLLECTIONS: CATEGORIES

Table 25.1   Type of Collection (ISO Categories)

1. Art Museum
2. History Museum
3. Archeology Museum
4. Natural History Museum
5. Science and Technology Museum
6. Ethnography and Anthropology Museum
7. Specialized Museum
8. General Museum
9. Zoo/Aquarium
10. Botanic Garden/Arboretum

Source: © ISO. This material is adapted from ISO 18461: 2016 with permission of the American National Standards Institute (ANSI) on behalf of ISO. All rights reserved, p. 21.

Table 25.2   Subdivision of Collection Counts (ISO Classification)

1. Natural Science Specimens
2. Art Objects
3. Cultural Artifacts (except art objects)
4. Printed Documents
5. Handwritten or Typescript Documents
6. Photographic Objects
7. Audiovisual Documents
8. Digital Objects (except audiovisual documents)

Source: © ISO. This material is adapted from ISO 18461: 2016 with permission of the American National Standards Institute (ANSI) on behalf of ISO. All rights reserved, pp. 33–35.

COLLECTIONS: USES

This section is based on writing by the American History Workshop and focuses on the use of collections in exhibits. It does not address collections as the basis for scholarly research.

Collection objects illustrate the concepts and narratives presented in thematic and storytelling exhibits.

Collection objects also provide information beyond what is conveyed in reproductions or images of them. They reveal a complexity of materiality that may not be visible on a computer screen or even an excellent photograph. (On the other hand, sometimes they obscure what an X-ray or a magnified image can show.) They may reveal a layering of human actions over time that is not equally visible in an image of the object.

Collection objects, properly displayed, provide an "aura" of authenticity that makes the museum site special and unique. They say that this place is not a copy, a themed attraction, endlessly replicated like other parts of the American commercial and experiential landscape.

Collection objects have the power to alter visitors' experiences, arresting their attention and redirecting their posture, and so they can contribute powerfully to the aesthetic qualities of a gallery presentation. In a way that images of or information about objects do not, original pieces seem to invite visitors to "complete" them. A pair of shoes invites the visitors' imaginations to walk a few steps in them. Such exercises of the imagination, by common observation, yield an emotional connection to the objects that is more difficult with copies or images.

Collection objects can become iconic originals, like the Hope Diamond and Betsy Ross's flag.

Every object is a remnant and reminder of human actions and therefore an entry point for reconstructing the senses and skills of the people who made it and used, preserved, and dispensed with it.

Collection objects, like all things, have a life history, dating from conception to disposal as waste or fuel, and these lives intersect and overlap with many human lives, forming a community that may stretch across long distances and many generations.

Unconventional objects, like 20th-century media products, may also spark a highly personal, empathetic visitor engagement. Contemporary audiences bring with them powerful strategies for interacting with, deciphering, and interpreting video images, for example. They know much more about how to "read" an eyewitness account of a natural disaster than how to use a 19th-century fireman's pump.

Section 26

Collections

Environmental Specifications

INTRODUCTION

Collections typically require storage and display conditions that can be demanding to meet with a building's environmental systems. The specifications are evolving: conservators want tighter, more constant temperature and humidity ranges, while environmentalists want to reduce the carbon footprint. Further, different collection materials need different specifications.

Hence, this section can give only a general overview, and you are encouraged to contact the agencies listed directly. See also "7. Architectural Standards and Green Resources."

COLLECTIONS: ENVIRONMENTAL SPECIFICATIONS

"The American Institute for Conservation of Historic and Artistic Works (AIC) has established interim guidelines [2014] for relative humidity for most types of cultural materials (45–55 percent/±5 percent daily drift) and temperature (59–77 degrees Fahrenheit ±4 degrees daily drift). Barbara Heller, chief conservator at the Detroit Institute of Arts and chair of an AAM Annual Meeting session on balancing collection needs and building energy consumption, says these parameters allow for slow seasonal gradients, but she also cautions that we do not know whether a change from the 50 percent/70 degree standard will realize energy efficiency improvements and maintain the integrity of collections care" (American Alliance of Museums, 2014).

Collection Environments

- National Park Service, Museum Collections Environment: Chapter 4 (PDF) (https://www.nps.gov/museum/publications/MHI/CHAPTER4.pdf)Collections Environments Standards

A comprehensive manual defining collections standard requirements and acceptable ranges for various degrees of vulnerability with links to a significant bibliography of literature on collections requirements (the latter viewable by members only):

- American Alliance of Museums, *Ethics, Standards and Best Practices: Collections Stewardship* (http://www.aam-us.org/resources/ethics-standards-and-best-practices/collections-stewardship)

  See "15. Bibliography for Museums" for citation references and further information.

Section 27

Community Needs Assessments

Process

INTRODUCTION

Community needs assessments are the foundation for a museum's planning: successful museums address significant community needs and aspirations. Museums grow and adapt in response to providing desired services to families, professionals, students, teachers, businesses, foundations, agencies, and other sponsoring investors. A market analysis forms the basis for a key element of strategic planning, assessing what the community needs and where it wants to go. Among other findings, a market analysis will help a museum do the following:

- Identify local, regional, and state community needs
- Identify community challenges and opportunities
- Stay abreast of city and regional priorities and initiatives
- Stay abreast of planned and potential construction and real estate development
- Identify major area industries and employers
  (continued next page)

Table 27.1   Sources of Community and Institutional Needs

Research Methodology/Source

External Input

Literature Review of regional visioning and analysis documents
Community Needs Interviews with civic leaders and spokespeople
Surveys and Visitor Studies
World Cafes, Interest Group Meetings and Open Houses
Brainstorming Sessions with Content Experts
Market Analysis: Demographic and Psychographic Market Profile
Best Practices in Peer Museums

Internal Input

Museum Performance Assessment and Recommendations
Operating Data Trend Analysis
Space Use Analysis and Recommendations
User/Non-User Focus Groups
Leadership Policy Guidance Workshop(s)
SWOT Exercise Results
Staff Project and Wish Lists
Database of Needed Upgrades and Capital Projects

Table 27.2   Types of Organizations with Which to Meet and Gather Data

Chamber of commerce	City overview, economic data, demographics, employers, major industries, city tourism data, list of public and private schools and colleges, list of museums and attractions, city master plans, number hotel/motel rooms
Convention and visitors bureau	Tourism data, demographics and visitor profiles, convention data, hotel/motel occupancy and seasonality, attendance at area attractions, motor coach industry data
State department of travel and tourism	Tourism data, demographics and visitor profiles, major reports, target markets, hotel/motel occupancy and seasonality, top state attractions and attendance, tourist breakdown by type of visitor (e.g., business and pleasure)
Major daily newspaper—market research department	Media packet given to potential advertisers, market psychographics and lifestyle, weekday and weekend circulation maps, customized search for location of population with specific demographics in line with the museum's visitation
Major television or radio station—market research department	Same as daily newspaper, definition of the designated market area
Cultural organization—private or public	Attendance at city and regional attractions, current and prior 5 to 10 years
School system	Enrollment, list of public and private schools, projected enrollment, testing and standards, curriculum
Community foundation and social service agency	Community needs and challenges
City planning and/or transportation department	List of other major development projects—definite and possible major current and projected construction (e.g., roads) that might have impact on attendance
Major area attraction and/or museum	Attendance data, seasonality, market data, visitor profiles

Table 27.3   Community Needs Interview Questions

What do you think of the museum so far? What is its image in the community?

What do you think the community needs, and what is the vision for its future?

How might the museum support those needs and aspirations in the future?

What needs are you addressing? How can the museum help you? (optional)

- Understand the region's economic trends and current status
- Identify potential organizational partners
- Track school enrollment trends and educational standards and initiatives
- Project attendance for a new museum, an expansion, or a multiyear strategic plan
- Identify the geographic parameters of the resident population and their characteristics
- Understand the tourist market and the best way to reach tourists
- Tailor marketing and advertising based on area demographics and psychographics
- Track attendance trends at local and regional attractions
- Assess whether ticket prices are in line with resident income profiles

The results of the market analysis will help project future attendance potential, set ticket and membership prices, target marketing and advertising more appropriately, develop programming that fits the needs of the market segments, and more. The market analysis presented here does not address fund-raising feasibility, though some of the findings may be useful in that regard.

This section is based on writing by contributing author Jeanie Stahl. See also "49. Market Demographics and Population Analysis."

MARKET QUALITATIVE ANALYSIS: COMMUNITY NEEDS AND ASPIRATIONS

Collecting Data and Conducting Interviews

A standard way to approach a market analysis is to set up a series of interviews with area organizations and to collect data from each of them. Tables 27.1 and 27.2 list the types of organizations to meet with and data to request. It is often worth asking for the same data from several organizations in case they have different reports and sources of data.

Almost all of the data identified in the tables should be available for free. Data that are not normally free include psychographic data, data regarding residents in the designated market area, and data by mileage or drive time. Often, media organizations, such as TV stations, newspapers, and radio stations, subscribe to those data and may be willing to provide them for free. It is also possible to ask the media organizations to run a specific demographic report with requested parameters, such as the number and location of households with incomes of $60,000 or more and with children ages 5 to 17.

Table 27.4   Generic Example of Summary of Opportunity and Challenges

Opportunities	*Challenges*
Area Attractions	
There are few other museums in the X region and none in the city. Will be able to build on the community support that the current museum and its partnering organizations have developed over the years. There are few indoor museums and attractions in the area targeting school groups. The museum's multi- and interdisciplinary focus will enable the museum to serve many different school grades.	Another museum in the area expanded and opened a 3D IMAX theater. The proposed new children's museum will compete for young audiences in a small residential market.
Tourism	
The convention and visitors bureau is an asset to the region and actively pursues increasing tourism. The sports complex attracts people to the downtown area.	The city's tourist population is small, with many of the tourists residing in the state and already included in the museum city's designated market area. The profile of the tourist visiting for gambling is not a good match for museum visitation.
Resident Population	
The profile of residents in the county where the museum is located is strong in regard to potential museum visitation.	County population growth is stagnant. A survey of designated market area residents indicated below-average interest in attending cultural and arts events compared to the United States as a whole.
Collaborations and Partnerships	
There is the potential to partner with a variety of area universities and colleges. There will be the opportunity for joint promotion and marketing with the civic center. The museum's status and branding as a Smithsonian affiliate is a great asset for marketing and programs.	Partnering and collaborating with others is time and staff intensive. There are few large corporations in the area.
Quality of Life	
Businesses looking to draw workers to the area view the museum as an important contributor to the area's quality of life. Interviewees indicated that there is not enough to do in the area for young adults and youth.	It's a big sports town, not a big museum town.
Market Reach	
The city already attracts residents from a large geographic area for shopping, conventions, and special events.	Residential growth is occurring north of the city, with new shopping complexes, moving the focus for some away from the museum's downtown location.
Site/Location	
The current park location is perceived as an upscale area of the city and perceived by some as a "snooty" part of town. Moving to the downtown will be more inclusive. Downtown development is continuing to occur.	There is a perception that people don't like "crossing the river," so it is more difficult to attract residents from the east side of the river.
Transportation	
City is centrally located in the state and is near I-XX, a major throughway between City A and City B. Improvements being done to I-XX include rerouting the highway so that it will no longer bypass the city. A downtown location will make it easier to access the site by public transportation.	

Table 27.5   Current and Projected Population by Market Segment

	Current	*Projected*	*Increase/(Decrease)*	*Increase/ (Decrease)*
Market segment	Population	20XX		
Primary market	440,300	490,200	49,900	11.3%
Secondary market	549,200	546,700	(2,500)	(0.5%)
School enrollment: K–12	81,700	88,236	6,536	8.0%
Tourists (overnight)	1,528,000	1,654,600	126,600	8.3%
Total	3,039,317	3,219,034	179,717	5.9%

Note: Population demographics are addressed in "49. Market Demographics and Population Analysis." Source: Alteryx Demographics USA, State Department of Education, State Tourism Department.

Table 27.6   Key Audience Segments

Visitor Segment	*Ideal Yearly Visitor Share*	*Ideal Yearly Program Share*	*Program Participant Segment*
Adults visiting with children			Regional households
School and youth groups			Professionals/hobbyists
Adults, ages 34 and up, visiting with adults			Businesses
Young adults, ages 18 to 34, without children			Community groups
Teens, ages 13 to 18			Schools and universities
Solo visitors, ages 18 to 75 and up			Other museums and public venues
Totals	100%	100%	

Hint: Don't worry about exact statistics or numbers at first. Use + + for prime segments and - - for the least frequent visitor. This is about whom you want to serve the most.

Table 27.7   Categories of Potential Museum Impacts and Benefits

	Current Priority	*External Demand*	*Future Priority*
Public impacts			
A Broadening participation			
B Preserving heritage			
C Strengthening social capital			
D Enhancing public knowledge			
E Serving education			
F Advancing social change			
G Communicating public identity and image			
Private impacts			
H Contributing to the economy			
I Delivering corporate community services			
Personal impacts			
J Enabling personal growth			
K Offering personal respite			
L Welcoming personal leisure			
Institutional impacts			
M Helping museum operations			
N Building museum capital			

Categories and definitions of these 14 impact areas organized by their precedented funding sources and kinds of impacts are described in "44. Museum Impacts and Benefits."

In all cases, when meeting with each organization, ask the questions identified in table 27.3. Question 1 would be omitted if you were planning a new museum.

Summary of Market Opportunities and Challenges

When the market analysis is complete, it is helpful to put together a table summarizing the opportunities and challenges. Sometimes it is useful to write a memo providing a more in-depth analysis of the findings and the data behind it. A memo might be organized under the following headings:

- Summary of market opportunities and challenges
- Regional overview and demographics (this might be at the state level or some larger geography than the primary and secondary resident markets)
- Overview of the city
  - Population growth
  - Downtown development
  - New projects and initiatives
  - Higher education
  - Crime statistics
  - Vision statements

- Area attractions and tourism
  - State and regional tourism
  - Local tourism
- Market segment population and demographics
  - Resident—primary and secondary and other markets, if applicable
  - School
  - Tourist

Table 27.4 presents an example of a summary of market opportunities and challenges.

Market Segment by Population

Table 27.5 is an example of a museum's population by market segment that is the basis for one of the methods of developing an estimate for a museum's attendance potential for a future operating year. Capture ratios are applied to each of the market segments resulting in potential attendance from each market (see "8. Attendance Potential Estimates").

Section 28

Community Needs and Museums

Rationale

INTRODUCTION

The social contract for a museum's nonprofit status—and often for the use of its public land or buildings—is that, in return, such museums will provide for the public good, even if there is no actual public funding in the operating budget. In short, providing at least some public value of the museum's choosing must be among a museum's services. Mission statements expressing that selected public value grow out of this foundational assumption.

Museums provide public, private, and personal values. Museums provide benefits and services to society as a whole and to private foundations, corporations, and donors, and they provide personal benefits and services to individuals and families (Hood, 1983; Jacobsen, 2016; Roberts, Morrissey, Silverman, & Perry, 1996; Scott, 2007). Managing the creative tensions between public, private, and personal values will be critical to museum development in the coming decades.

What are our community's needs? And which of those can our museum address most effectively? Museums operate in their community's *cultural ecosystem*. A museum can fill particular niches in our region's educational and cultural ecology. Informed by research into what is around us and what is missing (see "27. Community Needs Assessments: Process"), we can expand strategically and sensitively into undeveloped niches in our territory. In this, we should also help other neighboring institutions expand their learning and cultural services in their areas. Collectively, we will strengthen our community's resources and social bonds.

Each museum needs to discover how big its potential role should and can be in its cultural ecosystem and then make its best efforts at doing the best job of providing its range of quality services. This fully realized museum adds to the community, adds value to the other educational institutions, and adds essential services meeting more of the needs of a rich and diverse community.

The process of developing the museum's content and plans should be open to the community and involve key individuals and organizations as advisers, partners, and supporters. Visitor research will be used to inform management of public opinion about alternate exhibit and program choices.

The process of assessing community and institutional needs is outlined in "27. Community Needs Assessment: Process" and detailed in Jacobsen (2016, chap. 5).

COMMUNITY NEEDS AND MUSEUMS: RATIONALE

A Community Service Museum

Museums pursue many kinds of purposes. The late museum sage Stephen E. Weil (2002) observed that "museums can provide forms of public service that are all but infinite in their variety" (p. 89). There are historic shifts among categories of purposes— collection stewardship, education, lifelong learning, economic development, quality of life, and so on.

The current reality is that many U.S. museums already operate as community service museums and pursue multiple purposes, resulting in multiple kinds of outcomes. Such museums are constantly changing their mix in response to the interests and needs of their audiences and supporters.

This is good, and the museum community should not feel guilty about it but rather listen harder to the operating data and then look creatively for the common ground between the museum's intentions and its audiences' and supporters' intentions. Museums can track their changing value through the operating numbers and observe the shifting ratios among the multiple revenue sectors to inform planning and to keep the museum responsive to its external market and economy.

Museums as Civic Infrastructure

A city should be able to look across all its museums and other informal learning organizations and see, collectively, an inventory of public spaces that provide for the community's educational, cultural, social, and economic needs.

A community's strategy should be to end up with a full range of experience platforms in different subjects (e.g., art, history, and science) and for different ages and groups (e.g., school kids, families with children, and empty nesters), and for different learning needs (e.g., exploration, problem solving, understanding, and contemplation).

Museums as Civic Agoras

The Greeks used the term *agora* to refer to places in their cities where people came to exchange ideas, commodities, and values. Until World War II, town squares, pilgrimages, market days, churches, festivals, parades, town meetings, and other traditionally established places and events served the function of the agora in gathering the community. Today, the concept of agora is being redefined with new places and events, such as political rallies, festival marketplaces, mega-malls, community centers, libraries, and school sports events. Forward-thinking museums can further strengthen the bonds of their communities by adding another popular and relevant community gathering place and civic agora.

See "15. Bibliography for Museums" for citation references.

Section 29

Concept and Strategic Master Plans

INTRODUCTION

Integrated planning requires documentation that states a current set of planning assumptions that all agree on and that support each other in logical ways.

Early in the planning process, when not much is set down and known, a loose, top-down *concept development plan* will present the key assumptions in just enough detail to be able to quantify the capital and operating size of the envisioned project. Often, concept development plans have ranges of costs and a number of options that are useful in discussions with potential supporters—how large a project will they support? Which components are most supportable? Which site or concept?

Once the scale of the project is determined and some of the key planning is far enough along that cost and operating estimates can be made (e.g., the building size and costs are known), the museum can produce a much more detailed *strategic master plan*, which incorporates the *business plan*.

The strategic master plan integrates vision with economics, and the document reflects a synthesis of earlier work, including feasibility studies, visitor research, and conceptual plans.

Broadly, the order of the chapters reflects both the conceptual and the chronological sequences. In practice, the whole chain is constantly iterative and spiral, and each time planning goes through the sequence, more layers and more detail are added to the vision.

The full menu for a strategic master plan shown in tables 29.1 and 29.2 allows you to select what you will need in your eventual plan and to decide which chapters need to be addressed first.

Table 29.1   Concept Development Plan: Table of Contents

Project purposes and definition
Market research and assessment
Component descriptions and program themes
Attendance potential estimate
Site selection criteria
Preliminary sizing
Preliminary economic model
Operating and capital costs
Forms basis for detailed master plan
Provides basis for preliminary assessment of funding feasibility

Table 29.2   Strategic Master and Business Plan: Table of Contents

Table 29.2   Strategic Master and Business Plan: Table of Contents (Continued)

Table 29.2   Strategic Master and Business Plan: Table of Contents (Continued)

Section 30

Conceptual Framework

INTRODUCTION

A museum's *conceptual framework* is the theoretical foundation for everything it does. The conceptual framework has four main parts: *intentional purposes, guiding principles, stakeholders,* and the *business model.*

Purposes include mission, vision, objectives, goals, and desired impacts. Guiding principles include values (core and strategic), character, personality profile, and brand identity. Stakeholders include visitors, program participants, guests, customers, and supporters (public and private). Private supporters include funders, volunteers, partners, and collectors. The business model is also called and includes financial statement, operating budget, balance sheet, revenue mix, and business lines.

Broadly, purposes are about *why* a museum does what it does, guiding principles are about *how* a museum does what it does, stakeholders are *who* the museum serves, and the business model is the *value proposition* that sustains and grows the museum's services to its stakeholders.

This section looks at conceptual frameworks overall; see tables 30.1 to 30.3 for more detail. These samples are intended as starting tools, and you will want to edit and customize them to your needs.

Table 30.1   Elements of a Conceptual Framework

Traditional Model	Museum Manager's Compendium
Vision statement	Vision statement
Mission statement	Intentional purposes
Impacts and Objectives	Desired impacts and perceived benefits
Core and strategic values	Guiding principles
Market	Community
Visitors, users, guests, and customers	Audiences: visitors and program participants
Donors, funders, sponsors, partners, collectors, and volunteers	Public and private supporters

Table 30.2   Executive Summary Museum Description Template

[Museum Name]
The Museum's purposes are to [---What are your intentional purposes?---], and we will track and evaluate our impact by measuring [Which desired impacts will you measure?]. To achieve these purposes and impacts, the Museum will serve [---Who will you serve as visitors?---] as visitors and [Who will you serve as program participants?] as customers of our other services. The Museum will earn [Earned Revenue] % of its budget and attract support revenues of [---Support Revenue---] %, provided an endowment is established sufficiently to cover _____% of the yearly budget, expected to be in the range of $ [---Budget---], with a staff size of [---Staff---] FTEs. The Museum will pursue its purposes by using its [---Resources---] to offer a family of activities that share the brand's guiding principles [guiding principles] and collectively serve our key service markets in priority. These activities include [---Which activities and services will you offer?---]. The Museum will host these activities in a strategic selection of public spaces including [---Kinds of spaces---]. The Museum will take the following steps to implement this vision: [---What sequence of phases?---].

Table 30.3   Revenue Balance: How Will You Balance Your Four Masters?

Revenue Balance	Now	Future Vision
Earned revenue		
Visitor based	____%	____%
Program based	____%	____%
Support revenue		
Public sources	____%	____%
Private sources	____%	____%
Endowment income	____%	____%
	100%	100%

Sample Goal Statement

The museum will be a unique institution that serves [city] residents while also attracting tourists interested in experiencing the region. The overarching goal of the museum is to turn an engagement with the region's exciting human stories and historic places into a connection to the contemporary city, its evolving culture, and the people who are shaping its future.

Section 31

Content Development

INTRODUCTION

The development of the museum's exhibits and programs will be informed by scholarship, research, and fact checking of the highest standards. The museum's reputation will be based on the thoroughness of its content research and will be the basis of the public's trust in the brand. The public expects that the museum is an authoritative source of knowledge about the subjects in its repertoire of programs. However, it is quite unlikely that the organization can afford to maintain on its staff the range and depth of professional personnel with all the requisite knowledge.

The museum will, therefore, rely on procedures for acquiring the timely input from experts in the field, often from university, partner institutions, and corporate sources. The museum cannot function properly without some level of in-house subject matter expertise, but the professionalism required of the staff is to be able to communicate effectively with specialists and to translate their knowledge into a form that is appealing and comprehensible to the museum's audiences. Staff and project contractors will undertake research tasks defined by the museum's project teams and coached by volunteer advisers who are topic experts. Project teams may also contract with topic-specific experts for research and guest curator services.

CONTENT DEVELOPMENT

Content research will be guided by the needs of the envisioned programs and exhibitions, and the developers will be advised as to where to look for research by the following advisory groups:

- **Theme Advisory Groups:** Each major theme area, which may involve one or more experience platforms, will have a standing advisory group who will help guide the selection of scenarios and the appointment of scenario advisory groups.
- **Scenario Advisory Groups:** Each scenario will have an ad hoc advisory group composed of specialists on that scenario's topic.
- **Educator Advisory Committee:** Developing a close relationship with teachers and community educators is critical to collaborating with the local schools and developing appropriate programs. To facilitate this communication, an educator advisory committee will meet with the museum staff three or four times a year to share collective insights and discuss educators' needs. The educator advisory committee will also consult with teacher leaders (best practice teachers within districts), teachers who have shown great enthusiasm and energy for the museum, teacher educators from local colleges and universities; (subject) coordinators at the district level (or the administrative staff who make decisions about how professional development resources are spent in the district), stakeholders (e.g., funders and businesspeople), and retired teachers who have the time and energy to help the museum create partnerships and linkages to schools and school districts. Through focus groups, interviews, and surveys with teachers and administrators, the educator advisory committee will advise staff and the program committee on the content and creation of programming as well as services provided at the museum for educators.
- **Visitor Advisory Groups:** Comprised of volunteers in certain key visitor segments, these visitor advisory groups can be convened from time to time to react to ideas in development. Why and how is the content and experience beneficial to the visitor? To each key visitor segment? Advisory groups might include members, travel agents, parents of young children, and others who are familiar with the behavior of a particular segment.
- **Invited Visitors:** Before opening, once the museum is safe for invited guests, people can be invited to look at the exhibits as they are being installed and react to questions posed by researchers who will accompany them. Invited visitors will be helpful during shakedown and previews and, after opening, in summative evaluations of the opening scenarios. The invited visitors

Table 31.1   Volunteer Experts

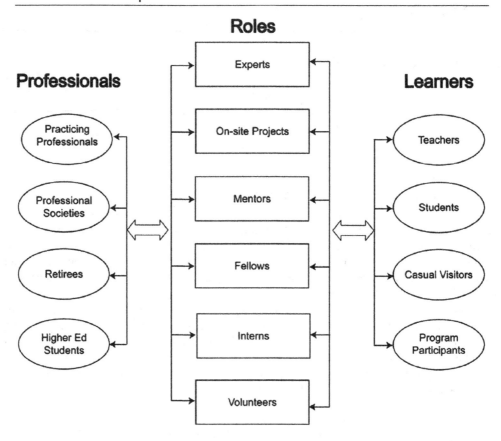

will be observed by researchers who will stop to ask questions from time to time and ask them to fill out a questionnaire before departure. In some instances, invited visitors will be asked for follow-up research by telephone.

These advisory groups will work on a voluntary basis, with individuals supplemented by project fees if substantial research tasks are required of the advisers.

Section 32

Education

K–12 Strategy

INTRODUCTION

The museum will be strategic and deliberate in the manner in which it prioritizes, develops, and implements its programs for the K–12 community. The following section summarizes the key approaches and impacts that the museum's school programs will have across elementary, middle, and secondary students.

Your museum can select and adapt from these components according to your resources and K–12 system's needs.

THE MUSEUM'S STRATEGY FOR IMPACT ON K–12 EDUCATION

This section is based on writing by Dr. David Chittenden, vice president of education at the Science Museum of Minnesota (retired).

Within the broad goal of providing support for K–12 education, there are different strategies (e.g., content, format, style, pedagogy, and location) for serving different ages. The museum will offer programs for all ages and will develop targeted programs for each of the following categories of students and their teachers:

- **Elementary School Programs:** Involvement with the museum at this stage will focus on school visits to the museum galleries, with pre- and postvisit material and teacher training to get the most out of each visit. Associated with the school visits to the museum, a core school outreach program will be initiated and piloted to help raise the visibility and familiarity of the institution in the K–12 community. The goal of the programs for this age is to build excitement and interest in XX at this impressionable time in student's lives. Students of this age are also candidates to visit the museum with their families.
- **Middle School Programs:** Research shows that this is a critical time for career directions, so this is an important audience for the museum. Middle and high schools are also difficult audiences to get to visit a museum, so the museum will have to go to their teachers, schools, and communities to reach them. The challenge at the middle school level is to keep interested students moving ahead with their education, and the museum's programs will support teachers and encourage these grades to work in teams doing projects using materials and equipment provided by the museum. Besides a core middle school outreach program developed and delivered by the museum outreach staff, additional programs may be implemented in collaboration with ones already run or offered by others.
- **High School Programs:** The museum will sponsor affinity clubs (e.g., rockets, animation, design, and Web publishing) and will train and support teachers and help students at this age work together on projects of their own choosing within a community of interest supported by the museum's equipment, resources, and people-to-people programs. High school students can also work as floor staff following the principle that teaching others is the best way to learn. The New York Hall of Science's Explainer programs are examples of intern programs that are successful at both science education and the development of job skills. Outside funds and partners will be sought to plan and implement a strong set of similar programs serving high school teens.
- **The Program Center:** The Program Center provides school and youth groups with specially equipped wet labs and other equipped learning spaces and provides teacher training programs for the region's teachers and their students. This facility will be operated in partnership and with the support of the region's public television and the state's public and private schools. The museum will work closely with the school system and other organizations to make sure its programs are integrated with the curriculum in the region and that efforts are not duplicated. The Program Center will also be very much involved with family learning in the public programs in the exhibit areas as well as in the themed program labs and classrooms. The Program Center's support for K–12 education is a high priority that complements the high priority of serving the general family visitors because the two audiences come at different times and in different contexts.

Section 33

Education

Learning Theory

INTRODUCTION

Learning is critical in a knowledge society. The market has already responded to (or perhaps instigated) a growing interest in lifelong learning. The traditional community resources for free-choice learning are being challenged by commercial entities: museums by top-quality theme parks, libraries by creative bookstores, and public broadcasters by focused cable and radio stations.

This competition does not mean that museums should shy away from the "learning market." Museums have strengths, assets, and responsibilities that give them considerable leverage against commercial competition: museums are America's most trusted source of information (Wilkening, 2015), and many museums have large capital investments in their buildings, collections, and exhibits. It does mean, however, that museums have to be very good at delivering learning services, focus on their areas of expertise and differentiation, and uphold the public trust in museums as authoritative sources.

Dewey, Piaget, Vygotsky, Spock, Gardner, Hein, Csikszentmihalyi, Bateson, and Langer have each contributed learning theory that has implications on museum learning. Inquiry-based learning, developmental learning levels, social learning, unstructured play, multiple intelligences, constructivist learning, flow experiences, spiral learning, and mindfulness, respectively, have each had their applications, and more theories are doubtless in the wings as neuroscience understands more about how the brain works. Museum educator Ted Ansbacher has observed that a good theory of learning not only describes and explains what takes place in a museum but also is needed as a foundation for developing new exhibits and programs. From the many theories and their variations, a consensus is emerging that John Dewey's experience-based approach—combined with current social and constructivist models that stress the individual's active participation in making meaning from direct experiences—is most appropriate for museums. This approach shifts the educational focus away from information transfer and onto providing meaningful experiences—the particular strength of museums with their real objects and phenomena.

There are many learning terms and theories relevant to museums, such as constructivism, free-choice learning, and inquiry-based learning. Many of these are defined by the Definitions Project (http://www.definitionsproject.com/definitions/index.cfm).

Museum learning theory is an extension of a museum's guiding principles. This section helps inform decisions about the museum's overall theory of action to advance education and learning. The section has options for learning concepts to select that fit your museum's resources and your community's needs. The following text and tables may be selected and adapted to suit your museum.

MUSEUM LEARNING THEORY

Museum Learning Is Experiential and Social

Like museums, public broadcasting, libraries, schools, and universities also offer many essential learning services. How do museums distinguish their services? The answer lies in a museum's unique physicality, which is traceable to our traditions in public buildings, physical collections, and exhibits. Unlike many other free-choice learning media, museums offer learning experiences in real time and real space with real objects and real phenomena. Museums offer direct experience in public spaces.

Experiential learning is a museum strength that clearly distinguishes what museums do from their free-choice learning cousins in libraries and public broadcasting. A museum's unique asset is *experiential learning*. A rearrangement of the same words shows another dimension of this core business: *learning from experience*.

The physicality of museum buildings that museums share with libraries but not learning media means that museums can serve social and civic needs. We experience museums socially, while walking and talking with the people we came in with, and sometimes with strangers. Museums are social places.

Table 33.1 Informal (aka Free-Choice) and Formal (aka School) Learning

Source: Falk and Dierking, 2010.

Lifelong Learning

John Falk and Lynn Dierking, Sea-Grant professors of science and math education at Oregon State University and experts on museum and other informal learning, observe that 95 percent of our learning time is spent outside of school, where we learn informally at work and at leisure as illustrated in table 33.1.

The National Advisory Group for Continuing Education and Lifelong Learning (NAGCELL) addressed an articulate report on lifelong learning to the secretary of education and industry in the United Kingdom. The following statement describes NAGCELL's approach to social reform during what they refer to as the "Learning Age": "We want to see lifelong learning becoming part of everyday life, in all sorts of contexts, in a variety of circumstances and for everybody at all stages in their lives. Where learning is concerned, this means shifting from those situations where it is mostly a minority or special kind of activity to ones in which, increasingly and happily, everyone integrates elements of learning into their lives. It means recognizing and cherishing those processes devoted to the generation and renewal of all forms of 'intellectual capital,' and devising appropriate mechanisms to measure and evaluate it" (Anderson, 1997).

Even within the museum niche, different kinds of museums may be needed to address different learning needs. A large city might support a science center, art museum, natural history museum, children's museum, aquarium, living history village, history museum, botanical garden, historic sites and houses, national parks, and numerous specialized museums and collections. Each of these museums provides a distinct gateway to learning that appeals to different visitors. According to Falk and Dierking, many visitors to a museum are already disposed and somewhat knowledgeable about the subject; museums can leverage their appeal to fans into wider topics, perspectives, and attitudes.

Theories of Knowledge versus Learning

"Educational theory is broader than learning theory and includes four components: how people learn, what they learn, how we go about implementing it (i.e., pedagogy or exhibit design, curriculum, etc.), and, most important, why we educate. Constructivism is an educational theory, not a learning theory. The distinction is important because we have to ask not only how people learn but what they learn. The crucial and controversial part of constructivism is that people construct their own meaning; it isn't only about how they go about this but what the result turns out to be" (personal communication with the author from museum educator George Hein, 2016).

Hein and Alexander (1998) observes that both the theory of knowledge and the theory of learning are continuous and that they can be organized orthogonally to define quadrants, as shown in figure 33.2. The two ends of the theory of knowledge are that all knowledge exists outside the learner versus that knowledge is constructed by the learner. The two ends of the theory of learning are that learning is incremental, added bit by bit, versus that learning is active, leading to restructuring.

Education Compared to Learning

Education and *learning*, terms often used interchangeably, have different meanings in this book, as shown in table 33.3. Education is about the desired transfer of a defined body of knowledge from a teacher to a student. Learning is about what an individual experiences and retains.

Contextual Model of Learning (aka Museum Experience Model)

Falk and Dierking (2000) illustrate that learning is a

Table 33.2   Theories of Knowledge versus Learning (Hein's Matrix)

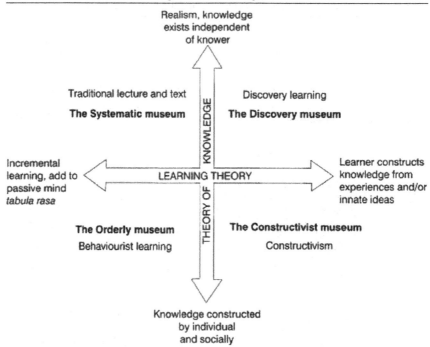

contextually driven effort by people to find meaning in the real world, an organic, situated, integrated process. The Contextual Model for Learning illustrates how meaning is constructed by the visitor through the interaction of three contextual factors:

- What the individual brings in terms of prior experience, knowledge, and interests (personal context)
- The interaction of the visitors with others, in their own group and outside, as well as cultural influences (sociocultural context)
- The architecture and physical elements of the exhibitions and programs as well as the subsequent experiences that visitors have (physical context)

The new model also includes a fourth and very important dimension—time. It is important to think about how the museum experience fits into the lifelong learning experience of the visitor as shown in table 33.4.

Note: In a liberal adaptation of Falk and Dierking's model, this book defines the physical context as including not only the architecture, exhibits, and collections but also the staffed museum programs run in and among exhibits, as the museum's human presence has become an integral part of the visitor's experience of museums.

Building on Falk and Dierking's three contexts, each can be subdivided into a strategic framework for museums to monitor and direct long-term outcomes and services:

- The personal context framework is based on nine individual learning levels by age as shown in table 33.5.
- The sociocultural context framework focuses on the six different types of visitor groups that arrive at a museum as shown in table 33.6.

Table 33.3   Education Compared to Learning

Education	Learning
Speaker driven	Listener selected
Top down	Bottom up
Objective driven	Outcome driven
Advisory board	Market research
Fact retention	Skill development
Content	Process

- The physical context framework defines 10 categories of museum exhibits, theaters, and programs and looks at each category's unique strengths to serve particular learning needs (see "73. Public Spaces: Categories").

STEM and STEAM Learning

Science, technology, engineering, and mathematics (STEM) are the disciplines many feel are critical to future employability and economic prosperity at both an individual and a societal level. Add the arts, and STEM becomes STEAM, with a recognition that the arts are as creative as the sciences and as necessary for a well-rounded community and mind. Some museums outside the sciences have elected STEM or STEAM programs at the instigation of funders.

With regard to STEM education, informal learning resources, including science museums, have been found to be effective in producing STEM learning outcomes by the U.S. National Research Council and reported by Bell, Lewenstein, Shouse, and Feder (2009). Their strands of science learning are listed in table 33.7

Table 33.4   Contextual Model of Learning (Falk and Dierking)

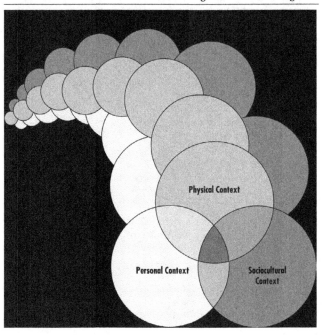

Table 33.5   Personal Context Framework

	Age	Share of Market	Share of Audience	Future Ideal
Toddler	0 to 3			
Early school age	4 to6			
Middle childhood age	7 to12			
Early adolescence	13 to18			
Later adolescence	19 to24			
Early adulthood	25 to34			
Middle adulthood	35 to64			
Later adulthood	65 to75			
Older seniors	75 and up			
		100%	100%	100%

The ECC Trilogy and the Museum's Role in the Educational Infrastructure

A metastudy of previous studies on factors influencing students' inclinations toward abilities in science and technology determined that there are three principal factors that need to be in place for a child to succeed in science—*engagement*, *capacity*, and *continuity*—which the authors called the "ECC Trilogy" (Jolly, Campbell, & Perlman, 2004). See table 33.8.

Engagement is about inspiring interest, particularly among youth, a natural territory for a museum. Building capacity—the cognitive knowledge of science and its theories—is the province of schools, and continuity—maintaining interest and continuing to develop capacity—is the province of families, youth groups, and a museum's teen and adult programs.

One of the many implications of this ECC approach to creating a science and technology–based economy is that different

Table 33.6   Sociocultural Context Framework: Key Visitor Segments

- **Adults visiting with children**

  Small family groups
  Extended families
  Tourist families
  Preschoolers and caregivers
- **School and youth groups**
  Elementary school
  Middle school

  High school
  Day care groups

  Home schoolers
  Scout and fellowship groups

  Summer camps
- **Teens, ages 13 to 18**
  After-school teens
  Groups of friends, ages 13 to 18

- **Adults, ages 34 and up, visiting with adults**
  Couples without children
  Empty nesters
  Seniors
  Group tours
  Business conferences
  Tourists
- **Young adults, ages 18 to 34, without children**
  Dating couples
  Groups of friends, ages 18 to 34
  College students
- **Solo visitors, ages 18 to 75 and up**
  Students on projects
  Singles
  Travelers
  Aficionados

Table 33.7   Strands of Science Learning

Strand 1: Excitement, interest, and motivation
Strand 2: Come to use concepts
Strand 3: Make sense of the natural world
Strand 4: Reflect on science as a way of knowing
Strand 5: Participate in scientific activities
Strand 6: Develop an identity as someone who knows about, uses, and sometimes contributes to science

Source: Bell et al. (2009).

Table 33.8   ECC Trilogy

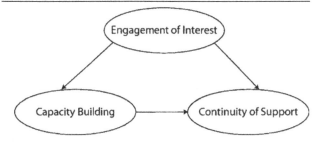

Source: Jolly, Cambell, and Perlman, 2004

organizations need to work together as part of a science education infrastructure, with both formal learning (schools and universities) and informal learning organizations, such as public television, libraries, scout clubs, and science centers. No one is sufficient on its own to do the job, but if we work together, with youths moving among the various programs throughout their formative years, the ECC Trilogy has a chance.

The museum's role in the partnership is to spark interest and help grow the culture of learning. The education system can do the capacity-building piece, but it does not have the resources or skills to do this kind of affective, emotional learning. A museum can complement the schools and help parents:

- *Engagement* is about inspiring interest.
- *Building capacity* is about the knowledge of science and its processes.
- *Continuity* is about maintaining interest.

Organizations working together in a science education infrastructure are needed to support a child.

PLANNING WORKSHEETS

Table 33.9   Summary of Learning Theories

	Relevance	Adoption
Experiential and social		
Lifelong learning		
Theories of knowledge and learning:		
Discovery		
Constructivist		
Stimulus–response		
Didactic expository		
Education: learning		
Contextual model of learning		
Personal context: stages of development		
Sociocultural context: key visitor segments		
Physical context: public spaces		
STEM and STEAM		
The ECC Trilogy		

Table 33.10   Target Learners: Key Visitor Segments (Sociocultural Context)

	Share of Market	Share of Audience	Future Ideal
Adults visiting with children			
School and youth groups			
Adults, ages 34 and up, visiting with adults			
Young adults, ages 18 to 34, without children			
Teens, ages 13 to 18			
Solo visitors, ages 18 to 75 and up			
	100%	100%	100%

See "15. Bibliography for Museums" for citation references.

Section 34

Education

Social Learning Concepts

INTRODUCTION

Exhibit halls will recognize that many visitors arrive as a social group and will allow for the interaction of visitors with each other around an exhibit. In this way, parents and/or groups of students will together facilitate each other's learning experience. This interaction with others will be achieved by designs that will recognize that we all have different learning styles and that we approach exhibits with different suppositions and kinds of interests.

SOCIAL LEARNING CONCEPTS

- Voices and Faces of Our Neighbors: Stories are told through audio and visual media in exhibits throughout the museum. They speak to our imaginations and our emotions in ways that can set a story deep inside us and inspire us to see.
- The Exploratorium's Group Inquiry by Visitors at Exhibits (G.I.V.E.) Project: This "concept engages visitors in social interactions and discussions about an inquiry-based exhibit. It encourages thinking of science as a group activity rather than a solo process."
- Contextual Clustering: Such clustering of exhibit units offers social groups, such as families, multiple perspectives on a topic: historical, technical, scientific, ethical, aesthetic, and biographical. These perspectives engage more members of a group and give each something to talk about (see also table 98.3).
- Family Social Learning: In particular, the family audience is unique, and it is the distinguishing characteristics of the family audience that are important to consider in planning family-oriented galleries. According to museum researcher Lynn Dierking (personal communication), there are five important points to keep in mind for the design of exhibits and programs that target families:
  1. A family comes to the museum with its own agenda, and we must try to accommodate it. We need to do everything we can to orient visitors to the institution, including in the exhibit spaces, restrooms, the café, and the store.
  2. The family visit is a social event, so we need to develop creative ways for families to be social together. We must also keep in mind that independent learning families like to do some things separately, so options in both exhibits and programs should be provided.
  3. Most visitors, including families, deal with exhibits in a very concrete fashion. A commitment to audience advocacy means that label copy must be clear and concepts emphasized that make sense to laypeople.
  4. Even though it may not always be obvious, visitors do come to our institutions to "look" at exhibits. Center staff should not be distressed if family guides are not used or families do not get excited about a program. We need to remember that families may perceive such programs as diverting them from their primary goal of "doing" the museum.
  5. Because of the diverse nature of families, we must provide a variety of options in exhibits and programs to accommodate varying learning styles, different knowledge levels, and uneven attentional levels.

See "15. Bibliography for Museums" for citation reference.

Section 35

Education

Strategies

INTRODUCTION

This section lists a selection of education strategies that your museum can adapt to achieve your educational purposes. See also "33. Education Learning Theory," "68. Programming," and "98. Visitor Experience."

EDUCATION STRATEGIES

- **Experiential Learning:** Participation and active engagement promote learning and fulfillment for the visitor. From a pedagogical perspective, hands-on/minds-on exhibits provide complementary learning gateways to classroom learning by offering spatial, kinesthetic, experiential, visual, and other intelligences to add reality to textbook principles.
- **Interpreters:** Throughout the exhibit halls, facilitators and explainers will add a friendly personal aspect to the visitor's experience. These individuals, who will include some staff but will be primarily volunteer based, will provide personal connections between individual visitors and exhibits and their contents. This customized human touch will be able to engage the visitor's specific interest and levels of knowledge and go on to inspire a greater understanding of the exhibit and subject in question.
- **Museum Educators and Docents:** These individuals facilitate meaningful dialogue with guests and guide them to discover things that are most meaningful to them.
- **Variety of Learning Spaces for Different Learning Styles:** A leading museum educator points out that a museum needs to offer its visitors a "wide range of possible experiences . . . recreation, spectacle, orientation and the chance to solve problems" (Grinell, 1992). If the museum is to serve a diverse audience and to operate fully during the year, then this range of activities becomes doubly important: different kinds of visitor and program experiences need to be formulated for the different kinds of learning styles and segments. The experience will blend a number of different kinds of learning spaces, some of which will be traditional history showcases that tell stories (of current interest to the paying visitors), while others will be like workshops or more informal hands-on arenas with clusters of exhibits whose elements can engage the whole family, from toddler to senior.
- **Building Connections:** The museum galleries are where you go to find out about yourself and your past and how your story is connected to the stories of others.
- **Inspiring Innovation:** The museum's unique approach to learning is to build innovation skills by looking at historical innovations in their social contexts using collection objects surrounded by interactives and encouraging kids to invent their futures by engaging them in the community's current challenges and opportunities. There is a logical sequence that the museum's exhibits, theaters, and programs can follow to build innovation skills: first *engage* their curiosity, which, it is hoped, leads to *investigation*, ideally resulting in a *discovery* (an aha! moment), which over time and if properly nurtured, can lead to *invention* and *innovation*. Exhibit and theater developers should consider this engagement sequence and find ways to catalyze the chain reaction. The first steps are in the museum's control, but the last ones happen inside our audience's minds—if we prime them properly.
- **Game-Based Learning Experiences and Cyberlearning:** These are realizing the power of virtual learning to transform education, exemplified by game skills and expectations in exhibition interfaces, such as NySci's network exhibit and Boston's Virtual Fish Tank ("design a fish that survives"), the Smithsonian's Art of the Game, and the Strong Museum's (Rochester, N.Y.) National Videogame Museum.
- **Visitor Monitoring and Interface Technologies:** Other sectors are developing digital sensing technologies that could be adapted to museums: retail, home medical alerts, social connection apps, augmented reality, employee tag sensors, security systems, intelligent thermostats, and house control systems. Time and tracking studies can result in metrics that are possible indicators of engagement and learning of individual visitors and exhibits.

- **Exhibitions as Learning Research Platforms:** If learning outcomes are a priority, then think about exhibitions as platforms for observing and documenting how and what visitors learn. A gallery equipped with visitor movement and response sensors that are linked to input from visitors using the interactive exhibits is capable of reporting visitor output, outcome, and impact data, as desired by either the show producer, the funder, or the museum. Such sensors can recognize each visitor, note dwell time at each station, record points of interaction and capture his or her responses to input prompts. These data are available privately to the visitor (souvenir record of the visit) and in anonymized management reports (e.g., time and tracking studies, weekly throughput, collected evaluation questions, and net promoters score). These data inform marketing, operations, and funders' evaluations.

See *"15. Bibliography for Museums" for citation reference.*

Section 36

Exhibit Evaluation Filters

INTRODUCTION

This section summarizes the main aspects to consider when evaluating designs and plans for future exhibits, from installation punch-lists to a summary evaluation after opening. In the case of contracted exhibits, the museum could edit and prioritize the choices in table 36.1 to attach to the contract in order to be up front about how the museum will evaluate work in progress. This framework is also useful evaluating existing gallery installations.

EXHIBIT EVALUATION FILTERS

Table 36.1   Exhibit Evaluation Filters

CORE VALUES (ALL MUST-FIT)	
Relates to science and technology	Universal access and design
Develops learning skills	Green thinking
Content is significant and accurate	Relevant to visitors and customers
Raises stimulating questions	Fits with brand identity
High value visitor experience	Engaging and appropriate design
Establishes visitor confidence	Incorporates visitor research
Fits approach designated for that space	Involves community program partners

LEARNING APPROACHES (MAY VARY WITH REASON)	
Engages and Inspires	Interdisciplinary (science, technology, art, and history)
Stimulus for conversations and participation	Intellectually accessible to all
Clarity of message and activity	Lifelong learning

VISITOR'S NEEDS (MAY VARY WITH REASON)	
Responds to participant's learning interests	Relationship to daily life—relevance
Appealing subjects	Engaging more than once
Appealing experience	Community gathering uses

WORKS FOR SMALL GROUPS (FAMILIES AND SOCIAL OUTINGS) (MAY VARY WITH REASON)	
See PISEC list below	

OPERATIONAL CONSIDERATIONS (MAY VARY WITH REASON)	
Flexibility (Delta change tactics used)	Cost effective
Low operating cost/hassle	Craftsmanship quality
Low staffing requirements	Storage capacity/low demand
Leverages in-kind services or equipment	Low noise and environmental impact
Environmental sensitivity	Dwell time appropriate to experience
Technical elegance	Does it work well?
Finishes	Fits design style of area
Accessible to special needs	Throughput/capacity
Supports sponsor/donor interests	Crowd management
Green fabrication and materials	Creates a longer dwell time

LOGISTICS (ALL MUST-FIT)	
Schedule/delivery	Actual cost versus perceived value
Budget/cost	Code compliance
Safety	

116

While all of the exhibit filters are useful, defining the target audience must happen first in order to prioritize the criteria. If the primary focus is targeting families, the PISEC characteristics of successful family exhibits are a thorough framework to begin with (Borun, 1998):

1. Multisided—family can cluster around exhibit
2. Multiuser—interaction allows for several sets of hands (or bodies)
3. Accessible—comfortably used by children and adults
4. Multioutcome—observation and interaction are sufficiently complex to foster group discussion
5. Multimodal—appeals to different learning styles and levels of knowledge
6. Readable—text is arranged in easily understood segments
7. Relevant—provides cognitive links to visitors' existing knowledge and experience

See "15. Bibliography for Museums" for citation reference.

Section 37

Facility and Security

FACILITY AND SECURITY

The General Facility Report (2011), updated periodically by the Registrars Committee of the American Alliance of Museums, is the most museum-specific comprehensive listing of museum facility and security considerations. While the document is a survey intended for museums to tell lenders about their situation, the questions and choices also help managers evaluate their museum's current and desired facility and security standards.

Instead of reprinting the entire set of considerations here, you can download your own copy from the product catalog at https://aam-us.org/ProductCatalog/Product?ID=891.

Section 38

Governance Policy Statements

INTRODUCTION

The adapted Carver Model of Policy Governance utilized by the museum can be characterized in the following two-part statement: the board sets policy. The CEO and staff implement that policy in accordance with certain guidelines.

This section can be adapted by your museum as a first draft of a board policy manual to be discussed by the board and eventually adopted. This section is based on writing by Bill Peters.

GOVERNANCE POLICY STATEMENTS

The Board of Directors' Role

The board of a not-for-profit organization has five primary responsibilities:

Vision (Strategic Direction, Mission Outcomes, and Strategic Priorities): Answers the question, "What kind of an organization, in terms of measurable outcomes, do we, board and stakeholders, want to have?" Establish broad standards for success.

Management: Acquiring and developing a CEO (and through him or her or senior managers) who delivers on the standards for success.

Fund-Raising and Advocacy: Through established credibility, track record, and advocacy with stakeholders, support staff in acquisition of the funding needed to deliver on the standards for success.

Board Development: Continuously increase the quality of the board membership, knowledge, training, and board processes. Monitor board performance and set objectives for board development.

Accountability: Approve policy and monitor that all financial, legislative, and due diligence responsibilities are met. Ensure that stakeholder expectations are met.

The board of directors' governance process consists of three functions:

- Planning
- Monitoring
- Evaluation

The board's planning focuses on what governance counsel and author John Carver calls "ends"—defining the outcomes to be achieved for the community as vision, mission, mission outcomes, and strategic priorities. When the ends are defined, it is the responsibility of management to bring forward, implement, and monitor plans that deal with "means" or the business plan. Translated to the museum theory of action, ends are the museum's intentional purposes and desired impacts, and means are its resources and activities. At all stages of the process, board members' involvement with management as partners in advocacy and fund-raising are vital to the ultimate success of the organization.

The board may, from time to time, retain expert consultants and advisers in each of the five responsibility areas and with the three process functions.

The current board of directors list is available online at XX and in the annual report.

Board Officers

Board directors are elected by a majority of members present at an annual general meeting of members. Every director serves for one term (three years) beginning the date of election. No director may serve more than three consecutive terms.

Officers of the board are appointed by the board at the first meeting of the board following the annual general meeting and serve a term of two years or such other period of time as the board may determine at the time of the appointment.

The officers of the museum are elected by the board. They include the following:

- Chair of the board
- Past chair of the board
- Vice chair of the board
- Committee chair(s)
- Secretary
- Treasurer, who shall be the chair of the Audit and Finance Committee
- Chief executive officer
- Chief financial officer
- Such other officers as the board may from time to time determine

Board and Committee Reports and Meetings

The board typically meets six to eight times per year with an annual, one-day planning retreat each January. Its annual general meeting is held each April. Due to the activity of a significant capital project, it is not uncommon to have one or two additional board meetings scheduled during the year.

Committees meet on an as-needed basis to carry out the activities of the museum. The Finance and Audit Committee typically meets prior to each board meeting, and the Executive Committee typically meets in the interval between board meetings, depending on project activity and required approvals. The External Relations Committee (aka Advocacy Committee), which drives fund development activity, typically meets on a monthly basis during the annual campaign portions of the year.

The museum publishes an annual board meeting calendar for board members that defines the annual cycle of activities (see table 38.1).

Board Committees

The Board Committee functions are as follows:

Finance and Audit Committee: Fiscal policy, financial due diligence, and review of financial aspects of business and project plans prior to board approval.

External Relations and Advocacy Committee: This is both a policy committee and a volunteer committee. As a policy committee, it is responsible for fund development, community relations, and government relations policy. In addition, it works with the senior fund development staff as a volunteer committee to raise the annual community support required for the operating budget, ensure that government support continues and expands, and guide and organize the capital campaign.

Capital Project Executive Committee: Facility development strategy and policy and review of project plans, budgets, and

Table 38.1   Outline of Annual Board Meeting Calendar

Meeting	Typical Major Activities
January: annual board retreat	Setting policy direction for operations and the capital project
March	Nominating Committee report and preparation for annual general meeting, approval of annual report, new facility project report (every meeting), and finance report (every meeting)
April: annual general meeting; board meeting following annual general meeting	Annual general meeting: election of board, election of chairs and officers, and board work plan for the year
June	Preview of operating business plan for the following year, second-quarter finance report, and capital campaign plan
September	Business plan direction, summer financial and attendance update, and new facility project report
November	Third-quarter financial report and year-end financial forecast, business plan and budget approval, and fund development campaign for year following

schedules prior to board approval. This committee has delegated authority from the board to make or approve project, schedule, and budget changes to a certain level within the total scope.

Governance and Nominating Committee: The Governance and Nominating Committee is established by the board of directors to assist the board in all issues relating to corporate governance: selection of board members and Board Committee members, the training and development of the board, and compliance with all applicable governance and regulatory requirements.

The Governance Committee's authority and responsibilities include the following:

- Monitor applicable corporate governance requirements and ensure compliance.
- Propose to the board director nominees who meet the board's predetermined qualifications.
- Ensure that there are appropriate orientation and ongoing education and training programs in place for directors.
- Propose to the board the members of each committee of the board and the chair of each committee.
- Ensure that the board and all committees of the board have documented mandates and that the mandates are reviewed and reassessed at least annually.
- Carry out a process to assess the effectiveness of the board and the committees of the board relative to their respective mandates and the contribution of individual directors.

Human Resources Committee: The Human Resources Committee was established by the board of directors to assist the board in all issues relating to the following:

- Human resources policies
- Compensation for the company's officers and directors

The Human Resources Committee's authority and responsibilities include the following:

- Create the CEO job description with input from the board.
- Review the appropriateness of current and future organizational structure at the request of the CEO.

- Annually review succession planning for senior executives.
- Periodically, but not less than annually, review the quality and effectiveness of members of the senior management team based on the CEO's assessment.
- Monitor compliance with legal requirements and corporate policy relating to human resources and compensation.
- Review and recommend to the board for approval the executive development programs for the CEO and senior management.

Section 39

Guiding Principles

Core Values

INTRODUCTION

This section covers what many call a museum's values. Core values (what you believe in forever) and strategic values (what you'd like to practice better in the future) are central to traditional museum planning. Value, however, has other meanings. In particular, economic value is also an important museum concept. To avoid confusion in this book, *value* is used only in its economic context, and *guiding principle* replaces the other terms for character and values.

GUIDING PRINCIPLES: CORE VALUES

The fundamental values that the museum will incorporate in all the changing scenarios that will play on its stages are shown in table 39.1.

Shorter-term considerations that reflect current community interests are *strategic values* that will also guide the development of the museum (see tables 39.2 and 39.3).

Table 39.1   Core Values

Education	Innovation
Accessibility	Scholarship
The power of the region's history	Authenticity

Table 39.2   Strategic Values

Freedom	Preservation
Honoring diversity	Defining the region
Partnerships	Fun visitor experiences
Community identity	An addition of architectural distinction
Cross-cultural community exchanges	Cleanliness

Table 39.3   Other Common Museum Values

Respect	Fun
Customer focused	Diversity
Engaging	Partnerships
Excellence	Quality
Passionate	Entrepreneurship
Creative	Thoughtful
Fiscal, ethical, and legal responsibility	

Section 40

Guiding Principles

Credos and Beliefs

INTRODUCTION

Guiding principles play a more foundational role in community service museums than in single-mission museums. Given changing purposes evolving in response to the community, a community museum's guiding principles may be a better place to anchor the corporate culture, brand identity, and public persona than on the mission and what you want to accomplish this year.

As an example, the U.S. Coast Guard proudly declares that it is a multiple-mission organization, but it unifies its diverse team and varied efforts under the guiding principle of *Semper Paratus* (Always Ready).

This section contains samples of guiding principles (aka corporate values) used by other museums. They are intended as starting drafts, and you will want to edit and customize them to your needs.

GUIDING PRINCIPLES: CREDOS AND BELIEFS

The museum will operate by the following guiding principles, promoting and incorporating them in all of its branded programs and activities (see table 40.1).

The Museum Will Be Responsive to the Community

The museum will be a public gathering place and a center of civic vitality, common ground where we can look together at our future. Through its programs and architecture, the museum will be a bridge between distinct neighborhoods and different cultures, and it will connect the central city to the metropolitan region. The museum will bring tourists to the region's other sites and tell the region's stories. At the museum, visitors will be able to visualize who is actually here, explore what we have brought with us to this place, and discover how we are constantly reinventing the city to reflect our diversity.

The Museum Will Be a Forum for Public Dialogue

The region has a vibrant tradition of public debate—sometimes polite, often rancorous, but always committed to principles and to putting ideals into practice. Passionate dialogue about social change, equal rights, cultural differences, and artistic and religious freedom has taken place in meetings throughout our history. For some time, the region has been at the forefront of movements for change. Strange and wonderful visionaries and resourceful and pragmatic leaders have all found constituencies here. Our tradition of public debate unites us even as it recognizes our differences.

The city needs a safe zone where, with equal doses of wit and high seriousness, we can look together at the future we face. The museum will invite inquiry into controversial issues and sponsor broadly inclusive dialogue, contributing to the reconstruction of civil society. By placing contemporary questions of civics and civic education in historical perspective, the museum will help us realize how where we stand shapes what we believe, enable us to identify with people who hold other viewpoints, and stimulate us to imagine ourselves making history.

The Museum Practices Triple Net Accounting

The museum will respond to three bottom lines: its economic well-being, its impact on staff and workplace conditions, and its impact on the environment.

The Museum Is Economically Sustainable

The vision is for a healthy operating institution, successful because of the value of the services offered to constituents, both public and private. The institution needs a realistic economic model to guide operations with careful, strategic planning given that a significant part of our annual budget will come from admissions and other earned revenues.

Outsiders, often including board members, assume that sustainability refers to covering a museum's operating costs through earned income, particularly gate admissions. For museums, however, the term needs to include sustainable support sources in addition to earned revenue. Economic sustainability—meaning steady sources of revenue and manageable levels of expense—is a moving target in the changing economy. Once established, few museums close, so in one sense they can be said to be sustainable; however, this is seldom a comfort to managers struggling to meet payroll or retire debt. Museums constantly need to shift emphasis to make up for increases or declines in some forms of revenue.

The Museum Will Be a Community Collaborator

Creating and operating a museum that is a representative reflection of the region requires partnership with many other organizations. The museum will collaborate with regional history organizations to provide them greater visibility, outlets for their collections, and promotion that will bring more visitors to their doors with a deeper initial understanding of how their stories fit into the larger fabric of the region's history. The museum will be a resource for schools, engaging students and teachers with the people who shaped the city and the traces of the past that remain in the landscape. Museums support a variety of learning styles, promote curiosity and imagination, and stimulate the development of critical thinking skills.

The museum will involve neighborhood groups, public interest societies, government agencies, academic and educational institutions, and community-based foundations and area corporations in the development and delivery of its programs and services. Social service organizations will be especially valuable collaborators, helping the museum build bridges to families and groups that are underrepresented in the city's existing historical institutions. The museum can serve as a unifying institution, bringing these resources together and serving the widest possible audience.

The museum will be an institution with affiliations with kindred institutions in the United States and other countries. There will be a physical representation of the museum in locations other than the region through these "affiliates" as well as virtually, thereby making the museum much more than just a single destination.

The Museum Will Nurture a Strong Sense of Place

We can no longer presume that local residents—particularly our children and grandchildren—will develop a strong attach-ment to the city just by being here. In the past, many identified with particular neighborhoods rather than with the city as a whole. Now, high migration rates, urban sprawl, and the growth of the megalopolises are undermining our connections to this place. Media technologies and virtual experiences allow us to lose touch with the physical world around us. The museum will develop attachments to the region and allow citizens to understand our city through the latest interactive technologies. Visitors to the region come here because they are looking for an experience that they cannot have at home or on the Internet, and the museum will offer them both encounters with authentic artifacts and links with historic sites and collections throughout the city and region.

The Museum Will Be a Catalyst for Social Change

Through its exhibits and programs and by working with its partners, the museum will deepen residents' commitment to civic responsibilities, equal rights, promoting understanding and acceptance of cultural differences, and enhancing intergroup relations through open dialogue. The museum will actively engage in the politics of equality and inclusion and provide opportunities for critical reflection on matters of identity and power. A widely representative board of directors and numerous advisory groups will help guide policies so that the museum's exhibits and programs respond to clear community needs and reinforce the museum's guiding principles.

The Museum Will Base Its Program on Scholarship and Collections

The museum will benefit from a reservoir of public trust in museums and uphold the values of authenticity and scholarship. The museum's use and care of artifacts and original documents will conform to the highest standards. Its interpretation will present multiple points of view and a diversity of voices, inviting visitors to draw their own conclusions from the evidence.

The Museum Is a Public Learning Resource

A leading educator points out that the design of any museum needs to offer its visitors a "wide range of possible experiences . . . recreation, spectacle, orientation and the chance to solve problems" (Grinell, 1993).

Different kinds of visitor experiences will be formulated for each of the different kinds of visitors: electronic, virtual, and actual. Expanded perspectives on what constitutes a visitor are central to the development of this institution.

Visitors will bring to their experience their personal frameworks of understanding and interests. The "visitor's experience" is an interaction among what the visitor brings to the museum, who they come with, and what the museum provides (Falk & Dierking, 1992). To avoid overwhelming visitors with a sequence of isolated "factoids," the experience will be organized around a story or a concept that will focus the visitor's understanding of the museum and its learning resources.

The Museum Is an International Institution

The museum's outlook will be international. Its services will be geared to a wide range of publics of all nations. In particular, the museum will maintain active digital sources and destinations and through electronic connections will have a virtual museum, a virtual library, and a virtual institute. At its physical setting, the museum will also serve international guests coming for education, training, study, and research.

The Museum Is a Delta Institution Built for Change

The museum will be a changing, visitor-focused learning institution and public forum and will involve visitors through dynamic and ongoing change. While some exhibits will remain for a long time to serve school groups and first-time visitors, most of the museum's programs will evolve to keep pace with changing public interests. With innovative technology and built-in support infrastructure, this will be a Delta museum—a vanguard museum format designed to facilitate change.

To change our programs regularly, we will build for change. Technology and programming are in such rapid change that the museum will have organizational and administrative systems to facilitate change.

The Museum Relies on Outsourcing

Provisions must be made for updating the content and technology using technical and production facilities of others, when appropriate, rather than acquiring and building internal staff and systems. Production management and outsourcing, rather than production personnel and on-site facilities, will be an organizational theme of the museum.

The Museum Relies on Internal Systems

Provisions must be made for updating the content and technology using in-house and internal technical and production facilities, when appropriate, rather than outsourcing in order to build internal capacity and brand control. Professional development and capacity building of internal staff and systems will be an organizational theme of the museum.

The Museum Will Be Popular and Visitor Focused

The museum will be of high quality and of sufficient scale to attract attendance and attention. Visitors are the touchstone for all planning and programming. The museum will offer the audience rich resources for an active engagement with the museum, allowing visitors to choose their own pathways as they explore changing themes and various perspectives. The museum will reach out to visitors of all economic and ethnic groups, recognizing what all have contributed, through their work and the richness of their culture, to the region's varied tapestry.

Research asking visitors why they come to a museum tend to focus on three prioritized values:

1. To have a good, comfortable time with friends or family
2. To experience something new
3. To learn something new

It is also important to understand some basics common to all museums and ingrained in public expectations. Museums are *social* and *physical*, and these characteristics distinguish us from public television, textbook learning, online experiences, and many other media in the educational infrastructure. Most museum visitors come in small social groups, such as a family or a group of friends. The interaction of this group should be encouraged by the exhibit and theater programs rather than isolated to individual experiences. The physicality is evident with hands-on activities and physical collections but is equally a factor in an immersive planetarium experience and in outdoor environments as well as architecturally distinct spaces and landscapes.

PLANNING WORKSHEET

Table 40.1   Guiding Principles: Samples

	Now	Future
The museum will be responsive to the community.		
The museum will be a forum for public dialogue.		
The museum practices triple net accounting.		
The museum is economically sustainable.		
The museum will be a community collaborator.		
The museum will nurture a strong sense of place.		
The museum will be a catalyst for social change.		
The museum will base its program on scholarship and collections.		
The museum is a public learning resource.		
The museum is an international institution.		
The museum is a Delta institution built for change.		
The museum relies on outsourcing.		
The museum relies on internal systems.		
The museum will be popular and visitor focused.		

See "15. Bibliography for Museums" for citation references.

Section 41

Human Resources

INTRODUCTION

This section looks at aspects of human resources that are unique to museums and includes the following:

- Staff organization chart
- Employee handbook: table of contents
- Job description template and sample
- Salary grading scale
- Benefits options
- Full-time-equivalent (FTE) calculations
- Sample indirect cost calculation
- Employee full cost calculation
- Nonstaff contractor options

Human resources are widely covered in traditional business publications, and you are encouraged to engage human resources experts from all sectors. Within the museum sector, there are publications with job descriptions and salary surveys segmented by sector, region, and size of museum.

This section written by contributing author Duane Kocik.

Table 41.1   Sample Staff Organization Chart (Large Museum)

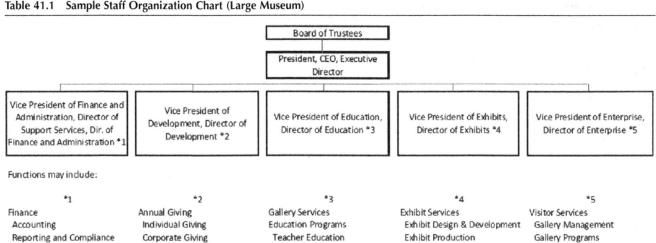

Functions may include:

*1	*2	*3	*4	*5
Finance	Annual Giving	Gallery Services	Exhibit Services	Visitor Services
Accounting	Individual Giving	Education Programs	Exhibit Design & Development	Gallery Management
Reporting and Compliance	Corporate Giving	Teacher Education	Exhibit Production	Gallery Programs
Contracts and Grants	Foundation Giving	Student/Youth Programs	Touring Exhibits	Public Operations
Financial Systems	Govt Relations	Adult Programs	Special Exhibits	Visitor Sales
Accounts Payable	Lobbyist	Learning Technologies	Media Design	Box Office
Accounts Receivable	Major Gifts	Live/Theatre Programs	Graphic Design	Call Center
Cash Receipts	Planned Giving	Community Engagement	Exhibit Maintenance	Web ticketing
Purchasing	Memberships	Large Format Theater	Collection Services	Marketing
HR	Retail memberships	Planetarium		Webmaster
Payroll	Donative Memberships	Evaluation and Research		Digital Marketing
Benefits	Capital Campaign	Special Events		Graphic Design
Talent Resources	Donor Events			Media Marketing
Training	Grant Writer			Public Relations
Building Services	Donor Data Base Mgmt.			Facility Sales (function rentals)
Bldg. Maintenance				Retail Stores
Safety				
Custodial				
Parking				
Mail Delivery				
Security				
IT				
Database Admin				
Network Admin.				
IT Service Desk				

Table 41.2   Sample Employee Manual: Table of Contents

FOREWORD
  Mission
  Vision
  Values
DIVERSITY
  Equal Employment Opportunity Statement
  Antiharassment Policy and Complaint Procedure
  Americans with Disabilities Act (ADA) and Amendments Act
  (ADA AA)
  EMPLOYMENT
  Employee Classification Categories
  Background and Reference Checks
  Internal Transfers/Promotions
  Nepotism, Employment of Relatives, and Personal Relationships
  Progressive Discipline
  Separation of Employment
WORKPLACE SAFETY
  Drug-Free Workplace
  Workplace Bullying
  Violence in the Workplace
  Safety
  Smoke-Free Workplace
WORKPLACE EXPECTATIONS
  Confidentiality
  Conflicts of Interest
  Outside Employment
  Attendance and Punctuality
  Attire and Grooming
  Electronic Communication and Internet Use
  Social Media: Acceptable Use
  Solicitations, Distributions and Posting of Materials
  Employee Personnel Files
COMPENSATION
  Performance and Salary Reviews
  Payment of Wages
  Time Reporting
  Meal/Rest Periods
  Overtime Pay
  On-Call Pay
  Employee Travel and Reimbursement
TIME OFF/LEAVES OF ABSENCE
  Holiday Pay
  Vacation
  Sick Leave
  Family and Medical Leave (FMLA)
  Personal Leave of Absence
  Bereavement Leave
  Jury Duty
  Voting Leave
  Military Leave of Absence
  Lactation/Breastfeeding
BENEFITS
  Medical and Dental Insurance
  Domestic Partners
  Flexible Spending Account
  Group Life Insurance
  Short-Term Disability Benefits
  Long-Term Disability Benefits
  401(k) Plan
  Workers' Compensation Benefits

Tuition Assistance
Employee Assistance Program (EAP)
DISCIPLINE AND TERMINATION OF EMPLOYMENT
    Performance Appraisals
    Discipline
    Immediate Dismissals
    Resignation
    Past Resignation/Termination Procedures and Protecting
    Working with Youth

HUMAN RESOURCES

This template by the HR Council for the Nonprofit Sector (Canada) provides the major categories that you should include in your job descriptions along with an explanation of what to include in each category.

Table 41.3   Job Description: Blank Template

Job title	*The formal title of the position*
Reports to	*The title of the position that the job incumbent reports to*

Job purpose
Provide a brief description of the general nature of the position, an overview of why the job exists, and what the job is to accomplish.
  • The job purpose is usually no more than four sentences long.

Duties and responsibilities
List the primary job duties and responsibilities using headings and then give examples of the types of activities under each heading.
Using headings and giving examples of the types of activities to be done allows you to develop a flexible job description that encourages employee to "work outside the box" and that, within reason, discourages "that's not my job."
  • Identify between three and eight primary duties and responsibilities for the position.
  • List the primary duties and responsibilities in order of importance.
  • Begin each statement with an action verb.
  • Use the present tense of verbs.
  • Use gender-neutral language, such as "s/he."
  • Use generic language, such as "photocopy" instead of "Xerox."
  • Where appropriate, use qualifiers to clarify the task—where, when, why or how often—for example, instead of "greet visitor to the office," use "greet visitors to the office in a professional and friendly manner."
  • Avoid words that are open to interpretation—for example, instead of "handle incoming mail," use "sort and distribute incoming mail."

Qualifications
State the minimum qualifications required to successfully perform the job. These are the qualifications that are necessary for someone to be considered for the position. All qualifications must comply with provincial human rights legislation. Qualifications include the following:
  • Education
  • Specialized knowledge
  • Skills
  • Abilities
  • Other characteristics such as personal characteristics
  • Professional certification
  • Experience

Working conditions
If the job requires a person to work in special working conditions, this should be stated in the job description. Special working conditions cover a range of circumstances from regular evening and weekend work, shift work, working outdoors, working with challenging clients, and so on.

Physical requirements
If the job is physically demanding, this should be stated in the job description. A physically demanding job is one where the incumbent is required to stand for extended periods of time, lift heavy objects on a regular basis, do repetitive tasks with few breaks, and so on.

Direct reports
List by job title any positions to be supervised by the incumbent.

Approved by:	*Signature of the person with the authority to approve the job description*
Date approved:	*Date on which the job description was approved*
Reviewed:	*Date when the job description was last reviewed*

Ideally, a job description should be reviewed annually and updated as often as necessary.

Source: HR Council for the Nonprofit Sector, http://hrcouncil.ca/home.cfm, accessed July 15, 2016.

Table 41.4 Job Description: Chief Financial Officer

Sample Position Description

Title: Director of finance and administration, vice president for finance and administration, chief financial officer (CFO)

Division: Administration/Support Services

Reports to: President (chief executive officer [CEO] or executive director)

Key Departments and Management Positions (directly reports to VP):

Human Resources: director of human resources, vice president of human resourcesFinance and Accounting: director of accounting, controller, director of reporting and compliance

Information Technology: director of information technologyFacilities Operations, Parking, Maintenance, and Engineering: director of facilities, building superintendent

Primary Objectives

- Accountable to the president (CEO or executive director) for all financial and accounting activities within the museum, including but not limited to fiscal controls, short- and long-range financial forecasting and planning, budgeting, investments, debt/borrowing, financial reporting, institutional insurance and risk management, and legal matters.
- Accountable for the physical plant of the organization's buildings and grounds as well as the safety of staff and visitors.
- Accountable for the design and implementation of systems to ensure effective and efficient use of human resources to accomplish organizational goals.
- Accountable for executive direction and guidance in all areas of information technology for the organization.

Major Areas of Accountability

- Serves as a member of the senior management team to the president (CEO, executive director) and on other management teams as needed.
- Works extensively with the board and key external stakeholders. This may include benefactors, banking relationships, creditors, vendors, and auditors.
- Leads and staffs various committees of the board, including finance, audit, information technology, compensation, and investment. Prepare financial and other reports to the board and other committees as needed.
- Works with the president (CEO, executive director) and the board to achieve institutional financial goals and objectives. Key goal: Keep the institution financially sound, including operating with a balanced or surplus operating budget.
  - As a key member of senior management, directs plans for the control of operations and administration. Plans would include financial planning and reporting, contingency planning, plans to build financial reserves and working capital, and other plans as needed to ensure financial sustainability and viability of the organization.
  - Institutional services include information technology services, human resources (staffing, compensation, employee benefits, training and development, retention, and evaluation), staff and visitor safety, physical plant maintenance, purchasing legal services, contract management, insurance, and investments.
  - Responsible for the management of all internal and external financial reporting. This includes all financial audits of the institution. Serves as chief liaison with the organization's external auditors and legal counsel.
  - Monitors the preparation and ongoing performance of the organization's finances: the operating budget, capital campaigns, and all special projects and grants. Responsible for overall financial management and reporting for the institution. Ensures that all projects and programs are established with budgets and monitored for compliance on an ongoing basis.
  - Manages the treasury functions of the institution as the chief liaison with banking and trust institutions. This would include debt and credit management, cash flow, and investments.
  - Responsible for maintenance of adequate insurance coverage for the organization. Monitors risk for the organization
  - Accountable for maintaining organization's tax-exempt status, including overseeing the institution's tax-exempt status and preparation of annual tax returns.
  - Keeps current on federal, state, and local tax laws and proposed changes. Keeps board of trustees and senior management informed.

Other Performance Standards

- Ensures that the organization's goal of being fiscally responsible is maintained.
- Oversees the investments and their returns with the Investment Committee as well as external investment consultants. Ensures that the organization's investments are prudent and that the returns meet or exceed the appropriate benchmarks.
- Keeps the museum a safe and clean for all.
- Maintains an adequate orientation, training, and staff development plan to grow a diverse staff.
- Maintains competitive employee total compensation plans in order to retain a strong workforce.

Qualifications, Education, Experience, and Skills

- Finance-related MBA desired (minimum requirement: BS in finance or accounting) with a minimum of XX years of senior finance and administrative management experience.
- Have experience with nonprofit sector organizations (operating budget >$XX million) with strong business process skills.
- Extensive experience in working with senior leadership and boards.

- Strong experience in management of human and financial resources with a solid understanding of complex operations and budgets. Demonstrate strong interpersonal and team-building skills.
- Understand the role of technology and how it can advance the organization.
- Solid work ethic, integrity, and high ethical standards required.

_____   _____
Employee Signature   Date

_____   _____
President Signature   Date

SALARY GRADING SCALES

Note: Pay ranges are an example of how a salary grading system works. Ranges may not reflect current wages scale and should be adjusted to local market conditions.

Table 41.5 Sample Staff Position Categories

Positions	Grades
President/CEO/Executive Director	10+
VP's	7-9
Director	7-8
Managers	5-7
Technical	4-6
Coordinator	4-5
Asst.	3-5

Table 41.6 Examples of Positions in Each Category

Grade 10 and up Top executive president/chief executive officer/ executive director/chief operating officer
Grade 9 Vice presidents
For this example, all positions are at the director level.
Grade 8 Directors
Director of development
Director of finance and administration
Director of communications/public relations/marketing
Grade 7 Director and manager
Director of exhibitions/programs
Director of collections/senior curator
Director of education
Human resources and volunteer manager/coordinator
Information systems/information technology manager
Grade 6 Managers and technical facility manager/engineer
Security manager
Web technician/designer
Box office manger
Retail store manager
Development officer (sponsorships/annual giving)
Publications/print graphics manager

Grade 5 Technical, coordinator, and assistants
Executive assistant to president/chief executive officer/ executive director
Facility rental coordinator
Memberships coordinator
Exhibitions/collections technician
Accounting assistant/bookkeeper
Accounting assistant payroll purchasing
Marketing coordinator
Assistant curator
Exhibit fabrications and repairs
Educators
Outreach coordinator
Grade 4 Technical, coordinator, and assistants
Facility technician
Security guard
Facility rental assistant
Sales and reservations coordinator
Special events coordinator
Receptionist
Human resources and volunteer assistant
Grade 3 Assistants
Custodians
Gallery staff
Grade 2 Hourly staff
Retail store clerks
Box office cashiers
Hourly staff for various exhibit/education and administrative positions
Grade 1 Not applicable

Table 41.7   Sample Salary Grading Scale: Small to Midsize Businesses

Grade	Pay Range							Hourly rates	
	Minimum	Midpoint Diff.	spread %	1st Quartile	Midpoint	3rd Quartile	Maximum	Min	Max
10	$ 100,000	20%	60%	$ 115,000	$ 130,000	$ 145,000	$ 160,000	$ 48.08	$ 76.92
9	$ 85,000	20%	50%	$ 94,500	$ 104,000	$ 115,750	$ 127,500	$ 40.87	$ 61.30
8	$ 72,000	20%	40%	$ 77,600	$ 83,200	$ 92,000	$ 100,800	$ 34.62	$ 48.46
7	$ 61,000	20%	35%	$ 63,780	$ 66,560	$ 74,455	$ 82,350	$ 29.33	$ 39.59
6	$ 49,000	20%	30%	$ 51,124	$ 53,248	$ 58,474	$ 63,700	$ 23.56	$ 30.63
5	$ 39,000	20%	25%	$ 40,799	$ 42,598	$ 45,674	$ 48,750	$ 18.75	$ 23.44
4	$ 29,000	20%	25%	$ 31,539	$ 34,079	$ 35,164	$ 36,250	$ 13.94	$ 17.43
3	$ 22,000	20%	20%	$ 24,631	$ 27,263	$ 26,831	$ 26,400	$ 10.58	$ 12.69
2	$ 18,000	20%	20%	$ 19,905	$ 21,810	$ 21,705	$ 21,600	$ 8.65	$ 10.38
1	N/A								

BENEFITS

Table 41.8   Benefit and Time-Off Options

Benefit Options	Time-Off/Leaves of Absence Options
Medical insurance	Holiday pay
Dental insurance	Vacation
Health savings account	Family and medical leave, personal leave of absence
Domestic partner	Bereavement leave
Group life insurance/accidental death and dismemberment	Jury duty
Short-term disability	Voting leave
Long-term disability	Military leave of absence
Flexible spending account	Lactation/breastfeeding
401(k), 403(b), or defined benefit pension plan	
457 plan	
Tuition assistance	
Employee assistance program	
Workers compensation	
Social Security and Medicare	
Unemployment compensation	

FULL TIME EQUIVALENT (FTE) CALCULATIONS

Note: Hours paid / worked should include hours an employee was paid, including vacation, holiday, and sick leave hours.

Table 41.9   Full-Time-Equivalent (FTE) Calculations

Employee	Status	Total Hours Worked/Paid - calendar year 2015	Comments
#1	Full Time	2,080	Full time employee, 40 Hrs/week
#2	Part Time	1,520	Hourly employee
#3	Full Time	2,080	Full time employee, 40 Hrs/week
#4	Part Time	940	Hourly employee
#5	Full Time	2,080	Full time employee, 40 Hrs/week
#6	Part Time	1,255	Hourly employee
#7	Full Time	2,080	Full time employee, 40 Hrs/week
#8	Part Time	650	Hourly employee
#9	Full Time	2,080	Full time employee, 40 Hrs/week
#10	Part Time	450	Hourly employee
	Total Hours	15,215	
	Divided by	2,080	
	# FTE's	7.3	

Table 41.10   Sample Employee Full Cost Calculation

Annual Salary (assuming full time)	Hourly Rate (before benefits and Indirect costs)	A plus Fringe benefits including Paid vacation, PTO (Assumed at 40%)	B plus indirect cost rate (assumed at 45%)	Fully Reimbursed Hourly Rate
A	**A-1**	**B=A*1.4**	**C=B*1.45**	**D=C/2080**
$ 30,000	$ 14.42	$ 42,000	$ 60,900	$ 29.28
$ 35,000	$ 16.83	$ 49,000	$ 71,050	$ 34.16
$ 40,000	$ 19.23	$ 56,000	$ 81,200	$ 39.04
$ 45,000	$ 21.63	$ 63,000	$ 91,350	$ 43.92
$ 50,000	$ 24.04	$ 70,000	$ 101,500	$ 48.80
$ 55,000	$ 26.44	$ 77,000	$ 111,650	$ 53.68
$ 60,000	$ 28.85	$ 84,000	$ 121,800	$ 58.56
$ 65,000	$ 31.25	$ 91,000	$ 131,950	$ 63.44
$ 70,000	$ 33.65	$ 98,000	$ 142,100	$ 68.32
$ 75,000	$ 36.06	$ 105,000	$ 152,250	$ 73.20

Table 41.11   Benefits Tally Worksheet

	Employee #1	Employee #2	Employee #3	Employee #4	Employee #5	Employee #6	Employee #7	Employee #8	Total staff benefit eligible	Total staff not eligible or partially	All employees	as a % of wages
Annual Wages	$70,000	$60,000	$50,000	$40,000	$30,000	$15,000	$25,000	$35,000	$250,000	$ 75,000	$325,000	
Annual Hours Worked	2,080	2,080	2,080	2,080	2,080	750	1,250	1,750	10,400	3,750	14,150	
Eligible for benefits?	yes	yes	yes	yes	yes	no	partially	partially	yes	no or partial		
Medical ($5,000/employee)	$ 5,000	$ 5,000	$ 5,000	$ 5,000	$ 5,000			$ 5,000	$ 25,000	$ 5,000	$ 30,000	9.2%
Health Savings Account ($1,000/employee)	$ 1,000	$ 1,000	$ 1,000	$ 1,000	$ 1,000			$ 1,000	$ 5,000	$ 1,000	$ 6,000	1.8%
Dental ($1,000/ employee)	$ 1,000	$ 1,000	$ 1,000	$ 1,000	$ 1,000				$ 5,000	$ -	$ 5,000	1.5%
Life Ins. (1% of wages)	$ 700	$ 600	$ 500	$ 400	$ 300				$ 2,500	$ -	$ 2,500	0.8%
Long & Short Term Disability (1% of wages)	$ 700	$ 600	$ 500	$ 400	$ 300				$ 2,500	$ -	$ 2,500	0.8%
Pension (4% of wages)	$ 2,800	$ 2,400	$ 2,000	$ 1,600	$ 1,200		$ 1,000	$ 1,400	$ 10,000	$ 2,400	$ 12,400	3.8%
Workers and Unemployment Ins. (1% of wages)	$ 700	$ 600	$ 500	$ 400	$ 300	$ 150	$ 250	$ 350	$ 2,500	$ 750	$ 3,250	1.0%
Social Security and Medicare (7.65% of wages)	$ 5,355	$ 4,590	$ 3,825	$ 3,060	$ 2,295	$ 1,148	$ 1,913	$ 2,678	$ 19,125	$ 5,738	$ 24,863	7.7%
Benefit Costs before Paid Time Off	$17,255	$15,790	$14,325	$12,860	$11,395	$ 1,298	$ 3,163	$10,428	$ 71,625	$ 14,888	$ 86,513	27%
Benefit % before Paid Time Off (PTO)	25%	26%	29%	32%	38%	9%	13%	30%	29%	20%	27%	
PTO (Vacation, Holiday, Sick, etc. 15% of wages)	$10,500	$ 9,000	$ 7,500	$ 6,000	$ 4,500	$ -	$ -	$ 5,250	$ 37,500	$ 5,250	$ 42,750	13%
Benefit Costs with PTO	$27,755	$24,790	$21,825	$18,860	$15,895	$ 1,298	$ 3,163	$15,678	$109,125	$ 20,138	$129,263	40%
Benefit % with Paid Time Off (PTO)	40%	41%	44%	47%	53%	9%	13%	45%	44%	27%	40%	

Notes to Table 41.11

1. Obtain a census of all employees listing annual wages and annual actual benefit costs for each employee. Benefit costs may vary per individual, depending on length of service, benefit eligibility, and so on. Some employers provide family medical coverage versus employee only.

2. Check with local and national laws for eligibility of benefits. Examples include the Affordable Care Act, pension laws as to eligibility, Social Security, and Medicare. Benefit tally worksheet can be used as a budgeting tool using average costs per different groups of eligible staff (full-time/part-time, benefit eligible/not eligible, or partially eligible). For example, full-time staff may have a benefit rate of 40 percent of salary and part time staff from 9 to 45 percent in the example above.

3. Worksheet can also be used for determining individual or group costs for grants. Strive to be reimbursed for all benefit costs, including paid time off.

4. Human resources can use the above for calculating total compensation statements

Note: In submitting grant requests, museums should strive to be reimbursed the full hourly rate in D as shown in Table 41.11. Museums should determine their benefit rates and indirect cost rate.

CONTRACTORS

Table 41.12   Staff/Contractor Options

Function	In-House Staff	On-Site Contractor	Off-Site Contractor	Business terms
Food service/catering				
Vending				
Information technology				
Window washing				
Custodial				
Facility engineering/mechanical				
Retail stores				
Payroll processing				
Month end accounting				
Grounds and landscaping (Snow)				
Parking lot operation				
Garbage hauling				
Printing				
Web and social media management				
PR/Ad agency				
Legal				
Accounting				
Museum counsel				
Fund raising counsel				
HR counsel				
Investment management				
Technical facility issues				
Pricing study				
Audience research				
Signs, labels, and graphics				

Section 42

Impact and Performance

Definitions

IMPACT AND PERFORMANCE: DEFINITIONS

1. There is overlap among the terms describing the results of a museum's activities. While there are distinctions, the following terms share the far right of the theory of action logic model (tables I.3 and 62.1), where the *results* of all this effort finally appear: *outcomes, ends, impacts,* and *benefits.*

2. *Outcomes, ends,* and *impacts* are words for the changes that the museum is making (or wants to make) to individuals and to society, with the underlying hypothesis that the museum is the active agent implementing these changes. Prepositions matter in their distinction: outcomes result *from* the museum's activities, and impacts are *on* the museum's community, audiences, and supporters.

3. In some cases, an accumulation of sufficient individual outcomes can become an impact on the greater social group, but this is neither a given nor a prerequisite of a societal impact.

4. The activities that the museum operates may result in *impacts on others* and *benefits to others*. Most impacts, we hope, will be beneficial, but others, such as a museum's carbon footprint, may not be.

5. A museum aspires to have *impacts* on its community, audiences, and supporters. The community, audiences, and supporters receive *benefits* from the museum. The benefits can be different from the impact: a family visiting an aquarium receives the benefit of a quality family experience, while the aquarium's desired impact on the family is to heighten their awareness of conserving biodiversity. Or the benefits and impacts can be aligned: new parents bring their toddler to a children's museum to see her develop and learn with new kinds of challenges; the children's museum's mission is child development. Studying the alignment between a museum's benefits and impacts may illuminate potentials and inefficiencies. It is useful to remember the distinction, which hinges on their prepositions: society, individuals, and organizations receive benefits *from* the museum. The museum has impacts *on* society, individuals, and organizations. Benefits are in the eyes of the receiver; impacts are in the desires of the museum.

6. Potential *indicators* of a museum's impacts and benefits on others and its performance in achieving those impacts include evaluation criteria, institutional success measures, foundation objectives, management resources, proposed indicators, research findings, and data collection fields from routinely asked surveys. Indicators are either quantitative or qualitative and may indicate to some expert audience potentially meaningful data related to measuring museum impact and performance. *Indicator* is the generic, encompassing term. A mission statement is an indicator of the museum's primary purpose; its annual budget is an indicator of the scale of operations, and its visitor satisfaction levels and supporter repeat levels are indicators of its impacts on visitors and supporters, respectively.

7. The Museum Indicators of Impact and Performance (MIIP 1.0) is a database of 1,025 indicators drawn from 51 sources (see Jacobsen, 2016) compiled by the White Oak Institute and available to all for free (see link on the copyright page). Every indicator is tagged by its category of potential impact and its step along the theory of action and the content of its data.

8. *Key performance indicators* (KPIs) are quantitative formulas, such as ratios, averages, and comparable benchmarks, that measure the effectiveness and efficiency of the activities. KPIs typically use evaluation and/or operating data in formulas that are meaningful to managers.

9. KPIs are a subset of all indicators in MIIP 1.0. They are tagged steps 6a and 6b. Step 6a KPIs tend to be *operational KPIs*, while step 6b KPIs may be *impact and performance KPIs*, depending on each museum's context. Most KPIs are mathematical formulas that incorporate two or more *data fields*. A data field can have *data entries* for different terms, such as this year and last year, and come from different sources, such as peer museums and market data.

10. *Performance* is a measure of efficiency and/or effectiveness. While a performance metric might be measurable at a moment in time, performance measures are useful mostly in comparison, such as to a museum's year-over-year measures and to the measures of peer museums. Performance is measured using KPIs.

Section 43

Impacts and Benefits

Category Summary

INTRODUCTION

Analysis of the database of 1,025 Museum Indicators of Impact and Performance (MIIP 1.0) reveals 12 broad areas of external impact and two of internal impact. These categories of potential museum contributions and benefits fall under four impact sectors and include seven categories of *public impacts* (broadening participation, preserving heritage, strengthening social capital, enhancing public knowledge, serving education, advancing social change, and communicating public identity and image), two *private impacts* (contributing to the economy and delivering corporate community services), three *personal impacts* (enabling personal growth, offering personal respite, and welcoming personal leisure), and two *institutional impacts* (helping museum operations and building museum capital).

Each of these categories can be looked at as the *impacts* desired by the museums and as the *benefits* perceived by the museum's audiences and supporters. Comparing the alignment between these two perspectives may lead to increased efficiency.

This summary section can be used as an overview of what the museum is currently providing its stakeholders and might add in the future.

Categories and definitions of these 14 impact areas organized by their precedented funding sources and kinds of impacts are described in "44. Museum Impacts and Benefits."

SUMMARY OF IMPACTS AND BENEFITS

Analysis of the MIIP 1.0 indicators reveals 12 broad areas of potential external impact and two of internal impact. Potential impacts to address community, audience, and supporter needs are divided into public impacts (seven categories), private impacts (two categories), personal impacts (three categories), and institutional impacts (two categories).

Public impacts benefit the public as a whole and tend to be funded by government and private philanthropy; *private impacts* tend to benefit businesses and corporations; *personal impacts* benefit individuals, families, and groups; and *institutional impacts* benefit the museum. Table 43.1 is a summary of the potential impact areas.

The direct beneficiaries are not always the funders. A foundation might pay for a teen workshop, benefiting teens directly while benefiting the foundation indirectly by serving its mandate. Internal impacts benefit the museum, either helping with operations or building capital resources.

Table 43.1   Categories of Potential Museum Impacts and Benefits

	No. of MIIP Indicators
Public impacts	
A Broadening participation	85
B Preserving heritage	47
C Strengthening social capital	76
D Enhancing public knowledge	43
E Serving education	56
F Advancing social change	40
G Communicating public identity and image	27
Private impacts	
H Contributing to the economy	85
I Delivering corporate community services	9
Personal impacts	
J Enabling personal growth	147
K Offering personal respite	4
L Welcoming personal leisure	11
Institutional impacts	
M Helping museum operations	308
N Building museum capital	87
Total indicators to the MIIP 1.0 database	**1,025**

Source: White Oak Institute.

PLANNING WORKSHEETS

Table 43.2   Categories of Impacts Desired by the Museum

	Staff Priority	*Board Priority*	*Future Priority*
Public impacts			
A Broadening participation			
B Preserving heritage			
C Strengthening social capital			
D Enhancing public knowledge			
E Serving education			
F Advancing social change			
G Communicating public identity and image			
Private impacts			
H Contributing to the economy			
I Delivering corporate community services			
Personal impacts			
J Enabling personal growth			
K Offering personal respite			
L Welcoming personal leisure			
Institutional impacts			
M Helping museum operations			
N Building museum capital			

Table 43.3   Categories of Benefits to Audiences and Supporters

	Audience Priority	*Supporter Priority*	*Future Priority*
Public benefits			
A Broadening participation			
B Preserving heritage			
C Strengthening social capital			
D Enhancing public knowledge			
E Serving education			
F Advancing social change			
G Communicating public identity and image			
Private benefits			
H Contributing to the economy			
I Delivering corporate community services			
Personal benefits			
J Enabling personal growth			
K Offering personal respite			
L Welcoming personal leisure			
Institutional benefits			
M Helping museum operations			
N Building museum capital			

Section 44

Museum Impacts and Benefits

INTRODUCTION

Museums are not manufacturers of stuff but, rather, community institutions that change people and places for the better (Museums Association, 2013). Museums provide services that add value to personal growth, serve the educational system, strengthen social capital, preserve heritage, communicate public image and identity, contribute to economic impact, enhance public knowledge, advance social change, deliver corporate community services, and broaden participation.

Many museum activities provide multiple services. A *Titanic* exhibition, for example, may provide personal growth and leisure benefits to its visitors, deliver corporate community services to its sponsors, and contribute to economic impact by generating tourism.

Impacts and benefits can be grouped under broad content umbrellas, such as *preserving heritage*, which covers more specific impacts, such as collection conservation, cultural identity, and access to history.

An actionable way of organizing a museum's potential impacts is to sort them by the kinds of funders that have supported them in the past. This perspective helps management connect ideas for impacts with potential funding sectors.

Analysis of 1,025 indicators in the Museum Indicators of Impact and Performance (MIIP 1.0) database reveals 12 broad areas of external impact and two of internal impact. The impact areas are divided into public impacts (seven categories), private impacts (two categories), personal impacts (three categories), and institutional impacts (two categories). *Public impacts* benefit the public as a whole and tend to be funded by government and private philanthropy; *private impacts* tend to benefit businesses and corporations; *personal impacts* benefit individuals, families, and groups; and *institutional impacts* benefit the museum.

Table 44.1 is a summary of the 14 categories potential impact.

Table 44.1   Categories of Potential Museum Impacts and Benefits

		# of MIIP indicators
Public Impacts		
A	Broadening participation	85
B	Preserving heritage	47
C	Strengthening social capital	76
D	Enhancing public knowledge	43
E	Serving education	56
F	Advancing social change	40
G	Communicating public identity & image	27
Private Impacts		
H	Contributing to the economy	85
I	Delivering corporate community services	9
Personal Impacts		
J	Enabling personal growth	147
K	Offering personal respite	4
L	Welcoming personal leisure	11
Institutional Impacts		
M	Helping museum operations	308
N	Building museum capital	87
Total indicators in the MIIP 1.0 database		1,025

Source: White Oak Institute.

The following text and tables may be selected and adapted to suit your museum. These samples are intended as starting tools, and you will want to edit and customize them to your needs.

The process for selecting intentional purposes and desired impacts is detailed in Jacobsen (2016, chap. 5).

CATEGORIES OF POTENTIAL MUSEUM IMPACTS AND BENEFITS

Public Values: Benefits to Society and the Public at Large

- Broadening Participation: The public benefit of increasing social justice and inclusion through audience diversity, access policy, inclusivity, community connections, management culture, and approach to learning.
- Preserving Heritage: Indicators about the public benefit of caring for and interpreting our past, both physically and culturally, through stewardship of collections, historic sites, and cultural neighborhoods. Heritage preservation contributes to a sense of belonging and where we come from; a place for communal archives, lessons of history, display of property, and collections; and the preservation of memory.
- Strengthening social capital indicators monitors the potential contributions that the museum makes to the health and structure of its community through its community connections and partnerships; serving as a place for different groups, generations, and cultures to come to learn from each other—each bringing diverse perspectives to a trusted, neutral environment; providing the means for communication and debate; serving as an honest broker through its partnerships with funders, companies, libraries, public agencies, and educational organizations; and being facilitator of events in cooperation with other organizations, resulting in expanded learning opportunities and trust in the museum's brand. Museums are part of a community's capital assets, adding to its cultural, educational, and economic infrastructure. Museums and other cultural facilities add public value and build public trust (Holden, 2004) by creating museum-quality brand relationships. As capital-intensive, physical structures open to the public, they add to a city's balance sheet. As collectors and stewards of a community's material culture, they maintain its valuable objects.
- Enhancing Public Knowledge: The research and reference contributions that the museum makes to the body of public and professional information, innovation, and scholarship and its access by individuals, the community, and the economy. Fifteen of the indicators refer specifically to the museum's contributions to scholarship. Reputation refers to the museum's trusted expertise and the quality of museum staff, exhibitions, and collections.

- Serving the Educational System: The museum's impacts to both formal education (schools) and museum professionals through student programs, educational initiatives and campaigns, STEM (science, technology, engineering, and mathematics) learning, school partnerships, and resources for educators.
- Advancing Social Change: The museum's potential impacts in leading people and communities to make changes deemed beneficial by society, such as addressing social problems, health initiatives, global environmental conservation, education initiatives, social justice, human rights, tolerance, fairness and equality, antidiscrimination, poverty, and reflecting on lessons from the past to envision new ways of living in the future (Museums Association, 2013).
- Communicating Public Identity and Image: Potential museum impacts that help a region, a community, or individuals think about, discuss, develop, and communicate their desired identity and image. At the city level, the museum can serve as a symbol, a statement of pride, an affirmation of a culture, and a reflection of local priorities. At the individual's level, the museum can become an important personal relationship, a symbol of who we are, a part of our identity, and a brand we trust.

Private Values: Benefits to Businesses, Government, and the Economy

- Contributing to the Economy: The museum's contributions to the regional and local economy by motivating tourism, increasing land and tax values, direct spending, neighborhood development, providing jobs, and developing the workforce and the quality of life. Generally, the museum's economic impact supports businesses and, in a ripple effect, generates jobs and incremental taxes.
- Delivering Corporate Community Services: Potential museum impacts to businesses that are fulfilling their community service responsibilities, networking with other civic leaders, or associating their brand with the museum through sponsorships and providing value to their employees by giving them museum access privileges.

Personal Values: Benefits to Individuals, Families, and Social Groups

- Enabling Personal Growth: The benefits that individuals, groups, and families get from their museum engagements that help them grow in abilities, awareness, and understanding. Enabling personal growth has the most indicators of the 12 external potential museum impacts, reflecting the museum field's focus on providing value to its free-choice audiences. Personal growth in museums can happen in many ways, and the most pervasive is learning, again reflecting the field's commitment as places of informal learning and to the priorities for education set forth by the American Association of Museums (Hirzy, 1992). Museums can help people learn and develop their capacities, knowledge, perspectives, sense of relevance, and social and family insights. This area also includes the intrinsic benefits that the museum can provide its visitors and program participants, such as affirmation, belonging, enlightenment, excitement and awe, insight, joy, perspective, reflection, satisfaction, and meaning. Museums can engage individuals in worthy purposes through volunteer opportunities.

- Offering Personal Respite: The benefits that individuals, groups, and families get from museum engagements that help them find comfort, spend time alone safely and quietly, or get away from their daily pressures.
- Welcoming Personal Leisure: The benefits that individuals, groups, and families get from their museum engagements that help them relax, have fun, and be entertained. These services are also offered by theme parks, movie theaters, and other entertainment centers.

Institutional Values: Benefits to the Museum Itself, Presumably to Increase its External Values and Performance

- Helping Museum Operations: The museum's yearly operating activities. Some are used for accounting and for assessing performance and efficiency. The data in these indicators tend to change periodically and are reported on at least yearly; some are reflected in the museum's statement of activities for a fiscal year. There are more indicators monitoring museum operations than any other area, reflecting a natural preoccupation with how the museum and its staff, collections, facilities, and budgets are running. Revenues, expenses, human resources data, attendance, activity listings, management culture, marketing, performance, and value judgments characterize this area of indicators.
- Building Museum Capital: The museum's long-term resources and assets, both tangible (e.g., facilities and endowment) and intangible (e.g., brand reputation, type of museum, and e-mail address). These categories list what the museum is and has. Some of these indicators are reflected in balance statements. These indicators tally capital assets, listings of community resources, and public value components; track capital campaigns, governance and parent organizations, institutional data (e.g., address, formal name, and Data Universal Numbering System number), long-term community trust, in-house expertise, and management culture; and provide counts of collections, square feet of space, acres of land, and dollars in reserve.

PLANNING WORKSHEET

Table 44.2   Current and Aspirational Impacts and Benefits

	Current	Future	Change
Public impact			
A Broadening participation			
B Preserving heritage			
C Strengthening social capital			
D Enhancing public knowledge			
E Serving education			
F Advancing social change			
G Communicating public identity and image			
Private impacts			
H Contributing to the economy			
I Delivering corporate community services			
Personal impacts			
J Enabling personal growth			
K Offering personal respite			
L Welcoming personal leisure			
Institutional impacts			
M Helping museum operations			
N Building museum capital			

See "15. Bibliography for Museums" for citation references. Museum Impacts and Benefits

Section 45

Implementation Phases, Schedules, Milestones, and Tasks

INTRODUCTION

Implementation will be organized into a series of phases in order to allow the museum and its advisers to manage the project and keep track of time and resources. While many teams will be working at the same time, the phase's name reflects the activity that is on the critical path at that time. Responsibility for the critical path will shift among the architects, operating staff, program team, investment team, and the other teams critical to completing a successful capital project.

If the project meets all of its milestones and deliverables at the end of each of these phases, groundbreaking is scheduled for XX, 20XX, when the majority of the funding should be committed, and the public opening will be in XX, 20XX.

The phase schedule is based on the experience of brand-new museums; your project may need only a selection.

IMPLEMENTATION PHASES, SCHEDULES, MILESTONES, AND TASKS

The *project milestones, management sectors*, and *phase schedule* developed in tables 45.1–45.3 provide a framework for the capital project's implementation.

Table 45.1   Critical Path Phases: Sample New Museum (e.g., Full Menu)

	Phase	On Critical Path	Duration
1	Preliminary research and planning	Founders	Varies
2a	Community needs assessment	Program team	Three months
2b	Opportunity assessment	Program team	Three months
2c	Planning stage investments	Investment team	Four months
3	*Concept development plan*	Program team	Four months
4	Campaign research and *plan*	Investment team	Three months
5	Organization and lead funding	Investment team	Varies
6	Program research and development	Program team	Three months
7	*Strategic master plan*	Program team	Four months
8	Predesign architectural program	Program team and architect	Two months
9	Schematic design	Architect	Three months
10	Design development	Architect	Four months
11	Construction documents	Architect	Five months
12	Construction phase investments	Investment team	Varies
13	Construction bids and awards	Building team	Two months
	Groundbreaking	Contractor	(+XX months)
14	Construction	Contractor	18 months
15a	Installation	Program team	Five months
15b	Shakedown	Operations team	One month
15c	Previews	Investment team	10 days
	Public launch	Marketing	(+XX months)
	Operations	Operations team	Ongoing
16	Summative evaluation	Program team	Four months

PROJECT MILESTONES

The milestones list principal tasks in chronological order, and it should be assumed that there is overlap among these tasks and that numerous additional tasks have been omitted at this level of detail.

The primary milestones are a few key achievements drawn for the fuller list in table 45.4 (key milestones are in bold in this table). The selection is intended for board and proposal use.

Table 45.2   Primary Milestones

Category	Task	Status
FUND	Identify sources of planning funds	
FUND	Task force (future board) development	
INST	Adopt *concept plan*	
FUND	Secure public funds	
OPS	Hire president and chief executive officer and support staff (first official hires)	
BLDG	Select architect	
INST	Complete *master plan*	
MKTG	Develop a corporate identity system and style manual	
BLDG	Architecture: building and model photos	
PROG	Experience platforms: design development	
PROG	Opening scenarios: schematic design	
BLDG	Building construction: start (actual site groundbreaking)	
PROG	Theaters and programs: construction documents	
LRNCT	Create school program catalog	
OPS	Pricing, ticketing, Web, marketing policy	
FUND	Campaign at 100%	
BLDG	Construction substantially complete	
PROG	Program installation substantially complete	
BLDG	Final occupancy certificate	
MKTG	New facility opens to public	
OPS	Approve year 3 budget	

Table 45.3   Categories of Project Management

Category	Project Management Area
INST	Institutional
PROG	Program: exhibits and theaters
LRNCT	Learning center
BLDG	Building, site, and architecture
OPS	Operations and administration
FUND	Fund-raising development
MKTG	Marketing and community relations

Table 45.4   Project Tasks and Milestones

1	Research and planning	Preliminary, very open vision and purposes
		Identify leadership (board)
		Incorporate
		Identify sources of planning funds (1% to 3% of funds raised)
		Identify interim project manager
2	Community needs	Retain museum planning counsel
		Retain fund-raising counsel
		Retain organizational coach
		Task force development

Table 45.4   Project Tasks and Milestones

		Visitor research: concept survey
		Discussions with community leaders and groups (ongoing)
		Implementation schedule and process
		Market analysis
		Prospect research
		Preliminary communications program
		Administrative setup
		Meet with other museums
		Interviews with potential funders and partners
		Community needs assessment
3	Concept development	Leadership retreat
		Organizational personality profile
		Select purposes and impacts
		Decision framework
		Develop museum concepts (visioning process)
		Interview stakeholders about alternative models
		Concept development workshop
		Preliminary program plan
		Preliminary architectural program
		Market assessment
		Economic parameters
		Concept development plan
4	Campaign research	*Campaign research and plan*
		Retain a public relations firm
		Quiet communications campaign
		Prepare case statement
		Attract key leaders
		Potential lead investments listed
5	Organization and lead funding	Homework and cultivation
		Targeted proposals and presentations
		Secure pledge commitments and public funds (30% to 50%)
		Select prime site
		Determine occupancy terms
		Organize board with chairman
		Implement new campaign committee and leadership
		Hire president and chief executive officer and support staff (first official hires)
		Identify campaign chairs
		Capital budget cash flow
		Architectural briefing package
6	Program development	Envision scenarios and programs
		Hold community planning workshop(s)
		Visitor research: define key visitor segments
		Visitor research: concept evaluation (ongoing)
		Start architectural search and selection process
		Prepare management and staff
		Special format theater recommendation
		Define organizational personality profile
		Maintain an *orientation package*
		Food service and function rental study
		Organize tours of other new museums
		Best practices research process
		Campaign communications plan
		Experience platform definitions

(Continued)

Table 45.4   Project Tasks and Milestones

		List of investment and naming opportunities
7	Strategic plan	**Strategic master plan and economic model**
		Finalize lease agreement and terms
		Revisit governance structure
		Institutional partnership framework
		Develop a shared sense of vision (ongoing)
		Start partnership programs
		Revisit *education and program plan*
		Select architect
		Prepare the board
8	Architectural program	*Room Book*: preliminary building requirements
		Outreach plan
		Commission land survey
		Start contractor selection process
		Grant and proposal writing
		Visitor research: theme concept survey
		Expand program design team
		Scenario development and evaluation
		React to community opportunities
		Complete contractor selection
9	Schematic design	Site planning and architecture concept
		Architecture: schematic design
		Preliminary cost estimate design revisions
		Architecture concept illustrations
10	Design development	**Architecture: design development and model**
		Preliminary program design workshop
		Name and image testing
		Program: concept development
		Corporate identity system: design
		Experience platforms: schematic design
		Select exhibit designers and theater suppliers
		Building model and photos
11	Construction documents	Architecture: construction documents
		Corporate funding commitments
		Building infrastructure program
		Experience platforms: preliminary specifications
		Visitor research: scenario testing
		Opening scenario selections
12	Construction investments	Investments continue up to groundbreaking goal
		Experience platforms: design development
		Advisory group presentations
		Museum peer reviews
13	Bid and award	Funds for building secured (70% to 100%)
		Board retreat
		Construction bids and awards
		Authorize contractor to proceed
		Start phased hiring plan
		Visitor research: design support
		Opening exhibit scenarios: schematic design
		Announce and run campaign
14	Construction	**Site groundbreaking (50% to 80% of funds raised)**
		Construction: site prep

Table 45.4   Project Tasks and Milestones

	Program operating plans
	Experience platforms: construction documents
	Visitor research: prototyping
	Program: construction documents
	Building construction—topping off
	Experience platforms added to contractors' scope
	Visitor research: pricing and positioning study
	Launch marketing plan and start implementation
	Operating systems specifications
	Pricing, ticketing, Web, and telemarketing policy
	Retail and food service plans
	Revise economic model
	Membership announced
	Campaign continues
	Hard hat tours
	Program: production and fabrication
	Board retreat
	Announce opening scenarios and films
	Launch membership drive
	Construction: weather tight
	Visitor research: shop testing
	Campaign pledges at 100%
	Construction substantially complete
	Experience platforms substantially complete
15 Installation	Start program installation
	Exterior programs installed
	Complete phased hiring plan
	Media software installation and programming
	Graphics installation
	Lighting installation
	Preliminary documentation
	Program installation substantially complete
	Staff training
	Shakedown
	Visitor research: test groups
	Party for cast and crew
	Final occupancy certificate
	Previews and opening galas
	New facility opens to public
16 Evaluation	Evaluation of programs
	Documentation
	Postopening adjustments
	Complete turnover to staff
	First operating year (called "FY 20XX")
	Refine programming schedule
	Approve year 2 budget
	Complete warranty periods
	Second operating year
	Evaluation of operations
	Selection and design of second-generation scenarios
	Approve five-year master plan

(Continued)

Table 45.4   Project Tasks and Milestones

Approve year 3 budget
Third operating year ("typical stabilized year")
Start recapitalization programs with new scenarios
Revisit five-year plan
Approve year 4 budget
Fourth operating year
Selection and design of third-generation scenarios
Approve year 5 budget
Fifth operating year

Section 46

Institutional Evaluation Concepts

INTRODUCTION

How will the museum be evaluated? How will the museum define success? Will its definition align with the community's definition of success?

How the museum conducts its processes of research and evaluation is an important strategic decision since the approach reflects how the organization conceives of its business and achieves its mission.

The following theories described in this section and listed in table 46.1 are options for museum evaluation.

Table 46.1   Museum Evaluation Theories

Theory-based evaluation
The museum theory of action (separate section)
Logic models
Infrastructure model
The community service evaluation model
Key service market appraisals
National Science Foundation evaluation worksheet templates
Community needs assessment (separate section)

INSTITUTIONAL EVALUATION CONCEPTS

Theory-Based Evaluation

If a museum wants to change the world in some way, what are its theories about how it will bring about and measure those changes?

> Theory-Based Evaluation ("TBE") is an approach to evaluation that requires surfacing the assumptions on which the program is based in considerable detail: what activities are being conducted, what effect each particular activity will have, what the program does next, what the excepted response is, what happens next, and so on, to the expected outcomes.[1] The evaluation then follows each step in the sequence to see whether the expected ministeps actually materialize. (Birckmayer & Weiss, 2000, p. 408)

TBE is based on a *theory of change* and/or a *theory of action*, which may be synonymous to some. Others draw a level distinction, meaning that a theory of change covers the big picture; for example, museums use their resources to change lives, while a theory of action details the pathway, steps, and actions the museum takes to effect its desired changes. Writing in *The Evaluation Exchange*, the Harvard Family Research Project periodical on emerging strategies in evaluation, Claudia Weisburd and Tamara Sniad from Foundations, Inc., further clarify the distinction: "A theory of change identifies the process(es) through which a given type of social change is expected to occur. A theory of action maps out a specific pathway in that theory of change, or an organization's role with respect to achieving that change, based on an assessment of how it can add the most value to the change process" (Weisburd & Sniad, 2005/2006). The more detailed and therefore more observable theory of action is the more useful of the two terms to address the complexity of the museum field and to provide a meaningful framework for evaluation, particularly TBE.

The Museum Theory of Action

See full description in "62. Museum Theory of Action."

Table 46.2   The Basic Logic Model

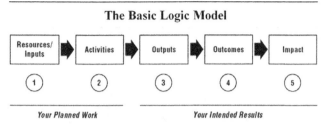

Logic Models

Very similar to theories of change and action, logic models add definition to the steps. The W. K. Kellogg Foundation (2006), in its evaluation handbook for grant applicants, defines logic models as "a picture of how your program works—the theory and assumptions underlying the program. . . . This model provides a road map of your program, highlighting how it is expected to work, what activities need to come before others, and how desired outcomes are achieved." This traditional, one-way logic model is a way of connecting a project's goals to resource investments, to activities, to outputs, to outcomes, and finally to impacts and social values. Kellogg diagrams it as a left-to-right sequence, shown in table 46.2, that horizontally connects the boxes in each step of the logic model in order to evaluate and measure a program's effectiveness and efficiency of transforming a funder's grant awards into community impacts and public value.

It is tempting to use logic models to evaluate entire museums as well as their individual grant-funded programs. However, a one-way logic model approach assumes the museum *versus* the world, where the intention of the museum (us) is to improve the world (them), and the museum is judged and valued on how well it succeeds in improving *them*. The richer and more socially beneficial reality recognizes the symbiotic relationship between the museum *and* the world: The world also wants to make us different. It has every right to: the world—our audiences, donors, society, city, culture, community, and/or market—is paying our bills. A museum logic model needs to be looping or two-way.

Infrastructure Model

In a convening of the leaders of the Association of Science-Technology Centers (ASTC) funded by the National Science Foundation (NSF) more than two decades ago, Perry, Huntwork, and St. John (1994) reflected on a different approach to museum evaluation:

> We see grants for exhibit development and other investments in informal science education as investments in infrastructure. Consequently, these investments should be evaluated against a set of criteria that are appropriate for evaluating infrastructure, not against criteria that assume direct and immediate "impacts" on the visiting public.

The Community Service Evaluation Model

A *community service model*, rather than a *mission-driven model*, may offer a more accurate way to measure performance based on each museum's prioritized, multiple purposes, each with its own set of indicators of success: How is the museum doing with learning outcomes? In community gathering? In heritage conservation? In educational support? In economic development? Which missions are the most important? The community service model recognizes the complexity and diversity of managing a contemporary museum that pursues several purposes. This requires moving beyond the idea of a single purpose, mission, intentionality, or core ideology as the museum's driver and sole evaluation test. The mission may remain a museum's primary purpose, but we need the museum's other purposes to show up fairly and be counted in any institutional evaluation.

Key Service Market Appraisals

For museums with jobs and public facilities to maintain, the pursuit of missions requires funding. The most likely and sustainable sources of that funding are the people and organizations that value the museum's benefits. The money a museum gets repeatedly (its recurring operating revenues) is an indicator of the value that people and organizations place on the museum's activities. These externally defined values can be unrelated to the museum's expressed intents, as museum funds come for many reasons and agendas, such as trade-offs between donors, merchandizing tie-ins, and so on. The museum as a whole serves multiple purposes for multiple revenue sectors, and a museum's yearly revenues are the sum of all the values purchased or funded that year by its audiences and supporters. This approach follows the subjective theory of economics, equating value with trading price (Menger, 1871).

Operating revenues are accurately reported in audited financial statements and are increasingly being made transparent (Stein, 2009). Annual revenues can be categorized into a museum's key revenue sectors, each sector defined by its different reasons and modes of funding or purchase. These are the stakeholders who are willing to pay the museum for the value they receive. One dimension of evaluation should ask, What are our revenue sectors valuing from their museum engagements, and do they see those engagements as good value for their money?

The sources of operating money can be broadly categorized by each museum into revenue sectors, such as grants, admissions, program fees, donations, economic development funds, and sponsorships. A revenue sector research framework offers several useful ways to evaluate a whole museum:

- Ranking, in share of total revenues, of each revenue sector (those are the key service markets)
- Degree of alignment of that ranking with the museum's prioritized purposes
- Changes in each sector's share of the museum's total operating revenues year to year
- Changes in overall tangible value of the museum's services year to year
- Market share in comparison to peer museums, which can lead to peer performance indicators

Table 46.3 The National Science Foundation's Advancing Informal STEM Learning Program Evaluation Framework Categories

Audiences
    Public audiences
    Professional audiences
Impact categories
    Awareness, knowledge, or understanding of a STEM concept or topic
    Engagement of interest in a STEM concept or topic
    Attitude regarding a STEM concept or topic
    Behavior regarding a STEM concept or topic
    Skills regarding a STEM concept or topic
    Other (specify)
Evaluation designs
    Qualitative, no comparison group
    Quantitative, no comparison group
    Quasi experimental
    Experimental
    Other (specify)
None (impact will not be measured)

Source: AISL Online Project Monitoring System, Baseline Screenshots, pp. 40–41; www.reginfo.gov/public/do/DownloadDocument?objectID=62363900.

Revenues are but one indicator of a museum's value, leaving room for the evaluation of its intangible public, private, and personal values to be made through other methodologies.

NSF Evaluation Worksheet Templates

In its *Framework for Evaluating Impacts of Informal Science Education Projects* (Friedman, 2008), the NSF's Informal Science Education program, now the Advancing Informal STEM Learning program, synthesized earlier evaluation experience to establish a language and set of expectations shared widely in the informal learning evaluation field, represented by the Visitor Studies Association and the Committee on Audience Research and Evaluation of the American Alliance of Museums.

The NSF established categories of informal learning impacts, such as changes in levels of "awareness, knowledge or understanding, engagement or interest, attitude, behavior, abilities, skills, and other" (Friedman, 2008, p. 21) and target audiences, such as professional or public. Given these categories of impacts and audiences, the NSF asked evaluators to state what indicators they will use to monitor whether the impact is happening as well as what kinds and level of indicator responses might show evidence of success (p. 23). See table 46.3.

Community Needs Assessment

See "27. Community Needs Assessments: Process" and "28. Community Needs and Museums: Rationale" for descriptions and options. This section is referenced here because assessing community needs and aspirations is a museum's foundational and most constant institutional evaluation activity.

See "15. Bibliography for Museums" for citation references.

NOTE

1.   The original cited Bickman (1990), Chen (1990), Chen and Rossi (1987), Costner (1989), Finney and Moos (1989), Suchman (1967), and Weiss (1972, 1995, 1997, 1998) at this point.

Section 47

Insurance Menu

INTRODUCTION

Museums need to consider a wide range of kinds of insurance to mitigate risk and buffer potential losses. Because of its role in protecting the institution and its people, insurance coverage is often a board-level choice.

You may use table 47.1 as a menu of possible coverage policies.

This section is compiled by contributing author Duane Kocik.

INSURANCE MENU

Note: Consult with a broker who ideally knows the museum business and has access to multiple underwriters and insurers. Seek coverage from highly rated insurance companies and underwriters.

Table 47.1 Sample Insurance Coverage

Line of Coverage	Comments	Name of Insurance Company	Insurance Company Rating— A. M. Best	Annual Coverage/Premiums			Deductible Examples
				Coverage Amount	Rate	Premium (Cost for Annual Coverage)	
Property							
Blanket building/business personal property	Seek replacement coverage for all structures and business property with appropriate deductible. Know rating of insurance company/underwriter.						$5,000 to $10,000
Business interruption/ replacement income	May have a high deductible and extends only 180 days. May include only business interruptions that were caused due to physical damage to building.						24 hours
Flood and earthquake	May have limits (10,000,000 as an example) if structures are in floodplain/earthquake area						$50,000 per 48 hours
Other property coverages	Seek coverage for debris removal, pollutant cleanup, fungus or dry rot, spoilage, ammonia, or hazardous substance. All may have lower limits for coverage.						$5,000 to $10,000
General liability							Typically none
General liability	Typical coverage is $1,000,000 to $2,000,000. Review terms of coverage carefully and know what is excluded from coverage from general liability and excess liability policies.						
First layer of excess liability/umbrella	May be a limit of up to an additional $5,000,000.						
Second layer of excess liability/umbrella	May be a limit of up to an additional $20,000,000 or level desirable. Limits may be combined under one or more insurance company.						
Sexual abuse	If museum involves children's programs, this coverage is recommended. Determine if coverage is on a claims-made basis						
Liquor liability	Typical limit is $1,000,000.						
Medical expense	Typical coverage limit may be $5,000 for any one person.						May be a limit of $5,000 per person
Products liability	Typical limit is $1,000,000 to $2,000,000.						
Personal and advertising injury liability	Typical limit is $1,000,000.						
Employee benefits liability	Typical limit is $1,000,000.						
Executive protection							None

Coverage	Description	Premium
Directors' and officers' liability insurance	Coverage may include directors and officers, staff, and volunteers. Coverage may include, on a claims-made basis, wrongful employment practices/termination, discrimination, sexual harassment, workplace torts, fiduciary coverage under ERISA, employee dishonesty, forgery, theft, disappearance and destruction, computer fraud, workplace violence, and defense costs. There may be a limit to defense costs.	$5,000 to $10,000
Employment practices liability		
Fiduciary liability		
Crime		
Workplace violence		
Internet liability		
Commercial automobile		
Vehicles	Seek appropriate coverage for liability, uninsured, personal injury, hired and borrowed auto, nonowned, and glass coverage.	$1,000
Garage keepers		
Parking garage property and liability (if owned and operated by museum)	Seek property and comprehensive liability and collision insurance with reasonable deductible.	$1,000
Other coverages		
Workers' compensation	Seek coverage for statutory limits.	None
Museum collection	It is difficult to place values on museum collections, as many items are one of a kind and irreplaceable. See coverage for collections that is broad and wall-to-wall coverage for items in transit and at other locations.	$5,000
Schedules property	Can include items such as computerized business equipment and software, cameras, films, audiovisual equipment, boats, trailers, video equip, ATVs, and miscellaneous equipment. See note below.	$1,000
Foreign package	If applicable, coverage should include general liability, auto, foreign workers' compensation, business travel accidental death and dismemberment, and kidnap and ransom.	None
Professional liability/kidnapping ransom/cyber risk	Coverage may or may not be needed. Review what is and is not covered in these types of policies.	$25,000
Total annual premiums		

Section 48

Key Performance Indicators

INTRODUCTION

A careful selection of key performance indicators (KPIs) can become a meaningful management dashboard. KPIs can combine quantitative operating, evaluation, and market data into formulas that track the relationships of data fields over time. For example, the number of teachers electing to bring their students to a museum (operating data) divided by the teacher population (market data) results in a market index KPI; factor that by the ratio of repeating teachers to get a satisfaction KPI. Of course, many other factors may be at work, and periodic evaluation needs to test the validity of such indicators.

Some KPIs may be able to indicate that the museum is achieving its desired impacts even though the KPIs are based on output counts from activities. Using the previous example, if we assume that teachers are expert educators, then their repeated selection of the museum is an indicator of an expert community's assessment of the museum's educational value compared to their other options. KPIs that might act as impact indicators are potentially new evaluation tools for measuring impacts.

This section starts with a sample selection of KPIs and then outlines a process for selecting KPIs that is more fully described in "Measuring Museum Impact and Performance", Jacobsen 2016, chap. 5.

As a case study of using KPIs, Heureka, near Helsinki, Finland, negotiated with their stakeholders which KPIs they would use to benchmark performance, impacts, and benefits, as shown in table 48.1.

Table 48.1   Case Study of Key Performance Indicators: Heureka, Finland

Indicators	Target Value
1. Heureka's visitors and their satisfaction	
a. Annual attendance	>250,000
b. Recommendable in visitor studies	>85%
c. Visitors from outside Helsinki metropolitan region	>50%
2. Economic efficiency	
a. Visitors per full-time equivalent	>2,800
b. Proportion of earned income	>42%
c. Economic result	25,000 euros
3. Heureka's content and its renewal	
a. Renewed exhibition surface	>50%
b. Number of organizational partners	>60
c. Number of innovative exhibition solutions	>10
4. Heureka as provider of learning	
a. Attractiveness of exhibitions in visitor studies	>80%
b. Intelligibility of exhibitions in visitor studies	>75%
c. Number of school visitors per annum	>60,000

Notes: The performance indicators have been defined in the contract between Heureka, the Ministry of Education and Culture, and the City of Vantaa, signed in 2010. The indicators are calculated as three-year annual means.

A closer look at Heureka's KPIs shows that some output-based KPIs can also serve as museum outcome indicators. Visitors are electing to spend their time, effort, and money in a learning institution, and studies that record their satisfaction are one source of evidence of value to the visitors. While the nature and depth of this value will vary among visitors and kinds of museum engagements, the annual accumulation of data becomes the definition of the museum's actual audience that year in measurable terms.

Their cumulative satisfaction is an indicator of successful outcomes in their eyes.

Similar user-based evidence exists in Heureka's number of partners (relative social bonding impact) and its exhibition intelligibility (message engagement impact). Other forms of evaluation are still needed to assess, for example, whether the partners see the relationship as mutually beneficial or whether the visitors were moved by the exhibition. Establishing a network of partners is a desirable public value on its own (organizational linkages add to the infrastructure of a community's social bonds), and the museum's impact value in this area is indicated by the size of its network. If that network is also seen by the partners as mutually beneficial, then the museum can claim an even higher impact value. Both are legitimate and evidenced impacts, even if one is counted using only output numbers.

Process for Selecting Purposes, Impacts, and KPIs

Brief governance on the need for your museum to establish prioritized intentional purposes and desired impacts. Research your community's needs and aspirations. Determine the museum's current key services markets and their perceived benefits. Review the museum's most recent strategic planning for objectives. Add other potential purposes and desired impacts, using Museum Indicators of Impact and Performance (MIIP 1.0) as a source of ideas. Import (a) your list of community needs and aspirations, (b) your audience's and supporter's perceived benefits, (c) your recent planning objectives, and (d) your other potential purposes and desired impacts into a combined database named "Potential Purposes and Impacts." Group purposes, desired impacts, and benefits that are alike into several umbrella content groups (e.g., family learning, tourism, and civic pride). Identify observable and measurable desired impacts for each content group (what measurable changes might we be able to see that we are achieving our purpose?) along with the data fields and KPIs suggested for measuring impact. Consolidate and synthesize the content groups down to 8 to 12 big ideas where the museum might serve a purpose, along with possible KPIs. Prioritize the museum's purposes and impacts by convening leadership in a facilitated workshop, such as a board retreat, to wrestle with the museum's most important questions, such as What are our main purposes, and what are we trying to achieve? Starting with the short-listed potential purposes and impacts, leadership should either combine or select the museum's top two to five intentional purposes and then assign to each a percentage priority, adding up to 100 percent. Formalize, circulate, and pursue your museum's prioritized purposes and impacts. Periodically review and update the museum's prioritized purposes and desired impacts.

See "15. Bibliography for Museums" for citation references.

Section 49

Market Demographics and Population Analysis

INTRODUCTION

This section focuses on how to divide a museum's market into geographic segments, define the territory parameters of each segment, and collect data and analyze each market's demographics and characteristics. The purpose is twofold: (1) to understand a museum's market and its potential impact on on-site visitor attendance and (2) to project future population from which a museum will draw visitors. Although the focus is on visitors, program participants will also be drawn from the resident and school markets.

This process does not include a fund-raising market analysis for ongoing operations or capital campaigns.

One of the goals of the data collection is to project the population by market segment for a museum's future "stable" or normalized year of operations after some contemplated change is complete (see "8. Attendance Potential Estimates"). The stable year is usually three to four years after the opening of a new museum, expansion, or renovation. It is a year in which attendance is based more on programming and marketing choices than on the excitement and additional marketing, public relations, and advertising surrounding the opening years. The estimated future population numbers by market segment form the basis from which to project capture ratios from each market, one of the methodologies for estimating future attendance potential. Table 49.3 later in this section presents sample current and future stable-year populations for each of the sample market segments.

This section covers a museum's market demographics and population. It is a quantitative analysis meant to complement the qualitative community needs assessment process (see "27. Community Needs Assessments: Process"), which also contains a comprehensive list of what data to collect and from which organizations.

This section is written by contributing author Jeanie Stahl.

MARKET DEMOGRAPHIC AND POPULATION ANALYSIS

Reasons to collect demographic and psychographic data include the following:

- Determine population trends that may have an impact on your museum.
- Analyze the population in relation to the potential and likelihood of visiting your museum.
- Determine the factors in your market that might increase or decrease the likelihood of visiting your museum and how your market's factors compare to the United States as a whole or to markets for peer museums.
- Use psychographic data to inform the development of exhibits and programming.
- Determine the population numbers for a future stable year of operations, which will be used as the basis for an attendance potential estimate.

Questions you should ask include the following:

- Do the demographics and psychographics of the resident population align well with the characteristics of museumgoers for your type of museum?
- Do the income and education demographics of residents align well with industry characteristics of typical museumgoers for your type of museum?
- Do your existing or planned exhibits and programs seem to align well with the lifestyle characteristics of your population?

Defining the Museum's Market Segments

A market segment is, essentially, a group of persons having similar characteristics, such as "area residents" and "tourists." Residential geography, or looking at visitors by where they live, is another way of segmenting the visitor market (see "Key Visitor Segments" in chapter 12) and is useful because it can be quantified. Residents and tourists vary from one another in age, party composition, and likelihood of engaging in various kinds of activities. By gathering data about each identifiable market segment, such as the size and age distribution of each segment and the year-to-year trend of the data, the total number of persons and their characteristics available to visit the museum can be estimated.

A standard way of looking at the museum's visitor market is based on the following three segments:

- Residents: Often divided into primary and secondary markets and occasionally with an additional core or tertiary market.
- Schoolchildren: Visiting as part of organized school and youth groups. This market is separately counted because children come to museums both with school groups and with their caregivers. Sometimes, this segment is geographically different and/or larger than the resident market and may be defined by county boundaries or by school districts.
- Tourists: Day-Trippers and Overnight Tourists: Day-trippers (optional market) are those who live outside a secondary resident market or the media market but not so far that they cannot drive round-trip the same day. Ideally, they live outside the defined resident markets, but in reality there is often an overlap.
  Overnight tourists live far enough outside the market to spend the night before traveling home, although, in

practice, tourists may include people who reside in the resident market.

The next step is to define the geographic parameters for each of the markets.

Resident Market

There are many ways of geographically defining a museum's resident market. The community interviews that the museum conducts can provide guidance on the most appropriate way to divide the market. The segments may be by metropolitan or micropolitan statistical area (MSA) or designated market area (DMA), based on county borders in groupings other than those of the MSA or DMA, or by drive time or mileage. It also depends on what data the museum can access:

- Core market (optional) may be included as an additional market, useful when the museum's immediate neighborhood or center-city location is distinct from the rest of its primary market. For midsize to large urban museums, the core market is often the population within city limits.
- Primary market refers to residents of the museum city's greater surrounding region, typically within commuting distance of downtown.
- Secondary market refers to residents who live outside the primary or core markets but are still within the larger media market reached by television stations.
- Tertiary market (optional) is useful for more remote markets or for counties between two cities.

Table 49.1 presents examples of how to divide the resident market. Definitions for the MSA and DMA appear after the table.

Table 49.1 Examples of Ways to Define the Resident Market

Primary Market	Secondary Market	
City limits	MSA	Good for small to midsize museums that will probably not draw from beyond the MSA.
MSA	DMA	Easy to collect free MSA data for current and past populations. Good for comparing to other museums and their MSA population when doing peer analysis. Population projections not always available for free.
		Usually have to pay to get DMA data. Good for comparing to other museums when doing peer analysis. Partner organizations, especially media partners, could provide data for free.
Drive time: up to 30 minutes	Drive time: 30 to XX minutes	Especially good for small museums and children's museums, whose visitors often have shorter travel times, especially with young children. Often have to pay to get data in this format.
Mileage: 0 to 20	Mileage: 20 to XX	Not as useful as drive time in minutes, as it does not factor in traffic and length of time to reach the museum.

The following definitions for MSAs are taken from the U.S. Census website:[1]

- Metropolitan Statistical Areas: Statistical areas with at least one urbanized area that has a population of at least 50,000. The MSA comprises the central county or counties or equivalent entities containing the core, plus adjacent outlying counties having a high degree of social and economic integration with the central county or counties as measured through commuting.
- Micropolitan Statistical Areas: Statistical areas with at least one urban cluster that has a population of at least 10,000 but less than 50,000. The Micropolitan Statistical Area comprises the central county or counties or equivalent entities containing the core, plus adjacent outlying counties having a high degree of social and economic integration with the central county or counties as measured through commuting.
- Metropolitan Division: Smaller groupings of counties or equivalent entities defined within a metropolitan statistical area containing a single core with a population of at least 2.5 million. Not all metropolitan statistical areas with urbanized areas of this size will contain metropolitan divisions. A metropolitan division consists of one or more main/secondary counties that represent an employment center or centers, plus adjacent counties associated with the main/secondary county or counties through commuting ties. Because metropolitan divisions represent subdivisions of larger metropolitan statistical areas, it is not appropriate to rank or compare metropolitan divisions with metropolitan and micropolitan statistical areas. It would be appropriate to rank and compare metropolitan divisions.

Data to collect based on the geographic parameters chosen include the following:

- Population—current, historic, and projected
- Population by race and ethnicity—current and projected
- Population by age range
- Number of households
- Income demographics
- Educational attainment
- Employment
- Psychographics

Sources for resident data include the following:

- American Community Survey, https://www.census.gov/programs-surveys/acs (based on the U.S. Census)
- American FactFinder, U.S. Census, https://factfinder.census.gov
- U.S. Census home page, https://www.census.gov/en.html
- U.S. Census county data, http://censtats.census.gov/usa/usa.shtml

- Statistics Canada and similar census data collected nationally by each country
- State, provincial, or similar research departments
- University research centers
- Nielsen list of DMAs and number of homes, http://www.nielsen.com/content/dam/corporate/us/en/docs/solutions/measurement/television/2013-2014-DMA-Ranks.pdf
- Community media organizations that collect population data: TV, radio, and newspapers
- City planning departments
- City economic development entities

School Market

The school market segment does not necessarily align with the geography of the resident market. Sometimes, the school market is geographically larger than the primary market but smaller than the secondary market. It can be defined by counties or by school districts.

Generally, this segment includes schoolchildren in K–12. In some cases, especially for children's museums, prekindergarten might be included and higher grades excluded.

Collecting data on future enrollment is often hard to get. (See table 49.9 on school enrollment data.) Sometimes, there are planning reports for future facility needs that include the data. Sometimes, university research departments have enrollment projections. If none are available, it is possible to take resident population projections by age and extrapolate data for 5- to 17-year-olds, but they will be only approximate.

Data to collect include, among other items, the following:

- K–12 public and private school enrollment by grade and defined geographic market, whether by county, school district, or other parameter
- Reports of projected facility needs, as they often include projected enrollment

Sources of data include the following:

- Local area school districts
- State departments of education
- National Center for Education Statistics
- University research departments

Tourist Market

The tourist market will have the same definition as the tourist market for the museum's town, city, or MSA. Overnight tourists are defined as those traveling to the area and spending the night. Day-trippers, as noted above, would typically reside beyond the museum's defined resident markets, but there is often an overlap. The day-tripper numbers, if collected, will originate from tourism entities and/or convention bureaus. If the definitions overlap, there are two options. One is to try to deduct the population that is in the overlap area, which would be based on rough estimates and will be inexact. The other is to not include a day-tripper market if it is a negligible portion of the market.

It is important to get multiyear historical data for the tourist market in order to see trends and high points and low points.

Tourism data are the most difficult to capture. Often, tourists are not tracked adequately, or numbers are inflated. They are counted differently in different markets and often by chambers of commerce and tourist and economic development agencies biased toward favorable numbers. Some tourist destinations can do an excellent job of counting tourists, such as Honolulu, and for others, it is not worth the effort. Definitions are not standardized as rigorously as resident populations. (See tables 49.10 and 49.11 for sample tourist data.)

Data to collect include, among other items, the following:

- Tourist population numbers—overnight and day-tripper, current and going back 5 to 10 years
- Reasons for visiting
- Composition of visitors (e.g., singles, couples, families with children, and average party size)
- Visitor origin
- Hotel or motel information—average annual and seasonal average occupancy, average party size, average annual and seasonal average length of stay, and number of hotel or motel rooms
- List of any new hotels or motels expected to be built and the number of rooms

Sources of data include the following:

- City, county, and/or state departments of tourism
- Convention and visitor bureaus
- Area attractions

Sample Tables of Demographic Data

This section presents tables of demographic data for a sample museum's three markets. It is useful to also collect, if applicable, MSA and DMA population data, even if the market segments do not use those definitions, as they will be helpful when comparing to peers.

Also included in one of the tables are psychographic data, a lifestyle segmentation system.

Psychographics take into account buying and spending habits, hobbies, attitudes, and values: "Psychographics analyze consumer lifestyles to create a detailed customer profile. Market researchers conduct psychographic research by asking consumers to agree or disagree with activities, interests, and opinions statements. Results of this exercise are combined with geographic (place of work or residence) and demographic (age, education, occupation, etc.) characteristics to develop a more 'lifelike' portrait of the targeted consumer segment."[2]

Psychographic reports are often purchased from vendors, such as market research agencies. They may use data from predetermined segmentation systems, such as Experian's Mosaic USA, Nielsen's PRIZM, SRI International's VALS (Value and Life Styles), or Acxiom's PersonicX system, or they may develop their own profiles based on Web usage and customer surveys. Some of these systems are only U.S. based. Some are international systems.

Data from the U.S. Census

Table 49.2 presents examples of some of the type of data available from the U.S. Census website. The data shown are for the United States as a whole. Data are also available by other geographies, such as states, cities, counties, MSAs. The U.S. Census website has extensive data on current and past populations by various geographies but has limited data on population projections by geography.

Table 49.2   Example of Data Available from the U.S. Census Website

	United States	Our Primary Market	Our Secondary Market
Population			
Population estimates, July 1, 2015 (V2015)	321,418,820		
Population, percent change, April 1, 2010 (estimates base), to July 1, 2015 (V2015)	4.10%		
Population, census, April 1, 2010	308,745,538		
Age and sex			
Persons under 5 years, percent, July 1, 2015 (V2015)	6.20%		
Persons under 5 years, percent, April 1, 2010	6.50%		
Persons under 18 years, percent, July 1, 2015 (V2015)	22.90%		
Persons under 18 years, percent, April 1, 2010	24.00%		
Persons 65 years and over, percent, July 1, 2015 (V2015)	14.90%		

Persons 65 years and over, percent, April 1, 2010	13.00%		
Female persons, percent, July 1, 2015 (V2015)	50.80%		
Female persons, percent, April 1, 2010	50.80%		

Race and Hispanic origin

White alone, percent, July 1, 2015 (V2015) (a)	77.10%
Black or African American alone, percent, July 1, 2015 (V2015) (a)	13.30%
American Indian and Alaska Native alone, percent, July 1, 2015 (V2015) (a)	1.20%
Asian alone, percent, July 1, 2015 (V2015) (a)	5.60%
Native Hawaiian and Other Pacific Islander alone, percent, July 1, 2015 (V2015) (a)	0.20%
Two or more races, percent, July 1, 2015 (V2015)	2.60%
Hispanic or Latino, percent, July 1, 2015 (V2015) (b)	17.60%
White alone, not Hispanic or Latino, percent, July 1, 2015 (V2015)	61.60%
Veterans, 2010–2014	20,700,711

	United States	*Our Primary Market*	*Our Secondary Market*
Population characteristics			
Housing units, July 1, 2015 (V2015)	134,789,944		
Owner-occupied housing unit rate, 2010–2014	64.40%		
Median value of owner-occupied housing units, 2010–2014	$175,700		
Median selected monthly owner costs—with a mortgage, 2010–2014	$1,522		
Median selected monthly owner costs—without a mortgage, 2010–2014	$457		
Median gross rent, 2010–2014	$920		
Building permits, 2015	1,182,582		
Families and living arrangements			
Households, 2010–2014	116,211,092		
Persons per household, 2010–2014	2.63		
Living in same house 1 year ago, percent of persons age 1 year and up, 2010–2014	85.00%		
Language other than English spoken at home, percent of persons age 5 years and up, 2010–2014	20.90%		
Education			
High school graduate or higher, percent of persons age 25 years and up, 2010–2014	86.30%		
Bachelor's degree or higher, percent of persons age 25 years and up, 2010–2014	29.30%		
Health			
With a disability, under age 65 years, percent, 2010–2014	8.50%		
Persons without health insurance, under age 65 years, percent	12.0%		
Economy			
In civilian labor force, total, percent of population age 16 years and up, 2010–2014	63.50%		
In civilian labor force, female, percent of population age 16 years and up, 2010–2014	58.70%		
Transportation			
Mean travel time to work (minutes), workers age 16 years and up, 2010–2014	25.7		
Income and poverty			
Median household income (in 2014 dollars), 2010–2014	$53,482		
Per capita income in past 12 months (in 2014 dollars), 2010–2014	$28,555		
Persons in poverty, percent	14.8%		

Businesses

Total employer establishments, 2014	7,563,085
Total employment, 2014	121,079,879
Total annual payroll, 2014	5,940,442,637
Total employment, percent change, 2013–2014	2.40%
Total nonemployer establishments, 2014	23,836,937

Geography

Population per square mile, 2010	87.4
Land area in square miles, 2010	3,531,905.43

Sample Demographic Data by Market Segment

Tables 49.3 to 49.7 are examples of the types of tables that can be developed from the collected data that will help inform the analysis of the market segments and the museum's attendance potential from each market.

Table 49.3   Sample Museum's Resident Market Population: Current and Projected

Year	Current 20XX	Projected 20YY	# Change 20XX-YY	% Change 20XX-YY
Primary market	440,300	490,200	49,900	11.33%
Secondary market	549,200	546,700	(2,500)	(0.46%)
Total	989,500	1,036,900	47,400	4.79%
U.S. data, 20XX				To fill in %

Source: Alteryx.

Table 49.4   Sample Museum's Resident Market Population by Race and Ethnicity

	White	Black	Asian/Pacific Islander	Other	Hispanic or Latino Origin
Primary market	93.3%	4.2%	2.2%		2.9%
Secondary market	95.8%	2.2%	1.7%		1.9%
U.S. data, 20XX	77.1%	13.3%	5.8%	3.8%	17.6%

Source: Alteryx.

Table 49.5   Sample Museum's Resident Market Population by Age Range

Year 20XX Age Range	Primary Market		Secondary Market		Total	
0-5	31,714	7%	33,910	6%	65,624	7%
6 to 11	40,114	9%	48,798	9%	88,912	9%
12 to 17	35,571	8%	46,223	8%	81,794	8%
18-24	39,347	9%	49,853	9%	89,200	9%
25-34	65,191	15%	62,263	11%	127,454	13%
35-44	73,974	17%	78,354	14%	152,328	15%
45-54	61,276	14%	70,701	13%	131,977	13%
55-64	37,827	9%	53,450	10%	91,277	9%
65+	55,286	13%	105,648	19%	160,934	16%
Total	440,300	100%	549,200	100%	989,502	100.0%
Children 0-17	107,399		128,931		236,330	
% 0- 17	24%		23%		24%	
Median Age: F	36.3		38.3		38.5	US 20XX
Median Age: M	34.0		35.3		36.1	US 20XX
Index Female	99		104		100	US
Index Male	99		103		100	US

Source: Alteryx.

Table 49.6   Sample Museum's Resident Household Effective Buying Income Distribution

	Less Than $25,000	$25,000 to $49,999	$50,000 or More	Total
Primary market	29%	35%	36%	100%
Secondary market	41%	36%	23%	100%
U.S. data, 20XX		To fill in		
Primary market	127,687	154,105	158,508	440,300
Secondary market	225,172	197,712	126,316	549,200
Total	352,859	351,817	284,824	989,500

Source: Alteryx.

Table 49.7   Sample Museum's Resident Market by Income

	Per Capita 20XX	Median Household 20XX	Median Effective Buying Income Index
Primary market	$18,813	$39,299	73
Secondary market	$16,624	$34,060	64
U.S. data, 20XX	$28,555	$53,482	100

Source: Alteryx.

Table 49.8 presents psychographic data for the sample primary market based on the segmentation system of Mosaic USA. The top psychographic cluster in the primary market is metro fringe. Descriptions are available for each of the clusters. For example, the description for metro fringe is

"a collection of five racially mixed, lower-middle-class Mosaic Types located primarily in satellite cities such as Kissimmee, FL, Flint, MI, Joliet, IL and Fresno, CA. Many of the group's households consist of young singles and couples who work at blue-collar and service industry jobs. They tend to live in older single family homes, semidetached houses and low-rise apartments. Overall, this group is relatively active and pursues sports-oriented lifestyles participating in activities such as soccer and softball, rollerblading, skateboarding, gocarting and video gaming. As shoppers, they patronize discount retailers where they buy the latest fashion and tech gear at low prices. In their homes, they're fans of electronic media, whether it's watching youth-oriented cable channels like Spike TV, FX and Cartoon Network, or going online to chat forums and Web sites for job listings or music downloading.[3]

Based on the description of this group, they are not necessarily a good match for visiting a museum or becoming a member. They are far more sports and outdoors oriented. As they are such a large part of the primary market, the sample museum will need to factor this into the planning of exhibits and programs, the design of some of its galleries, and determining the best way to reach them through marketing and advertising."

Table 49.8   Sample Museum's Psychographic Profile for the Primary Market

Metro fringe	113,168	26%
Rural villages and farms	78,054	18%
Blue-collar backbone	55,514	13%
Upscale America	51,048	12%
Affluent suburbia	31,153	7%
Small-town contentment	29,562	7%
Struggling societies	28,246	6%
Urban essence	23,277	5%
Aspiring contemporaries	18,776	4%
American diversity	9,452	2%
Varying lifestyles	2,050	0%
Remote America	0	0%
Total	440,300	100.0%

Source: Alteryx and Mosaic USA from Experian Business Strategies.

Table 49.9   Sample Museum's School Enrollment by Market Segment

	K-5	6 to 8	9 to 12	Total
Current Year 20XX				
County A	28,771	13,728	17,534	60,033
County B	3,803	1,991	2,323	8,117
County C	3,294	1,786	2,422	7,502
Subtotal	35,868	17,505	22,279	75,652
Plus estimated private school enrollment			7.4%	6,052
Total Current Enrollment				81,704

Projected Stable Year 20XX				
County A	31,071	14,826	18,936	64,832
County B	3,724	1,950	2,275	7,949
County C	3,916	2,123	2,879	8,919
Subtotal	38,711	18,899	24,090	81,700
Plus estimated private school enrollment			7.4%	6,536
Total Projected Enrollment				88,236

Projected Increases				
County A	2,300	1,098	1,402	4,799
County B	(79)	(41)	(48)	(168)
County C	622	337	457	1,417
Subtotal	2,843	1,394	1,811	6,048
Plus estimated private school enrollment				484
Total Enrollment Increase				6,532

Source: U.S. Department of Education.

Table 49.10   Tourism Characteristics

Average length of stay in nights	2.77
Average number of persons in party	3.75
Average staying in hotels or motels	65%
Primary reason for visit:	
Sightsee/vacation	57%
Visit family/friends	36%
Visited for other reason	24%
Business reasons	15%

Table 49.11   Tourism Population

	Current Year	Projected Stable Year	Projected Increase
Day-trippers	2,500,000	2,625,000	125,000
Overnight visitors	1,528,000	1,573,840	45,840
Total tourists	4,028,000	4,198,840	170,840

MARKET SEGMENT BY POPULATION

Table 49.12 presents an example of total population by market segment that becomes the basis for one of the methods of developing an estimate for a museum's attendance potential for a future stable operating year. To estimate future attendance, capture ratios are applied to each of the market segments, resulting in potential attendance from each market (see "8. Attendance Potential Estimates"). In the sample markets below, the day-tripper tourist market was excluded because of too much overlap with the secondary market. In general, it is very hard to differentiate the day-tripper market from a secondary or tertiary market because of some degree of overlap. In developing the attendance potential by market segment, it is better to be conservative and err by excluding the day-tripper market and, instead, factor up the capture ratio for the outer resident market.

Table 49.12   Current and Projected Population by Market Segment

Market Segment	Current Population	Projected 20XX	Increase/(Decrease)	Increase/(Decrease)
Primary market	440,300	490,200	49,900	11.3%
Secondary market	549,200	546,700	(2,500)	(0.5%)
Public school Enrollment: K–12	81,700	88,236	6,536	8.0%
Tourists (overnight)	1,528,000	1,654,600	126,600	8.3%
Total	3,039,317	3,219,034	179,717	5.9%

Source: Alteryx Demographics USA, State Department of Education, State Tourism Department.

Some salient points derived from the tables for the sample museum are the following:

- Projected population growth in the primary market is very strong.
- The population in the secondary market, which is larger than the primary market, is projected to decline.
- Both resident markets are far less diverse than the country as a whole.
- The primary market is younger than average, and the secondary market population is close to the U.S. averages.
- Per capita and median household income in the primary and secondary markets are below the data for the United States as a whole.
- A large percentage of the secondary market has household effective buying incomes of less than $25,000. Residents will have far fewer discretionary dollars to spend on leisure activities.
- The top psychographic clusters for residents of the primary market are metro fringe, followed by rural villages and farms, none of them fitting the typical characteristics of some museumgoers. Other comparatively large markets are blue-collar backbone and upscale America.
- The majority of schoolchildren reside in County A.
- The majority of tourist visits are for sightseeing and to visit friends and relatives, good target markets for a museum.
- The day-tripper tourist population is projected to increase in size. The overnight visitor market is expected to increase only a small amount.

NOTES

1. http://www.census.gov/econ/census/help/aff/what_geographies_are_available_for_economic_data.html#Metro accessed 7/18/2016.

2. http://www.businessdictionary.com/definition/psychographics.html, accessed July 21, 2016.

3. Mosaic USA Group and type descriptions by Experian, http://www.appliedgeographic.com/AGS_2010%20web%20pdf%20files/MosaicUSA_06_definitions.pdf, accessed August 2, 2016.

Section 50

Marketing

INTRODUCTION

The museum's marketing and communications initiatives fall into four overlapping domains, reflecting the four major categories of ongoing revenue: consumer marketing to *visitors*, consumer marketing to *program participants* (both are earned revenue), fund-raising support for *private donors*, and community relations and advocacy for *public support*. Each communications domain has its own needs, sub-audiences, key messages, and media, even though all four communication domains may be handled by one individual in a small museum or separately by the marketing and development departments in large museums. The last two are most active during fund-raising campaigns seeking private and public funds. Plans and budgets for these are covered by the development office.

This section focuses on consumer marketing to visitors and program participants; both are earned revenue sources. The section outlines the goals, messages, audiences, and strategies to be covered by the marketing plan, to be written by staff. The activities are covered by the marketing budget.

This section is based on writing by Mary Jane Dodge.

MARKETING

Marketing: General Objectives

The primary objectives of the marketing plan for the museum are the following:

- To help the museum achieve operational earned revenue goals from visitors and program participants.
- To build broad public awareness of the museum and to inspire positive attitudes toward the museum among the residents of the region by communicating its mission, products, and services.
- To attract XX (budget minimum) to XX (ideal target) site visitors to the museum in 20XX at or above the budget minimum average ticket price.
- To attract the target program participation numbers detailed elsewhere in the plan, both in people served and in gross sales.
- To establish the museum as a premier family museum in the region.
- To analyze the audience and forecast their attendance and interests and to use that information and other market research to be a "learning organization," constantly improving its relationship with its customers.
- To define the goals, strategies, budgeting, and implementation of each of the integrated communications campaigns (e.g., advertising, publicity, and promotions).
- To demonstrate to the financial and political leadership of the region that the museum is capable of mounting an effective, efficient, and professional customer marketing campaign.
- To partner with others on mutually beneficial promotions.
- To support fund-raising and development efforts and to acknowledge donors and promote their participation in an appropriate manner.
- To support community relations and advocacy efforts and to acknowledge partners and promote their participation in an appropriate manner.

Marketing Assumptions

- The museum will pay full attention and commitment to the quality and appeal of the visitor's and participant's experience, not only in the exhibit galleries, theaters, and program spaces but also in the gift shop, ticketing areas, websites and social media sites, parking areas, restrooms, and so on.
- The museum will develop of a carefully conceived schedule of offerings that maximizes attendance, accounts for the needs of diverse audiences, and maximizes repeat visitations.
- The museum will obtain a significant share of its revenues from earned revenue categories. Therefore, marketing will play a key role in the management and economic health of the facility.
- The museum will establish and support with sufficient resources a strong marketing plan, highly integrated with program plans and visitor services, taking into account the nature and value of the offerings the museum presents.

Communications Goals

A successful marketing program communicates many things—ideas, information, a sense of the experience, and, most significant, a call to action. This multifaceted message determines exactly what to say, how to say it, and who to say it to. Every effort should be made to keep the messages from becoming garbled or lost, and the right messages should be communicated at the right time through the right media to the right audiences as per the *marketing plan*.

To present a clearer picture of exactly what makes up the complete marketing message, we have divided these messages into five categories, each containing pieces and goals of the complete marketing message:

- Key Messages: Describe how the museum will be positioned in the marketplace, what differentiates it from its competition, and how it is perceived in the marketplace. This positioning is akin to staking a claim in the market.
- Key Image Statements: Guidelines to help the people who will create the "look and feel" of the museum in a variety of areas, including everything from the logo and brand, the corporate identity system, signs, and staff uniforms or dress code.
- Promises: What we want the audience to believe they will receive by visiting the museum. These are the ideal *benefits* that the marketing campaign offers and communicates to the public. Audiences exchange their money, effort, and time for benefits (see "Possible Brand Promises" below).
- Ideal Visitor Reactions: The desired feelings and perceptions of the visitors to the museum. These are the comments we want to hear as people leave the museum. Ideally, these reactions are produced when the promises

are delivered. This is what we want the "word of mouth" to be.
- Key Facts: The details and logistics, such as prices, parking, show times, directions, and so on, that will be communicated through publicity and collateral materials.

Possible Brand Promises

The following are potential benefits that a visitor to the museum will get in return for his or her time, effort, and money. All are expressed from the visitor's view, as "You will ———."

- Learn about ———
- Have a good time
- Construct meaning from your experiences
- Exercise mentally (mental nautilus)
- Exercise physically (walking and rock wall climbing)
- Experience awe, beauty, insight, and other intrinsic joys
- Apply critical thinking (solve puzzles)
- Be creative (make something)
- See new frames and perspectives on the world
- Develop new skills or develop the skill of ———
- Be inspired to ———
- Engage intellectually and/or socially
- Help yourself improve (assist the stages of change)
- Develop your family's core competencies
- Prepare for the future
- Spend quality time with friends and family
- Have new experiences
- Get away from your world
- Connect with your world
- Relax in an oasis of safety and refreshment
- Find romance and/or new friends
- Enhance your relationships
- Belong to something worthwhile
- Form cultural connections
- Strengthen your identity
- Enjoy and engage in active leisure
- Escape with passive entertainment
- Be actively entertained
- Learn together across generations
- Travel to other times and places
- See and stand beside rare icons
- Explore career options
- Find comfort and solace
- Connect spiritually
- Honor a memory
- Develop your sense of relevance and connection
- Find affirmations and belonging to a sense of shared identity
- Be enlightened
- Be excited and inspired
- Have an excellent visitor experience
- Engage in worthy purposes

- Be moved by beauty
- Be affected by history

Marketing Strategies

Note: The following strategies cover the most complicated case: the launch of a new museum. Existing museums will select operating versions of some of the strategies.

1. Communicate the Mission: Nonprofit organizations, such as the museum, will receive greater benefits from people and businesses if the institution is service driven. A clear message should be communicated as to how and why the organization is enriching the cultural fabric of the region.

2. Plan a Successful Opening: Planning a strong opening for the new museum is one of the most important decisions that can be made to ensure success. The complex of new attractions will open only once, and it must be fully ready and properly positioned at the beginning. If it is to be regarded as a world-class attraction, it needs to open in a big way, utilizing advertising, promotions, publicity, exclusive previews, corporate support, direct mail, new collateral materials, and other means to develop a campaign that is as exciting and professional as the new facility itself. Concentrating attention into the launch period is the most efficient way of generating community awareness and strong word of mouth.

3. Mount a Major Marketing Campaign: As part of the preopening budget, a launch campaign should be defined that includes the following areas:

   a. Market research
   b. Public relations plan
   c. Internal relations plan
   d. Customer relations plan
   e. Publicity plan
   f. Advertising plan
   g. Promotions plan
   h. Web and social media plan
   i. Special events and previews plan
   j. Collateral materials/distribution plan
   k. Group sales plan
   l. Direct-mail plan
   m. In-house marketing plan
   n. Speakers bureau

4. Launch Marketing Plan: This should be commissioned and fully developed at least two years prior to the opening of the new facility.

5. Adopt a new Corporate Identity System in 20XX: Once the marketing plan is complete, graphic designers should be engaged to design a logo and graphic system that meets the demands of the key image statements. A secondary logo should also be designed for the feature theater. This work should be done with an awareness of the current logo. All collateral materials should follow the guidelines of this graphic image. If necessary, the strategy is to produce fewer materials but of top quality with professional graphics.

6. Focus on the Major Attractions during the Launch Campaign: These new components will be key to attracting new audiences as well as attracting those who have attended the museum previously.

7. Develop an Operational Marketing Campaign Mirroring the Launch Campaign: The museum's marketing operation should be a continuation of the elements in the launch campaign at a more modest scale of media expenditure.

8. Focus on the Changing Programming and New Exhibits during the Operational Campaign: The key to attracting visitors to the museum on an ongoing basis is giving them new and exciting reasons to visit. By focusing messages on the changing exhibitions, as well as new programs, the museum will be able to maximize the effectiveness of the marketing campaigns.

9. Market Both Learning and Fun Concurrently: This seeming dichotomy can be most successfully managed by relying on public relations efforts to market the mission while advertising and promotion efforts are devoted to emphasizing the fun factor.

10. Take Advantage of the Museum's Unique Position in the Market.

11. Develop Word-of-Mouth Advertising: Word of mouth is the best form of marketing for any attraction. Immediately after opening the facility, it will be important to get as many community influencers in to see the museum as possible. Exclusive previews are designed to make sure everyone has a first-rate experience so that they will make positive comments to their friends. Developing good word-of-mouth endorsements should be part of all aspects of the marketing of the museum.

12. Coordinate with Other Campaigns: The launch and operating marketing plans should be coordinated with membership and development activities.

13. Develop Cross Promotions with Major Sponsors: A key strategy will be for the museum to align itself and develop long-term relationships with corporations, major employers, media organizations, retail stores, other cultural attractions, and the tourism industry. Cross promotions will be organized in a variety of ways to gain exposure and ultimately to increase attendance.

14. Know the Market and the Visitors' Needs: It is extremely important to know who the audience is and what their needs are. In this way, the audience can be built and maintained. Having an ongoing market research program is of paramount importance in order to understand the audience. An extensive ongoing market research program should be implemented, including monitoring of psychographic groups.

15. Special Programming Strategies:

a. Plan programs for a variety of audiences such as the following:

   i. Members—frequent attendees, family based
   ii. Tourists—seasonal attendees
   iii. Schoolchildren—programming related to various curricula.
   iv. Seniors—films, lectures, off-peak opportunities, special members category

b. Develop marketing components in the museum's outreach programs. Lectures, teacher training, and classroom activities and projects are effective ways to reach out into the community and attract them to the museum.

c. Develop special programming for seniors. A group sales effort and other activities will attract older citizens provided that the programs (e.g., exhibits, films, and lectures) are selected to serve their interests. To attract the senior groups, special programs, such as declaring February as "Senior Citizen's Month," offering special events, promoting the senior discount, and perhaps serving tea in the afternoons, might be of interest to them.

d. Convert visitors to the current facility into ambassadors for the future by displaying models and renderings of the new museum to the current visitors.

16. Become Part of the Region's Tourism Campaign: Take advantage of local and state tourism funds by participating in campaigns developed to attract tourists to the region.

17. Orchestrate the Medium and the Message: The audience will be segmented into key focus segments. Different media reach different audiences. What are the key messages for each visitor market? How should these messages be delivered for each market? To communicate these messages, the most effective and efficient media should be selected and the right "product" offered. A matrix looking for intersections of product, market segment, and promotional vehicle should be created and analyzed as a part of planning.

18. Involve the Key Players: It is essential to build support among business and community leaders. The museum should establish this support by communicating its mission and progress on its expansion to these groups.

19. Involve Celebrities: For its opening, the museum should utilize celebrities to attract media attention and create excitement and to position the museum as a world-class facility.

20. Use "Leverage" to Increase the Impact of the Marketing Campaign: Involve other resources in the marketing campaign that have something to gain by association with the launch of the newly expanded museum. Some groups that would benefit include the following:

a. Corporate sponsors
b. Suppliers to the museum, construction firms
c. Local media outlets
d. Local retailers
e. Other cultural organizations
f. Hotels, restaurants
g. Community and fraternal organizations
h. Local utilities

21. Claim the High Ground from the Start: Become the top-of-mind association with world-class attractions from the start. Associate only with other quality organizations. Attract function rentals to the museum that have the best cachet, especially high-profile events.

22. Make Communication *the* Key Ingredient:

a. Develop community pride in the project.
b. Focus on key hooks to attract audiences.
c. Communicate a world-class image.
d. Utilize key spokespersons.

23. Develop Strategies to Fill Attendance Valleys and Build on Shoulders: When analyzing how to increase attendance, focus on these strategies. Attract available audiences during seasonal valleys through value-added special programming and discount opportunities. Senior citizen and school group audiences are likely targets for building valleys. Shoulder seasons occur just before or after peaks. They frequently can be built on with increased media, promotion, or special programs.

24. Prepare Annual Marketing Plans and Seasonal Work Plans: Advance planning is critical to achieving long-term marketing success. These plans must be developed in tandem with institutional strategic plans.

25. Involve Community Resources: There are many organizations that will be supportive of the museum's mission and plans and might be interested in participating in joint ventures or brokering introductions. These may include the following:

a. Economic development council
b. Chamber of commerce
c. Tourist development council
d. Hotel association

26. Accessibility to the Museum: Attention must be given to building the perception that access to the museum is simple.

27. Individual Venue Champions with Separate Marketing and Programming Budgets and Revenue Reporting.

28. Market Segmentation and Coverage: The museum's visitor venues and program offerings will together serve the museum's overall potential audience, with each venue and business line targeted at one or more of the museum's key visitor and program segments.

Table 50.1   Table of Contents for a Marketing Plan

1. Executive Summary
2. Mission and Objectives: Overview
3. Environment Analysis
4. Market Analysis
5. Influencing the Product
6. Audience Potential Analysis
7. Projected Market Penetration and Attendance
8. Seasonality and Traffic Patterns
9. Breakdown of Estimated Audience Attendance
10. Messages to Be Communicated
11. Marketing Strategies
12. Market Research
13. Public Relations Plan
14. Internal Relations Plan
15. Customer Relations Plan
16. Publicity Plan
17. Advertising Plan
18. Promotions Plan
19. Web and Social Media Plan
20. Special Events and Previews Plan
21. Collateral Materials/Distribution Plan
22. Group Sales Plan
23. Direct-Mail Plan
24. In-House Marketing Plan
25. Speakers Bureau
26. Integration of Plans
27. Implementation and Budgeting
28. Scope for Ad Agency
29. Scope for Public Relations/Social Media Agency

29. Combination Ticketing Strategies: Admission to two or more venues will be discounted XX percent off the combined solo prices as a way of encouraging combination tickets. Additionally, combination packages will be promoted through signs and marketing.
30. Coordinated Graphic Identities: All the museum's programs and venues will share the museum's brand identity. In some cases, subidentities might be developed for the main venues to indicate different appeal to different audiences.

Section 51

Membership

INTRODUCTION

Museums have membership programs to build deeper relationships with their closest advocates, supporters, and customers. Membership programs are the formal interface between the museum and its primary audiences and supporters; the informal, of course, are the personal relationships members develop with museum personnel.

At the ground level, most membership programs are essentially discounted museum admission tickets that pay off after about 2.8 visits in a year. Base-level membership revenue should be counted as earned revenue. Higher levels of membership count as support revenue. Attendance for all categories should be counted, even if free.

The following text and tables may be selected and adapted to suit your museum.

Membership Program Objectives

The membership program should meet the following objectives:

1. To create and develop a membership program that serves the educational mission of the museum
2. To develop a base of popular and ongoing financial support for the future development of the museum
3. To help create a familiar bond with the museum's most active visitors and program participants
4. To expand members' use of the museum's other learning services, in other words, to build on frequent visitors by converting them into program participants as well
5. To identify and cultivate a base for potential annual donors
6. To build a membership base that will contribute significantly to the museum's present and future operating budget
7. To serve as an essential communications link with visitors and provide critical feedback

Member Benefits

Individual Membership: $XX; Student Membership: $XX

- Free unlimited admission to the museum for members only
- Subscription to the museum newsletter
- Discount on purchases in the shop
- Invitation to special events
- Discounts on program fees and subscriptions

Family Membership: $XX

All of the benefits listed above for families plus two free passes to the feature theater, invitation to special family festivals, and discounts on birthday party rooms and other function spaces

Supporting Membership: $XX

All of the benefits listed above plus listing in the museum's annual report, invitation to private reception for supporting members, two free one-time guest passes, and free rental of a birthday party room

Contributing Membership: $XX

All of the benefits listed above plus behind-the-scenes tour of the museum and six one-time guest passes

Patron Membership: $XX

All of the benefits listed above plus special reception with the museum director, recognition in the museum's lobby, and eight one-time guest passes

Corporate Membership

The corporate membership program for the museum should be designed to attract support from local corporations and businesses as well as national and international corporations.

In addition to providing funds, the local sector will add to the important visibility of the museum. Often, volunteers will be identified through this solicitation mode.

As with individual memberships, benefits might include the following:

- XX free admission passes to be distributed to company staff and employees.
- Invitations to special events and exhibits
- VIP passes (gold cards) to be used by the chief executive officer or president enabling free admission and special privileges at all times to all areas
- Honor roll of annual corporate members displayed in the museum
- Free (once per year) and reduced cost in the use of the facility for corporate training and events
- Receipt of the newsletter, with appropriate recognition of the corporate members in the publication

PLANNING WORKSHEETS

Table 51.1   Membership Pricing

	Current		Future	
	$	Number	$	Number
Individual				
Student				
Family				
Supporting				
Contributing				
Patron				

Table 51.2   Corporate Membership—Annual Price (XX or Fewer Employees)

	Current		Future	
	$	Number	$	Number
Corporate—patron				
Corporate—sponsor				
Corporate— associate				
Corporate—director				
Corporate—member				

Table 51.3   Summary Membership Goals

	Rate $	Average Rates	Number	Revenue
Individual memberships				
Individual				
Family				
Supporting				
Contributing				
Patron				
Corporate memberships				
Patron				
Sponsor				
Associate				
Director				
Member				
Totals				

Note: Categories are typically proportional to the number of employees.

Section 52

Multimode Operations

INTRODUCTION

If technology is embedded in the building operation, spaces can be conceived as multimode spaces, capable of being operated for different kinds of functions for different kinds of audiences at different parts of the day or week through the use of automated presets for lighting, window shades, audiovisual ambience, and access to the equipment in that space.

With these capabilities, the museum can have an exhibit area that operates in closed-door school program mode in the morning, in public visitor mode that afternoon, and then as a part of an evening function rental or as an overnight camp-in site. Each of these modes has different operating parameters.

Managers decide on operating modes for each space, ideally communicated through a centralized schedule. Most public spaces have at least two modes: closed and open. Depending on built-in systems for changing modes, the demand for multimode operation, and your museum's programming strategies, any given public space may be capable of operating in one of two to more than 10 operating modes, as listed in table 52.1 and described in this section.

MULTIMODE OPERATIONS

- Public Visitor Mode: Daytime, during all weekends, holidays, and during the summer months—non–school days.
- Adult Mode: A period of time, typically an evening, when children's discounts are not offered. Children are not forbidden, but the incentive is removed, and adult-rate tickets must be purchased for them.
- Program Mode: Open to groups and reserved individuals for scheduled programs offered during the school days available for road trips. It is assumed that school and youth groups will come to the museum and book a sequence of several programs, with lunch, theater, and recreation breaks as part of their visit schedule. In program mode, non–group members are not allowed to join the program in progress—that is, the space has a door, which is closed in program mode.
- Food Service Mode: Set up with tables and chairs, service stations, and access to catering support spaces. This mode can be as informal as a school group lunchroom to the formality of a black-tie awards dinner.
- Special Event Mode: A special day or weekend when much of the museum is taken over by a promoted public event (see "Function Rental Mode" below for private events), such as Community Day and Inventors' Weekend.
- Community and Cultural Center Mode: During the late-week evenings, the museum will transform itself and its theater into a nighttime social ambiance packaged around a theme ("Art and Science in Food") and/or an audience ("Young Leaders"). In this mode, the museum offers films, lecture series, a café/social scene, gift shop, and access to the temporary exhibits.
- Camp-In Mode: After the museum closes, troops of Girl Scouts, Boy Scouts, and other youth groups spend the night in the museum with parent chaperones. After an evening of programs, dinner, films, and time in the galleries, camp-in participants sleep in their sleeping bags on the gallery floors, using the public washrooms. Spaces must be darkened and near washrooms. Museums may need to meet additional safety and fire codes to accommodate overnight sleeping. After breakfast and a conclusion in the theater, caregivers drive in to pick up their children and their sleeping bags in the early morning before the museum opens.
- Function Rental Mode: In the evening and nights, particularly early in the week and during the December holiday season, the museum will transform itself off-hours into a facility ideal for receptions, sit-down dinners, and other events. Museums with separate, dedicated function rental spaces can rent them during public visitor hours.

Table 52.1   Multimode Operations Matrix: Typical School Week

- Meeting Mode: A cluster of program spaces, conference rooms, and theaters operated as a museum conference hall or meeting venue, serving organizations that need neutral ground to meet together and in breakout groups. Spaces in this mode must be quiet and private and with seating and media support.
- Maintenance Modes: The media equipment should allow the building to be put in several other modes to facilitate maintenance and cleaning.
- Shift and Setup Mode: The time between modes for staff to prepare for their shift and make whatever changes to the space that is needed to change modes. Investing in infrastructure and systems to support changing modes may pay off in fewer staff and shorter mode changes. Automatic access controls, lighting presets, storage closets, window treatments, catwalks, media equipment, and prewiring are examples of infrastructure that can make mode transfers more efficient.
- Dark Mode: Totally closed with security systems activated.

Given centralized media controls, it is possible to inexpensively create additional modes simply through writing new programming.

This mixture of changing programming should mean that regional residents will come to use the museum for a variety of reasons, many entirely independent of the mission. Through exposure to the museum, however, it is hoped that they will come back during the daytime and make use of its education programs.

PLANNING WORKSHEET

Table 52.2   Multimode Operations: How Will You Run Your Museum?

Modes	30 Active School Weeks	7 Slow School Weeks	15 Summer and Holiday Weeks	52 Weeks, Yearly Totals
Student group mode				
Public visitor mode				
Cultural center mode				
Special event mode				
Subtotal visitor hours				
Program mode				
Food service mode				
Camp-in mode				
Meeting mode				
Function rental mode				
Subtotal program hours				
Preparation and maintenance modes				
Shift and setup time				
Dark time				
Subtotal staff and dark hours				
Total hours per week	168	168	168	8,736
Total hours per year	5,040	1,176	2,520	8,736

Section 53

Multiple-Mission Museums

INTRODUCTION

This section describes the transition from traditional ways of thinking about a museum's mission to the new reality of multiple-mission museums. The rationale underpins the use of prioritized intentional purposes in this book.

MULTIPLE-MISSION MUSEUMS

The Limiting Tradition of Mission Focus

The concept of mission is deeply ingrained in the museum culture and is closely tied to the idea that museums exist for the public good. The National Standards and Best Practices for U.S. Museums, set forth by the American Alliance of Museums, includes an evaluation standard establishing the primacy of mission: "All aspects of the museum's operations are integrated and focused on meeting its mission" (Merritt, 2008, p. 34).

The Reality of Multiple-Mission Museums: Limitations to the Mission Tradition

Today, many organizations of all sizes have missions. From corporations to military maneuvers to churches to museums, they all have missions. Why question them now? Because museums serve multiple masters and may need multiple missions. Corporations get revenues from customers, the military from the government, and churches from their parishioners. Museums, in contrast, get support revenues from both private and public sources in combination with earned revenues from visitors and program participants. Our embeddedness in our community's economic money flow makes the myth of a solitary-focused mission an anachronism from days when the funding sources were fewer and perhaps more passive.

Museums Offer More Outcomes Than Our Mission Outcomes, and We Pursue More Purposes Than Our Mission Purpose

Externally, communities see museums and use them for more purposes than the mission purpose. Museums are increasingly providing public and personal values (Scott, 2007) beyond their mission statements. Weil, however, said that everything a museum does should be a means to the museum's purpose, or it is not worth doing (Weil, 2005). A museum's communities, on the other hand, value it for its means as well as its mission purpose. A zoo's mission might be biodiversity conservation, but families value it for outings, employers for its quality-of-life contributions, economic development agencies for its jobs and tourism impacts, and corporations for its community relations benefits. Learning is one of a visitor's values, but it is often secondary to other personal values, such as using the museum for quality leisure time with friends and family (Hood, 1983; Roberts, Morrissey, Silverman, & Perry, 1996).

These are all valid and beneficial community values and not inherently in conflict with biodiversity conservation. They also show up among the zoo's annual revenues as admissions, memberships, public funds, and corporate sponsorships. There is nothing wrong with the public valuing a museum for some benefit it provides outside its mission purpose. Further, the public will likely get even better value if the museum becomes purposeful and intentional about providing that benefit.

Hence, both the museum and its publics benefit once the museum becomes intentional about more than one mission and recognizes that, far from being eternal, a museum's missions should evolve with the times and the community's needs.

Build Long-Term Identity, Character, and Brand on Your Beliefs (Guiding Principles), Not on Your Changing Intentional Purposes (Mission)

If a museum has multiple intentional purposes rather than one mission and if it evolves those purposes in response to changing community needs, then it should look to its guiding principles as the museum's constants. The museum's brand and values should express the museum's long-term, core beliefs and character and not tie such timeless aspects of the museum's changing purposes.

Some museum mission statements are already essentially value statements, such as the Smithsonian's "the increase and diffusion of knowledge." Museums with a strong commitment to a discipline, such as a museum of art or a museum of aviation, can shift their love and respect for art or aviation into a value statement. For example, a science museum can list scientific accuracy and processes among its core guiding principles, allowing its intentional purposes to change as needed but always within the methods and findings of science.

See "15. Bibliography for Museums" for citation references.

Section 54

Categories (Types) of Museums

INTRODUCTION

This book adopts the categories established by the American Alliance of Museums, as listed in table 54.1, because they make up a mature, field-based system. These categories are also known as types of museums. Art museums will have art historians as curators, while planetariums will have astronomers.

The ISO list (table 54.2) is new (2016) and shorter but has significant omissions (children's museums) and includes virtual museums as a separate category. The Wikipedia list (table 54.3) is included to communicate the diversity of the museum field, not as a shared classification taxonomy. It is expansive and inclusive and may help your museum find closer subcategories of peer museums.

The National Taxonomy of Exempt Entities (NTEE) system is used by the Internal Revenue Service and the National Center for Charitable Statistics to classify nonprofit organizations. The Foundation Center uses a similar system but with additional codes. A museum's NTEE codes are sometimes requested on forms. To determine your museum's code, go to http://nccs.urban.org/classification/NTEE.cfm.

To answer surveys and to start to identify your peer museums, your museum should select one category from table 54.1 that fits your primary identity and purpose, recognizing that you may have secondary characteristics, such as a historic site including a visitor center and a historic house.

CATEGORIES OF MUSEUMS

Table 54.1   Types of U.S. Museums

• Aquarium	• Military Museum/Battlefield
• Anthropology Museum	• Nature Center
• Arboretum/Botanical Garden/Public Garden	• Natural History Museum
• Art Museum/Center/Sculpture Garden	• Planetarium
• Children's or Youth Museum	• Presidential Library
• General or Multi-disciplinary Museum	• Science/Technology Center/Museum
• Hall of Fame (e.g., sports, entertainment, media)	• Specialized Museum (single topic/individual)
• Historic House	• Transportation Museum
• Historic Site/Landscape	• Visitor Center/Interpretive Center
• History Museum	• Zoo/Animal Park
• Historical Society	

Source: American Alliance of Museums, Museum Benchmarking Online 2.0.

Table 54.2 Types of Museums (ISO Categories)

- Aquarium
- Arboretum
- Archaeology museum
- Art museum
- Botanic garden
- Ecomuseum
- Ethnography and anthropology museum
- General museum
- Herbarium
- History museum
- Living history museum
- Natural history museum
- Open-air museum
- Science and technology museum
- Specialized museum
- Virtual museum
- Zoo

Source: © ISO. This material is adapted from ISO 18461: 2016 with permission of the American National Standards Institute (ANSI) on behalf of ISO All rights reserved. pp. 2–4

Table 54.3   Wikipedia Museums by Type (to Illustrate Diversity of Field)

Advertising museums	Folk museums	Open-air museums
Aerospace museums	Food and drink museums	Opera museums
Agriculture museums	Forestry museums	Performing arts museums
Amusement museums	Fossil museums	Petroleum museums
Anthropology museums	Gas museums	Pharmacy museums
Archaeological museums	Geology museums	Photography museums and galleries
Architecture museums	Glass museums and galleries	Planetaria
Armor collections	Halls of fame	Poetry museums
Art museums and galleries	Historic house museums	Postal museums
Astronomy museums	History museums	Prison museums
Automobile museums	Horological museums	Puppet museums
Bank museums	Hospital museums	Quilt museums
Beer museums	Human rights museums	Religious museums
Bible-themed museums	Industry museums	Research museums
Biographical museums	Insectariums	Rural history museums
Bus museums	Museums of Japanese culture	School museums
Business museums	Jewelry museums	Science museums
Canal museums	Jewish museums	Science centers
Cannabis museums	Language museums	Scouting museums
Carriage museums	Law enforcement museums	Sex museums
Ceramics museums	LGBT museums and archives	Shell museums
Children's museums	Lighthouse museums	Museum ships
Cinema museums	Literary museums	Society museums
Circus museums	Living museums	Sports museums
City museums	Local museums	Steam museums
Civilian Conservation Corps museums	Magic museums	Tea museums
Civilization museums	Masonic museums	Technology museums
Computer museums	Media museums	Telecommunications museums
Costume museums	Medical museums	Textile museums
Cycling museums	Military and war museums	Theatre museums
Museums of Dacia	Mill museums	Tourism museums
Decorative arts museums	Mineralogy museums	Toy museums
Dental museums	Modern art museums	Transport museums
Design museums	Motorcycle museums	University museums
Dinosaur museums	Music museums	Urban planning museums
Ecomuseums	Law museums	Video game museums
Museums of economics	Museums in India by type	Viking Age museums
Education museums	Museums of human migration	Virtual museums
Equestrian museums	National museums	Wax museums
Ethnic museums	Natural disaster museums	Whaling museums
Ethnographic museums	Natural history museums	Wine museums
Farm museums	Nature centers	Women's museums
Fashion museums	Numismatic museums	Toy museums
Firefighting museums	Nursing museums	

Source: Wikipedia.

Section 55

Museum Definitions

INTRODUCTION

What is a museum? What is not a museum? We cannot count museums until we define what counts and what does not. At a time of fertile innovation (many new museum concepts have been launched during the Museum Boom [1980s to 2008]) and at a time of coattailing on the popular respect for museums (the Lizzie Borden Bed and Breakfast and Museum, museum-quality reproductions, virtual museums, and private collector museums), the museum field needs definitions that are both liberal enough to encourage innovation and clear enough to exclude commercial and private appropriations.

There are two definitions in wide use (there are also multiple dictionary, Internet, and association definitions): the International Council of Museums (ICOM) definition (global) and the Museum Services Act (United States). Central to both these definitions and all sections of this book is the specification that a museum is a nonprofit institution with a primary purpose of public service.

MUSEUM DEFINITIONS

The frameworks in this book build on the ICOM definition of museums because ICOM is international, museum-field based, and active in updating its definition from time to time. According to ICOM, a museum is

a non-profit, permanent institution in the service of society and its development, open to the public, which acquires, conserves, researches, communicates and exhibits the tangible and intangible heritage of humanity and its environment for the purposes of education, study and enjoyment. (ICOM Statutes, 2007)

ICOM defines these terms broadly enough to include science centers, children's museums, zoos, and planetariums.
According to the Museum and Library Services Act, a museum is

a public or private nonprofit agency or institution organized on a permanent basis for essentially educational or aesthetic purposes, which, utilizing a professional staff, owns or utilizes tangible objects, cares for them, and exhibits them to the public on a regular basis. (Public Law 111-340, 2010)

Additionally, the definition of museum includes four concepts that museums in North America, the United Kingdom, and the Eurozone might agree with, though the implications may not be clear:

1. Stephen Weil's introduction to John Cotton Dana's selected writings from the 1920s quoted Dana's maxim that museums should find what the community needs and fit the museum to those needs (Peniston, 1999, p. 16).
2. Weil's own theory of museums bases a museum's worth on the good it has accomplished, and the museum's resources are the means to that end. The performance evaluation is then of the museum's effectiveness at achieving its purposes and of the efficiency of its resource use (Weil, 2002, 2005).
3. John Falk and Lynn Dierking, in describing their contextual model of learning, place emphasis on the museum's unique business model of free-choice learning that meets personal and sociocultural needs in physical contexts (Falk & Dierking, 2000, p. xii; 2012, p. 33; Sheppard & Falk, 2006). Free choice means that museums are in a competitive marketplace dependent on voluntary engagements. No one has to visit. No one has to give museums money. This is a fundamental difference between museum business models and schools, where attendance is enforced by truancy laws. While private schools and higher education are consumer choices, once a student is enrolled, attendance is expected and ritualized. This is not so in museums. Museums must attract and benefit our audiences and supporters for each engagement.

4. George Hein (2006, p. 349) builds a wide mission on John Dewey's progressive education that is sharable by all museums: the mission of building a better and more democratic society.

These conceptual foundations have implications for today's museum leaders:

1. Dana's Implication: Museums are responsible for offering their communities services that address their needs and aspirations.
2. Weil's Implication: Museums should use their resources (means) to achieve their purposes (ends) and be evaluated on how effectively and efficiently they do that (performance).
3. Dierking and Falk's Implication: Museums operate in a competitive, free-choice marketplace by offering physical and social services valued by their audiences and supporters.
4. Hein's Implication: Museums aspire to make the world better and more democratic, such as advancing community development and social good.

Synthesized, these concepts underlie museum economic theory: The community funds the museum to use its resources to provide effective services back to the community. The museum provides these services efficiently and, instead of privatizing its net revenues, contributes to community development and social good.

These frameworks do not define or limit museums any further than these broad generalities.

See "15. Bibliography for Museums" for citation references.

Section 56

Museum Engagements

Definitions

1. A *museum engagement* is defined as one physical person-trip to a museum or to a museum sponsored program off-site by a person not employed or contracted by the museum to be there. The person-trip is a measure of effort spent by the person (time and often money are also spent).

2. The umbrella definition of *museum engagements* collects a museum's many potential kinds of activities—gallery attendance, lecture series attendance, volunteer shifts, board meetings, interactions with partners, outreach participants, and so on—into one number across all the museum's activities. Annual engagements are an indicator of the effort that the museum's beneficiaries are willing to make in return for the personal, private, and public benefits they receive. To date, no association is counting total engagements, only total attendance.

3. Engagements can be *physical* face-to-face, both *on-site* at a museum facility and *off-site*, or *virtual*. Virtual engagements are not yet included in most reporting of attendance.

4. The most common and counted engagement is a museum *site visit*. A site visit is one individual who comes on-site to visit the museum's galleries or to participate in a program. Each person-trip is counted as one museum engagement or site visit, even if the trip involves more than one activity or venue. For example, an admissions ticket that combines two *visitor venues* (e.g., galleries + garden tour) during a single site visit is counted as one *site visit* but two *venue visits*. A *visit* has a narrower meaning than site visit, as it assumes only exhibit and theater attendance, whereas site visits include those visits plus all the other reasons to come to the museum site.

5. People also come to museums to participate in *programs*. A museum can hold its programs *on-site*, *off-site*, and *virtually*—the last two are also called *outreach*. While one of the goals of outreach is to reduce audience effort, there is still some effort to attend an off-site program, so each *program participation* is counted as one per person-trip, even if it is off-site. If a ceramics workshop has six sessions and a *program participant* attends all of them, that counts as six museum engagements.

6. Any museum engagement that is not a *visit* is a *program participation*. By this definition, board meetings, volunteer shifts, meetings with grant officers, and event rentals are programs, and the individuals attending them are *program participants*.

7. *On-site attendance* includes both visitors and program participants counted by person-trips to the museum's site. The motivation to make the trip is the distinction between visitors and program participants—did they come primarily for a visit or a program?—and usually shows up in the museum's transaction records—did they buy an admission ticket or pay for a program or get a pass to attend a meeting? Many exhibit *gallery admissions* get programs included for free, some school groups add fee-based programs to their base admission, and some patrons buy combo tickets. These multiple *venue visits* do not increase on-site attendance, as they do not increase the number of person-trips.

Section 57

Museum Field Counts

INTRODUCTION

This section reports some of what is known about the museum field as a whole—the number of museums in the United States and elsewhere and total attendance.

Unfortunately, none of these counts is very accurate. There is no census of U.S. museums. Internationally, each nation has reasonably accurate counts of their publicly funded museums but less accurate estimates of the purely privately funded museums. These include a wide variety with prestigious museums, such as the Courtauld Gallery (London) and for-profit tourist ventures, such as the Salem Witch Museum (Salem, Massachusetts).

The Institute of Museum and Library Services (IMLS) attempted a museum census ("Museums Count") but could not get approval to burden the museum community with its survey. Instead, the IMLS aggregated existing museum listings and directories to assemble a *museum universe data file*. This is available online from the IMLS at https://www.imls.gov/research-evaluation/data-collection/museum-universe-data-file. The data file lists both museums and museum-related organizations (hence the "museum universe"); even though the IMLS reports 33,072 museums and museum-related organizations (IMLS, February 2017), so the number of museums will be less. The IMLS updates the data file periodically, as errors, duplicates, missing, and closed museums are submitted.

MUSEUM FIELD COUNTS

Museum participation has grown in America beyond population growth in the past three decades for which data exist. A 1979 IMLS survey reported 350 million on-site visits annually, or 1.5 visits per American. A 1989 survey conducted over 1986–1988 found a 5 percent annual growth from 1986 at 515 million to 1988 at 566 million, or 2.3 visits per person (Grogg, 1994, p. 63). An IMLS study (Griffiths & King, 2008) recorded the figure in 2006 as 701 million adult in-person visits, holding at 2.3 visits per person,[1] but that study added 542 million online visits, bringing the public engagement ratio up to 1.2 billion and 4.0 engagements per year.[2] The American Alliance of Museums factored the 701 million adult visits for children and other adjustments to arrive at a total on-site visitation of 850 million visits per year to all U.S. museums, or 2.8 physical visits per person (Merritt & Katz, 2009). To summarize, 1979 had 1.5 physical visits to a museum per capita in America. By 2006, the number had increased to 2.8.

Museum growth is also international, as the *Economist* (U.K.) reported:

> Globally, numbers have burgeoned from around 23,000 two decades ago to at least 55,000 now. In England over half the adult population visited a museum or gallery in the past year, the highest share since the government began collecting such statistics in 2005. In Sweden three out of four adults go to a museum at least once a year (though not all Europeans are equally keen). The Louvre in Paris, the world's most popular museum, had 10m visitors last year, 1m more than in 2011. China will soon have 4,000 museums—still only the quarter the number in America, but it is racing to catch up. (Rocco, 2013)

In the 1990s, the IMLS estimated 17,500 museums in the United States alone. The number of U.S. museums has clearly grown during the museum boom, perhaps to around 23,000 to 27,000 museums that fit the IMLS's legislated definition, most of them small, some of them very large. Globally, museums continue growing, most dramatically in China and the Middle East.

In the United States, however, the boom is over. Who survived? Who may not continue to survive? It is fun to build a museum but challenging to sustain its operation. How many museums can our economic, educational, and cultural ecosystems support? Sustainability will depend on delivering important benefits, measuring impact and performance, and constantly tuning the museum's mix of community services to respond to changing community needs.

Data from the Internal Revenue Service show museums and other arts nonprofits in the middle of all nonprofits with regard to the makeup of their financial structures: museums receive on average roughly 60 percent support revenues (government and private), with the balance coming from program services, membership, and other substantially earned revenues (Raymond, 2010, p. 9). Health organizations, such as hospitals, are operated primarily with earned revenues from program services, while religious institutions, such as churches, are primarily support revenues. Museums fall in the middle, with a wide range in the field, as some aquariums are close to all earned revenue and some art museums are almost fully endowed or support funded.

See "15. Bibliography for Museums" for citation references.

NOTES

1. Based on the U.S. population midpoint in 2006, which was 299,398,484 (Web capture on October 25, 2012, http://www.infoplease.com/ipa/A0764220.html).

2. These numbers do not include additional outreach and off-site engagements, and the figures need to add children to the adult numbers.

Section 58

Museum Planning

Conceptual Diagrams

INTRODUCTION

Table 58.1 to 58.5 may be selected and adapted to suit your museum.

EXAMPLES OF MUSEUM CONCEPTUAL DIAGRAMS

Table 58.1   Sample Core Ideology. Source: Roy Shafer for the Science Center of Iowa in 20020

Core Business

| Providing informal science learning opportunities. |

Our vehicle by which we pursue our aspiration

To Engage and Inspire

Our aspiration for 100 + years

Core Values

| Resourcefulness |
| Freedom |
| Discovery |
| Interactive Learning |
| Fun |

Our essential tenets and their signal behaviors

Mission Statement
To be the highest quality resource inspiring scientific exploration through interactive education, exhibits and programs

- Develop the People…Build the Team
- Build SCI's Capacity to more effectively serve and reflect the community of Iowa
- Establish SCI as a valuable resource and forum for informal science learning in Iowa… The Science Center of Iowa
- Learn from and with others…Research, Development, and Partnerships
- Execute sound/effective strategic and financial planning to support SCI's Core Ideology and planning model

__WHAT__ we do to best pursue our aspiration for the next 3 – 5 years

Strategies Annual Operating Plan

What we do, how we do it and how we allocate our resources to blend strategic objectives and strategic values over the next yearly cycle

Strategic Values

| Partnerships |
| Safety |
| Stewardship |
| Innovation/Uniqueness |
| Strategic Planning |
| Teamwork |

__HOW__ we do what we do to best pursue our aspiration in the next 3 – 5 years

Table 58.2 Sample Logic Model

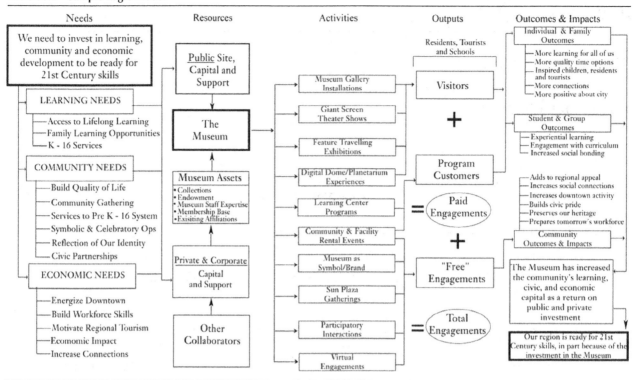

Table 58.3 Two-Way Logic Model

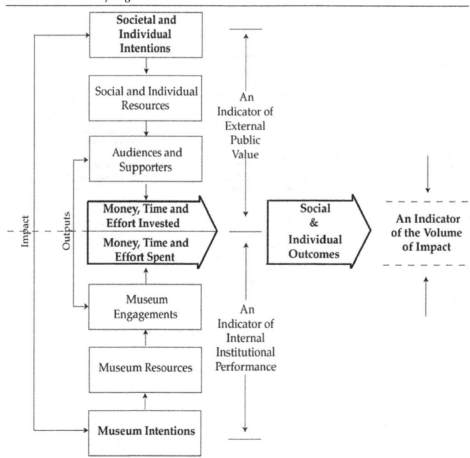

Table 58.4   Purpose and Business Model

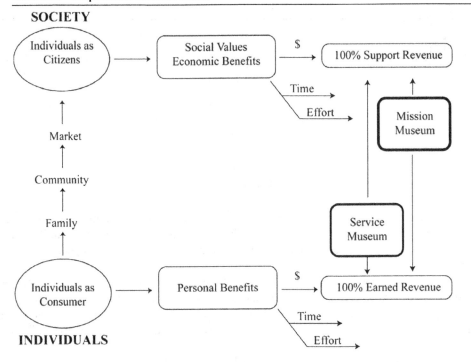

Table 58.5   Integrated Economic Model

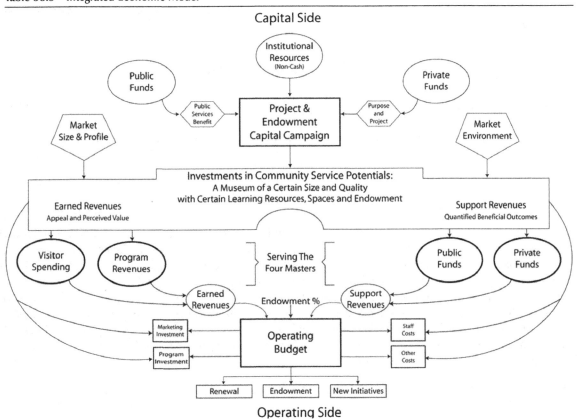

Section 59

Museum Planning

Frameworks

INTRODUCTION

Planning is a process that helps a museum prepare for and take advantage of the future. Strategic planning is envisioning a desired future and then determining the best path to that end. Planning happens all the time, not only when scheduled. Planning happens during the morning floor staff meeting, during office chats, in board retreats, and in architectural offices. As planning is ongoing, it should be budgeted and staffed.

The common advice from museum directors who have been through capital projects before is, "Don't design for opening day." Design, instead, a viable and sustainable operating institution playing a central role in the community and its infrastructure.

Planning is an iterative and ongoing process. While it has a deliverable—the *plan*—it is constantly evolving. Mostly, the evolution is in-depth (a more detailed plan), but, importantly, it can also involve changes in direction as the museum knows more or faces changed circumstances.

This section provides ways of visualizing the planning process that have helped other museums understand the planning process and keep track of where they are.

You may adapt these diagrams to your context. They are particularly useful in presentations to board members and other stakeholders. The planning worksheets may help you make the most significant decisions about your museum's future and then to visualize your museum's plan in a logic model.

PLANNING FRAMEWORKS AND DIAGRAMS

Research conducted by Association of Science-Technology Centers (1993) of successful start-up science museums found that the healthy case studies shared five factors, listed in table 59.1.

Planning is ongoing in a constant cycle of research, planning, implementation, feedback research, planning, and so on, as shown in tables 59.2 and 59.3.

PLANNING WORKSHEETS

Leadership has a number of key choices to make with regard to a projected future for the museum. Once these policy decisions are made—"stakes in the ground"—many other aspects of a complete future model fall into place. Table 59.4 lists some of the key policy choices to be made early in planning by leadership. The list needs to be cross-referenced and integrated, and this process requires dialogue and compromise to evolve a model for the future that will work on all fronts.

The museum is in competition with other museums and activities in its market. While it may seem nice to dominate in all categories, business advisers suggest that this is inefficient and can be counterproductive. It is hard to have the best product, the best service, and the best experience as well as the lowest price and easiest access. Better, they suggest, to dominate in one area, be distinguished in another, and be acceptable in the rest as listed in table 59.5 (Sheppard & Falk, 2006).

See "15. Bibliography for Museums" for citation references.

Table 59.1   Requisites for Success

- Vision
- Leadership
- Community involvement
- Models to study
- A "can do" mentality

Source: Association of Science-Technology Centers (1993).

Table 59.2   Planning Cycle

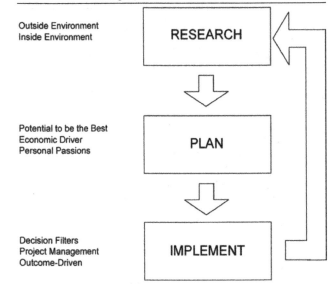

Table 59.3   Planning Sequence

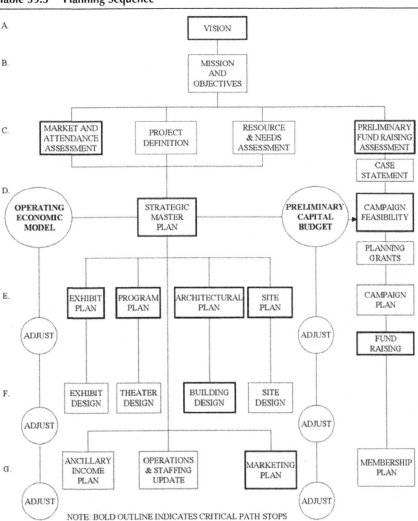

Table 59.4   Key Characteristics of a Museum Model

Planning Worksheets	Status	Action
Key service markets		
Community role		
Profile of visitors, program participants, and supporters		
Market size		
Purposes		
Mission and vision		
Intentional purposes and desired impacts		
Guiding principles		
Museum type and accreditation goals		
Values and corporate culture		
Brand positioning and reputation		
Earned/support revenue balance by policy		
Resources		
Ownership: leadership and governance		
Collections (e.g., yes/no, what kind?, where?)		
Capital assets (site, building, endowment)		
Facility size in gross square feet		
Components (galleries, theaters, program spaces)		
Public spaces in net square feet		
Human resources (in number of full-time equivalents)		
Activities		
Community needs assessment		
Programming plan		
Operations		
Operating economic model		
Marketing and development strategies		
Analysis		
Attendance potential		
Planning		
Schedule and implementation		
Capital and preopening costs		
Next steps		

Table 59.5   Choosing Where to Excel

Level	Product	Access	Experience	Price	Services
Dominate—choose only one					
Distinguished—choose another one only					
Acceptable—make sure other three are here					
Unacceptable—none in this row					

Source: Sheppard and Falk (2006).

Table 59.6   Logic Model Template

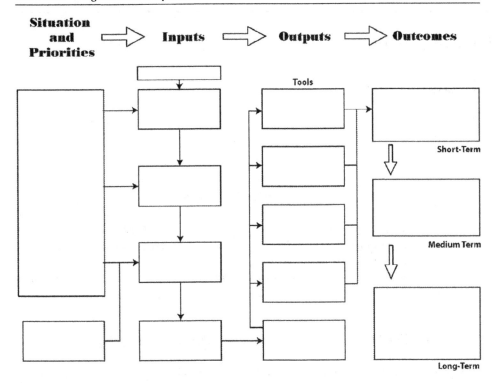

Section 60

Museum Planning

Process and Scope

INTRODUCTION

Museums contemplating a planning process need to think through the scale and detail of the process. Is this a master planning process involving a year of consensus building among a large number of stakeholders, documented in formal reports? Or is this a quick-action turnaround on a pressing issue or something in between?

You can use this questionnaire as a discussion outline among your museum's leadership to identify the planning process that is right for your museum and your resources.

MUSEUM PLANNING: PROCESS AND SCOPE QUESTIONS

1. What is the purpose of this analysis and planning initiative? How will the results be used, and by whom? (start with this question first but revisit at the end)
2. How are we defining "analysis and planning?" How many years? What are we planning?
3. What research steps should inform this process?
   - ☐ Market demographic and psychographic profiles by zones
   - ☐ Visitor and nonvisitor research (quantitative and qualitative front-end evaluation)
   - ☐ Crowdsource opinion analysis
   - ☐ Gap analysis for access to cultural and educational facilities
   - ☐ Community needs analysis (stakeholder interviews and report)
   - ☐ Virtual presence analysis and assessment (Web, social media, cyberlearning)
   - ☐ Opportunity assessments (brief studies comparing options and economics)
   - ☐ Best practices: models to consider (slide show and briefing)
   - ☐ Potential creative transformational ideas (workshop and slide show)
   - ☐ Current space use and infrastructure analysis and recommendations (report)
   - ☐ Current museum operating data versus comparable museums and recommendations (report)
   - ☐ Feasibility of economic model and business plan (report and workbook)
   - ☐ Campaign feasibility
4. Who should be involved in which parts of the planning process?
5. What process best suits the museum and the Strategic Planning Committee (SPC)? (assume a combination of board and staff managers)
   - ☐ A hands-on SPC engagement in researching, creating, and writing the plan
   - ☐ A series of workshops where the SPC members guide an evolving, facilitated plan
   - ☐ An external creative process presented periodically to the SPC for review
   - ☐ A staff- and consultant-driven process with only key policy questions brought to the SPC
6. What final output will best serve the museum's needs and meet stakeholder expectations?
   - ☐ A PowerPoint presentation of the top-level plan summary
   - ☐ A short, attractive written executive summary of the plan
   - ☐ A short, informal concept plan with a transformational vision creatively presented
   - ☐ An illustrated, large-format museum vision booklet for potential supporters

☐ A straightforward master plan listing mission, vision, values, four to six strategic goals, and around five years' worth of objectives, initiatives, and tasks under each goal

☐ A multichapter strategic master plan integrating all aspects in an implementation blueprint

☐ Economic pro formas and budgets: operating and capital

☐ Architect's and site developer's proposed site design

☐ A final document that the SPC recommends for adoption by the museum's full board

7. What resources, time, and attention do we want to invest in our analysis and planning process? What impact do we wish it to have?

Section 61

Servant of Four Masters Model

INTRODUCTION

The four categories that make up the museum's audiences and supporters—visitors, program participants, public supporters, and private supporters—are also the museum's sources of potential revenue. A museum with regular revenues from all four *service market sectors* must be a *servant of four masters*, as illustrated in table 61.1.

SERVANT OF FOUR MASTERS MODEL

In table 61.1, the horizontal axis is support revenue, and the vertical axis is earned revenue. This table illustrates the need to find the sweet spot: a museum plan that provides enough benefits efficiently to enough sectors to sustain operations.

Table 61.1   Servant of Four Masters

Section 62

Theory of Action

Definitions

1. Theory of Action: "Theory-Based Evaluation in Practice (TBE) is an approach to evaluation that requires stating the assumptions on which the program is based in considerable detail: what activities are conducted, what effect from each activity, what the program does next, what the expected response is, what happens next, and so on, to the expected outcomes"[1] (Birckmayer & Weiss, 2000).
2. The museum theory of action hypothesizes that a museum, in service to its community, decides on its intentional purposes. Then, guided by its principles, the museum uses its resources to operate activities for its community, audiences, and supporters that result in benefits and other impacts. Engagements with these activities generate operating and evaluation data that can be incorporated into key performance indicators (KPIs) that monitor the museum's effectiveness and efficiency.
3. A museum's *intentional purposes* (aka mission, vision, goals, strategies, and objectives) aspire to lead to its *desired impacts* (aka outcomes, impacts, benefits, and ends). There are also other unacknowledged and *unintended impacts* from a museum's operation, some of which may be beneficial.
4. A museum uses its long-term *resources* to pursue its purposes. Resources include a museum's *capital resources*, such as its endowment, land, buildings, collections, equipment, and exhibits; *human resources*, such as staff, leadership, contractors, and suppliers; and *intangible assets*, such as its reputation, location, community relationships, brand identity, and historic legacy. Resources are long-term and capital considerations.
5. *Resource indicators*, such as the number of staff and the square feet of a gallery space, report status at the end of the fiscal year, with an explanation of any significant changes in status.
6. A museum uses its resources to produce and deliver its operational *activities*, such as its visitor experiences, conservation work, exhibitions, research, theater presentations, marketing campaigns, projects, and programs. Activities aspire to have effective impacts and benefits and to achieve these with efficient resource-to-output ratios. Activities are operational considerations.
7. Activities are the vehicles or instruments for the delivery of the museum's *impacts* and *benefits*. An activity, such as curating an artist's retrospective exhibition, is not an impact or benefit per se, but the process of producing it and the eventual public engagement with the exhibition can have outcomes including preserving heritage, enhancing public knowledge, developing economic impact, and enabling personal growth. To what degree the activity actually generates such impacts and benefits is an evaluation question, parallel to the larger question of whether the museum actually achieves its purposes.
8. With a few exceptions, such as catalog publications and educational kits, a museum's activities deliver *services*, not *products*. Museums are in the service sector as well as in the cultural and educational sectors. Weil (2002) flips the emphasis from mission to services: "The emerging public-service-oriented museum must see itself not as a cause but as an instrument . . . [and] to be of profound service, to use their competencies to enrich the quality of individual lives and to enhance their community's well-being" (p. 49).

See "15. Bibliography for Museums" for citation references.

Section 63

Museum Theory of Action

Rationale

INTRODUCTION

The museum theory of action assumes that a museum produces its values through a sequence of steps. In this theory, a museum produces its impacts and benefits through iterations of a sequence of logic model-like steps, as described in the following constructed narrative: (1) museum leadership (and/or other forces), in response to perceived community needs and aspirations, determine the museum's intentional purposes; (2) leadership and staff filter the many possibilities for achieving those purposes by the museum's guiding principles to select the museum's desired impacts and their target audiences and supporters; and (3) staff, with their knowledge of the museum's resources, produce (e.g., plan, design, test, fabricate/create, market, deliver, and operate) (4) the museum's activities, using a constantly iterative cycle of (5) evaluation and operating data that feed into (6) the museum's key performance indicators that monitor (7) the impacts and benefits the museum is providing its audiences and funders, which feed back to the beginning as one source of their perceived community needs and aspirations (see table 63.1).

The museum theory of action is useful in three ways: (1) provide a framework to see what a museum is actually doing now and evaluate the alignment between intentions and results ("documentation"), (2) provide guidance to museum managers about decisions about the future ("planning"), and (3) provide researchers and evaluators with a shared framework for evaluating the impact and performance of museums ("evaluation").

You can adapt the museum theory of action as a template for narrating how your museum will achieve its purposes. For a complete description and rationale for the museum theory of action, see Jacobsen (2016, chap. 1).

MUSEUM THEORY OF ACTION: FROM INTENDED PURPOSES TO PERCEIVED BENEFITS

The museum theory of action follows the sequence of a classic logic model, revised to loop back to the beginning. There are feedback cycles even within the seven steps. The museum evaluates the outputs and outcomes of all its activities in order to prove and improve their efficiency and effectiveness at delivering the museum's intentional purposes.

Of course, audiences and funders have other ways of voicing their needs and aspirations, and museum practice often veers from this linear sequence. In practice, decisions and actions within the museum culture seem more weblike than linear: The marketing department wants to engage teens, development is courting a collector of animation cells, education wants to script some teen workshops, and a curator has been itching to do a popular culture show, and suddenly the museum has booked the *Pixar* traveling exhibition. Such webs of interest can drive decisions that escape the theory of action's intentional sequence, particularly when staff initiate activities ahead of leadership, but this theory of action intends to reflect the fullest, most responsible and thoughtful sequence.

See "15. Bibliography for Museums" for citation reference.

Table 63.1   The Museum Theory of Action: Logic Model Version

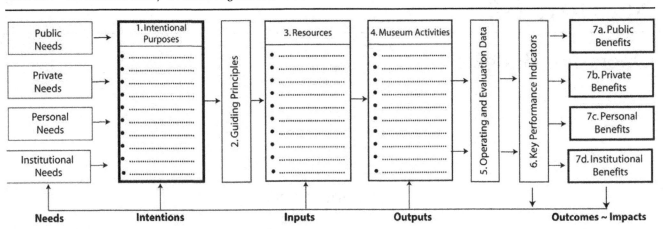

Section 64

Operating Budgets

INTRODUCTION

As in any business, financial planning is critical to sustainability. Institutional budgets and projections will be developed annually and updated periodically during the fiscal year. Monthly reports will be shared with management staff and, at minimum, quarterly reports shared with the board.

A large organization will involve department heads in the process. A small organization may require only the museum's director and finance officer to be involved. In all cases, the board, often based on the recommendation of the Board Finance Committee, will approve the annual budget as well as budget revisions during the year. An ongoing goal should be set to operate with a surplus in the black.

This section provides a broad overview of operating budgets. It includes sample budgets and reports from a number of museums to illustrate the formats that you might adopt.

This section written by contributing authors Duane Kocik and Jeanie Stahl.

OPERATING BUDGETS

Budgeting Process

Following are aspects of the budgeting process, including suggested time frames for meetings and budget updates:

1. Assemble budget teams.
2. Affirm and circulate the museum's strategic plan and institutional objectives.
   a. Ask each department how they plan to support the plan and objectives.
   b. Discuss these as a group and decide on priorities.
3. For existing museums:
   a. Review trends performance in prior years.
   b. Review current-year budget to prior-year actual performance and include meetings with department heads and managers.
   c. Analyze the real cost of existing programs and whether they result in a net surplus or deficit.
   d. Based on historic data and projected trends, set preliminary financial goals to be achieved by each division or team.
4. Review any plans for exhibit or program changes to core components of the museum and any impact they might have on attendance and revenue.
5. Review prebooked films and temporary and traveling exhibits and likely appeal and impact on the budget year(s).
6. Consider having a pricing study to help determine the market value of program offerings. National and local comparisons may be helpful.
7. Align institutional goals with actual revenue and expense streams.
8. Develop departmental budgets ideally based on preliminary financial goals.
9. Develop an overall institution budget that tests the preliminary budget goals.
10. Develop monthly cash flow.
11. Develop dashboard of key performance indicators and key data.
12. Track dashboard daily, weekly, and/or monthly.
13. Track budget to actuals on a monthly or weekly basis for some major components.
14. Update projections monthly based on actual year-to-date performance.

Table 64.1 Sample Summary Five-Year Budget for a New Museum

Fiscal Year End:	Yr 1	Base Yr 1	Year 2	Year 3	Stable Yr Year 4	Year 5	Yr 4
On-Site Attendance		xx	xx	xx	xx	xx	
Attendance Index		xx	xx	xx	100	xx	
REVENUE							
Visitor Earned Revenue	%						%
Program Earned Revenue	%						%
Public Support	%						%
Private Support	%						%
SUBTOTAL EXTERNAL REVENUE	%	$	$	$	$	$	%
Endowment and Interest Income	%						%
Transfers - Operating Support Fund	%						%
TOTAL SUPPORT/REV	100%	$	$	$	$	$	100%
EXPENSES							
Visitor Services & Programs	%	$	$	$	$	$	%
Overhead & Support	%	$	$	$	$	$	%
TOTAL EXPENSES	100%	$	$	$	$	$	100%
SURPLUS/(DEFICIT)		$	$	$	$	$	
Transfers to Reserve Fund		$	$	$	$	$	
SURPLUS/(DEFICIT) after Transfers		$	$	$	$	$	
Wages & Benefits		$	$	$	$	$	
Wages/Benefits % of Exps pre Transfers		%	%	%	%	%	

15. Present quarterly budget-to-actual to the Board Finance Committee.
16. Adjust budget as needed if significantly off from projections.
17. Seek board approval of budget and any midyear revisions

Sample Budget Templates

There are many resources available that address operating budgets and financial management in depth. Books on finance and budgeting are available from museum associations and publishers that focus on the museum industry. In addition, museum associations post resources on their websites. Basic information can be found for free online.

Tables 64.1 and 64.2 are samples of a summary and a detailed institution-wide departmental operating budget for a midsize to large museum. Staffing costs are usually embedded in each department, though it is important to develop side calculations to monitor total staff and benefit costs versus nonstaff or OTP (other than personnel) costs. Smaller organizations usually develop budgets by functional expense and not by department, as shown in table 64.3.

The budget template in table 64.1 is for a new museum, and the format is based on the suggested ways to analyze revenue as presented in this book. It uses the definitions of visitors and program participants.

Note that under revenue, there is a line for "Transfers from the Operating Support Fund." This fund is to support the museum in the first years after opening, as donors to the capital campaign will still be paying off pledges from the campaign. As a result, annual giving and often sponsorship in the first few years are likely to be lower than in future years.

In both the larger and the smaller museum budgets, the presentation is for internal purposes and is not the format used for reporting on audited financial statements or IRS 990 tax returns. One significant difference is that amortization and depreciation are generally not included in museum budget templates, but this is an ongoing concern. Many museums are not funding items like building repairs and then are forced to launch capital campaigns to pay for long-overdue repairs. It is recommended that a building reserve fund be established and funded.

Table 64.2 presents a detailed version of the budget. Note that in this budget, sponsorship is counted as support revenue, whereas in the sample board-approved budget in table 64.4, it is counted as earned revenue. Different museums categorize it differently. Some museums count grants as earned revenue, as grants often have deliverables, such as outreach programs or programs for schoolchildren.

Table 64.2 Sample Five-Year Budget for a Noncollections Museum

	Yr				Stable Yr		Yr
Fiscal Year End:	1	Base Yr 1	Year 2	Year 3	Year 4	Year 5	4
On-Site Attendance		*xx*	*xx*	*xx*	*xx*	*xx*	
Attendance Index		*xx*	*xx*	*xx*	*100*	*xx*	
REVENUE							
Earned Revenue	%						%
Admissions Revenue	%						%
All Program Rev (no grants)	%						%
Membership	%						%
Ancillary Income	%						%
Store (net income)	%						%
Café and Vending (net income)	%						%
Function Rentals (w. catering net)	%						%
Miscellaneous	%						%
Interest Income	%						%
Support	%						%
Annual Giving & Major Gifts	%						%
Corporate Grants & Sponsorships	%						%
Grants - Foundation	%						%
Grants - Government	%						%
Grants - Program Specific	%						%
Government Funding	%						%
Special Fund-raising Events (net)	%						%
Endowment Income	%						%
Transfers - Operating Support Fund	%						%
TOTAL SUPPORT/REV	100%						100%
Ratio of earned to total rev.	%	%	%	%	%	%	
Earned revenue dollars	$						$
Support & Endowment (excl. Transfers)	%						%
EXPENSES							
Visitor Services & Programs	%						%
Exhibits and Multi-Purpose Thtr	%						%
Education Center	%						%
Theater	%						%
Visitor Services	%						%
Function Rentals	%						%
Membership	%						%
Overhead & Support	%						%
Development	%						%
Admin & Finance	%						%
Information Services	%						%
President's Office	%						%
Marketing and Community Relations	%						%
Facilities	%						%
TOTAL EXPENSES	100%						100%
SURPLUS/(DEFICIT) pre Transfers to Reserve Fund							
Wages & Benefits as % of Exps pre Transfers		%	%	%	%	%	

Table 64.3   Sample List of Functional Expenses for a Small-Museum Budget

Personnel:
  Salaries
  Employee benefits
  Health insurance
  Payroll taxes
  Payroll services
Personnel expenses:
  Advertising
  Bad debt expense
  Bank charges
  Computer software
Conferences, conventions, and meetings:
  Contract labor
  Dues and subscriptions
  Exhibit supplies
  Equipment rental
  Exhibit rental
  Insurance
    General liability
    Board of Directors and Officers
    Other
  Interest expense
Information technology, Internet, and communications:
  Meals and entertainment
  Miscellaneous
  Occupancy
    Utilities
    Groundskeeping
    Building repairs and maintenance
  Office supplies
  Postage
  Printing and reproduction
  Professional development
  Professional services (legal, accounting)
  Promotions
  Program supplies
  Purchases for resale, gift shop
  Recruiting
  Repairs and maintenance
  Special events
  Shipping and freight
  Telephone
  Travel
Nonpersonnel expenses
Total expenses

Reporting to the Board

Financial reports for the board are often in a different format than those used by museum management and department heads, but regardless of the format, all the numbers must align in the different versions. Table 64.4 is an example of a fiscal year budget presented for board approval.

In this example, "Visitor Services and Programs" expenses include exhibits, programs, membership, and retail. Earned revenue includes sponsorships, another example of different ways of categorizing what is earned revenue. The purpose of the template is to present format and math, not the specific numbers, which, though adapted from an existing museum, are somewhat arbitrary.

It is useful to add accompanying footnotes to the board reports. Some will include historical data as well as current projected data. Following are selected templates for footnotes:

1. Admissions: Attendance will be driven by two traveling exhibits, one on Da Vinci (September 15 through January 15) and a Rodin exhibit (April 5 through July 5). Overall admissions in fiscal year 2017 is expected to decrease compared to the prior year, as fiscal year 2016 included a blockbuster traveling exhibit.
2. Membership: Membership generally increases and decreases with attendance, but that trend can be altered with special holiday membership sales and by pushing membership during the Da Vinci and Rodin exhibits.
3. Federal Grants: The increase for the future budget year is based on a grant recently awarded, which makes up 85 percent of the budget line item. Three other grant proposals are outstanding, and we anticipate that one of them will be granted.
4. Visitor Services and Programs: These include operations related to earned revenue, including all attendance-related revenue, such as admissions, membership, ticket fees, retail, function rentals and catering, marketing, and public relations. *(Note: Some organizations do not include marketing and public relations as part of this grouping, but those expenses drive visitor attendance and program participation, and it is reasonable to include them here.)*

Table 64.8 is a sample board report showing current year-to-date performance as compared to the budget and also includes adjustments to the year-end forecast based on current-year performance to date. This report should be presented to the board at least quarterly.

Indirect and Overhead Cost Calculations

Granting organizations, such as the National Science Foundation, often award grants on the basis of reimbursing *direct expenses* plus an overhead rate, called *indirect expenses*, to cover the organization's general operating expenses. Table 64.9 is one accepted method for a museum to calculate and justify its indirect rate, in this case 45 percent. In principle, for every $100 in direct expenses, the museum can invoice the agency for $145; in practice, there are many rules and exclusions.

Indirect costs can typically be included in federal grant requests and be reimbursed to the organization. This same method can be used for other grants and is becoming more acceptable with state funding as well as some private funding sources. It never hurts to ask for reimbursement of all or some indirect costs in all grant requests. Check with grant authorities for the latest regulation as to what qualifies for indirect costs and request approval of your organization's indirect cost calculations.

Table 64.4 Sample Final Board-Approved Operating Budget

	PRIOR FY YY ACTUAL	CURRENT FY XX FORECAST	FUTURE FY ZZ BUDGET	VARIANCE: FY ZZ vs FY XX FORECAST		FOOTNOTES
REVENUE:						
Earned Income:						
Admissions	$ 2,200,000	$ 2,240,000	$ 1,650,000	(590,000)	-26%	A
Museum Stores	$ 440,000	$ 430,000	$ 410,000	(20,000)	-5%	B
Memberships	$ 890,000	$ 940,000	$ 940,000	-	0%	C
Food Service	$ 80,000	$ 80,000	$ 70,000	(10,000)	-13%	D
Program Fees	$ 420,000	$ 390,000	$ 420,000	30,000	8%	E
Sponsorships	$ 340,000	$ 380,000	$ 420,000	40,000	11%	F
Exhibit Sales/Rentals	$ 320,000	$ 280,000	$ 230,000	(50,000)	-18%	I
Total Earned Income:	**4,690,000**	**4,740,000**	**4,140,000**	**(600,000)**	**-13%**	
% of Total Income	*46%*	*49%*	*43%*			
Contributed Income:						
Public Funding:						
Federal	$ 2,260,000	$ 1,970,000	$ 2,420,000	450,000	23%	J
State	$ 1,160,000	$ 950,000	$ 920,000	(30,000)	-3%	K
Local	$ -	$ 10,000	$ 10,000	-	0%	
Total Public Funding:	**3,420,000**	**2,930,000**	**3,350,000**	**420,000**	**14%**	
Private Funding:						
Annual Giving	$ 1,140,000	$ 1,110,000	$ 1,200,000	90,000	8%	L
Project Grants	$ 550,000	$ 500,000	$ 530,000	30,000	6%	M
Total Private Funding:	**1,690,000**	**1,610,000**	**1,730,000**	**120,000**	**7%**	
Total Contributed Income:	**5,110,000**	**4,540,000**	**5,080,000**	**540,000**	**12%**	
% of Total Income	*50%*	*48%*	*53%*			
Endowment/Interest Income	**380,000**	**420,000**	**440,000**	**20,000**	**5%**	N
% of Total Income	*4%*	*4%*	*5%*			
TOTAL REVENUE	**10,180,000**	**9,700,000**	**9,660,000**	**(40,000)**	**0%**	
EXPENDITURES:						
Visitor Services & Programs	$ 6,050,000	$ 5,440,000	$ 5,280,000	(160,000)	-3%	O
Development	$ 740,000	$ 860,000	$ 890,000	30,000	3%	Q
Support Services	$ 2,680,000	$ 2,630,000	$ 2,730,000	100,000	4%	R
Contingency	$ 230,000	$ 250,000	$ 230,000	(20,000)	-8%	S
TOTAL EXPENDITURES	**9,700,000**	**9,180,000**	**9,130,000**	**(50,000)**	**-1%**	
SURPLUS / DEFICIT	**480,000**	**520,000**	**530,000**	**10,000**	**2%**	

Table 64.5   Footnotes to Board-Approved Fiscal Year 2017 Budget: Admissions

	Fiscal Year 2014 Actual	Fiscal Year 2015 Actual	Fiscal Year 2016 Projected	Fiscal Year 2017 Budget	2016–2017 % Change
Attendance					
Admission revenue					
Average ticket price					

Table 64.6   Footnotes to Board-Approved Fiscal Year 2017 Budget: Membership

	Fiscal Year 2014 Actual	*Fiscal Year 2015 Actual*	*Fiscal Year 2016 Projected*	*Fiscal Year 2017 Budget*	*2016–2017 % Change*
On-site attendance					%
Total membership revenue	$	$	$	$	%
Membership expense	$	$	$	$	%
Membership net surplus/(deficit)	$	$	$	$	%
No. of memberships at end of fiscal year	#	#	#	#	%
No. of household memberships	#	#	#	#	%
No. of dual memberships	#	#	#	#	%
No. of memberships, % of attendance	%	%	%	?	%

Table 64.7   Footnotes to Board-Approved Fiscal Year 2017 Budget: Federal Grants

	Fiscal Year 2014 Actual	*Fiscal Year 2015 Actual*	*Fiscal Year 2016 Projected*	*Fiscal Year 2017 Budget*	*2016–20177 % Change*
Federal grants					
No. of federal grants					

Table 64.8   Sample Operating Budget, Year to Date versus Actual

	CURRENT FY XX			2ND QUARTER ENDING CURRENT FY XX						PRIOR YEAR
	Annual Budget	Forecast changes	Annual Forecast Budget	YTD Budget	YTD Forecast	YTD Actual	YTD Actual Variance from Budget	YTD % Ahead (Behind) Budget	YTD Variance from Forecast	2ND QTR PRIOR YR ACTUAL
REVENUE:										
Earned Income:										
Admissions	1,880,000	210,000	2,090,000	800,000	920,000	940,000	140,000	18%	20,000	930,000
Museum Store	370,000	30,000	400,000	170,000	180,000	200,000	30,000	18%	20,000	190,000
Memberships	870,000	70,000	940,000	300,000	330,000	370,000	70,000	23%	40,000	360,000
Food Service	60,000	20,000	80,000	30,000	30,000	40,000	10,000	33%	10,000	30,000
Program Fees	470,000	(50,000)	420,000	210,000	210,000	210,000	0	0%	0	200,000
Sponsorships	360,000	0	360,000	180,000	180,000	170,000	(10,000)	-6%	(10,000)	180,000
Exhibit Sales/Rentals	340,000	(60,000)	280,000	170,000	150,000	100,000	(70,000)	-41%	(50,000)	190,000
Total Earned Income:	4,350,000	220,000	4,570,000	1,860,000	2,000,000	2,030,000	170,000	9%	30,000	2,080,000
Contributed Income:										
Public Funding:										
Federal	2,030,000	80,000	2,110,000	810,000	990,000	840,000	30,000	4%	(150,000)	1,080,000
State	1,030,000	(60,000)	970,000	460,000	490,000	440,000	(20,000)	-4%	(50,000)	440,000
Local	0	0	0	0	0	0	0	100%	0	10,000
Total Public Funding:	3,060,000	20,000	3,080,000	1,270,000	1,480,000	1,280,000	10,000	1%	(200,000)	1,530,000
Private Funding:										
Annual Giving	1,180,000	0	1,180,000	650,000	650,000	660,000	10,000	2%	10,000	690,000
Project Grants	830,000	(240,000)	590,000	340,000	340,000	250,000	(90,000)	-26%	(90,000)	220,000
Total Private Funding:	2,010,000	(240,000)	1,770,000	990,000	990,000	910,000	(80,000)	-8%	(80,000)	910,000
Total Contributed Income:	5,070,000	(220,000)	4,850,000	2,260,000	2,470,000	2,190,000	(70,000)	-3%	(280,000)	2,440,000
Endowment/Interest Income	420,000	0	430,000	210,000	210,000	210,000	0	0%	0	190,000
TOTAL REVENUE	9,840,000	10,000	9,850,000	4,330,000	4,680,000	4,430,000	100,000	2%	(250,000)	4,710,000
EXPENSES:										
Visitor Services & Programs	5,660,000	(230,000)	5,430,000	3,180,000	2,900,000	2,460,000	(720,000)	-23%	(440,000)	2,480,000
Development	810,000	(40,000)	770,000	400,000	380,000	310,000	(90,000)	-23%	(70,000)	280,000
Support Services	2,880,000	(110,000)	2,770,000	1,450,000	1,410,000	1,240,000	(210,000)	-14%	(170,000)	1,320,000
Contingency	260,000	30,000	280,000	110,000	110,000	100,000	(10,000)	-9%	(10,000)	90,000
TOTAL EXPENSES	9,610,000	(360,000)	9,250,000	5,140,000	4,800,000	4,110,000	(1,030,000)	-20%	(690,000)	4,170,000
SURPLUS/DEFICIT	230,000	370,000	600,000	(810,000)	(120,000)	320,000	1,130,000		(940,000)	540,000

Table 64.9 Indirect Cost Calculations

	AUDITED EXPENSE	MUSEUM ADMIN.	MUSEUM BID & PROPOSAL TIME (Grant Writing time)	TOTAL AUDITED EXPENSE	(A) ADJ'S	(B) Unallowed adjustments for transactional review	TOTAL ACTUAL
DIRECT COSTS OF OPERATIONS							
Galleries and Exhibition Halls	1,000,000	-	-	1,000,000	-		1,000,000
Collections	500,000	-	-	500,000	-		500,000
Live Performances	250,000	-	-	250,000	-		250,000
Exhibition Design and Development	2,000,000	(50,000)	(25,000)	1,925,000	(75,000)		1,850,000
Large format theater	1,000,000	-	-	1,000,000	-		1,000,000
Education Programs	1,500,000	-	(25,000)	1,475,000			1,475,000
Marketing & Public Relations	1,000,000	-	-	1,000,000	-		1,000,000
Membership	200,000	-	-	200,000	-		200,000
Retail Store	750,000	-	-	750,000	-		750,000
Fundraising - Development	500,000	(25,000)	-	475,000	-		475,000
Volunteer Service Costs	100,000	-	-	100,000	100,000		200,000
Parking Ramp	500,000	-	-	500,000	(100,000)		400,000
TOTAL DIRECT	**9,300,000**	**(75,000)**	**(50,000)**	**9,175,000**	**(75,000)**	**-**	**9,100,000**
INDIRECT COST OF OPERATIONS							
Bid and Proposals	-	-	25,000	25,000	-		25,000
Human Resources	350,000	-	-	350,000	-	(50,000)	300,000
Finance	525,000	-	-	525,000	(75,000)		450,000
Museum Administration	750,000	75,000	-	825,000	-		825,000
Interest Expense	495,000	-	-	495,000	-		495,000
Building Operations/Maint.	1,000,000	-	-	1,000,000	(500,000)		500,000
Information Technology Services	500,000	-	-	500,000	-	-	500,000
Depreciation	2,000,000	-	-	2,000,000	(1,000,000)		1,000,000
TOTAL INDIRECT	**5,620,000**	**75,000**	**25,000**	**5,720,000**	**(1,575,000)**	**(50,000)**	**4,095,000**
TOTAL EXPENSES	**14,920,000**	**-**	**(25,000)**	**14,895,000**	**(1,650,000)**	**(50,000)**	**13,195,000**
% INDIRECT COST							**45.00%**

PLANNING WORKSHEET

The museum's business lines—its admissions venues, gift shop, program revenues, grants, fund-raisers, and so on—have a strategic mix of sources of revenue based on maximizing the types of revenue available to each business line.

You can use table 64.10 to plan relative revenue shares for your museum's main and contemplated business lines.

Table 64.10 Aligning Revenues to Business Lines

Revenues	Business Lines		Total
	Museum Galleries	Retail	
Earned $—visitors			
Earned $—programs			
Support $—public			
Support $—private			
Subtotal: external revenue			
Endowment income			
Totals			

Section 65

Operating Data Standards

INTRODUCTION

Do you count visitors or visits? Do you count them once or twice if they buy a combination ticket? How do you measure average dwell time? How many partnerships do you have today? Do you include function rental guests in your annual attendance? How are you doing compared to your peers?

The only way you can answer the last question is if your peers answer the previous types of questions using the same definitions. To improve individual museums as well as the field as a whole, we need shared data definitions and data collection methods.

The philanthropic sector now demands metrics through donor-funded initiatives, such as the Cultural Data Project (by Data-Arts) and Charity Navigator. Charity Navigator's system focuses on "the two most important questions ever to face the sector: how to define the value of all the work we are doing, and how to measure that value . . . [in pursuit] of how to identify high-performing nonprofits and how to better direct donors' contributions to them" (Berger, Penna, & Goldberg, 2010). In addition to their ratings based on fiscal metrics, Charity Navigator is working on approaches based on measuring impact.

The Cultural Data Project's (CDP, now by DataArts) 2013 analysis by Sarah Lee and Peter Linett of the use of data in the cultural sector, which includes museums, performing arts, and other cultural nonprofits, found that

we face an abundance of data about the cultural sphere. But it is not yet clear that the cultural sector is making effective and strategic use of all of this data. The field seems to be approaching an inflection point, where the long-term health, sustainability, and effectiveness of cultural organizations depend critically on investment in and collective action around enhancing the field's capacity for using data strategically and thoughtfully to inform decision-making. (Lee & Linett, 2013)

The CDP's report also found issues with nonstandardization of data definitions, which means that all these data cannot be aggregated easily.

This section reports on efforts to establish museum operating data standards. As this is a dynamic field, you should research the current status, see if your most relevant associations have adopted any set of definitions, and then reflect their selections in your internal data collection standards.

MUSEUM OPERATING DATA STANDARDS (MODS)

There are existing standards and initiatives looking at aspects of the larger challenge of standardizing museum data definitions:

- DataArts (formerly the CDP) established rigorous standards and reporting mechanisms for collecting, aggregating, and reporting on financial data from grant-seeking, cultural nonprofits, and they are adding programmatic data fields.
- The American Association for State and Local History has standardized comparison and assessment resources in their Visitors Count! survey and StEPs program.
- The Association of Science-Technology Centers and the Association of Art Museum Directors have established definitions for member surveys in the science center and art museum sectors, respectively. The American Alliance of Museums (AAM) has a set of definitions for its online member survey.
- The Association of Children's Museums (ACM) established its online ACM Benchmark Calculator, which goes further to suggest shared key performance indicators.
- The Museum of Science (Boston) established a national Collaboration for Ongoing Visitor Experience Studies to develop shared metrics related to the visitor experience and its learning outcomes.

- The White Oak Institute (WOI), partnered with the Museum of Science's evaluation department to develop the Museum Indicators of Impact and Performance evaluation model.
- The MODS initiative of 2007–2011 was an AAM and White Oak Institute joint initiative that successfully engaged other museum associations to support the goal of shared definitions; this led to the following:
    - Recommended Data Definitions for the census of the Institute of Museum and Library Services (IMLS), which IMLS contracted WOI and AAM to

develop with the field. This resulted in the IMLS's Draft Museums Count Survey Instrument (2012; unused so far)
- ISO 18461: 2016 International Museum Statistics with definitions and data collection methods developed by the Swiss international standards organization in collaboration with ICOM and EGMUS (European Group on Museum Statistics) and referencing the IMLS's survey instrument

See "15. Bibliography for Museums" for citation references.

Section 66

Peer Performance Assessments

INTRODUCTION

Comparing a museum's key performance indicators with those of peer museums is an informative exercise that helps museum leadership see where your museum excels and where there may be growth or efficiency potentials. Comparing a museum's metrics to the average and mean of a sample of peer museums becomes more meaningful as the definition of peer gets closer to the museum's unique definition and as the sample size gets larger.

Your museum is likely to have lessons to teach and some to learn. A corollary idea is to establish a positive and collaborative relationship among your peers. From this network you will learn their best practices and use that information to improve your impact and performance, raising the bar for your network and for the museum field as a whole. If you are in separate markets, you are not competing but rather helping each other. You have a lot to share with your peers, ideally with collective gain over the years, expanding and shifting the membership of the peer group as each museum evolves in purposes and resources.

The management approach called *appreciative inquiry* starts such comparisons on a positive note, asking more about what is going well and how to maximize it than the alternative *deficit inquiry* model, which investigates what is going poorly and focuses on fixing it.

This process is about comparing your performance in your selected areas of impact and performance to that of your peers. Find out what you do better than the norm and what you could improve. This outline is detailed in Jacobsen (2016, chap. 7).

This section includes contributions by Jeanie Stahl.

PEER PERFORMANCE ASSESSMENTS

Peer museums are as follows:

- The Same Type, Discipline, or Sector of the Museum Field: This includes other collection-based art museums or other historic house museums or municipal zoos.
- Funded by Similar Business Models: Peer museums will have similar revenue sources, which can be approximated by looking at their share of earned to support revenue and, within support, to the relative share of public or private funding. A government or university museum with free admission is not a peer to a museum dependent on admissions revenues.
- Operators of Similar Resources: A museum's operating data are shaped by its physical resources (site, facility, collections, and exhibits), human resources, and endowment. Ideally, meaningful comparables should have roughly the same components, building size, staff size, annual budget, and/or capital assets.
- Located in Contexts as Similar as Possible: Comparable museums should be in cities, communities, or markets of similar size, ideally in the same climate and with similar disposable household incomes and similar education levels (two key indicators of museum attendance). Similar governance and control are needed, as university, government, and nonprofit mandates are different. Location is also a factor: urban or suburban, unique building or tenant in a complex, or coastal or central.

When enough museums share these filters, they form a peer group that can start to make meaningful comparisons and assess relative performance for specific key performance indicators (KPIs). Such data comparisons have been useful to several sectors of the museum field to guide management, evaluation, and advocacy.

We can compare performance among peer museums once we make some basic assumptions or rules about the sample of peers:

Table 66.1   Facility Size—Total Square Footage

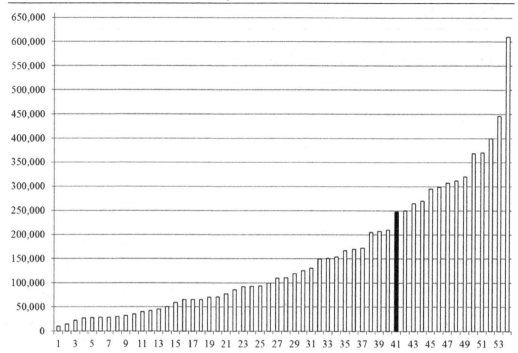

Source: Data are derived from various years of ASTC Science Center Statistics, copyright © Association of Science-Technology Centers, Washington, DC, http://www.astc.org.

Table 66.2   Interior Exhibit Square Footage

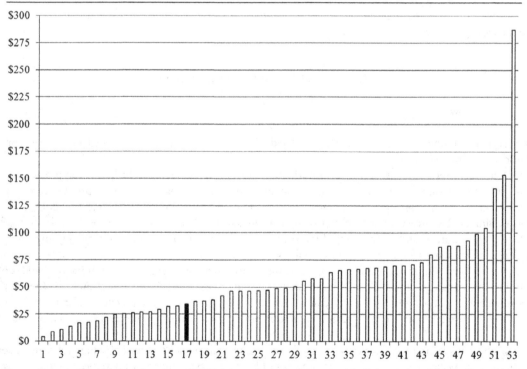

Source: Data are derived from various years of ASTC Science Center Statistics, copyright © Association of Science-Technology Centers, Washington, DC, http://www.astc.org.

Table 66.3   Gate Attendance to Exhibit Square Footage

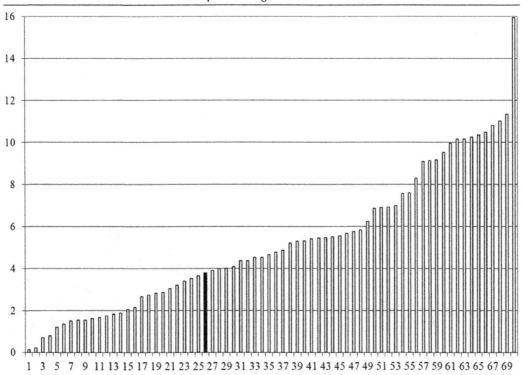

Source: Data are derived from various years of ASTC Science Center Statistics, copyright © Association of Science-Technology
Centers, Washington, DC, http://www.astc.org.

Table 66.4   School On-Site Attendance to Metropolitan Population

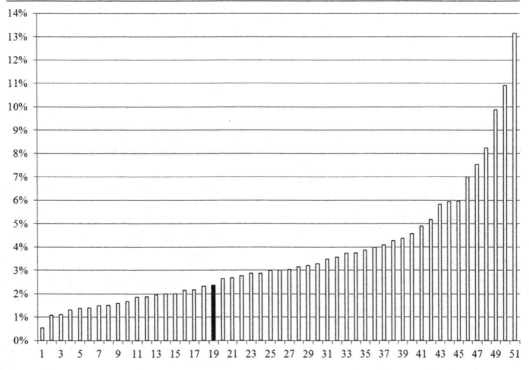

Source: Data are derived from various years of ASTC Science Center Statistics, copyright © Association of Science-Technology
Centers, Washington, DC, http://www.astc.org.

Table 66.5   School Percentage of Gate Attendance

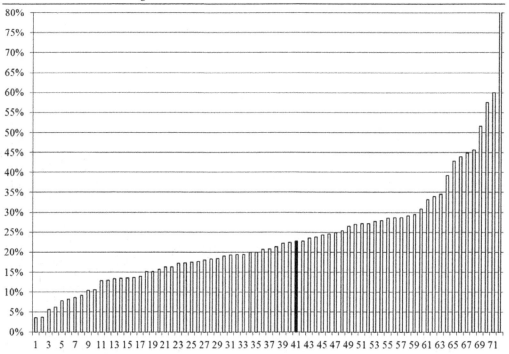

Source: Data are derived from various years of ASTC Science Center Statistics, copyright © Association of Science-Technology Centers, Washington, DC, http://www.astc.org.

Table 66.6   Revenue by Category

	Sample Study Museum	ASTC Data (N = 75)	Museum Variance
Earned	78%	49%	29%
Public	15%	18%	3%
Private	7%	28%	21%
Endowment	0%	3%	(3%)

- The sample will contain peer museums of the same type and with similar business models, resources, and contexts, with anomalies noted. Your museum is included in the sample of peer museums, appearing near the middle of the sample when sorted by population, budget, or size.
- You and your peers use identical data definitions for all compared data fields and ideally share data for the same year or, at most, one year apart.
- The museum participates in relevant data-sharing systems, particularly those run by the museum associations, the government (the Institute of Museum and Library Services and the Internal Revenue Service in the United States), and DataArts (formerly the Cultural Data Project in certain U.S. states).
- Enough of your peers have reported these data fields to create a meaningful sample.

The Process of Peer Comparisons

1. Select an existing or create a new museum database with consistent sources for peer museum operating data.
2. Identify standard sources of high-quality community and other external data, such as metropolitan population, community diversity, and household income.
3. Filter the database for peer museums by using bracketed filters for this first cut: type of museum, business model (similar share of earned to support revenue), market population (the context), and the museum's scale and resources (size or annual expense budget).
4. Look at the museums on the list if they are named. Do you think of them as peers?
5. Create other kinds of museum groups for other kinds of comparisons.

Table 66.7   Earned Revenue Percentage of Total Revenue

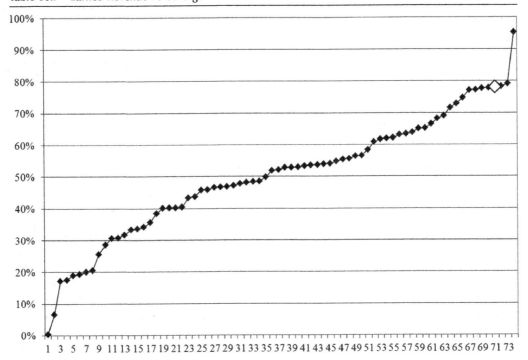

Source: Data are derived from various years of ASTC Science Center Statistics, copyright © Association of Science-Technology Centers, Washington, DC, http://www.astc.org.

Table 66.8   Earned Revenue per On-Site Visit

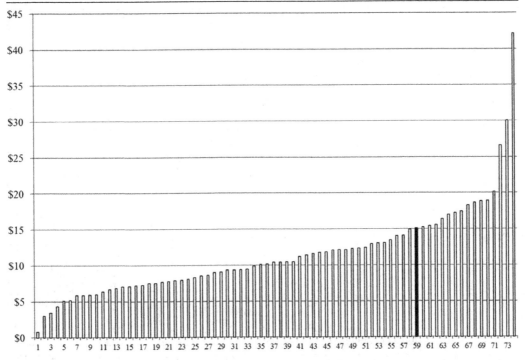

Source: Data are derived from various years of ASTC Science Center Statistics, copyright © Association of Science-Technology Centers, Washington, DC, http://www.astc.org.

Table 66.9   Public Funding per On-Site Visit

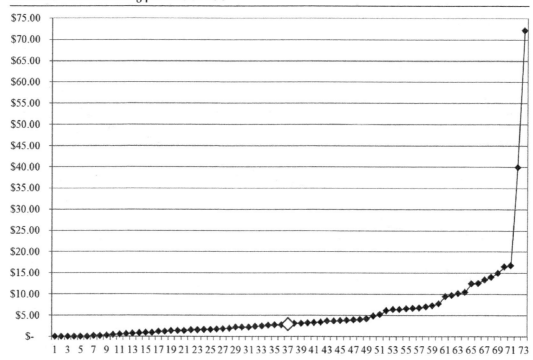

Source: Data are derived from various years of ASTC Science Center Statistics, copyright © Association of Science-Technology Centers, Washington, DC, http://www.astc.org.

Table 66.10   Expenses per Building Square Foot

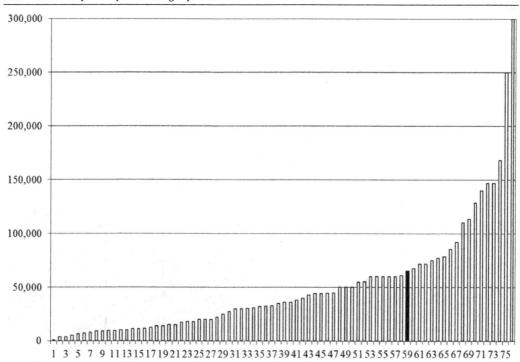

Source: Data are derived from various years of ASTC Science Center Statistics, copyright © Association of Science-Technology Centers, Washington, DC, http://www.astc.org.

Table 66.11   Personnel Expenses Percentage of Total Expenses

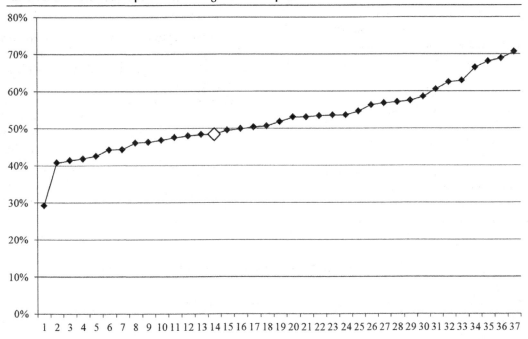

Source: Data are derived from various years of ASTC Science Center Statistics, copyright © Association of Science-Technology Centers, Washington, DC, http://www.astc.org.

Table 66.12   Membership Renewal Rate

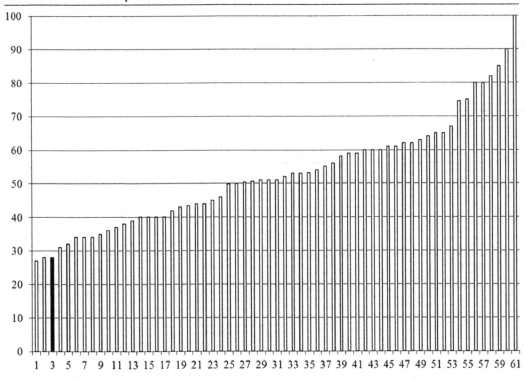

Source: Data are derived from various years of ASTC Science Center Statistics, copyright © Association of Science-Technology Centers, Washington, DC, http://www.astc.org.

6. Circulate a draft list of peer museums to the core team and others knowledgeable about other similar museums.
7. Import peer museum data already in your selected database into an Excel worksheet for analysis.
8. Ask your peer museums to review, proof, and add to their data.
9. Calculate the KPIs for each peer museum.
10. Determine the median and average of the sample.
11. Compare your KPIs.
12. Research and analyze why your museum may be performing outside peer norms.
13. Study peers' best practices and incorporate lessons learned into planning and implementation
14. Share your experiences with the museum field so that your sector and all museums can improve.

Sample Peer Sector Comparison Charts for a Family Museum

This section compares data for one Association of Science-Technology Centers (ASTC) member museum to others of the same discipline, as opposed to a small group of peers with similar characteristics.

The data in tables 66.1 to 66.12 are derived from various years of ASTC Science Center Statistics (copyright © Association of Science-Technology Centers, Washington, D.C., http://www.astc.org). The black bar or white diamond in each chart represents the same member museum.

These data are for family science centers. Do not assume that the numbers apply to other disciplines and key visitor segments.

PLANNING WORKSHEETS

Table 66.13   Peer Museums: Data Entry and Key Performance Indicator (KPI) Calculations

Museum Name	City	State	Country	Total Indoor Facility Sq. Ft.	Total Interior Exhibit Sq. Ft.	Exh Sq. Ft. % of Total	Fiscal Year End	On-site Atten-dance	Operating Expenses	Payroll and Benefit Exps	Exps per Tot. Sq. Ft.	Expenses per Visit	Payroll % of Expenses	# Full-time Employees	# Part-time Employees	# Full-Time Equivalent Employees	# FTE per Visit
Data	*Data*	*Data*	*Data*	*Data*	*Data*	*KPI*	*Data*		*Data*	*Data*	*KPI*	*KPI*	*KPI*	*Data*	*Data*	*Data*	*KPI*
Museum A																	
Museum B																	
Museum C																	
The Study Museum																	
Museum D																	
Museum E																	
Museum F																	
Excluding the Study Museum																	
Average																	
Median																	
High																	
Low																	

Museum Name	City	Adult Tx Price	Total Earned Income	Total Public Funds	Total Private Funds	Endowment Income for Operations	Total Operating Revenue	% Earned Revenue of Total Rev.	% Public Funds of Total Revenue	% Private Funds of Total Revenue	% Endowment of Total Revenue
Data	*Data*	*Data*	*Data*	*Data*	*Data*	*Data*	*Data*	*KPI*	*KPI*	*KPI*	*KPI*
Museum A											
Museum B											
Museum C											
The Study Museum											
Museum D											
Museum E											
Museum F											
Excluding the Study Museum											
Average											
Median											
High											
Low											

Note: Shaded sections are calculated KPIs.

It is extremely useful to compare the museum's performances to that of its peers, with the caveat that it is important to know the anomalies for each museum. One museum might have free admission, another a large endowment, and another a large tourist population. There are many more data points and KPIs that can be tracked.

See "15. Bibliography for Museums" for citation reference.

Section 67

Policy Choices

INTRODUCTION

In the Carver model of policy governance (see "38. Governance Policy Statements"), a museum's board establishes policy, and the staff, led by the chief executive officer, develop strategies to implement the policies. The board's policy guidance becomes management's intentional purposes and guiding principles.

Policy, however, is a broad term. Governance must be guided to articulate policy in the areas most needed by management: What are our purposes? Whom should we serve? How should we serve them? What resources do we pursue, and what components do we offer the public? What is our business model? How do we evaluate our impact and performance? What is our capital fund-raising capacity? These policy questions should be addressed by the museum's governing body; in mature museums, management and staff can then implement their policy directions.

This section contains a wide selection of policy-scale exercises that may be selected and adapted to suit your museum (see tables 67.1 to 67.34). These have been used in board-level policy guidance workshops. Each is intended to be printed out on 11- by 17-inch paper and taped to the walls surrounding the boardroom table. Facilitators introduce each group of questions with the pros, cons, and definitions, showing case studies of different options. Discussion follows. Participants then place specified numbers of small dots along the scales, indicating where they would like to see the museum be in the future (sometimes a star indicates where the museum is now). At the end, the facilitator goes around the room interpreting the pattern of dots: If all dots cluster, there is consensus on policy direction; if they are dispersed, either participants want some of everything along the scale or more discussion is needed to arrive at consensus. Sample interpretation: "On this Resident–Tourist scale, it looks like most of you want the museum to serve about three-quarters residents and one-quarter tourists. On this one about age range, however, there is enough difference of opinion about the museum's age focus that this topic should be reviewed at a future meeting." A four-hour workshop typically can handle 30 to 40 policy scales.

POLICY SCALE EXERCISES AND CHOICES

Table 67.1   Categories of Purpose

Broadening participation
Public knowledge
Identity and image
Social capital
Education
Social change
Economic value
Heritage preservation
Corporate community service
Personal growth, leisure, and respite

Table 67.2   Learning Outcomes (National Science Foundation Framework)

Knowledge
Awareness
Understanding
Skills
Attitudes
Behaviors
Interest and engagement

Table 67.3   Museum Outcomes

Empowering people
Enriching places
Inspiring ideas

Table 67.4   Add to the Quality of Life

A. Add to the Community's Quality of Life

Minimally Important |——————————————| Very Important

Table 67.5   Create Economic Value

B. Create Economic Value

Minimally Important |——————————————| Very Important

Table 67.6   Contribute to Heritage Preservation

C. Contribute to Heritage Preservation

Minimally Important |——————————————| Very Important

Table 67.7   Serve as a Center for Lifelong Learning

D. Serve as a Center for Lifelong Learning

Minimally Important |——————————————| Very Important

Table 67.8   Partner with Formal Education

Effect on Individuals

Ignite Learning |——————————————| Build Character

Table 67.9   Serve as Places of Memory

E. Partner with Formal Education

Minimally Important |——————————————| Very Important

Table 67.10   Effect on Individuals

F. Serve as Places of Memory

Minimally Important |——————————————| Very Important

Table 67.11   Social Context Framework

Adults visiting with children
   Preschoolers
   Ages 5 to 12
   Adolescents
School and youth groups
Adults ages 34 and up visiting with adults
Young adults ages 18 to 34 without children
Teens ages 13 to 18
Solo visitors ages 18 to 75 and up

Table 67.12   Adults with Children

Adults with Children
(YEARS DEVELOPMENTALLY)

| 0-2 | 3-5 | 6-8 | 9-10 | 11-12 |

Table 67.13   Primary Focus

Primary Focus

Family Focused |——————————————| Adult Focused

Table 67.14   Visitor Source

Visitor Source

Tourist |——————————————| Resident

Table 67.15   Audience Mix

Audience Mix

Visitors |——————————————| Program Participants

Table 67.16   Visitor Segments

Visitor Segments

General Visitors |——————————————| School Groups

Table 67.17   Symbiotic Partners

Tourism development
Corporate community
Public agencies (government)
Academic and university community
Cultural and community organizations
School and educational systems
Media partners
Community groups
Retail promotional partners
Other museums

Table 67.18   Relevant Museum Categories

Art museum/center/sculpture garden
Children's or youth museums
General or multidisciplinary museum (several subjects)
History museum/historical society
Science technology center
Visitor center/interpretive center

Table 67.19   Degree of Institutional Change Desired

Degree of Institutional Change Desired

Revolution |————————————————| Evolution

Table 67.20   What Kind of Museum

What Kind of Museum

Commercial Attraction |————————————————| Accredited Museum

Table 67.21   Educational Goals

Educational Goals

Skill Development |————————————————| Content Transfer

Table 67.22   Visitor Experience

Visitor Experience

Easy/Fun |————————————————| Challenging/Serious

Table 67.23   Visitor Experience

Visitor Experience

Low Tech |————————————————| High Tech

Table 67.24   Ability to Change Galleries

Ability to Change Galleries

Delta Museum |————————————————| Built to Last

Table 67.25   Ability to Change Galleries

Ability to Change Galleries

Experience |————————————————| Content

Table 67.26   Learning Spaces

Contemplative galleries
Showcases
Tunnels of wonder
Theaters/demonstrations
Immersion environments
Hands-on arenas
Discovery worlds
Workshops and studios
Icons and open spaces
Virtual spaces

Table 67.27   Overall Feel

Overall Feel

Quality |————————————————| Quantity

Table 67.28   Type of Museum

Type of Museum

Self-Sufficient |————————————————| Partnerships

Table 67.29   Financial Objectives

Financial Objectives

Support Revenue |————————————————| Earned Revenue

Table 67.30   Earned Revenue Portion

Earned Revenue Portion

Visitor-Based |————————————————| Program Based

216 Section 67

Table 67.31   Support Revenue Portion

Support Revenue Portion

Private
Funding ————————————————— Public
Funding

Table 67.32   Capital and Preopening Campaign

Capital and Pre-Opening Campaign

0
Million ————————————————— XX
Million

Table 67.33   Physical Expansion

Physical Expansion

No
Growth ————————————————— Growth

Table 67.34   Operating Revenues: Sources

_____%	Earned revenue
_____%	Private support revenue
_____%	Government support revenue
_____%	Endowment and investment operating revenue
_____100%	Total operating revenue (will be automatically calculated)

Section 68

Programming

Categories

INTRODUCTION

If the exhibit halls are the heart of the museum, its programs will be its soul. While exhibits happen in space, programs happen in time and typically involve educators in the guise of hallway interpreters, demonstrators, actors, lecturers, presenters, greeters, and other roles designed to add a human dimension to the museum. The museum's staff and volunteers will be involved in the delivery of educational services both on-site and in the community through a structured series of programs planned to reach different audiences with different parts of the museum's message. Educational programs will happen in the exhibit halls for the general visitor but will also be very active behind the scenes, serving school groups, continuing education programs, school outreach, teacher training, and numerous other activities. See table 68.1 for a list of possible programs.

Through its programs, the museum will serve the region regardless of where the main facility is physically located.

The museum will work closely with the school system in order to make sure that its school programs are integrated with the curriculum in the region and that efforts are not duplicated. For example, other organizations may have a kits program, and it would be useful to standardize the museum's approach and to make sure that museum does not offer subjects already covered by any other regional educational institution.

The museum's educational programs can be particularly active in reaching out to underserved communities who are not used to going to museums and are perhaps uncomfortable with the museum's content. Its outreach programs can go into schools that might not be able to afford travel to museum.

See also "72. Programming: Menu of Options" and "81. Earned and Support Revenue: Checklist."

Programs: Ways of Organizing

The brief descriptions of potential programs in "72. Programming: Menu of Options" are organized into the following categories according to where the program takes place. Programs can also be categorized by their audience, business model, and frequency:

- On-site programs
  - Floor and theater programs
  - Other on-site programs
- Off-site outreach programs
- Web and virtual programs

Programs Categorized by Business Model

- Fee-Based Programs: This category of programming is based on the program participants paying a fee to register and attend the program, which can be a single program or a weekly series. Summer camps are likely to be the largest revenue source in this category. Arriving at the right mix of programs that serve a wide range of out-of-school audiences and use the time slots unfilled by schools will take time and flexibility. Programs will be developed for specific audience groups that are important to the mission of the museum, including youth and families, home schoolers, youth groups, downtown residents and employees, community groups, professional audiences, adults, and a variety of government or private sector audiences. Programs will be marketed in a course catalog mailed to members and others or through specific program brochures and paid advertisements. Scholarships will be pursued for programs targeting disadvantaged and at-risk youth and family participants.

Table 68.1   Summary of Potential Programs (On-Site Only)

Informal education experiences in galleries/grounds ("floor programs")
Site and gallery tours
Live interpreters
Demonstrations
Activity carts
Discovery zones
Visit enrichment (audio guides, wands, mobile apps, etc.)

Regularly scheduled education programs
Art school
Film series (other than giant-screen or planetarium screenings)
Learning programs
Overnight camp-in programs
Preschool/day care sessions
Summer and/or holiday camps
Professional development programs for teachers
Special needs programming
Auditorium presentations

Community service(s) and public events
Meet-ups at the museum for Web-based social communities/groups
Open public events (e.g., blood drive or a rally for local sports team)
Affinity group events (enactments, vintage auto shows, craft shows)
Performances or concerts
Community group meetings
Ethnic/cultural fests
Polling place
Wi-Fi or other computer access areas

Private rental events
Birthday or other parties
Conferences or corporate meetings
Private functions on a rental basis

Partner programs
Charter magnet or other school facilities
Public library branch
Adult education center
Programs run by others but held at the museum

Research library and conservation services
Conservation projects for outside collectors/museums
Public access computer labs or terminals
Public access to research libraries and facilities
Animal or plant rescue center
Collections research access for researchers and scholars

- Grant-Funded Programs: This category of programming is based on agencies, foundations, and other sources of funding underwriting programs that typically serve audiences who would not—or could not—pay the cost themselves. Grant-funded programs are likely to include after-school workshops for teens, summer training camps, English-as-a-second-language courses, and social service programs.
- Fee-Based Group Programs: These will be developed to take off-site or to offer to organized youth groups, such as Girl Scouts, Boys and Girls Clubs, or to after-school community education sites. In addition, programs will be offered during school holiday periods when parents need structured experiences for their children. The burgeoning home school market will also provide opportunities to redeploy the existing repertoire of youth classes and activities. Enrichment programs for home schoolers will complement the use of the program center spaces by school groups.

Programs Categorized by Audiences (Key Program Participants)

- Youth and Family Programs: These will develop and offer a wide range of enrichment classes, workshops, and weeklong science camps for preschool children, youth, and families covering a broad array of topics. These programs will enable youth to develop an understanding of processes and principles so that they can use them in everyday life. They will be designed to strengthen problem-solving skills and build higher self-esteem and confidence to engage in those skills and to help kids realize that they can be done by anyone and that it can be fun.
- Adult Programs: These will offer lectures, classes, and domestic and international study tours as well as daylong field trips for the adult community and the museum's membership. In cultivating the adult audience, the museum will actively promote partnerships with colleges, continuing education centers, and professional societies. The museum might also collaborate with elder hostel programs or conference organizers to offer tours for spouses of conference participants. One could develop programs for older visitors by developing programs, such as "Technology Then and Now—A Look at the 'Cutting Edge' Technology of the 50s and 60s." Special programs may be developed for the "electronic classroom" to be used by senior citizens.
- Volunteer Programs: In order to operate successfully, the museum will have a very active volunteer program that will be coordinated by the programs division because so many of its activities will be in the delivery of educational services. These volunteers will also be active in the gift shop, as entrance greeters, and as market researchers and in several other areas of the museum's operation. Volunteers will receive training in their areas that will amount to a continuing education program during their involvement with the museum. Volunteers will be made up of college and high school students, professionals currently employed in the region's scientific and technological areas, and retirees who are interested in passing their accumulated experience onto future generations.
- Group and School Programs: On-site, the museum's educational staff will deliver programs that will complement a group's visit to the museum with focused

presentations on human health, laser and lights, electricity, and numerous other curriculum-integrated demonstrations. These group programs will happen in specially designed laboratories and classrooms that will feature technologies and architecture significantly different from traditional schoolrooms. After school and on weekends, museum will offer continuing education programs with a menu of topics reflecting both the visitors' interests and the region's desire to inspire interest in particular future technologies. museum will also work with adults, expanding domestic technological literacy and opening doors to new skills. museum will host special interest clubs and groups as well as overnight camp-ins whereby children can spend the night in museum with sleeping bags on the floor.

PLANNING WORKSHEET

Table 68.2 Program Categories

	Business Model	Annual Participations		
		On-Site	Off-Site	Virtual
Floor programs	Included	100%	—	—
School and group programs	Fees			
Public programs	Fees			
Educator programs	Fees			
Public events	Sponsors			
Private events	Rentals			
Educational services	Grants			
Community services	Sponsors			

Section 69

Programming

Changing

INTRODUCTION

Relevance changes. What is relevant today is seldom as relevant a year or two later. To be relevant carries an obligation to change programming.

Audiences also pressure museums to change: "What's new? Why should I come back?"

History museums feel the same pressure to change to reflect current perspectives as do science museums. Art museums have always been able to change paintings in galleries without big construction and exhibit costs, but other museums need to spend more to redo exhibit galleries.

While most want changing exhibits and programs, some donors, exhibit designers, and teachers are interested in permanent exhibits because of their longer impact, greater budgets, and constant message. Museum leadership needs to decide how much should be permanent and how much should change and how often.

An *exhibition* is a group of exhibits addressing a theme or topic and integrated aesthetically into a visitor experience. Long-term and permanent exhibition galleries are addressed in "74. Public Spaces: Entry and Galleries." This section focuses on *changing exhibitions and shows*, also known as traveling exhibitions, retrospectives, films, presentations, scenarios, feature exhibitions, biennales, travelers, and installations.

Market research that asks visitors why they come to a museum and why they come back finds that changing exhibitions are an effective attractor. For mature community museums with residential rather than tourist audiences, changing exhibitions are more effective motivators of visits than are the permanent exhibitions.

This section looks at options for changing the museum's content and experience from the perspective of the long-term resources needed to facilitate changing programming. The programming itself is addressed in "72. Programming: Menu of Options."

Changing Programming: Exhibitions and Theater Shows

The following management research questions may inform programming strategy for the visitor venues:

- What are our yearly programming strategies with regard to the following?
  - In what months are which audiences available?
  - When can the museum communicate to the community most effectively?
  - What is the return on investment on the cost of changing programming?
  - What are the best windows to launch and run changing exhibitions?
  - How often should the shows in the feature theater and exhibition gallery change?
- What are the weekly programming strategies suggested by which days of the week that each key visitor segment is available? School groups are not available on Friday evenings, but adults are.
  - During the day, when do our visitors arrive and depart? What is the peak time?
  - What is the dwell time for each audience segment?
  - When during that dwell time are they ready to sit down?
  - When are the galleries most crowded so that a scheduled program might help relieve crowding?
  - What is the ideal orchestration of daily programs with the rest of the visitor experience? From a purpose/impact perspective? From a visitor/benefit perspective?

The factors listed in Table 69.1 may increase the likelihood that a prospective exhibition will attract attendance. Each museum should set its own priorities among these criteria and use them as filters to select among options for changing exhibitions. Table 69.2 lists options for business models.

Table 69.1 Changing Exhibitions: Factors Affecting Appeal/Draw

Sufficient size, dwell time, or importance to justify a repeat visit to the museum
A marketable and relevant topic/theme
A natural and available audience
A mission and sense of quality aligned with the museum's purposes and guiding principles—enthusiastic staff support
A good fit with the museum's spaces, facilities, schedule and other resources
A good fit with the community's schedule, attention span, and communications media
A supportable and realistic business model
Scale of potential returns versus risk exposure
An appealing case for support, sponsorships, and partnerships
A clear connection to the community's needs and aspirations
Existing brand recognition
Appeal to multiple audiences and identities

Table 69.2 Categories of Changing Exhibitions: Business Models

Change Strategy	Business Model
Traveling exhibitions: blockbuster	Negotiated agreement typically including gate share with guaranteed minimum; share of ancillary revenues; security, transit, conservation, and insurance demands
Traveling exhibitions: large	Lease plus stipulated costs; sponsorship and product line visibility
Traveling exhibitions: medium	Lease plus shipping and other expenses
Traveling exhibitions: small	Flat fee plus shipping
In-house exhibitions	Staff, contractors, and expenses
Delta galleries	Routine changing scenarios covered by the operating budget to develop and install new scenarios on long-term experience platforms
Exhibition transformers	Amortization of costs among a peer network for new scenarios (software and objects) to be installed on shared experience platforms (in-place hardware and cabinetry)

Note: Individual exhibitions are bound to vary from these broad distinctions.

- Marketable Change: This is something so new, important or big that it is worth another visit. While there are many reasons to change, attracting repeat and new visitors has been a principal driver. Traveling exhibitions and giant-screen (e.g., IMAX) films are marketable changes, as are new scenarios with new content in specially outfitted, large exhibit galleries.
- Traveling Exhibitions, Giant-Screen Films, Art Film Theaters, and Fulldomes: These have different models for changing content and attracting repeat and/or new audiences. Traveling exhibitions start with bare, simple spaces and move truckloads of stuff around to fill them. Giant-screen theaters and fulldomes have very expensively equipped specialized spaces and ship multiple copies of hard drives to many theaters at the same time.

Informal Learning Experiences (ILE): Run by Dr. R. "Mac" West, ILE hosts forums on traveling exhibitions at the Association of Science-Technology Centers and the American Alliance of Museums, where producers describe upcoming exhibitions to potential venues. ILE also operates an interactive subscription database of available exhibitions.

- Transmedia Leverage and Multiplatform Production: Producers of digital museum learning experiences are increasingly thinking about releasing different versions of the same content or theme on different platforms. In theory, this leverages the content, research, and brand and increases exposure as it reaches different audiences though different media—some on mobile, some on TV, some in museums, and some on the Web. Social media can interlink these audiences. The potential downside is that producing for all platforms may compromise the excellence and impact of each platform.

Flight of the Butterflies: This appears in giant-screen film, fulldome, video, and other platforms, thereby leveraging the brand.

- The Programmable Museum: Many museum spaces are underutilized much of the time. Exhibit halls and school program rooms may be jammed at some times but empty the rest of the time. A programmable museum uses technology and staff to change the operating mode of its public spaces so that more audiences can utilize them for more purposes at more times. Multiple operating modes can include public visitors, member hours, group programs, function rentals, docent tours, camp-ins, and maintenance modes.
- The Delta Museum: This is a concept for changing the content and experience of museum galleries using similar approaches to the way theaters change plays. Delta thinking and its strategies, tactics, and processes are described in "70. Programming: Delta Approaches."

The exhibit halls should be designed with several uses or modes in mind: as traditional hands-on, interactive exhibit halls and as mission-simulation "laboratories" and electronic classrooms to be run on a scheduled basis with reserved groups. Lighting, audio, projections, computer software, video monitor feeds, and other electronic tools will be used to transform the public spaces from one mode to another.

PLANNING WORKSHEETS

Table 69.3   Categories of Changing Exhibitions

	Business Model	*Our Strategy*
Traveling exhibitions: blockbuster	Negotiated agreement typically including gate share with guaranteed minimum; share of ancillary revenues; security, transit, conservation, and insurance demands	
Traveling exhibitions: large	Lease plus stipulated costs; sponsorship and product line visibility	
Traveling exhibitions: medium	Lease plus shipping and other expenses	
Traveling exhibitions: small	Flat fee plus shipping	
In-house exhibitions	Staff and expenses	
Delta galleries	Routine changing scenarios covered by the operating budget to develop and install new scenarios on long-term experience platforms	
Exhibition transformers	Amortization of costs among a peer network for new scenarios (software and objects) to be installed on shared experience platforms (in-place hardware and cabinetry)	

Table 69.4   Changing Exhibitions: Factors Affecting Appeal/Draw

Rank	Factor	Assessment
	Sufficient size, dwell time, or importance to justify a repeat visit to the museum	
	A marketable and relevant topic/theme	
	A natural and available audience	
	A mission and sense of quality aligned with the museum's purposes and guiding principles—enthusiastic staff support	
	A good fit with the museum's spaces, facilities, schedule, and other resources	
	A good fit with the community's schedule, attention span, and communications media	
	A supportable and realistic business model	
	Scale of potential returns versus risk exposure	
	An appealing case for support, sponsorships, and partnerships	
	A clear connection to the community's needs and aspirations	
	Existing brand recognition	
	Appeal to multiple audiences and identities	

Table 69.5   Rate of Program Change: Yearly Strategy

Component	Year 1	Year 2	Year 3
Gallery A			
Gallery B			
Gallery C			
Sample gallery	Scenario A (18 months)		Scenario B (15 months)
Feature theater			
Magic box			
Traveling exhibition A			
Traveling exhibition B			

Section 70

Programming

Delta Approaches

INTRODUCTION

Remodeling or building museum galleries can no longer be about first creating great exhibits and then enclosing them with space. The exhibits need to change faster than architecture. If we are to be responsible stewards of our community's scarce capital dollars, then we should invest our supporter's funds in flexible learning spaces that host a succession of compelling visitor experiences and powerful learning resources. The Delta museum is an approach to adding change infrastructure to galleries to facilitate scenario change (see table 70.1).

Table 70.1   The Delta Museum: Key Attributes

- "A museum or gallery built for change"
- Modeled on theaters, retail stores, libraries, and sports arenas
- Program change is routine
- Community trained to expect change
- A focus on change and flexibility at all levels
- Separate hardware (long term) from software (easily changeable)
- Interchangeable inventory of parts among galleries and theaters

The Delta museum approach tries to reduce the cost of each change by building in long-term support for changing the exhibits, theater shows, and programs more economically. The layers of the Delta museum model are shown in tables 70.2 and 70.3.

Table 70.2   Delta Museum: Layers and Rate of Change

Layers of Delta in an Exhibit Gallery

223

DELTA APPROACHES TO CHANGING PROGRAMMING

Table 70.3   The Delta Museum: Two Layers in Comparison

Experience Platform The Stage	Scenario The Play
Built in	Changeable
Capital budget	Operating budget (goal)
Funding theme	Promotion opportunity
Background	Foreground
Neutral or iconic	Visually striking
Platform designer	Exhibit/media designer
Code engineering	Unlicensed designers
Building contractor	Exhibit fabricator
Built in place	Built off-site

Delta Tactics

Each Delta gallery should have tactics for change. Some exhibit installations are long-term investments intended to change through *gradual evolution*, such as a hands-on arena. While staff and volunteer *floor programs* are labor intensive, they are easily changeable aspects in exhibit galleries. Some exhibits, particularly collections, can be reinterpreted by a curator with new *labels and lighting*. Other learning spaces change scenarios by rearranging their *kit of parts* and filling them with new contents, such as showcases and contemplative galleries. Some change in a large, marketable way by installing new exhibits and environments on long-term *exhibit structures*, and some are open, neutral spaces for *traveling exhibitions*. Theaters are also learning spaces, and the *new shows*, films, and demonstrations are the scenarios that change on their stages. Workshops and libraries can be used in many ways or have a wealth of information, and their repeat-use strategy is to be *open ended or deep*. Each learning space can have one or more of these change tactics assigned to it, and it will be designed with built-in systems and infrastructure—the *experience platform*[1]—to facilitate changing content according to that strategy. The principal tactics are shown in table 70.4. The process and sequence are outlined in tables 70.5 and 70.6.

Table 70.4   Delta Tactics

Change Tactic	Marketable Change?	Separate Scenario?
Traveling exhibition	Yes	Yes
New show/film/content/new experience	Yes	Yes
Gradual evolution	No	No
New floor programs	No	Yes
Rearranged kit of parts	Possibly	Yes
New scenario on exhibit structure	Yes	Yes
Open ended or deep	No	No
Change context/environment	Possibly	Yes
Reinterpret (guest curator)	Possibly	Yes

Table 70.5   Development Process for Delta Galleries

1. Assess community needs and identify significant needs that this space can address.
2. Articulate the theme and community benefit.
3. Decide on audiences to be served.
4. Envision multiple contexts of use.
5. Decide on content lifecycle (e.g., change every 24 months).
6. Decide on change tactic(s).
7. Envision a range of scenarios.
8. Define the experience platform.

Table 70.6   Sequence of Delta Designers

1. Management: change cycle objectives	Management
2. Project team planners: how to meet objectives	Staff
3. Design of the public space (Delta gallery)	Architect
4. Experience platform designers: support for change	Engineers
5. Exhibit (scenario) designer(s)	Exhibit designers
6. Content installers	Fabricators
7. Floor program developers	Staff

NOTE

1. I credit this term to the late Roy L. Shafer.

Section 71

Programming

Feature Theaters

INTRODUCTION

Museums have used feature theaters to communicate in a different medium, to attract new and repeating audiences, to generate net revenue, to offer new experiences, and to provide the museum with a venue for changing content.

Theaters complement exhibits as learning resources because they reach learners at different levels. Theaters permit the development of a linear, sequential logic and story where exhibits encourage random exploration and connections. Theatrical presentations can be much more experiential and emotional, complementing the more rational and interactive engagement with exhibits. Museum fatigue sets in after an hour, and theaters provide a chance to sit down. Both theaters and exhibits can be effective and popular learning resources; they just work differently and are each suited to different content.

This section helps you set expectations, decide among programming options (see table 71.1) and schedule shows (see table 71.2). See "77. Public Spaces: Theater Options" for the selection of theater formats.

FEATURE THEATER PROGRAMMING

Show Evaluation Checklist

Table 71.1   Criteria for Show Selection

	Priority	Show A	Show B	Show C
Quality of show				
Is it a good show?				
How has it performed at other theaters?				
Does it show off the feature theater experience?				
Mission driven				
What is the educational content?				
Will it work for schools?				
Marketing				
Is it marketable?				
How will it be marketed?				
Is it entertaining?				
Will it create positive word-of-mouth advertising?				
Is there marketing support from the distributor?				
Is there marketing support from the national sponsor?				
Will it be attractive to potential sponsors?				
Will you be able to find promotional partners to support it?				
Financial aspects of lease				
What is the lease cost?				
What are print costs?				
How much flexibility will there be in the schedule?				
Will there be a test preview?				
How did the show test with the public?				
How did the show test with schools?				
Market factors				
What is the timing?				
Is it attractive to the core audience?				
Or will it attract a new audience?				

Fulldome and Planetarium Programming (Sample to Adapt to Other Formats)

The fulldome is conceived as a space that remains fully flexible to subject matter, enabling programming that extends well beyond the stars. The fulldome programs will cover a range of topics, including the earth sciences, social sciences, energy, astronomy, space exploration, and our role in the universe. Given an array of equipment, including a star-field projection system by Sky Skan, Evans and Sutherland, Spitz, Zeiss, or another supplier, the fulldome can be used for the following kinds of presentations:

- Planetarium shows
- Leased fulldome shows
- Educational media shows
- "The Sky Tonight" demonstrations using the remote from the telescope

- Lectures and live demonstrations
- Concerts and performing arts
- Nighttime laser and animation shows

If the fulldome is also equipped with an audience response system in each seat, then it can be used for the following:

- Function rentals for training or corporate meetings where the audience votes
- Issues-oriented programs asking for visitors' votes
- Interactive presentations steered by visitors' votes

These various kinds and levels of presentations will be scheduled to serve the needs of a wide variety of audiences, from school groups to weekend family visitors to evening lectures and adult education classes. The model assumes that the fulldome will be separately ticketed.

SAMPLE SHOW SCHEDULE

Table 71.2   Show Schedule and Allocation

	Mon.	Tue.	Wed.	Thu.	Fri.	Sat.	Sun.
9:00							
10:00							
11:00	F	F	F	F	F	F	F
12:00	F	F	F	F	F	F	F
1:00							
2:00	F	F	F	F	F	F	F
3:00	I	I	I	I	F	F	F
4:00			F	F	L	L	L
5:00					I	I	I
6:00						F	P
7:00	P	P	P	F	F	F	P
8:00				F	F	F	F
9:00				L	L	L	L
10:00					L	L	

Legend	Type of Show	Slots in Peak Week	Ratio of Total Schedule
F	Feature show	32	46%
I	Interactive show	7	10%
	Astronomy	14	20%
L	Laser shows	9	13%
P	Special programs	8	11%
	Shows/peak season	70	100%

Section 72

Programming

Menu of Options

INTRODUCTION

These brief descriptions of potential programs are organized into the following categories according to where the program takes place. Programs can also be categorized by their audience, business model, and frequency (see "68. Programming: Categories"):

- On-site programs
  - ° Floor and theater programs
  - ° Other on-Site programs
- Off-site outreach programs
- Web and virtual programs

This section is based on writing by Dr. David Chittenden.

PROGRAMS: MENU OF OPTIONS

On-Site Programs

Floor and Theater Programs

- Floor Programs: These occur in the museum galleries and are included in the visitor experience as part of the admissions. Staff and volunteers engage visitors in the exhibit halls to complement their interaction with the exhibits and presentations. Much of this hallway interpretation will be delivered by a diverse group of volunteers, ranging from high school students to senior science mentors who can help customize an exhibit to the particular interests and learning levels of different groups of visitors. Interpreters will work in many of the presentation stages and small laboratories that will be integrated into the exhibit theme areas to facilitate visitors creating their own experiments and discovering their own routes toward the information and understanding they seek. Public programs will include hallway demonstrations, activities in the exhibit hub, visitor information stations, live demonstrations, theme weekends, and numerous other floor activities that will bring life and constant change to the exhibit hall for the visitor.

Program Center and Other On-Site Programs

- Special Events, Festivals and Carnivals: In its role as a community citizen, the museum should offer its facilities and park to the community as an ideal setting for special events, festivals, promotions, carnivals, and other gatherings, even if the museum's themes are not the focus. The museum should maintain an active yearly schedule of different events, with something happening practically every week during the high season. Some events will be more significant than others and might be several weeks long. Others might be simply a single evening party. The purpose of this schedule of activities is to attract to the park a much wider range of people than would normally come to the museum. These sponsored activities, many of which will be free, should attract family groups that might not normally come to a museum because of lack of money or because they are not interested in the subject. In this way, the museum can make these casual park visitors aware of the offerings and perhaps introduce them to the fun and enriching experiences available within the museum. Any time there is a significant event in the park, the museum's café, remote food service stations, gift shop, and feature theater (at least) should be open for business. It is expected that the organization and operation of many of these events may be handled by outside groups on a voluntary basis. In this way, for example, the regional police association, a neighborhood church, or any other civic group might take on the sponsorship of an event, perhaps in conjunction with a local retailer or bank to help with the promotion. The museum will provide services, limited staff support, and some amount of resources to the event sponsors in return for their ability to attract crowds to the site that might then use the museum's revenue-generating facilities.

• Family Sunday Program for Community Access: Modeled on the very successful Bishop Museum (Hawaii) program, the museum will throw open its theme pavilions for free the first Sunday of every month or so and invite the community to come in very casual attire for a festival-like atmosphere of musicians, food tents, dancing, speeches, exhibits, craft sales, and so on. Each family Sunday will be cosponsored by a different community organization (e.g., the police, the Elks, or local hospitals) in return for getting their messages out and the chance to do some fund-raising. In Hawaii, the community organization takes on the role of organizing the programs and putting the word out. Each event typically also has a different corporate sponsor that handles the publicity. A strong Sunday attracts 8,000 to 10,000 visitors. While there will be no exhibit admission income, the gift shop and food services could do good business, and tickets could still be sold to the theater.

• Extended Programs
  ° Kite Festival and Competition: The open site with a prevailing wind from the south is ideal for flying kites from the banks out over the river. Kites are also excellent teaching tools to develop skills in aeronautics and engineering as well as design and construction skills. The museum could stage an annual competition and plan a series of promotional weekends (e.g., Open Skies Weekend, Invitational Weekend, and Semifinalist and Finalist Weekend) and offer kite-building workshops beforehand.
  ° Riverfest participation
  ° Radio-controlled model boat regatta
  ° Inventors' weekend
  ° Ham radio operators' weekend
  ° Cinco de Mayo celebrations
  ° Solstice and equinox celebrations: When the sun strikes reflective structures in the park to achieve Stonehenge-like alignments
  ° Maker fairs
  ° Art walk
  ° Family free Sunday program for community access

Any time there is a significant event in the campus, the museum's other components should be open for business:

• Education Programs for Students and Teachers: A significant area of the museum's educational services will be in the training of teachers. Numerous such programs exist on the region at the moment, and the museum will serve to complement those, perhaps even serving as an umbrella organization that will be a gateway for interested students seeking involvement at other institutions that are providing science education. The museum's library and media center will be a resource listing all the offerings available in the region. The museum will work closely with the school systems and cooperatively with the region's universities to develop in-service training programs for teachers as well as preservice courses for future teachers in science education. The museum will also be capable of offering internships on the floor in order to give teachers hands-on experience.

• Teacher Workshops: Special content and teaching practices workshops will be offered at the museum at affiliated university campuses and on-site in the schools. These programs will help link the museum's exhibits to the curriculum and will foster increased confidence in utilizing an inquiry-based, hands-on approach to teaching.
  ° Teachers will be awarded continuing education units or, when possible, graduate credits for their training efforts.

• Teacher Resource Center: The Teacher Resource Center will include examples of activity kits for classroom use, pre- and postvisit materials, virtual science center tours, science content, and educational methods that will be available for rental or purchase by teachers. Teachers can access a catalog of the Resource Center's holdings via the museum's website, reserve their materials, and either pick them up or have them mailed or downloaded. Samples of all materials will be available for teachers to inspect, and a resource facilitator will be on hand to process loan requests and assist teachers in finding the information they need. Registered participants in Program Center programs can also use the Resource Center to find more information about topics, access a variety of home projects, and research projects for fairs and reports. Students, families, and children who have signed up for hands-on workshops in the themed program labs and classrooms can purchase supplies at the Resource Center.
  ° Career Center: This is a resource room and support facility focused on job skills and employability as well as continuing adult education programs operated in partnership with local agencies. Through liaisons with other organizations, the career center will keep up to date on the region's career needs.
  ° Curriculum Development Think Tank: The Resource Center will also serve as a planning workshop for a think tank of educators working together to develop curriculum, surrounded by reference materials and samples of other curriculum support materials.

- Inquiry-Based Training Programs and Teacher Institutes: The museum will develop and deliver a core set of training programs that enable teachers to develop their inquiry-based instructional skills. Hands-on inquiry is a staple of the museum learning environment.
- Teacher Internships and Teacher-in-Residence Programs: The museum will bring practicing teachers into the museum for extended periods to gain museum learning experience and to provide a consistent and sustainable linkage to school districts and teacher leaders with whom the museum will partner on projects and new school-based initiatives. Some potential relationships could include informal collaborative agreements, joint appointments with the school system, teachers on special assignment, teacher sabbaticals, program/project internships, and student teaching assignments.
- Camp-In Programs: Overnight camp-in programs have become popular in family museums nationwide. They provide a tremendous opportunity to increase the visitation and engage the young visitor. Girl Scout camp-in programs have been successful educationally and financially lucrative for many museums. Museum camp-ins will be an intensive, fun, hands-on, overnight experience for youth groups. Visitors will have the exclusive use of the museum so they can explore the facility to their heart's content. They also have the opportunity to participate in specially designed hands-on workshops.
- Themed Parties: These will include time for the party group to explore the exhibits, a choice of an age-appropriate hands-on workshop, and a short use of a birthday party room. These group parties have proven popular and profitable.
- Special Events and Programs Using the Whole Museum: These can tie in with annual celebrations or be stand-alone, one-time initiatives. They can be used for general publicity, fund-raising, soliciting community support, and coordinating with regional festivities. Holiday and special weekends will be designed to include parades or "invention conventions" or to coincide with exhibit openings. These events will be excellent opportunities to collaborate with discipline-based societies and regional professional associations. Depending on need, feasibility, and support funding, the following events might be held:
  ° Inventors' weekend
  ° Outdoor celebrations
  ° High-tech holiday trees
- After-School Programs: These programs are effective with at-risk teen audiences but require considerable community and philanthropic subsidy. After-school programming continues to emerge as one of the top priorities for youth advocates.
- Scholarly Research: Some museums are associated with research organizations, with the museum functioning as their public outreach program. The American Museum of Natural History (New York City), the Minnesota Historical Society (St. Paul), and the Getty Museum (Los Angeles) all operate museums as one of several activities in their organization chart. Over time as funding shifted, some research institutions have shifted priorities toward more public museum activities and less pure research. Nevertheless, art museums, natural history museums, history museums, and other collection-based museums continue to conduct original research, publish peer-reviewed papers, and contribute to public knowledge and understanding.
- Learning Research: Given heightened interest in out-of-school learning, some museums are conducting research into how and what visitors and program participants learn in informal environments like museums. The Whitney Museum (New York City), the Exploratorium (San Francisco), the Holocaust Museum (Washington, D.C.), and the Museum of Science (Boston) exemplify museums that have conducted and published grant-funded and peer-reviewed research into learning outcomes for public and professional audiences.

Off-Site Outreach Programs

Off-site, the museum personnel and volunteers will take school programs out to the community, in particular to schools that might have difficulty reaching the museum for either distance or economic reasons. These auditorium presentations will use many of the same subjects used on-site to familiarize students with what kinds of education the museum can offer.

- Hub-and-Spoke Concept: An important metaphor for the outreach programs is the idea that the museum works with partners throughout the region to offer grassroots programs that happen in the schools, library, and affiliated science centers. The intent of the hub and spoke is to be a two-way program distribution center, respecting the considerable experience that existing organizations, particularly the science centers, have in developing education programs and operating them effectively.
- Neighborhood Programs: As part of its collaborative and community development goals, the museum will operate various neighborhood programs. These programs will work with neighborhood groups to develop activities, special events, and exhibits about specific neighborhoods, ethnic groups, and public interests. These will involve volunteers from the community, working with professional historians and local historical societies from the region's neighborhoods, to research and locate artifacts or neighborhood characters that represent the history of that neighborhood in a way that evokes lifestyles and stories from the recent past that all of the museum's visitors can enjoy. The neighborhood programs will be changing on a frequent basis in order to allow for coverage over time of the region's many diverse communities.
- Tour Programs: The museum will operate interpretive tour programs to both local and distant destinations. Lo-

Table 72.1   The Physical Outreach Network

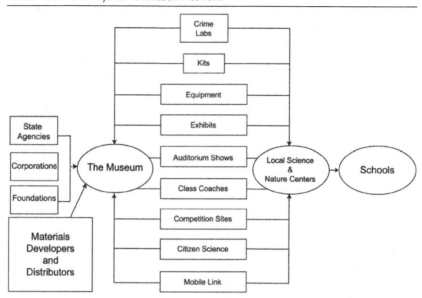

cal bus tours will take groups of people to area sites connected to the museum's stories, and travel programs will partner with tour operators to more distant destinations thematically connected to the museum.

- In-School Programs: Auditorium assembly programs, based on a van from the museum arriving with one or two demonstrators; a coach who helps a teacher run a number of experiments with a class; a hallway kiosk with relevant information on health care or other current issues; and a parking lot van with exhibits are all useful. The Science Museum of Minnesota has found that taking science assemblies (large science demonstrations and content-focused presentations) into elementary schools has been the most well received and profitable for them. Schools love large, entertaining science demonstrations that they can't do themselves. Such assemblies are the most cost effective as well. Once a set of science assembly programs have been developed, they can be used for a variety of out-of-school audiences, including program events sponsored by community centers, libraries, Cub Scouts, Girl Scouts, and so on. Specific outreach array of programs and services needs to come out of a planning process with the schools.

- Field Projects and Citizen Science/History: Involving students, teachers, and parents in the process of actual scientific and history research is a role that family museums are increasingly playing. Citizen science projects, such as Project Feederwatch from the Cornell Laboratory of Ornithology or the Spider Survey at the Denver Museum of Nature and Science, are examples of museum-led field research projects in which students and others collect data and make observations according to specific scientific protocols and contribute their information to an ongoing scientific investigation. Such programs can be integrated

with other outreach efforts that the museum initiates and can help strengthen and sustain relationships with participating schools.

- School Kit Service: A library of activities, experiments, and equipment will be developed by the museum staff or contract staff for distribution to schools through a kit rental program. Kits will be developed through grants and will focus on specific topics relating to the exhibits for multiple age-groups. Some of these could include the following:
  ○ Elementary level: "Color Magic," "Popcorn Math," and "Magnets"
  ○ Middle/junior high level: "Creative Thinking," "Communication," and "Weather"
  ○ High school level: "Careers in Science and Technology," "Lasers," and "Debate a Current Issue in Science and Technology"

Web and Virtual Programs

- Website: The museum has a website (http://www.--.org) that includes the following:
  ○ A compilation of relevant lesson plans and curriculum guides with images and archives.
  ○ An online library with access to the other library collections.
  ○ Online activities, such as creating their own experiences and exploring the region's history from home or school.
  ○ Using an education database, teachers (or parents) will type in a specific subject to be searched, and the database will provide a list of all of the best lessons, activities, and museum tours related to the subject.

○ Information on museum programming and services.

○ Links to relevant websites that target specific audiences; for example, programs for tourists and a list of function rental spaces can be linked to the region's Convention and Visitors Bureau website.

The qualities of the museum's branded website and the scope of work expectations for Web designer include the following:

○ The website should be formatted to be able to work off an existing database so that information can be transferred between modes and requires a minimum of data entry.

○ The templates provided by the vendor should be able to be easily updated by the museum staff without the future assistance of a Web designer.

○ The "information architecture" is to be part of a collaborative effort between the museum and the information technology designer. This "skeleton" of the Web pages is a fundamental portion of the scope of work.

○ The museum will provide a portion of the images and graphics, the designer will acquire and provide the rest of the images and graphics.

○ The types of reports of visitor usage that the museum would like to generate off the website includes at least the usual data collected from users (e.g., what link they came from and where they went from there).

• Social Media Sites: The museum will maintain an active presence on Facebook, Twitter, Instagram, and other social media sites provided that the cost and resources are appropriate for the outcomes:

○ Blogs and external reviewers

○ Virtual sites

○ Augmented reality

○ Mobile apps

○ Crowdsourcing

○ e-fund-raising

• Distance Learning Programs: Distance learning will connect the exhibits and programs to the public, parochial, and private schools as well as the higher education facilities throughout the region. The museum will adapt its most popular science demonstrations and science class experiences into distance learning programs that can be marketed to schools locally, regionally, and nationally on a self-supporting basis. A number of programs will engage emerging and new technologies that can broaden

the opportunity to reach off-site school audiences in engaging and interactive ways, including high-definition broadcasting, videoconferencing, and webcasting. Some of these distance learning programs may involve on-site demonstrations using exhibits, and others might be interactions between groups of students on-site and those in remote locations.

Table 72.2   Sample Summary of Programs

Programs and Services	Implementation Schedule	Funding Category
In-school programs	Currently	Core funding
School science kit service	Within two years	Sponsorship only
Distance learning programs	Within three years	Foundation grant
Field projects and citizen science	Within four years	Research grant
Hub-and-spoke network model	Within five years	Legislature funding

PLANNING WORKSHEETS

Table 72.3   Program Development Summary

Programs and Services	Implementation Schedule	Funding Category

Table 72.4   Potential Programs by Location

Program Location	Audience	Business Model	Facilitator
On-site programs			
Floor and theater programs			
Other on-site programs			
Off-site outreach programs			
Web and virtual programs			

Section 73

Public Spaces

Categories

INTRODUCTION

These sections describe a museum's potential public spaces and its major components in the order listed in table 73.1.

The public spaces use a classification system described in table 73.2 at the end of this section. The categories are identified by name and code.

The classification system is based on analyzing the architectural characteristic and built-in systems of a database of more than 500 existing public spaces and components currently operating in a wide range of museums. The analysis looked for commonalities in characteristics, audiences, and operating modes, resulting in 14 categories of public components. Additionally, a museum has non–public service and support components.

The classification system is an elaboration of Falk and Dierking's Museum Experience Model (see table 33.4), specifically the *physical context.*

Table 73.1   Menu of Potential Public Spaces, Venues, and Components

Exterior spaces	Program center
Outdoor park and festival grounds	Orientation center (commons)
Outdoor exhibits	Themed program labs/classrooms
Parking	Teacher resource center
Open zone and entrance lobby	Media and network control room
Entrance vestibule	Kit preparation and distributions
Visitor orientation and reception lobby	Education staff offices
Marketing kiosks and racks	Digital visualization lab
Visitor amenities	Library and resource center
Washrooms	Community library branch
First-aid/family room	Preschool learning laboratory
Coat check/locker room	Hands-on laboratories
Ticketing and admissions	Digital history center
Welcome center	Observatory
Café and food service	Volunteer restoration workshop
Gift shop	Collections center
Admission venues	Function rental spaces
Exhibit halls/museum galleries	Support facilities (offices, shops, storage, etc.)
Exhibit hub and function rental space	
Theme galleries	
Traveling exhibition and gallery	
Early learning discovery center	
Theater options	
Giant-screen theater	
Fulldome (planetarium)	
Art film theater	
Auditorium and presentation theater	
Object theater	
Simulation center	

Table 73.2   Public Spaces: Physical Context Framework

Learning Space Category	Sample Application	ArchitecturalSnapshot	Daylight	Learning Skills Strengthened
Open spaces and lobbies	Lobbies, atria, rotundas, hallways	Views and daylight in calm rest areas	Yes	Synthesis, framework building, questioning, evaluating
Temporary exhibit galleries	*Titanic, King Tut, Pixar*	Neutral box lighting system	No	Varied approach
Showcase galleries	Interpretive displays and graphics	Spotlit cases and rare artifacts, mixed with photos, labels, and videos	Seldom	Understanding, synthesis
Contemplative galleries	Art and collections	Light, quiet, calm, formal, and open	Diffused	Reflection, appreciation, identity development
Hands-on arenas	Science and technology centers with interactive exhibits	Open informal spaces encouraging activity	Possible	Problem solving, experimenting, discovering
Immersion environments	Historic rooms, space capsules, botanic gardens	A complete and convincing surrounding reality	No	Discovery, engagement, inspiration
Tunnels of wonder	Dioramas, period rooms, aquaria	Dark corridors with lit windows into stage sets	No	Exploring, observing
Discovery worlds	Storyland, climbing structures, minivillages	Playful, fantasy, clean, light with small spaces	Possible	Exploring, discovering, creating
Theaters and presentation spaces	Auditoriums, demo stages, IMAX	Audience/stage areas supported by lighting and sound systems	No	Linear narratives, empathy, emotional experiences
Workshops, studios, and meeting rooms	Art studios, reference rooms, classrooms	Focused work spaces out of main flow	Possible	Critical thinking, team building, confidence building
Icons and symbolic object spaces	Dinosaur, *Mona Lisa*, Liberty Bell	Prime focus of an open area	Possible	Reflection, kinesthetic understanding
Dedicated function rental spaces	The d'Arbeloff Suite	Open gallery-like space with staging spaces	Views	Networking
Virtual spaces	Cyberlearning, social networks	Anywhere	Yes	Social networking, imagination building, identity development

CATEGORIES OF PUBLIC SPACES: THE PHYSICAL CONTEXT FRAMEWORK

Some of the categories shown in table 73.2 can be successfully combined. Hands-on elements, for example, can be brought into showcases, immersion environments, or other learning spaces, but discovery worlds are poor mixes with contemplative galleries. How a museum's learning spaces are orchestrated and their relative scale are key brand and management decisions that ultimately determine the character of the institution. Science centers tend to use lots of hands-on arenas; aquariums have tunnels of wonder and immersion environments, and art museums tend to have contemplative galleries. The choices also affect which learning needs and audience segments the institution is most likely to serve best.

Showcase galleries with a rich array of graphics, artifacts, and photos, as might be found in a history museum, can help adult visitors build their skills synthesizing images and ideas into observations. A light and airy art gallery may help build contemplation, appreciation, and reflection skills in the same adult, while a museum workshop setting in a science center might help develop problem-solving and teamwork skills.

Some museums specialize in just one or two of these categories of public spaces; others offer a number of very distinct galleries and approaches, each with its visitor fans. Some go with a variety of formats but then graphically brand all labels and signs for consistency and clarity of institutional voice.

PLANNING WORKSHEETS

Note: "Venue" assumes controlled access zone, often by admission tickets.

Table 73.4 groups galleries and program spaces by type of space, allowing a look at the total area currently devoted to each type of learning style and illuminating the degree of diversity of space usage.

Table 73.3   Venues by Key Visitor Segments

Visitor Venues	Adults with Children	Adults with Adults	School and Youth Groups	Teens	Young Adults	Solo Visitors

Table 73.4   Categories of Learning Spaces

Category	Symbol	Current		Future	
		No. of Spaces	Size	No. of Spaces	Size
Open spaces and lobbies	OS				
Temporary exhibit galleries	TE				
Showcase galleries	SHW				
Contemplative galleries	CG				
Hands-on arenas	HO				
Immersion environments	IE				
Tunnels of wonder	TW				
Discovery worlds	DW				
Theaters and presentation spaces	TH				
Workshops, studios, and meeting rooms	ST				
Icons and symbolic object spaces	ICON				
Dedicated function rental spaces	FR				
Virtual spaces	VR				

Section 74

Public Spaces

Lobby and Galleries

INTRODUCTION

This section is a menu of possible public components (spaces) that a museum might consider incorporating into its core museum experience, covering the exterior and entrance components, parking, the lobby, and the museum galleries.

You can select and adapt these spaces from the menu to fit your museum's needs and future plans. You are likely to have some spaces already in some degree. The menu contains spaces and facilities requested by museums in the past; there are bound to be additional facilities desired.

DESCRIPTIONS OF POTENTIAL LOBBY AND GALLERY SPACES

Exterior Spaces

The exterior grounds will be the museum's free front-end attraction, drawing *park casuals* for walks, picnics, and play activities. The outdoor areas will include some of the following public spaces:

- Open-air, gazebo-like structures where testing and analysis and other learning programs can be held as well as celebrations, such as weddings
- A flat plaza for outdoor festivals, activities, and programs: smaller tents, food trucks, and kiosks; and support for occasional large pavilion tents for significant traveling exhibitions
- Herb garden
- Bocce ball and horseshoe pitch and other small-scale outdoor activities
- Amphitheater
- Site sculpture and public art envelopes (see below)
- Regional pathway system (see below)
- Environmental landscaping (see below)
- Outdoor program support space

Public Art Envelopes (Icons)

Conceptually distinct from both site and building, public art envelopes are platforms for artistic or sculptural installations of public art coordinated with the site and the building's exterior that will define the public's visual perception from key viewing points.

Each installation will be created by a public art team working in close collaboration with the museum and intended to produce a work of art or science that is stunningly eye-catching, memorable as a form, arrestingly provocative, and unique to the region. Most installations will be limited terms, with the work either sold or reverting to the artist to own or recycle.

Regional Pathway System

The site is an excellent gateway to the regional pathway system. From an interpretive plaque at the hub of the pathways, visitors, walkers, bikers, and others can orient themselves to choices, maps, degrees of difficulty, and nature interpretation along a selection of pathways, both on nearby circuits and to the broader pathways around the region.

Environmental Landscaping

A more formally laid out area allows for the interpretation of native vegetation, interspersed with interactive recognition monuments and large samples of regional rocks and minerals.

The landscape and building renovations will be guided by LEED environmental principles, and an interpreted section of the campus will serve as a live demonstration of environmental restoration in progress. An area allows for the interpretation of native vegetation, interspersed with clean-energy interactives and large samples of regional rocks and minerals that reveal the deep time of the region, while the pattern of rock placement allows kids to imagine the shapes connected by the dots or for families to come celebrate the solstices in Stonehenge-like alignments. The following will be considered:

- Agricultural technology area
- Wetlands area
- Bioswales and other rainwater conservation and treatment features
- Sustainable development demonstration projects
- Regional rock samples
- Interpretive native vegetation
- Public art installations
- Petroglyph and geology park
- Outdoor program support space

Parking

Immediately adjacent, clean and safe parking is important to achieve sustainable attendance levels. Parking will be free and inexpensive. Parking will be for XX spaces (XX visitor cars and XX staff, contractor, and volunteer cars) plus XX slots for buses/RVs in a surface lot adjacent to the museum. The parking study by XX recommended a minimum of XX car stalls for visitors.

The walkway connecting the parking to the entrance will establish pathways and sight lines. The pathway is an opportunity to educate arriving audiences on their choices.

Parking Options

- Parking will be an on-site surface lot.
- Parking will be an on-site garage.
- Because of its densely crowded site, the museum will build a multistory garage that will have the benefits of justifying parking fees more easily and of controlling the traffic flow into the building through a concourse that might permit an enticing introduction to the museum's many offerings along the way. This concourse might be at a second level, providing a more dramatic entrance to the museum's lobby and exhibit hall overviews.
- On-grade parking is also available in a large surface lot contiguous to but separate from the museum's main parking areas.

- A tertiary lot handles staff and overflow parking.
- Current planning is to rely on street surface spaces and parking lots in and around the museum site. More parking capacity might be handled by adjacent lots.
- Parking fees will be charged, the quality and pricing of the operation will be controlled by the museum, and revenues will benefit the museum.
- Parking fees will seldom be charged, and, when they are, the quality and pricing of the operation will be controlled by the museum, and revenues will benefit the museum.

Open Zone and Entrance Lobby

The museum's entrance lobby will set the tone for the visitor's experience as well as serve numerous practical objectives. The lobby will be connected to a series of spaces that collectively will be known as the open zone, which is free access to everyone during all opening hours for no charge. As a result, the lobby will be spectacular and appealing as well as durable and operationally workable. It will contain information booths, ticketing counters, membership booths, and controlled-access gateways into the controlled-admission areas (aka venues), such as the exhibit halls, the feature theater, and entrances to the gift shop and the café. Visitor amenities will be immediately available, including bathrooms, coatrooms, telephones, benches, and other services. Security and fire safety issues are prime considerations in the layout of these passageways and of the entrance. Graphics, both directional and marketing, are an essential component of the entrance lobby in order to guide visitors through their experience and to encourage them to utilize the facility fully.

The following will be included in the open zone and entrance lobby:

1. Main entrance
2. Information booth (optional)
3. Ticket booth/admissions counter
4. Membership booth (optional)
5. Museum galleries entrance/exit gateway
6. Temporary exhibition gallery entrance gateway (exit option to exhibit hub)
7. Feature theater lobby and entrance gateway
8. Gift shop
9. Café/vending area
10. Visitor amenities and washrooms
11. Security (optional or at loading deck)
12. Administration and human resources reception

Optional Lobby Components

- What's Happening at the Museum: A walk-in kiosk that welcomes and orients visitors to the museum and its current features using posters, videos, brochure racks, LED signboards, and ATM-like ticketing machines.

Ever-changing "What's Happening?" stations will allow visitors to design their own experience—and send themselves event reminders, activities, and other information at home. The purposes are to do the following:
○ Welcome visitors
○ Communicate that something new and exciting is always happening
○ Allow visitors to create unique, individual profiles that will enable them to plan their visits, record their own data from a range of exhibits, and download websites or other information for further investigation at home
• Welcome and Orientation Center (aka Partners' Showcase): The bright and airy Welcome Center contains attractively displayed information and promotional material about all of the recreational and interpretive experiences that are available in the region. In particular, the Welcome Center will allow the museum to reveal its deep connections to the community by illustrating its partners' shared missions and services to the community. From here, visitors to the region can board special shuttle buses that will take them to these regional destinations. Attraction and shuttle operators will operate counters in the Welcome Center where visitors can sign up for specific tours. During the high season, visitors and casuals will find that there is usually some interesting tour that leaves within the hour.
• Digital Family History Center: An important supporting element of the museum is the ability for visitors to add names, images, and their own stories to the Digital Family History Center, a multimedia database that can be accessed by visitors for generations to come. The revenue-generating digital database, modeled on the U.S. Navy Log at the U.S. Navy Memorial in Washington, D.C., will allow families to enter "family scrapbook pages." Future generations can receive color printouts of these records. While all visitors can see records for free, entering, maintaining, and printing out family histories will involve nominal sums. Recording their history on this digital log is a way for new arrivals and old-timers to pass along their stories to their children's children.
• Muslim Prayer Rooms: Male and female enclosed spaces with water and sinks meeting Muslim expectations. Orientation toward Mecca is critical.

Exhibit Halls/Museum Galleries

The museum galleries will be the museum's major programmatic component for most visitors. Full of different kinds and styles of exhibits organized into XX theme areas, the museum galleries will be designed to hold the average visitor for approximately XX minutes.

Exhibit halls are the heart of any museum. The nature and appeal of the exhibits can vary widely and include artifact cases with scholarly interpretation; restored interiors; aesthetic appreciation of works of art; hands-on interactive exhibits;

spectacular dioramas and live animal habitats; demonstration stages and theaters, programs, activities, and workshops; and immersion environments and combinations of the above.

Exhibit halls can be small if they are associated with some other activity, and a separate charge is not levied; however, once a separate admission charge is established, exhibit halls should be a minimum of 10,000 net square feet and can go over 250,000 square feet in large museums. Different subject matters and approaches require different amounts of space: an industrial museum requires more space than a jewelry museum, and young children require different spaces than adult audiences. Live animals and fish require support systems, and interactive exhibits require maintenance shops and repair areas.

In exhibit halls, visitors appear to enjoy the ability to elect where they spend time and to move freely among different exhibits. Hence, the exhibit experience is typically self-directed, although some museums and aquariums use a story line route to take visitors in a planned sequence, perhaps following a chronology of development.

Visitor groups create their own experience when they select a sequence of galleries and theaters to move through, in addition to their experiences entering and exiting the museum. Asking "what does each visitor segment want from their succession of learning spaces?" should be foundational to any museum trying to be responsive to visitors' needs. Do visitor groups want a sequence of galleries that are similar or distinct in meaningful ways? How does their sequence work as an overall experience? At what point do they get the most spectacular gallery? Are there issues with vision adjustments from dark to light spaces? Do visitors get lost, distracted, and disoriented?

Because exhibits are standing experiences and demand close mental engagement and constant choice, visitors typically experience museum fatigue after about 60 to 90 minutes, regardless of how much more there might be to see. For this reason, museums that offer opportunities to sit down and relax, such as a theater or a café, are able to hold their audiences longer. Longer dwell times for visitors usually correlate with visitors spending more on-site, larger market basins, and greater efficiencies of scale in operations (see also "97. Venue Capture Rates").

Basic architectural specifications, such as windows or darkness; ceiling heights; acoustic qualities; heating, ventilating, and air-conditioning systems; security features; load-in access; and lighting, make some galleries more appropriate for certain kinds of exhibits and programs than others. For example, a room for paintings is not a room for a starfish touch tank. Add to the basic architecture a series of long-term built in systems and support spaces—the experience platform layer, borrowing a Roy Shafer term—and a gallery becomes a flexible stage geared to support certain kinds of learning. The water play area at the Boston Children's Museum has views of the Fort Point Channel that relate to the shape and challenges of several large water tables that fill the gallery inside the windows. Each water table is surrounded by safety flooring, drains, and hooks full of rain slickers for the kids. This is a room designed and outfitted for water play. It is also a learning stage that successfully nurtures collaborative problem-solving and adaptation skills.

See "98. Visitor Experience: Concepts" for other exhibit and gallery concepts.

Exhibit Hub

The number of galleries (and a two-story structure) suggests that the museum galleries need a central orientation place, or hub, that will continually orient the visitor. Theme galleries and other components of the venue can be off this hub, which also acts as the central circulation spine for people moving between the two levels. This circulation hub also underscores the visitor's connection to views of XX and features an inlaid map of the region on its floor. The exhibit hub can also be left empty for function rentals, public art, and extra-large temporary exhibitions and feature scenarios provided that the hub is an open space and not a long hallway or spine.

Theme Galleries

There will be XX theme galleries within the museum galleries, each ranging in size from XX to XX net square feet. Aside from a few long-term galleries, most theme galleries have management-assigned cycles of content change. Each changing theme gallery (aka Delta gallery) will have built-in support for changing scenarios in that theme. Each gallery should have its own architectural identity based on what kind of learning space it wants to be.

Feature Exhibition Center and Multipurpose Galleries

The feature center will host temporary exhibitions in a wide range of subject matters that are relevant to the region's interests. Some exhibitions will be oriented to families with children (e.g., dinosaurs and giant insects), and some will be geared to appeal to adults by offering exhibitions featuring the latest trends in contemporary science and art, new perspectives on culture, and new ways of looking at history and culture.

The feature center is a multipurpose gallery whose primary use will be for temporary exhibitions but will be flexible enough to be used in other ways. Visitors will enter and exit the feature center from the main lobby and the exhibit hub. The feature center may include the following components and capacities:

- Two adjacent temporary exhibit galleries totaling XX square feet. The active programming of these spaces, both independently and combined, will be designed to attract repeat visitation and to complement the permanent exhibits with contemporary topics.
- Fully programmable to be capable of conversion into immersion environments involving light, sound, projec-

tions, movable walls, and other features that will allow the creation of scenic settings for traveling exhibits, such as for dinosaurs, *Titanic*, and other popular traveling exhibitions.
- It is likely that traveling exhibitions will occur primarily during the shoulder and peak seasons and that some of this space might be closed for winter storage or be used as school program and brown-bag lunch space during the school year.

Through temporary exhibits, the museum will present itself to its residential community as a vital organization in touch with relevant trends. Many of these temporary exhibits will come from peer museums and independent producers. In time, the museum will join the network of producers of such shows and will be able to get its content out to other communities.

Early Childhood Discovery Gallery

More and more attention is going to preschool education as research on brain development helps parents understand how much learning is going on before their children get to school. Museums are starting to include areas and programs for preschoolers and their parents, such as the Denver Children's Museum's Center for the Young Child and the Cleveland Children's Museum's Early Learning Center. These areas combine exhibits, programs, and discovery centers to develop children's learning skills as well as their parents' parenting skills.

The early childhood discovery gallery will engage children in learning at an early age. All exhibits will stimulate constructivist learning through multiple learning styles. Exhibits will provide a suite of learning opportunities by providing experiences that will encourage full-bodied play (sometimes encouraging a feeling of "safe danger"); provide hands-on experiences for direct learning; foster role playing; create emotional connections; provide context for content; encourage social, family-based learning; provide real objects and themed environments; and mix changeable elements with the familiar and safe.

A toddlers' area is tucked away in a quiet, safe nook. Entrance is permitted only to those under a certain height and to their caregiver. Here, the youngest visitors can play safely in a soft environment.

Discovery Centers

This section is based on writing by Charles Howarth.

Family discovery centers,[1] typically separate rooms opening onto the exhibit halls and featuring staff-assisted activities based on kits and other items that require some amount of supervision and handling, are popular features of science centers and children's museums; art and history museums are also implementing the concept. In history museums, children can put on period costumes and play roles using mirrors and theatrical settings. In science centers, older children can explore a kit containing items related to smoking, such as models of a smoker's lungs and throat, tubes of extracted tar, microscope slides, and other items to illustrate the effect of smoking. Younger children can play with model fossil parts to assemble their own pterodactyl.

Family discovery centers are not day care; in fact, parental participation in the experience is a key component of family learning, and discovery centers are developing specific roles for parents with their children in these settings. Discovery centers can be configured for different age ranges, such as for toddlers, 4- to 7-year-olds, 8- to 12-year-olds, and teenagers. Because of the age-specific nature of these learning resources, these age ranges are seldom combined, and large institutions will have several discovery centers. Discovery centers can be compact, ranging from 1,000 to 2,000 square feet.

A *swap shop* similar to the one at Science North in Sudbury, Ontario, might be a feature of the discovery centers. A swap shop is a place where children can bring items they have found or collected and turn them in for points that can be used to "purchase" items that other children have brought in or that have been supplied by the museum.

PLANNING WORKSHEETS

The following matrices show how the museum thinks the components will be used:

Table 74.1   Venues and Components by Age (Personal Context)

Age Range (Years)	Public Components
	Museum Galleries
1. 0 to 2 plus parents	
2. 3 to 6	
3. 7 to 12	
4. 13 to 17	
5. 18 to 24	
6. 25 to 34	
7. 35 to 54	
8. 55 and up	

* If subject or theme of the program appeals to this group and their age range

Table 74.2   Venues and Components by Key Visitor Segments

Key Visitor Segments	Public Components
	Museum Galleries
Adults with children	
Pre-K–12 school and youth groups	
Adults ages 34 and up visiting with adults	
Young adults ages 18 to 34 without children	
Teens ages 11 to 18	
Solo visitors ages 18 to 75 and up	

Table 74.3   Options for Admission Venues

Venues	Current	Future
Museum exhibit galleries		
Feature exhibition galleries		
Early learning discovery center		
Giant-screen/large-format theater		
Planetarium/fulldome		
Art film theater		
Multipurpose auditorium		
Other ticketed theater(s)		
Large-scale artifact(s)[1]		
Live animal habitats[2]		
Other performance space(s)		
Historic houses/sites		
Outdoor exhibits[3]		
Outdoor gardens or park		
Rides[4]		

[1] For example, a submarine, historic structure, or whaling ship.
[2] For example, an insectarium or butterfly pavilion.
[3] For example, interpretive trails, zip line, canopy walk, or climbing structure.
[4] For example, miniature trains, simulators, or pony rides.

Table 74.4   Sample Feature Center

Space	Sample Size (Net Square Feet)	Current Size (Square Feet)	Future Size
Feature gallery A	4,500 to 5,400		
Feature gallery B	3,000 to 3,600		
Entrance and preshow	750 to 1,200		
Exit gift shop	750 to 1,200		
Support spaces	500		
Totals	9,500 to 11,900		

☑   Mild interest and use
☑☑   Occasional use
☑☑☑   Regular use

NOTE

1.   The term *discovery center* is also used as the name of a whole museum, such as the Discovery Science Center of Orange County, California.

Section 75

Public Spaces

Program Center

INTRODUCTION

The program center (aka learning center, education center, or museum school) is described here as a series of connected spaces, but they could also be dispersed physically around your museum but connected administratively into one department, typically the education or program department.

The program center will have a number of outfitted spaces that will enable it to offer programs in the museum and across the region. Some of these spaces are intended as support, but most are intended to be semipublic, available by reservation to school groups or registered *program participants*. The program center will be accessible from the public entrances as well as connected to the museum galleries. This allows school groups and others to arrive at the museum, enter through the program center, receive broad orientation in the commons (an open area), proceed through the exhibit experience, and possibly return to the program center's program spaces for lunch in the commons and/or more in-depth programs in the labs before reassembling for departure. The program center will have loading facilities for its outreach programs.

THE PROGRAM CENTER

The museum's program center will have the following components and facilities:

- The Commons (Group Orientation and Lunchroom): The commons will be an open, flexible area immediately off the group entrance that will be used as an orientation area to introduce school and other organized groups to their experience at the museum. It will also serve as a community and social gathering place. During school visits, the commons can be used as a place to eat lunch, and it will have places for groups to store their lunches, backpacks, and other items as well as some vending machines. At other times, the commons can be used to hold meetings, science fairs, competitions, and workshops for larger groups and for a staging area for projects and informal community exhibits, particularly during the summer or holiday season. Further, the commons can be used for short-term overflow space needs. It will be equipped to operate in a range of modes, including screening of video orientation programs, hosting evening receptions, and corporate conferences.
- Themed Program Studios and Classrooms: At one level, the themed program studios are classrooms, each capable of hosting 35 students or registered participants. Yet each program lab is enhanced with equipment and capabilities that distinguish it from a typical classroom and enable a range of flexible programs to be offered through its facilities. Further, the equipment is built-in and can be covered, leaving a space appropriate for other uses, such as adult education and corporate rentals. The actual choices for equipment capabilities will be determined based on assessing the needs of teachers, scout groups, summer camps, adult education programs, and the function rental market, including area corporations and the convention center. Through careful scheduling and appeal to a number of audiences, the program studios can be kept active day and evening all week long. A menu of offerings will be developed and a schedule of participation fees charged; this course catalog will be marketed to appropriate audiences, and staff will adapt each program laboratory to suit the needs of a particular program and its audience. Program presenters, workshop facilitators, and project coaches will be drawn both from the staff and from outside contractors, many of whom will be graduate students, part-time teachers, and retired professionals. Current program has space for XX themed studios that can be divided into XX smaller spaces.
- Teacher Resource Center: This will be conveniently located in the program center and be accessible during the museum's open hours. It will provide display and demonstration space for teacher activity kits and other classroom materials that teachers may purchase, lease, or borrow. The participants in workshops may buy or pick up their workshop materials here. The resource center will also function as a flexible workshop space for small programs and meetings.

- Media and Network Control Room (Support Space): This will house the equipment to connect the museum to the regional educational network. This facility will be the center for two-way teleconferencing, production support, and other technical requirements to enable the museum to broadcast programs recorded anywhere in the museum to libraries and schools across the state that are equipped with appropriate materials and to the museum's mobile van to reach places that are not so equipped. The control room will also have a one-way mirror into the commons to serve as a distance learning studio for managing stage events in that facility.

- Kit Preparation and Distribution (Support Space): This is space and a loading dock for the museum's inventory of educational kits, including space to plan, assemble, repair, check in, and ship out kits to schools and other partners who will use the kits in their classrooms and programs. The on-site kit depot will have a modest inventory of loan kits. As funding for the program center grows, this space will need to be complemented by an off-site warehouse and workshop for the assembly and storage of the complete inventory. The off-site facility will be used for shipping and receiving, while the smaller on-site space will serve as an adjunct to the resource center and a supply location for the program studios that are using kits.

- Education Staff Offices (Support Space): This is an open office plan and meeting room with reference materials will support the museum's staff and provide preparation and relaxation space for the contractors presenting programs. Storage space will be included to support staff activity.

- Library and Resource Center: The museum will operate a library and resource center. This space will house the museum's book and media collections that relate to the museum's programs and collection. In addition to supporting in-house curators and scholars, it will welcome outside scholars, students, and the interested public to study the books in the library at reading tables and carrels. One of the features of the library will be a *career center* where visitors can research potential professional involvement in XX and a database that would allow youth to connect their interests with possible careers. For adults, the career center will be a resource for learning about retraining opportunities. Through a liaison with regional organizations, the career center will keep up to date on the economy's career needs.

- Community Library Branch: There are several libraries that operate branch facilities within museums, such as the Carnegie Science Center and the Indianapolis Children's Museum. There are also plenty of examples where museums provide libraries with temporary exhibits and with borrowable membership cards for library patrons. The Institute of Library and Museum Services has studies and publications on library–museum partnerships.

- Museum Preschool: The museum will run a preschool within the museum. Museum preschools use dedicated and specially equipped classrooms in conjunction with tours out to areas within the museum galleries. Thus, the child's experience is enriched by the museum's offerings, differentiating it from other preschools. Special provisions vary by state and may include child-sized bathroom fixtures and furnishings, safety surfaces and edges, an outdoor playground, and a dedicated entrance within the line of sight of the parents' drop-off curb. The Science Center of Iowa operates a preschool that is so much in demand that some parents reserve a place for their children as soon as they are born.

- Observatory: A rooftop shed with a retractable roof will contain an array of telescopes usable by groups to view the night sky. During the day, this flexible space can be used as another program studio in the program center.

- Collection Archive and Access Center: This will be a front door and reception to the museum's collection vaults. Here, scholars, amateurs, and students can come to request access to the collections physically. This interface between storage and public access potential is critical to maintain, though the demand is likely to be low. Most of the center's access routes to the collection are likely to be virtual. The center will focus its activities on increasing digital access to the full collection over time, prioritizing those aspects related to XX. The center currently includes a conservation lab. Collector groups and affinity clubs can hire these facilities to care for their own collections during scheduled workshop sessions.

- Volunteer Restoration Workshop: This is a place in the museum where community volunteers take on rebuilding and refurbishing large-scale artifacts that are part of the region's story, such as a grape press or a historic structure. The restoration activity will be a feature on public display. While visitors should be kept away from the work floor, a mezzanine where visitors can watch volunteers work on the current project and talk with them about the artifact will be appealing. The concept demands that the volunteers be willing to keep a relatively constant level of activity. There are many precedents for volunteer groups restoring historical objects. One example is the EAA Museum (Oshkosh, Wisconsin), which displays many airplanes that have been restored or built by its members all over the country and then flown or shipped to Oshkosh for display. The volunteers who undertake these restoration tasks are often retired individuals who had experience with the original in its heyday. Once the artifact is restored, it will go on display for a period of time, after which it will revert to the group that owned the artifact and undertook its restoration. Proposals for projects will be submitted by volunteer groups to the museum; the museum will select among the proposals and determine the guidelines for process and terms.

Section 76

Public Spaces

Retail and Functions

INTRODUCTION

This section is a menu of possible retail and function facilities (spaces) that a museum might consider.

You can select and adapt these spaces from the menu to fit your museum's needs and future plans. You are likely to have some spaces already in some degree. The menu contains spaces and facilities requested by museums in the past; there are bound to be additional facilities desired.

PUBLIC SPACES: RETAIL AND FUNCTIONS

Museum Shop

The XX-square-foot museum shop will be filled with fun games, kits, books, tools, and educational toys. The decor and overhead graphics will remind visitors that the gift shop is connected to the educational mission of the museum and that its offerings provide the visitor with an opportunity to extend his or her interest outside the museum. Staff at the shop will be able to make helpful connections between exhibits and programs that interest a visitor and items in the store that may help extend the learning experience at home.

Café

The museum's café will offer simple selections in a restful environment with self-service tables. The café will be designed as a fast-service family restaurant featuring hamburgers and French fries but also salad bars and information about nutrition.

The Museum Restaurant

A full-service restaurant with menu, tablecloths, and waiters will appeal to adult audiences with the time to relax and enjoy a meal themed to the museum. A few museums are able to operate a restaurant that also attracts nonvisitors, thereby expanding the museum's drop-in and community service. Museum restaurants can be sustainable in larger museums, but careful economic analysis by an experienced food service consultant is advised. Most such operations are subcontracted, as running a restaurant is a risky venture unless run by professional restauranteurs.

Function Rental Spaces

The museum will have dedicated event spaces available for private rentals at all hours, including when the museum is open to the public. These spaces will be adjacent to support and catering spaces with access to loading and garbage docks. The design and outfitting of the function rental spaces will be done with the advice from an advisory group of local event planners: Are dressing rooms needed for weddings? What equipment should be built in to catering support? What audiovisual functions are marketable? What is the inventory of tables and chairs?

Function Rental Space Options

- The building will be designed to permit simultaneous evening functions to XX small groups or XX large groups.
- The museum will not have dedicated function spaces but rather will make available for rental many of its public and semipublic spaces during off-hours. The exhibit halls, for example, can be rented by businesses holding award ceremonies, a university course

may rent a program lab for an evening course, a training firm may rent the feature theater's media and audience-response systems to run interactive training sessions for employees, and associations could rent the museum's boardroom for meetings on neutral territories.

- The functions will be supported by catering services adjacent to the café, which is likely to be run by the same concessionaire under contract to the museum to provide both food service to the general public and food and drink to function renters.

- Walk-in pantries, refrigerators, freezers, and secure, cooled garbage-holding rooms will be considered for the architectural program.

Section 77

Public Spaces

Theater Options

INTRODUCTION

Live demonstrations brought theater into museums from the beginning, and theater and exhibits have been complementary interpretation media for a long time. Theaters complement exhibits as learning resources because they reach learners at different levels. Theaters permit the development of a linear, sequential logic and story, whereas exhibits encourage random exploration and connections. Theatrical presentations can be much more experiential and emotional, complementing the more rational and interactive engagement with exhibits. Museum fatigue sets in after an hour, and theaters provide a chance to sit down. Both theaters and exhibits can be effective and popular learning resources; they just work differently, and each is suited to different content (see table 77.1).

This section is a menu of possible theater formats meant to complement a museum's other offerings. The section includes worksheets to help list and decide on formats that meet the museum's objectives. While some museums are part of performing arts complexes, this section does not include operas, orchestras, ballet and dance theaters, live stages, or other performing arts theaters.

You can select and adapt these spaces from the menu to fit your museum's needs and future plans. You are likely to have some spaces already in some degree. The menu contains theaters requested by museums in the past; there are bound to be additional facilities desired, and you may elect to combine formats into a new format.

Table 77.1   Theater and Exhibits as Learning Resources

Exhibits	Theaters
Random	Linear/sequential
Interactive	Experiential
Rational	Emotional
Concrete	Magical
Stand-up	Sit-down
Cognitive	Affective

PROGRAMMING A MUSEUM THEATER

Theaters can be usefully categorized by audience appeal/draw and by their role in the museum's business plan:

- Destination Theaters: These offer changing content and immersive or social experiences that are capable on their own of attracting visitors as the prime motivation for their site visit. Typically separately ticketed (also available in combination), destination theaters often require premium leases for regularly changing content, films, and experiences and significant marketing and advertising. Many destination theaters are expected to post a net operating margin. Examples are the Simons IMAX Theater at the New England Aquarium (Boston).
- Secondary Theaters: These depend on capturing some share of the visitors dawn to the museum site primarily by its other attractions or draws. Admission is typically charged as an "up-sell" or combination ticket. Many planetariums and documentary film theaters are secondary theaters. Some generate revenue; of those, some are net contributors to the museum's budget.

- Enrichment Theaters: These are typically included in the general admission prices. The launch of such theaters can justify an increase in general admission; thus, they can enrich both the visitor's experience and the museum's earned revenue. In later years, cost–benefit calculations are challenging, as enrichment theaters have varying capture rates and their impact on visitor engagements is hard to predict and quantify. Examples are object theaters, performed dramatizations, introductory media presentations, auditorium demonstrations, and live animal encounters.

Theaters can also be categorized by their source and supply of content:

- Library Theaters: These share a sufficiently large inventory of leasable "shows" that can play in a large enough number of compatible theaters to justify amortizing the cost of producing and distributing changing content that draws audiences. Giant-screen, fulldome, and DCI-compliant film theaters are examples.
- In-House Theaters: These have unique setups and technologies not shared by enough others to justify amortized production. While content can change, production and installation are nonstandard tasks produced by the museum for just its one theater with custom content, unique results, and experience. Examples are The Works (Carnegie Science Center, Pittsburgh, Pennsylvania), older planetariums, and some object theaters.
- Dedicated Theaters: These have unique setups specially designed for one show. This approach is well suited to museums and settings where the audience is constantly changing, such as tourist sites or schools and colleges. Examples are the Salem Witch Museum, the Imperial War Museum's blitz simulation in London, and *Freedom Rising* at the National Constitution Center (Philadelphia).

PROGRAM SPACES: THEATER OPTIONS

Giant-Screen Theater

A giant-screen film theater with a projection system installed by IMAX or another supplier will be able to show large-format films, such as *Everest*, *Grand Canyon*, and *The Living Sea*.

Giant-screen film theaters have worked well in museum settings, although the novelty is definitely declining. Much of the film programming is produced for educational institutions and will be appropriate for the museum. Subjects tend to feature science, nature, and travel, and there are few history-oriented films; however, positioning the giant-screen theater to be able to show all educational films will broaden its appeal and its library.

Giant-screen theaters come in both flat and dome screens. The Giant Screen Cinema Association maintains the technical specifications called DIGSS 1.1 (Digital Immersive Screen Specifications, developed originally by the White Oak Institute with support from a National Science Foundation grant).

Giant-screen films have developed into a powerful learning experience, supported by curriculum materials, websites, merchandise, and other dimensions that continue the learning experience beyond the film itself. But IMAX Corporation has now changed its focus to commercial applications, and attendance has declined at many institutional theaters, as the format is no longer unique. Nevertheless, educational films are still produced at the rate of more than 10 titles annually, and everyone focuses attention and marketing on making theaters do the best they can.

Programming a giant-screen theater to maximize its educational and economic impact is a skill learned after years of experience selecting films, negotiating distribution deals, and arranging for marketing and promotions. Prime-time slots should be given to giant-screen film presentations, and required marketing dollars should be focused on the launch and support of feature films. When the museum is closed or in late evening or other off-peak time slots, the giant-screen theater can be used for other purposes, such as meetings, media presentations, and lecture series; however, the steeply banked seats and large screen make live presentations and panels difficult—more so in giant-screen dome theaters than flat-screen versions. Moreover, projection of less detailed and/or smaller-scale projections often look weak on the large screen. High-quality digital video imagery, however, is more recently helping to offset such perceptions.

The Fulldome

Many planetariums, with their hemispherical dome screens, have evolved to *fulldomes* to fill all 180 degrees with projected digital imagery as well as a projected star field.

The fulldome will be a multipurpose auditorium serving a variety of needs and covering a range of topics. Given an array of equipment, including a star-field projection system by Sky Skan, Evans and Sutherland, Spitz, Zeiss, or another supplier, the fulldome can be used for the kinds of presentations listed in chapter 5 under "Fulldome."

The fulldome will be separately ticketed.

Digital Visualization Lab

This small dome theater can serve as a study planetarium, but because of its digital visualization and projection technologies, it can do so much more. Images and databases developed by the associated digital visualization studio will allow guests and renters to see live and real information on an immersive dome.

The digital visualization lab will allow guests operating an adjacent jukebox-like kiosk to create their own minishows and then go inside to experience them moments later.

Auditorium and Presentation Theater

A multipurpose auditorium and presentation theater seating XX to XX will be a useful addition to the community as well as an important resource for the museum. The museum will use the auditorium for school programs, public demonstrations, and evening travel and member series; during the weekends, children's theater could be performed. The community will use the auditorium on a rental basis for awards and presentations, corporate meetings, public forums, and other community events. The auditorium will be adjacent to open spaces capable of hosting dinner parties and/or receptions.

Object Theater

The museum will use the XX collection as the basis for a dramatic, surrounding "object theater" that combines collection cases and mounts in settings with high-definition video and other media to tell the story of XX. This is a high-tech sound-and-light show with a serious scholarly story, taking advantage of creative lighting, sound effects, and a rapidly moving story line. The XX-minute presentation will be fun and dramatic in a comfortable, seated theater.

3-D and 4-D Theaters

These are specially equipped theaters with high-definition 3-D films, sometimes adding motion-base seats synchronized with physical effects, such as water spritzes. Much smaller than giant-screen theaters and using traditional screen aspect ratios, these theaters offer a relatively low cost source of programming, which some museums have used as a revenue stream by ticketing separately. Caution must be used so that this theater does not cannibalize other theater revenue.

Interactive Theaters

Digital technologies also offer the promise of audience participation, using approaches such as virtual reality, mobile apps, enhanced reality, in-seat polling, social media contexts for programs, group gaming, and audience competitions. Some museum theaters have interactive technologies, but shows with interactive sequences or menus have not established a strong demand. With 21st-century participation trends, however, digital technologies have potential for museums experimenting with new formats of audience participation.

PLANNING WORKSHEETS

Table 77.2   Summary of Theater Formats

Network theaters (library of shows exchanged)	
a. Giant-screen film theaters	Ticketed
b. Planetariums/fulldome/ digital dome theaters	Ticketed
c. Art film theater	Ticketed
d. Multipurpose community auditoriums	Rentals
e. 3-D theaters	Up-charge
Unique and added-value attractions (fixed, unique show/ experience)	
a. Customized film theaters	Included
b. Digital visualization labs	Included
c. Object theaters	Included
d. Interactive theaters	Included
e. Wide formal theaters	Up-charge
f. Themed audio tours	Up-charge
g. High-tech illusion theaters	Included
h. Live story theaters	Included
i. Regional experience shows	Up-charge
j. Experience simulators	Ticketed
k. Ride experiences	Ticketed
l. Artisanal craft studios	Rentals
m. Special tours (e.g., a coal mine)	Ticketed
n. Large objects (e.g., a submarine)	Ticketed

Table 77.3   Business Objectives for the Theater

	Priority
Major changing programming to attract repeat visits from residents	
Increase on-site dwell time and spending	
Increase educational impacts/learning outcomes	
Increase overall attendance	
Significant contribution to net income	
Maintain the current standards of brand quality	
Increase the perceived value of the visitor's experience	
Support additional ancillary income sources	
Develop tourism and its economic impact	
Broaden appeal and audiences	
Expand community services	
Change, update our image	

Table 77.4   Theater Format Evaluations

	Importance Factor	1 Theater Option	2 Theater Option	3 Theater Option
Quality of experience				
Appeal of the format				
Appeal of the shows				
Library of software				
Production cost and quality				
Flexibility of use				
Inventory of compatible theaters				
Quality of theater association				
Educational impact				
Service to educational mission				
Learning methodology effectiveness				
Range of content possible				
Fit with context				
Net revenue generation capabilities				
Operating constraints				
Market positioning strategy				
Box office appeal				
Fit with market				
Competition in region				
Perceived value/ticket price				
Scale and cost of operation				
Net revenue potential				
Risk of loss				
Capital considerations				
Capital cost and process				
Proven track record				
Architectural fit				
Quality of vendor product and support				
Terms of ownership				
Upgradability				
Risk				
Terms of business arrangements				
Reliability				
Donor appeal				
Case statements				
Naming opportunities				
Sponsorship opportunities				
Recognition benefits				

Section 78

Purposes and Impacts

Definitions

INTRODUCTION

This book uses a family of terms based on the museum theory of action and on the idea that museums pursue multiple, prioritized purposes. The terms also recognize that a museum's desired impacts may be different from the benefits perceived by its stakeholders.

This section defines mission, purposes, impacts, benefits, and key performance indicators.

INTENTIONAL PURPOSES AND DESIRED IMPACTS

A museum aspires to have *impacts* on its community, audiences, and supporters. The community, audiences, and supporters receive *benefits* from the museum. The benefits can be different from the impact: a family visiting an aquarium receives the benefit of a quality family experience, while the aquarium's desired impact on the family is to heighten their awareness of conserving biodiversity. Or the benefits and impacts can be aligned: new parents bring their toddler to a children's museum to see her develop and learn with new kinds of challenges, and the children's museum's mission is child development. Studying the alignment between a museum's benefits and impacts may illuminate potentials and inefficiencies. It is useful to remember the distinction, which hinges on their prepositions: society, individuals, and organizations receive benefits *from* the museum. The museum has impacts *on* society, individuals, and organizations. Benefits are in the eyes of the receiver; impacts are in the desires of the museum:

1. *Mission* and *Purpose*: These terms are used interchangeably, recognizing that readers may have different associations, including expectations that *mission* is singular and that *purposes* is often pluralized and generally thought to be subservient to mission. *Multiple-mission museum* may be a more challenging term than *multiple-purpose museum*, but it makes the distinction clear between this new plural form and the traditional singular *mission-focused museum*.
2. Intentional Purposes: These are the public, private and personal values the museum commits its resources to generate.
3. Desired Impacts: These are the prioritized outcomes, impacts, and benefits the museum hopes to observe and measure if the museum is successful at achieving its purposes.
4. Perceived Benefits: These are what the audience and supporters think they receive from the museum in return for their money, time, and effort.
5. Key Performance Indicators: These are quantitative formulas, such as ratios, averages, and comparable benchmarks, that measure the effectiveness and efficiency of the activities. Such indicators typically use evaluation and/or operating data in formulas that are meaningful to managers.

Section 79

Purposes

Samples and Options

INTRODUCTION

This section contains packages of impacts and benefits. The packages are genericized samples from museum master plans. You may wish to copy those closest to your aims into first drafts of intentional purposes, case statements, and other planning and development documents, but please customize them to your museum's context.

Unlike the previous list of 14 categories of potential museum impacts and benefits (see #43 and #44) the selection in this section is not comprehensive. There are many more possible packages of impacts and benefits than are listed here. You will want to adapt these and use them as models to define your own intentional purposes. Intentional purposes do not need to align perfectly with one of the 14 categories. Most likely, your intentional purposes will be packages of impacts and benefits.

For example, the first sample, "Deliver STEM Learning Outcomes," has aspects of the following categories:

- *Broadening participation*
- *Serving education*
- *Contributing to the economy*
- *Enabling personal growth*

Many of the samples are written for informal science education (ISEs) institutions, also known as science museums and centers, aquariums, natural history museums, and, often, children's museums. Other disciplines will want to shift language and intent as appropriate to your discipline and context.

The following text and table 79.1 may be selected and adapted to suit your museum.

SAMPLE PACKAGES OF INTENTIONAL PURPOSES AND OBJECTIVES

Deliver STEM Learning Outcomes

The museum will seek to illuminate science, technology, engineering, and math (STEM) and to act as a bridge between science and the public of all ages. A special emphasis will be placed on career information that may encourage children to select science and engineering professions that will help supply the region's future with well-prepared professionals. An important component of this challenge is education about the effects of science and technology on our lives and demonstrations of the ways in which individuals can usefully apply their learning. A major new populist museum will add an important option for residents who are trying to educate and excite themselves and their children about the joy of discovery:

- Stimulate visitors' interest and expand their understanding of science and technology through the use of hands-on, participatory exhibits, programs, and school and community outreach initiatives.
- Offer a safe, excellent, and rewarding experience for all visitors.
- Encourage participation in science and technology in all sectors of the population, especially underserved communities, including women, minorities, the economically disadvantaged, and the physically challenged.
- Relate science to everyday experiences and real-life applications in order to engage nonscientists and to illustrate ways in which an appreciation of science, nature, and technology can enhance one's daily life.
- Communicate the beauty, power, and importance of science and technology and improve attitudes toward these fields and toward scientists and engineers.
- Work with schools and teachers to enhance science education in the region.

250

- Represent science as a creative human enterprise open and accessible to all people.
- Be the focal point for public understanding of science and technology, be a creditable forum for public policy debate on issues in science and technology, and give visitors an opportunity to wrestle with complex social issues related to science and technology.
- Foster dynamic learning and program collaboratives with other institutions, including universities, the region's secondary and elementary school system, science-related associations, and other science centers and museums worldwide.

Enable Excellent Experiences for Our Visitors and Program Participants

The museum should serve our visitors and program participants by offering them excellent experiences. If we do that job well, our investors and community partners will also be well served. Earned revenue will be over XX percent of our total revenues, and our visitors and program participants will be our primary revenue source.

No one answer will meet all visitor needs. Not only are visitors different in their interests, but research has shown that individual visitors like a variety of different kinds of experiences. A full menu of types of experiences—including exhibits, demonstrations, films, and outdoor activities as well as food services and relaxing amenities—can be offered; visitors will assemble their own sequence of experiences according to their interests, time, stamina, and group makeup.

Provide a Community Learning Resource

The vision is for a center for human creativity, an open house, a forum for societal debates, and a marketplace of ideas. Learning resources will be focused on developing lifelong learning skills, not only transferring information. As a part of our commitment to provide learning resources for the community, the museum will do the following:

- Stimulate visitors' interest and expand their understanding of XX through the use of firsthand experiences with engaging exhibitions, theaters, programs, and school and community outreach initiatives.
- Develop core skills or competencies, such as problem solving, abstract and system thinking, teamwork, organization, experimentation, and adaptation.
- Commit to firsthand, lifelong learning through do-it-yourself, spontaneous learning experiences.
- Strengthen the learning infrastructure of society, not as a frill but as a foundation.
- Work in partnership with the region's universities, community colleges, private and public schools, and other educational organizations so that the museum's learning resources will complement their efforts.

Become a Common Meeting Ground

The museum will help the greater region achieve the goal of broader unity by becoming a significant place for community gathering. From board-level committees to activities for visitors, we will bring people together. The museum will engage in long-term community building by establishing and maintaining collaborative partnerships with specific communities, including neighborhoods, cultural groups, regional businesses, the educational system, sponsoring investors, and numerous others who share our passion for learning skill development and cultural exchange. The museum will become part of the essential regional infrastructure.

Museums will serve as a social and cultural bridge, encourage a feeling of local community ownership so that all feel welcome, and utilize the facility as a focus for intercultural programs, professional associations, public debates, and other community events.

In order to create an institution that is a key member of the community and a vital part of its learning infrastructure, the museum will do the following:

- Bring people together and attract groups and other community gatherings, thereby serving as a social and cultural bridge.
- Encourage a feeling of local community ownership of the museum so that all will feel welcome. Utilize the facility as a focus for intercultural programs, professional associations, public debates, and other community events.
- Develop a community relationship that encourages repeat visits by offering multiple contexts of use, repeatable experiences, and changing programs.
- Establish open and trusting visitor relationships based on a history of good experiences and an open dialogue that continually reinvents ourselves with our customers.
- Be clear about who we are and the value for what we offer.

Commit to Firsthand Science and Technology

Given the region's rich tradition of invention and industry, one of the principal focuses of the hands-on exhibits and theater programs should be on the heritage of engineering and applied science that has made the region one of the world's centers for innovation. Further, given the region's desire to retain strength in this area for future generations, these topics should be high on the list of objectives and should be addressed through a variety of exhibits and programs focusing on creativity and problem solving.

In particular, the state department of economic development listed the following industries as major players and/or potential growth areas for the region's economy: XX and XX. As a part of its commitment to XX, the museum will do the following:

- Represent science and technology as a creative human enterprise open and accessible to all people.

- Highlight XX as "something people do," as a cultural process, and as an unending debate.
- Foster the spirit of ingenuity that characterizes the region and celebrate the invention and creativity that has been responsible for the region's technology heritage.
- Humanize the people who made the difference in the region—their dreams, their successes, and their failures.

Inspire Tomorrow's Workforce

The wealth of possibilities for tomorrow's careers goes well beyond "doctor," "lawyer," and "banker." Students need to know the possibilities but also need to realize that most of the higher-paying jobs involve some aspect of science, technology, engineering, and/or math. Tomorrow's economy and workforce needs to open young and transitioning adult minds to exciting career options, to meet role models, and to explore developing science and engineering skills and acquiring introductory knowledge about a field.

Integrated learning is needed for well-rounded citizens, who also need the basic working and living skills that will be needed in the near future—what some call 21st-century learning skills, such as problem solving, critical thinking, communication, teamwork, and project design.

New interdisciplinary approaches that layer science with arts and humanities are in tune with the kinds of social innovation that will be prized in the future. In a report published by the National Academies of Science, Hill (2007) observes that culture, the arts, and social sciences may be more important in the future than mastery of physical sciences and mechanical engineering.

A postscientific society will have several key characteristics, the most important of which is that innovation leading to wealth generation and productivity growth will be based principally not on world leadership in fundamental research in the natural sciences and engineering but rather on world-leading mastery of the creative powers (and the basic sciences) of individual human beings, their societies, and their cultures (Hill, 2007):

- Increase the awareness of and encourage the choice of careers in the fields of XX and XX, thereby inspiring the next generation.
- Reflect the region's excellence in the fields of XX, XX, and XX and support the region's continued leadership in these disciplines.
- Serve as springboard or gateway for learning about the region's target industry sectors.
- Help maintain and enhance national and regional competitiveness in skills, abilities, and productivity.
- Address workforce readiness and technical preparation initiatives, such as job training, career issues, technology transfer, skill development, and other educational programs designed to help with the transition into new economies, technologies, and industries.
- Improve the image of the city.

- Showcase important developments by the industries of the city, featuring the region's strengths.

Develop Tourism

Museums, with their unique facilities and educational exhibitions, provide exciting attractions, particularly with large-scale exhibitions. As a tourist facility, a museum can broaden its base of public support by attracting distant visitors, making the region more attractive to visitors and more able to prevent "leakage" by keeping some residents from traveling away for their leisure activities.

To maximize the economic benefits, the museum will do the following:

- Set high standards of accommodation for distant visitors and make each visit a recreational and learning success.
- Offer a safe, excellent, and rewarding experience for all visitors.
- Showcase regional stories, character, environment, and achievements in science and technology.
- Work with the state tourism division and with other regional attractions and private organizations to develop more tourism to the city.

Provide Informational Services to XX Industry Professionals and Scholars

In addition to its public visitors, the museum will serve a specialized audience of individuals who are professionally and academically interested in the XX industry. The museum's objectives for this audience will include the following:

- Encourage, facilitate, and provide training, applied research, information, and database services and consulting to the XX industry on issues related to business operations, management, strategic consumer marketing, planning, programming and engineering, and technology.
- Develop continuing education programs for the industry that are not now being provided by others, with emphasis on the use of distance learning and contemporary distribution technologies.
- Provide support to the academic community for academic research and curricular development at the undergraduate- and graduate-degree levels in programs related to the XX industry.
- Develop career information about XX and serve as a resource on the topic.
- Disseminate findings resulting from research to corporate members, the general public, and the academic community as appropriate through print, video, or other media.
- Be a resource about educational and informational resources for the XX industry.

Conserve and Interpret Collections and Artifacts

The museum serves as a conservator for XX's key documents and artifacts. A collections management policy will accept items that are of significance to XX or that can be used to support the museum's educational objectives.

Guidelines for fulfilling the museum's responsibilities in heritage recognition and commemoration include the following:

- Establish and implement a collections acquisition and maintenance policy that will obtain, conserve, and interpret items of significance to the heritage of XX.
- Maintain with the highest preservation standards the XX industry's comprehensive archive. All appropriate media and formats are collected and cataloged with contemporary technology.
- Develop the economic benefits of the intellectual property rights of the items owned by or loaned to the museum in a manner consistent with the museum's purposes and guiding principles.

Support Readiness for the Future

The region's economy is undergoing fundamental structural shifts. High-tech and service-oriented industries are playing an increasingly important role in the state's economy, while traditional manufacturing and defense industries are shifting their focus. This economic reorientation has important implications for the future, including the creation of new kinds of jobs for the region's workforce in coming generations. A special emphasis will be placed on career information that may encourage the region's children to explore and potentially select science and engineering professions that will help supply the region's future with well-prepared individuals. The museum will serve as a catalyst and be part of the infrastructure that develops programs to serve these changing needs and give competitive advantage to the region's industry. The museum will do the following:

- Reflect the region's excellence in the fields of XX, XX, and XX and support the region's continued leadership in these disciplines.
- Help maintain and enhance national and regional competitiveness in skills, abilities, and productivity.
- Increase the awareness of and encourage the exploration of careers that include XX, XX, and XX skills, thereby inspiring the next generation to be comfortable with their processes.

Quality of Life

One of the main contributions that the museum makes is to add to the cultural life of residents. The region is undersupplied, for a region of its size and sophistication, with other large cultural facilities geared toward informal family education. A day at the museum with all the kids and perhaps the visiting in-laws is an attractive leisure-time option. The museum is also a resource for parents and teachers to help their children and students understand the world they live in.

Through active programming, museums develop a community relationship that encourages repeat visits by offering multiple contexts of use, repeatable experiences, and changing programs. They establish open and trusting relationships based on a history of good experiences and an open dialogue so that they continually reinvent themselves with their customers. The museum will do the following:

- Provide a regionally focused attraction and improve the quality of life.
- Provide an educational and excellent experience for all visitors and especially encourage the frequent return of all visitors.
- Encourage a feeling of local community ownership of the museum so that all will feel welcome and utilize the facility as a focus for programs, professional associations, public debates, and other community events.
- Support and cooperate with other agencies and individuals in the region and nationally, working to improve public understanding of XX.
- Bring people together and attract groups, thereby serving the community as a social and cultural umbrella.

Create a Sustainable Organization

The overarching financial objective is to create a viable and sustainable organization capable of operating smoothly and attracting recapitalization funds to remain connected to the community. The museum will do the following:

- Operate from a business structure that will allow the museum to best achieve its mission and objectives for its visitors, program participants, and supporters.
- Generate sufficient earned and support revenues to operate the facility as envisioned in the master plan.
- Ensure that earned revenues are at least XX percent of total revenues and that support revenues are the remaining XX percent.
- Attract a minimum of XX visitors in the first year of operation and XX visitors in a stabilized operating year.
- Secure long-term, continuing support revenues from organizations and agencies that are served by and support the museum's educational mission and other objectives.
- Total revenues should exceed total expenses by at least XX percent; the balance shall be rolled over to a capital improvement fund.
- An operating cash fund should be maintained at XX percent of total expenses, to be used and replenished as fluctuations

in cash flow demand or permit. Surpluses beyond this amount shall be transferred into the capital improvement fund. Initial funds shall be provided by the capital budget.

Raise the Necessary Capital

In terms of raising necessary capital, the following will be done:

- The capital improvement fund shall address new and replacement exhibits, equipment, and other ongoing capital expenses, which would be the equivalent of depreciation costs. Assuming an average 15-year life, the fund should be prepared to spend XX percent per year of the capital cost of the physical plant and the exhibits starting in year 5. Surpluses to these amounts shall be transferred into the endowment fund.
- The endowment fund shall be seeded with a principal of $XX from the capital budget. The museum will spend the income (but not principal) for operations through the annual budget approved by the trustees.
- Incur no long-term capital debt, although some degree of short-term pledge financing may be expected.

PLANNING WORKSHEET

Table 79.1   Sample Intentional Purposes

	Now	Future
Deliver STEM learning outcomes		
Enable excellent experiences for visitors and program participants		
Provide a community learning resource		
Become a common meeting ground		
Commit to firsthand science and technology		
Inspire tomorrow's workforce		
Develop tourism		
Provide informational services to industry professionals and scholars		
Conserve and interpret collections and artifacts		
Support readiness for the future		
Build the quality of life		
Create a sustainable organization		
Raise the necessary capital		

See "15. Bibliography for Museums" for citation reference.

Section 80

Revenue

Categories

INTRODUCTION

Just as there are many types of museums, there are many financial operating models. The range varies depending not only on type of museum but also among similar museums, such as art museums or history museums.

This section is written by contributing authors Duane Kocik and Jeanie Stahl.
See also "61. Servant of Four Masters Model."

CATEGORIES OF REVENUES

Table 80.1 groups revenue by external and internal sources.

Table 80.2 presents average revenue by museum discipline for U.S. museums and is sorted by highest earned revenue. The balance among earned, support, and other revenue also varies by country. Non-U.S. museums generally receive substantially more funding—and sometimes all of their funding—from governments.

The median data for all respondents in table 80.2 are skewed by the large number of respondents in two categories: history museum/historical society (typically very low earned revenue) and art museums (typically higher revenue from endowments). The low number of respondents in some of the categories may also skew data. For example, children's/youth museums generally have a very low—and sometimes zero—percentage from investment income. Most likely, the data were skewed by one of the few children's museums with a very large endowment.

Table 80.3 shows the broad range of performance among museums of the same discipline. In the table, each data point indicates the percentage of annual earned revenue for one of the 72 science centers that are U.S. members of the Association of Science-Technology Centers (ASTC) and responded to the ASTC 2014 survey. The range of earned revenue is from 0 percent to almost 100 percent, showing the great diversity even among similar types of museums.

Table 80.1   Six Revenue Sectors: Four External and Two Internal

Earned revenues (external)
    Visitors
    Program participants
Support revenues (external)
    Public
    Private
Capital asset income (internal)
    Endowment income
    Leases, intellectual property, and other asset income

256

Section 80

Table 80.2   Funding Sources by Type of Museum

Funding Sources by Segment Median	Government	Private	Earned	Investment	No. of Respondents
Science/technology center/museum	19.3%	28.9%	48.8%	3.0%	22
Children's/youth museum	11.7%	27.8%	48.3%	12.1%	14
Specialized museum	19.9%	37.7%	33.2%	9.3%	46
Historic house/site	23.0%	34.6%	31.7%	10.7%	49
Natural history/anthropology Mus.	24.2%	38.3%	31.1%	6.4%	21
Living collections	35.4%	20.3%	30.0%	14.3%	12
General museum	32.6%	33.7%	24.8%	8.8%	52
History museum/historical society	36.4%	31.0%	24.0%	8.5%	114
Art museum	13.3%	46.6%	21.5%	18.6%	123
All, 2009 report	24.4%	36.5%	27.6%	11.5%	453
All, 2006 report	24.1%	35.2%	31.0%	9.6%	693

Source: American Association of Museums, 2006 and 2009 Museum Financial Information, pp. 63 and 58.

Table 80.3   Earned Revenue Percentage of Revenue for 72 U.S. Science Centers

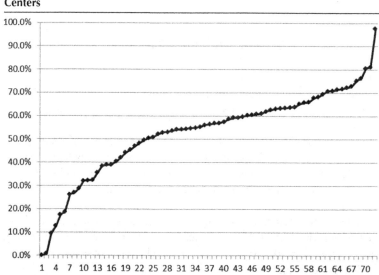

Source: Data are derived from the 2014 ASTC Science Center Statistics, Copyright © Association of Science-Technology Centers, Washington, D.C., http://www.astc.org.

Section 81

Earned and Support Revenue

Checklist

INTRODUCTION

Table 81.1 lists some of the typical categories of a museum's potential earned and support revenue. Each of these market sectors is explored in more detail in other sections of this book.

Table 81.1   Core Potential Revenue Sources

	Current	Future
Visitor-based earned revenues		
Admissions revenue from visitors		
Museum galleries		
Planetarium/feature experience		
Visit enhancement options (special exhibition up-charges, audio guides)		
Festival and event fees		
Retail shop and food service revenues		
Memberships (basic)		
Program-based revenues		
Preschool		
Charter or magnet school		
Facility rentals		
Fee-based programs (films, courses)		
Camps		
Ceremonial, memorial, and honorary induction events		
Fees for school and youth group programs		
Grant-funded educational programs (e.g., after-school workshops)		
Teacher professional development programs		
Outreach programs		
Web, social media, and virtual programs		
Private support–based revenues		
Donor bequests and gifts		
Annual campaign		
Memberships (higher level)		
Fund-raising events		
Private foundation grants		
Corporate membership		
Corporate sponsorships		
Public support–based revenues		
City		
County		
State		
Federal		
Public foundation/agency grants		
Asset income		
Leases to tenants		
Intellectual property income		
Endowment income		

Section 82

Earned Revenue

Business Lines

INTRODUCTION

Museums have many precedented and potential sources of earned revenue. The options listed in table 82.1 are a menu for you to consider when trying to expand earned revenue. No one is predicting that any option will be a net revenue generator in your context, and economic feasibility analysis should precede development.

POTENTIAL EARNED REVENUE BUSINESS LINES

Table 82.1   Earned Revenue Options (Partial Listing)

Visitor Revenues (All Branded)	*Program Revenues (All Branded)*
☐ Exhibit galleries	☐ Mission simulations
☐ Long-term galleries (ideally, free)	☐ Challenger centers
☐ *Scenario change galleries*	☐ BUBL (Rochester, New York)
☐ Temporary exhibit galleries	☐ Information and interpretation services
☐ Theaters	☐ Cell phone interpretation (e.g., talking streets)
☐ Giant-screen (e.g., *IMAX*) theaters	☐ *Special interest blogs (online clubhouses)*
☐ Planetariums and fulldome	☐ *Relationship-building programs*
☐ *Digital visualization theaters*	☐ Appraisal and authentication services
☐ Digital dome/fulldome	☐ Learning and conference center
☐ High-definition digital theaters	☐ Program fees
☐ 3-D cinema	☐ Camps (on- and off-site)
☐ Motion simulators 4-D	☐ Corporate meetings
☐ Multipurpose community auditoriums	☐ Teacher development
☐ Interactive theaters	☐ *Dialogue center and breakout rooms*
☐ Experience theaters	☐ Conference center
☐ Feature exhibits	☐ Team project centers
☐ Feature exhibition center	☐ Digital family history centers
☐ Children's museum	☐ *FabLabs*
☐ Maker spaces	☐ Teen clubhouse
☐ Outdoor exhibit areas	☐ *Planning and production studios*
☐ Ride experiences	☐ Citizen science/history
☐ Insectariums/butterfly pavilions	☐ Recognition, award, and challenge programs
☐ Special tours of large objects	☐ Competitions, contests/rallies
☐ Miniature golf course	☐ Seal-of-approval licensing
☐ Miniature trains	☐ Sponsor recognition programs
☐ Membership	☐ Topical fairs (science, history)
☐ Added learning value	☐ Coproduction events
☐ Mobile/MP3/iPod/audio guide rentals	☐ *Digital visualization labs and forums*
☐ *RFID follow-through connections*	☐ Added-value catering and functions
☐ Events	☐ Themed singles events
☐ Ethnic/cultural events	☐ Food service to functions, programs, and events
☐ Artisan craft fairs	☐ Facility and site partnerships
☐ Theme weekends	☐ Museum residential

☐ On-site retail
  ☐ Museum shop
  ☐ Theme shop
  ☐ Crafts center
  ☐ Book fair
☐ Visitor support services
  ☐ Café, vending, etc.
  ☐ Member centers
☐ Satellite facilities
  ☐ *Family centers*
  ☐ *Community galleries*
  ☐ Corporate lobbies
  ☐ Prototype studio
☐ Learning resources production
☐ Learning resources distribution
  ☐ Off-site branded retail

☐ Lease space to affiliated organizations
  ☐ Magnet or charter schools
☐ Early learning services
  ☐ Preschools
  ☐ Parenting centers
☐ Outreach
  ☐ School programs
  ☐ Library programs
  ☐ Community services
  ☐ Travel/tour programs
  ☐ Satellite facilities
☐ Services to museums and collectors
  ☐ Conservation centers
  ☐ *Online collections links*

Section 83

Site Selection

INTRODUCTION

The evaluation of proposed sites for a new or relocated museum will require multiple perspectives, each with its own set of parameters. The principal perspectives below (not prioritized) are presented with sample questions to be asked of the site.

You can use the evaluation matrixes to compare sites by your selected and prioritized criteria.

This section is written by contributing author Victor A. Becker.

SITE SELECTION

As soon as enough has been determined about the contents of the facility to begin to project its likely total scale, the process of site selection can begin. There are situations, of course, in which a favored site is already in mind, but commitment to that site should be withheld until it can be verified that it will satisfactorily accommodate the architectural program. In due diligence, the site evaluation process described below should be conducted on the favored site to ensure its adequacy before investing resources on architects' and engineers' time to come to the conclusion that the site is inadequate for the envisioned museum.

Physical Potential of Site

- Does it accommodate the architectural program size comfortably, ideally on one level, and with room for future expansion? It is highly recommended that sites be large enough to accommodate a one-story building so that the project can invest a greater portion of the available space in net program space. When evaluating site size, all of the site requirements need to be defined (see table 83.1).
- Is it a stand-alone building with its own driveways (very desirable control), or will the museum be in a development or buildings with others (compromised by tenant restrictions)?
- Is the site easy for first-time visitors, both locals and tourists, to find?
- Is it easily visible to a high volume of passersby (on foot and/or in cars)?
- Does it offer potential for turning the museum building into a landmark?
- Does it offer good school bus access with ample room for drop-off and pickup with sufficient nearby bus-parking potential?
- Does it offer potential for outdoor exhibits and programs, especially during the summer?
- Is there space within (or adjacent to) the site for building equipment and materials?
- Is there satisfactory access to the site for heavy construction equipment and 55-foot semi-trailer trucks delivering traveling exhibits?

Neighborhood and Community Support

- Will the site offer a good fit with the immediate neighbors?
- Does it have the potential to increase the attendance numbers?
- Is the character of the surrounding neighborhoods inviting and accommodating to outsiders?
- Is the character of the surrounding neighborhoods appropriate for the museum's likely visitors?
- Does it provide a comfortable environment for use by projecting a clear sense of security and safety, especially at night?

Table 83.1   Minimum and Desirable Site Requirements

Space	GSF
Building gross square foot footprint	XXX
Exterior site components	
Exterior exhibits/programs	XXX
Icons/public art, etc..	XXX
Circulation	
Parking for XX cars	XXX
Parking for XX buses	XXX
Public vehicle access	XXX
Service vehicle access	XXX
Total minimum usable area required	XXX
Future expansion	XXX
Total desirable usable area required	XXX

- Is it supported by nearby activity (e.g., restaurants, shops, and parks) that can create a longer and more attractive experience for the visitor?
- Does it risk excluding certain neighborhoods from access?

Marketing Appeal

- Does the site have general appeal to neighboring residents?
- Does it have general appeal to tourists who may not have been to the region before?
- Will the site facilitate capital fund-raising?
- Does the site risk losing current visitors or membership of an existing museum?
- Are there natural features, appealing landscaping potential, or other environmental features?
- Is there the possibility for a gift shop to serve a wider market?
- Is there the possibility for a cafeteria to serve a wider market?
- Does it have good pedestrian access?
- Does it offer convenient access to public transportation?
- Is it close to other public or cultural attractions that might bring potential visitors to the museum?
- Is it perceived as serving the region?

Capital Cost Requirements

- What is the capital cost of the site? (Most museums are on free land.)
- Are there any natural features that will negatively affect the construction budget?
- Are there any zoning requirements that will negatively affect the construction budget?

Operational Requirements

- Does the site present any challenges to maintaining manageable operating costs?
- What will annual lease costs add to the operating budget? (Most museums are on free land.)
- Is there the potential for assistance from other agencies for building upkeep and maintenance?

Business and Zoning Terms

- Will the site be donated, purchased, or leased? If leased, what are the terms?
- Will the site be dependent on unfunded work or uncertain commitments by others?
- What constraints are there on the building size, shape, or height? (Note that if a museum is planning to include a giant-screen theater, the top of the exterior of the theater is likely to be 55 feet or more in height and is likely to become a significant architectural element in the neighborhood.)
- Is there the possibility of rent-producing development parcels within the site?
- Are there any zoning requirements that affect the construction or operation of the museum?

Site Evaluation

As the attractiveness of each potential site can be unique and difficult to compare with the others, an evaluation process will be helpful to facilitate making decisions.

The first step in this process will be to prioritize the various factors noted above to fit the specific museum's goals and constraints by, for example, assigning a relative weight to each factor from 1 to 10 in value. The factors with the same weight can then be grouped and put into an order of importance. This provides a clear path for a relatively objective comparison of the evaluations of very different sites.

If the outcome of this exercise seems wrong or unsatisfactory, it is probably because the weighting of the site potential factors doesn't reflect the true values of the museum and suggests that the process of assigning weight to the factors should be carefully reviewed.

The sample matrix shown in table 83.2 illustrates one possible way to organize the site evaluation process. Note that not all factors will apply or be weighted the same for all museums.

OTHER SITE CONSIDERATIONS

Relative Capital Costs

The process of acquiring or leasing land by a 501(c)(3) must be achievable within the limitations of its campaign fund. Property adjacent to the selected site may increase in value, and the process of acquiring this land should be done very carefully. Most nonprofit museums are located on donated or rent-free land.

Relative Attendance Potential

Each site will appeal differently to the museum's audience segments with factors such as adequate parking and easy access for parents with young children or for seniors, influencing which site has the potential to attract more visitors and to achieve higher earned revenue.

Tourists and residents are important subsets, as each might find different sites the most attractive.

Table 83.2   Sample Site Evaluation Matrix

Group 1 (rate from 0 to 10 points)	Current Site	New Site A	New Site B	New Site C
General appeal to residents				
General appeal to tourists				
Attendance potential				
Least risk				
Perceived appeal: visitor experience				
Easy to find for first-time visitors				
Character of surrounding neighborhood				
High visibility to lots of passersby				
Total group 1				
Group 2 (rate from 0 to 8 points)	**Current Site**	**New Site A**	**New Site B**	**New Site C**
Sufficient adjacent parking				
Earned revenue potential				
School bus access				
Perceived as a safe area				
Annual lease costs low				
Potential for building support				
Total group 2				
Group 3 (rate from 0 to 6 points)	**Current Site**	**New Site A**	**New Site B**	**New Site C**
Potential for expansion				
Ongoing private support/giving				
Potential for outdoor exhibits/programs				
No special building site restrictions				
Easy rehabilitation or construction				
Appealing landscaping and site				
Appealing architectural potential				
Total group 3				
Group 4 (rate from 0 to 4 points)	**Current Site**	**New Site A**	**New Site B**	**New Site C**
Possibility for wider access to gift shop				
Close to other public/cultural attractions				
Fit with immediate neighbors				
Perception of serving the region				
Total group 4				
Group 5 (rate from 0 to 2 points)	**Current Site**	**New Site A**	**New Site B**	**New Site C**
Good pedestrian access				
Possibility for wider access to café				
Time frame to occupy building				
Total group 5				
Total of all groups (maximum possible score = 192)				
	Current Site	**New Site A**	**New Site B**	**New Site C**
Site percentage rating (divide each total by maximum possible score)				

Relative Fund-Raising Feasibility

As part of the planning, the museum should engage fund-raising counsel to conduct a campaign feasibility study. During the interviews with potential sponsoring investors and donors, counsel should assess what scale of campaign is appropriate for each of the considered sites.

Different visions will have different appeals to potential funders, and it is not necessarily true that the least expensive option among the sites studied will be the easiest to fund. For example, several projects have become reality because the promise of a new building on a prominent site with signature architecture has been instrumental in moving a campaign forward, even at a higher cost than less exciting proposals. In short, a final decision about which site to pursue might wait until after the potential donors have been interviewed.

Business Terms with a Landlord

Before making final selections of sites, the museum should have discussions with any site landlords to determine tenancy terms. Most nonprofit museums and science centers are located on free land with no annual lease fee. Many receive additional benefits, such as maintenance, utilities, and other services from the landlord. Many museums are located on government-owned land, and government agencies provide these services.

Occupancy and Development Assumptions

The museum may be open to arrangements with developers who are developing a larger site that will include the museum as a tenant. The following factors should be negotiated by most museums that go into partnership with a developer of a larger complex:

- There is no rent.
- Any lease required must be very long to honor naming opportunities.
- The museum will be a stand-alone building with its own distinct identity and separate main entrance at street level with a bus drop-off nearby.
- The museum's visitors will have access to an agreed-on number parking spaces provided by others within 1,000 feet of the entrance and without streets to cross, plus additional spaces for school buses. An additional agreed-on number of spaces will be needed for staff.

- Most museums are not in the position to help any developer secure construction financing or provide ongoing revenues to pay off debt that might be incurred in any aspect of a development.
- The museum should require that there be no other museum-like tenants in the development appealing primarily to the museum's target audiences.
- The museum must be permitted to develop and promote ancillary income sources, including food service and museum shop retail, that are typical of museums.
- Ticket sales must be entirely in the control of the museum with 100 percent of the museum's admission sales being retained by the museum.
- Most museum operating budgets are extremely limited and depend on ongoing support from the community for survival. In this context, the museum cannot cover unlimited assessments for ongoing maintenance charges. Some cities express their ongoing support of their museums' activities by providing utilities, maintenance, grounds care, security, and other such services in addition to arranging a free lease.
- The museum's capital budget will be locked to a fixed number, and the museum will have to accomplish all of its tasks within these strict budget limits. The museum will not be able to cover any capital cost overruns.
- The developer's start-up permitting, financing, and organizational costs should not be shared by the tenants.

Relative Neighborhood Support

The museum should take pains to determine if the immediately surrounding neighborhoods support the plans. Dialogue with residents is likely to result in some amount of accommodation to their needs.

Section 84

Space Use Analysis

INTRODUCTION

A comprehensive study of a museum's existing space utilization is required to better inform the decisions that will improve the effective use of existing space and provide an enhanced visitor experience for years to come. Aspects of this process are similar to the development of an architectural program for a new facility as described in "5. Architectural Planning."

You can adapt the processes outlined in this chapter to determine how you currently use the spaces in your building and how your museum might want to reassign them to other functions. The section also helps you create an analysis report.

This section is written by contributing author Victor Becker.

SPACE USE ANALYSIS: PROCESS

A current space use analysis focuses on three processes. The first is an examination of the current uses of the net museum interior spaces and grouping them according to use. The components of this analysis are the following:

- An inventory of spaces is a comprehensive listing of all existing net spaces in the facility, grouped primarily by function and secondarily by adjacency. It closely resembles the architectural program outlined in table 5.5 in section 5. It is a list of the existing spatial resources with which the museum can observe inefficiencies, reassign or reprioritize functions, eliminate circulation bottlenecks, rethink the relationship between exhibit spaces, or otherwise improve the visitor experience.
- A summary of the inventory of spaces is organized by category of use, showing each category's current aggregate net area expressed both in net square feet and in its percentage of the total net building area. This summary provides the most succinct statement of the current commitment to each function of the museum's current operation.

The second process is an evaluation of the current flexibility of those museum spaces and their ability to provide the appropriate infrastructure for a succession of varied exhibits and programs. While this process can be a bit subjective—an architectural feature of an existing space can be an obstacle to one exhibit designer while being a blessing to another—it will help describe the current "palette" of spaces with which the museum can work. The goal of this assessment is to determine if the flexibility of the spaces—the degree of *Delta*—as they currently exist matches the range of flexibility required by the policy and schedule of changing exhibits and programs required by a master plan or vision statement.

The third process is the comparison of the aggregate museum areas to the facilities of peer institutions in a manner very similar to the confirmation of an architectural program discussed in space allocation step 4 in section 5. These comparisons are intended not to "rate" the museum's spaces against either an ideal or an average but rather to help illustrate what is and is not worthy of more scrutiny or investigation.

Process 1: Analysis of Current Use

Overview

Because the study of a museum's current space use will involve comparison to other museum facilities, a good place to begin is to take a fresh look around the existing spaces and identify characteristics that make them what they are.

Some of the questions that might be asked are the following:

- Is the museum a freestanding facility, or is it part of a larger development or structure?
- How many entrances are there to the facility, and who uses each?
- Is the visitor experience on one floor or on multiple floors?
- If the facility is multistoried, is there a visual connection between the floors, or do the floors rely on graphics and signage to make their presence known?
- Is the facility completely accessible in the spirit as well as the letter of the Americans with Disabilities Act?
- Is there a great deal of natural light in the exhibits and programs areas, or are they predominantly windowless?
- How much variation is there in clear ceiling heights—both in the exhibit areas and throughout the facility?
- Is the current visitor experience self-directed, or is it a linear experience of spaces?
- Are there issues with the current circulation?
- Are there program spaces where a capture ratio is reduced in any way by the physical location or layout of the space?

Museum Gross Area

The first quantitative measure of a facility is the determination of its total space—its gross area—which is determined by a number of guidelines that apply to all facilities, even if they have multiple levels and/or walls shared with tenants or other institutions:

- Gross area is measured from the exterior perimeter of all exterior walls where they define a clear "edge" to the museum space.
- Gross area is measured from the center of any interior wall that defines a clear edge of the museum space shared with neighboring non–museum tenants.
- Areas within the museum's "boundary" used exclusively by non–museum tenants are not included; the excluded area is measured to the center of all shared walls.
- Stairways are included in each level they service; the area of elevator shafts is included on only one level no matter how many levels they serve.
- Multistoried spaces are included as only one level.
- Duct spaces, chases, voids, storage areas, and other "hidden" spaces are included.
- Exterior space is not included.

For the purposes of this kind of analysis, it is advantageous to reduce the often complex architectural drawings of a facility to simpler drawings that show clearly what has been included in the gross area calculation (see table 84.1).

Museum Net Area

The total usable area of a facility—its net area—is determined by a number of guidelines that apply to all facilities:

Table 84.1 Sample Gross Area Drawing

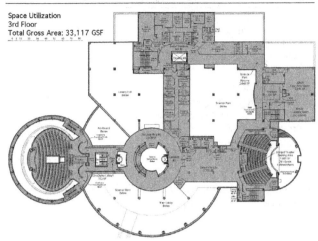

Space Utilization
3rd Floor
Total Gross Area: 33,117 GSF

- Net area is measured from the interior perimeter of all walls of a particular space.
- Multistoried spaces are included as only one level.
- Net area generally does not include restrooms unless they are particular to a museum's visitor experience (e.g., family restrooms and baby-changing rooms). In no case does it include plumbing access spaces.
- Net area does not include the footprint of any architectural element that is within the space (e.g., columns).
- Net area does not include any spaces outside the building (e.g., terraces and courtyards).
- Net area does not include the wall thickness occupied by a door or entry portal.
- Net area does not include MEP spaces; heating, ventilation, and air-conditioning ducts; chases; voids; or structure.
- Net area does not include circulation corridors that provide access to exhibit or program spaces. Stairways, ramps, and elevators are not included in the net area unless they are integral components of the program use of the space.
- Net area does not include spaces off-site used by the museum unless they are integral to the visitor experience.

The total net area can be determined from the as-built drawings that are usually an accurate record of the components of the museum. The individual net area figures may also be derived by simply measuring each space and adding them together. The latter process is much slower, but it ensures accuracy, especially in an older building in which both the architecture and the functions of spaces have changed over time.

And while the total net area is useful in assessing, for example, the metrics of attendance and expenses, a more informative analysis of the net area can be produced by identifying the function of each space as one of 10 categories of net space.

Color coding the function of each net space on a drawing can produce a document in which the degree of efficiency of each function's spaces can often be assessed simply by

Table 84.2 Categories of Spaces

- Free zone circulation
- Free zone amenities
- Paid zone circulation
- Exhibit galleries
- Theater spaces
- Program spaces
- Collections spaces
- Administrative spaces
- Program support
- Building support

observing the layout of colors. It will also make the next step in the process easier to approach.

Inventory of Spaces

The inventory of spaces is a spreadsheet—similar to an architectural program—that lists the net area of the spaces and groups them in one of the 10 categories of operating function. It is basically a written version of the colored floor plans that allows more manipulation of the net areas than does a drawing and can offer insight into how each of the functions is working.

In one sense, the inventory process is the opposite of the architectural program process; instead of breaking large ideas down into individual discrete spaces, the inventory of spaces looks at the myriad spaces, searching for larger patterns or relationships that would inform a rethinking of the function of spaces and/or their relationships to each other.

Table 84.4 is an excerpt of a five-page inventory of a large museum with over 250 individual net spaces. It includes the room's number (where available), the room's name, the level of the museum on which it is located, and its net area. The net-square-foot numbers in the exhibit portion of the excerpt also have subtotals to help further identify basic differences in function.

Inventory of Existing Spaces Summary

As with the architectural program, a summary of the inventory can be a helpful tool to understanding the data. The sample summary in table 84.5 includes all of the net spaces in the museum used in the sample above.

Process 2: Inventory of Delta Flexibility and Learning Style

Current Delta Inventory

The heart of a museum experience is in the exhibits and programs it offers to visitors. Most museums can capitalize on their size to offer more activity and engagement than is likely to be "consumed" by the visitor in a single visit. But to ensure that a first-time visitor becomes a repeat visitor, the museum

Table 84.3 Sample Net Area Drawing

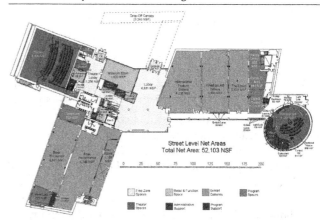

must invest in *flexible learning spaces* that host a *succession* of compelling visitor experiences and powerful learning resources.

A Delta museum is a museum with built-in infrastructure to facilitate change. Conceptually, this approach treats a gallery or program lab much like a theater, where its stage, lights, suspension grid, and other built-in systems allow for a relatively economic changeover from play to play. While it costs more to build Delta infrastructure at the start, subsequent program changes will be more economically manageable to allow the museum to stay in touch with its community and to respond more quickly to new interests, stories, and opportunities. A Delta museum has implications for architecture, infrastructure, exhibit design, staff culture, and operating budget as well as for the institution's relationship with the community it serves.

To evaluate the degree of Delta in a museum, it is useful to start by describing the basic components of the nature of the spaces. In a matrix format, each of the areas is described by the following:

- Its floor level
- Its net area
- Its height (expressed in clear ceiling height measurements or in the number of floor levels)
- The presence or absence of natural light
- Its degree of Delta flexibility (e.g., expressed in the range of 0 = no flexibility to 4 = high flexibility)

The first four characteristics are objective facts or measurements. The degree of Delta is more subjective but can be estimated by asking questions such as the following:

- Could the space be transformed from a dark experience to a light one?
- Could the space be transformed from an intimate personal experience to a grand public one?
- Could the space be transformed from a quiet reflective environment to a loud celebratory experience?

Table 84.4 Sample Inventory of Spaces (Excerpt)

D.		Exhibit Galleries	Level	Area Net Square Feet (NSF)
		Core Exhibit Galleries		
		Nature Works		
		Nature Works Gallery	1	6,101
		Nature Works Program Area	1	193
		Kids Town Exhibit Gallery	1	2,847
		Science Park Gallery	2	9,380
		All Aboard Gallery	2	1,494
		Careers for Life Gallery	3	2,375
		Dino Digs Gallery	4	9,541
		Science of Toys Gallery	4	5,717
		Subtotal		37,648
		Traveling Exhibit Gallery		
		Lowery Hall Gallery	2	6,912
		Subtotal		6,912
E.		Exhibit Support Spaces	Level	Area NSF
		Nature Works Animal Support	1	inc.
		Nature Works Filter Room	1	inc.
	1052	Fab Lab	1	2,543
	1054	Electronics Shop	1	254
	1055	A/V Storage	1	130
	1056	ProtoZone	1	1,391
		Nature Works Aquarium Support	1	79
	1068	Reptiles	1	220
	1094	Nature Works Manager's Office	1	133
	2013	All Aboard Storage	2	106
		Lighting Storage #1	3	119
		Exhibit Storage #1	4	802
		Lighting Storage #2	4	119
		Exhibit Storage #2	5	674
		Subtotal		6,570

• Could the space be transformed from an experience consisting of a multitude of individual exhibit components to one immersive environment that occupies the entire space?

In evaluating Delta qualities, it is not important whether such ranges of space are conceivable; rather, what is important is whether such changes are feasible within the museum's standard exhibit and program budgets.

In some components of the visitor experience, there is a significant difference in Delta flexibility between the physical hardware that delivers the content and the content itself. In those cases, the hardware and content are evaluated separately.

The two sample Delta inventories shown in tables 84.6 and 84.7 illustrate a facility that was conceived and designed as a comparatively static, non-Delta institution. It is apparent that in most aspects (except for natural light), there is a higher degree of flexibility in the program spaces than in the exhibit spaces.

Current Range of Learning Spaces

In addition to an assessment of the Delta flexibility of the range of the museum's exhibit and program spaces, it is useful to assess the range of learning styles that those spaces present to a visitor.

In addition to the broad distinctions in character present in differing categories of space use (e.g., public lobbies, exhibit areas, and back of house), it is important to understand that a range of learning spaces will also require a variety of learning environments. These environments are created chiefly by the various physical elements—in addition to its net area—that create the character of each area.

Table 84.8 summarizes the general relationship between learning styles, learning spaces, and architectural character.

Of course, a single exhibit gallery or program space may well have a number of different learning styles/spaces within it. This results from various combinations of architectural features with specific choices of scale, height, natural light, exterior views, interior views, finishes, acoustic energy, and similar variables.

The two matrixes shown in tables 84.9 and 84.10 identify the type of learning space/style that is inherent in each of the existing exhibit and program spaces in the museum described in tables 84.6 and 84.7.

Table 84.11 groups the existing museum galleries and program spaces above by their type of space as noted in the previous tables. This allows a look at the total area currently devoted to each type of learning space/style and illuminates the degree of diversity of space usage that is the central goal of the Delta concept.

Table 84.5 Sample Inventory of Spaces

Entrance areas		
Public entrance and lobby spaces	13,472	10.23%
Public amenities	215	0.16%
Entrance support spaces	1,067	0.81%
Subtotal	14,754	11.20%
Retail and function spaces		
Science store	3,058	2.32%
Café	8,524	6.47%
Founders' room and support	2,946	2.24%
Subtotal	14,528	11.03%
Exhibit galleries		
Core exhibit galleries	37,648	28.58%
Traveling exhibit gallery	6,912	5.25%
Exhibit support spaces	6,570	4.99%
Subtotal	51,130	38.81%
Theaters		
CineDome lobby	1,669	1.27%
CineDome	6,299	4.78%
Science adventure theater	4,754	3.61%
Film theater	450	0.34%
Subtotal	13,172	10.00%
Enclosed program spaces		
Lobbies	2,239	1.70%
Clubhouse and support spaces	2,819	2.14%
Learning labs	9,031	6.85%
Preschool/early childhood learning	4,679	3.55%
Birthday rooms	915	0.69%
Observatory	1,424	1.08%
Program support spaces	2,777	2.11%
Subtotal	23,884	18.13%
Administrative areas		
Open administrative offices	3,143	2.39%
Enclosed administrative offices	4,570	3.47%
General administrative service areas	1,996	1.52%
Administrative office support spaces	740	0.56%
Subtotal	10,449	7.93%
Facility support areas		
Facility administration	3,828	2.91%
Subtotal	3,828	2.91%
Total net museum space (net square feet)	131,745	100.00%

Process 3: Comparison of Use to Peer Institutions

Every museum is unique in ways that should be maintained and strengthened, but there is much value to be gained by a detailed comparison of its facility to those of museums considered to be peers. This is not an effort to compare it to an "ideal" museum or to make it conform to the "average" museum. It is a process of identifying what makes a museum different from other and evaluating whether those differences represent strengths or weaknesses.

A museum's data about its facility are first compared to the data made available by an appropriate association. The Association of Science-Technology Centers (ASTC), for example, offers data sufficiently detailed to determine a context for understanding the institution's overall facility size.

The data are then compared to very detailed data from the analyses of a number of particular ASTC institutions chosen by the museum as it peers. The specific comparison institutions should be chosen both for their similarity in purpose and for their ability to reveal as much as possible about the museum's physical characteristics. It is important that the comparison data are accurate and comprehensive; it may be necessary to rely on a museum-planning consultant to get these data in an efficient manner.

All of the following comparisons are drawn from the same five peer institutions.

Gross Facility Size

The first pass at putting the museum's facility into perspective is to compare its gross area (in gross square feet) with a median; the ASTC, for example, calculates the median museum facility of many members to have about 78,000 gross square feet. The second comparison would be to the average ASTC facility of 167,500 gross square feet.

Net-to-Gross Ratio

The *net-to-gross ratio* is an expression of the relative efficiency of a building, calculated by dividing the total gross area of the building by the total usable net area. A smaller number describes a more architecturally efficient building. A larger number usually results when a building has an "excessive" amount of space dedicated to corridors, mechanical spaces, voids, and/or other spaces that cannot be programmed to enhance the activities of the visitor.

The net-to-gross ratio of museums usually ranges from 1.333 (a very efficient building) to 1.600 (a very inefficient building that may require some rethinking).

The museum and its five peer institutions can be compared in the order of their net-to-gross ratios (see table 84.12).

Comparison of Space Allocation Summaries by Percentage

To provide a fair method for comparing these data, all subsequent comparisons of the museum and its five peer institutions are expressed in terms of the percentage of a building's total net space that is devoted to each of the functions listed. While this method may be a bit skewed when facilities of extremely different gross sizes are compared, the desired end products of this process are more qualitative than quantitative in nature.

In table 84.13, any specific number in bold in the comparisons indicates that there is something worth investigating about the number, usually because there is a meaningful variance between the museum and one or more of the peer institutions that bears some examination. A sampling of the kinds of comments and suggestions derived from an examination of these matrixes is included at the end of this section.

Table 84.6 Sample Delta Inventory: Principal Exhibit Spaces

Exhibit Areas	Level	Net Square Feet	Height	Natural Light	Delta
Orientation area	5	377	1	No	1
Tools Gallery	5	1,423	1	No	1
World without XX	5	2,493	1	Possible	1
Time Machine Gallery	5	574	1	No	0
Formation Gallery—hardware	4, 5	5,991	2	Possible	0
Formation Gallery—content	4, 5	Not applicable	2	Possible	2
Exploration Gallery	4	3,920	1	Possible	1
S Gallery	4	2,145	1	No	2
Platform Gallery	4, 5	6,618	2	Possible	0
Speed Gallery	4	4,114	1	No	2
Kid's Gallery	4	2,339	2	Yes	2
Molecule Gallery	5	1,230	1	Yes	2
Future Gallery	5	1,502	1	Possible	2
M Gallery	5	1,190	1	No	2
Traveling Exhibit Gallery	4	7,050	1	No	2
Total		40,966			

Table 84.7 Sample Delta Inventory: Principal Program Spaces

Program Areas	Floor	Net Square Feet	Height	Natural Light	Delta
Dark Ride—hardware	4, 5	10,032	1	No	0
Dark Ride—content	4, 5	Not applicable	1	No	4
Galeria 1	4	2,116	1	No	3
Metre City	5	1,270	1	No	3
Round Program Space	5	723	1	No	2
Simulation Theater—hardware	4	2,167	2	Yes	0
Simulation Theater—Content	4	Not applicable	2	Yes	2
Documentary Theater—hardware	5	853	1	No	1
Documentary Theater—content	5	Not applicable	1	No	2
Total		17,161			

Comparison of Space Allocations by Categories by Percentage

The matrixes shown in tables 84.14 to 84.18 break down the components from table 84.13 into a finer level of detail to enhance the understanding of the museum's spaces. These matrixes cover the following categories:

- Entrance areas, lobbies, and retail spaces
- Exhibit spaces
- Theater spaces
- Education/program spaces
- Administrative and facility support spaces

SAMPLE SUMMARY OF FINDINGS

The sample observations, comments, and recommendations that follow are based on the data in the previous tables derived from comparison of the museum with its five peer institutions. All are intended to provoke further questions and discussions that will inform the improvement of the visitor experience.

General

- It is interesting to note in table 84.12 that the net-to-gross ratio for the museum shows that it is a comparably "lean" building but also that it ranks in the middle of the group. This suggests that it may be possible to increase the efficiency of the museum's space usage to "free up" space for new and/or enhanced visitor experiences.
- The first suggestion raised in table 84.13 is that the museum's café, store, and other retail spaces may be able to be increased in area. An increase in area could increase earned revenue from those functions and/or provide opportunity to add new elements to the visitor's retail experience. Table 84.14 identifies that the café, café support areas, and function spaces offer the largest opportunity for increased allocations of space.
- It is interesting that of the six institutions under study, table 84.13 shows that the museum has the largest allocation of space to theaters. It is worth examining whether this commitment of space is justified by visitor participation. The theaters may be a prominent feature of

Table 84.8 Learning Spaces: Physical Context Framework

Learning Spaces	Sample Application	Architectural Snapshot	Daylight	Learning Skills
Contemplative galleries Showcases	Art and collections Interpretive displays and graphics	Light, quiet, calm, formal, open Lighted cases and rare artifacts, mixed with photos, labels, videos	Diffused Seldom	Reflection, appreciation Understanding, synthesis
Tunnels of wonder	Dioramas, period rooms, aquaria	Dark corridors with lighted windows into stage sets	No	Exploring, observing
Theaters and presentations	Auditoriums, demo stages, IMAX	Audience/stage areas supported by lighting and sound systems	No	Linear narratives, empathy, perspectives
Immersive environments	Historic rooms, space capsules, botanic gardens	A complete and convincing surrounding reality	No	Discovery, engagement, inspiration
Hands-on arenas	Science and technology centers with interactive exhibits	Open informal spaces encouraging activity	Possible	Problem solving, experimenting, discovery
Discovery worlds	Storyland, climbing structures, minivillages	Playful, fantasy, clean, light with small spaces	Possible	Exploring, discovering, creating
Workshops and studios	Art studios, reference rooms, classrooms	Focused work spaces out of main flow	Possible	Problem solving, team building, confidence building
Icons	Dinosaur, *Mona Lisa*, Liberty Bell	Prime focus of an open area	Possible	Reflection, kinesthetic understanding
Open spaces	Lobbies, atria, rotundas, hallways	Views and daylight in calm rest areas	Yes	Synthesis, framework building, questioning, evaluating

Table 84.9 Sample Learning Space/Style Overview: Principal Exhibit Spaces

Exhibit Areas	Floor	Net Square FReet	Type of Space
Orientation area	5	377	Hands-on arena
Tools Gallery	5	1,423	Hands-on arena
World without XX	5	2,493	Hands-on arena
Time Machine Gallery	5	574	Showcase
Formation Gallery—hardware	4, 5	5,991	Showcase
Formation Gallery—content	4, 5	Not applicable	Showcase
Exploration Gallery	4	3,920	Showcase
S Gallery	4	2,145	Hands-on arena
Platform Gallery	4, 5	6,618	Immersion
Speed Gallery	4	4,114	Hands-on arena
Kid's Gallery	4	2,339	Hands-on arena
Molecule Gallery	5	1,230	Showcase
Future Gallery	5	1,502	Showcase
M Gallery	5	1,190	Showcase
Traveling Exhibit Gallery	4	7,050	Traveling exhibits
Total		40,966	

the museum's experience, or they could be an "also-rans" whose capture ratio doesn't justify their size. It also needs to be asked if any of the types of learning space listed in table 84.11 are being "shortchanged" by the commitment to theater space.

- Table 84.13 also suggests that the space the museum has allocated to programs may be insufficient. A clear understanding of the museum's commitment to programs and a differentiation between "passive" theaters and "hands-on" program spaces may reveal areas of the visitor experience that might be strengthened.

- Table 84.13 clearly suggests that the administrative spaces are either oversized or extremely inefficient. Few, if any, types of museums need nearly a quarter of their net area committed to administration. An in-depth examination of the reasons for this is certainly warranted.

Table 84.10 Sample Learning Space/Style: Principal Program Spaces

Program Areas	Floor	Net Square Feet	Type of Space
Dark Ride—hardware	4, 5	10,032	Theater
Dark Ride—content	4, 5	Not applicable	Showcase
Galeria 1	4	2,116	Workshop/studio
Metre City	5	1,270	Workshop/studio
Round Program Space	5	723	Workshop/studio
Simulation Theater—hardware	4	2,167	Theater/presentation
Simulation Theater—content	4	Not applicable	Theater/presentation
Documentary Theater—hardware	5	853	Theater/presentation
Documentary Theater—content	5	Not applicable	Theater/presentation
Total		17,161	

Table 84.11 Sample Learning Space/Style by Percentage

Type of Space	Net Square Feet	Percent
Theater/presentation	13,052	26.2%
Icon, showcase	14,407	23.6%
Hands-on arena	12,891	21.1%
Traveling exhibit space	7,050	11.5%
Immersion environment	6,618	10.8%
Studio/workshop	4,109	6.7%
Discovery worlds	0	0%
Total	58,127	100.0%

Table 84.12 Sample Building Size and Efficiency Comparison

	Net Area (Net Square Feet)	Gross Area (Gross Square Feet)	Net-to-Gross Ratio
Peer A	131,745	204,962	1.56
Peer B	96,000	144,000	1.50
Peer C	82,368	120,190	1.46
Museum	94,895	133,518	1.41
Peer E	149,129	205,280	1.38
Peer D	101,442	136,788	1.35

Table 84.13   Sample Comparison of Summaries of Space Allocations

Net square feet	94,895	131.745	96,000	82,368	101,442	149,129	102,889
Gross square feet	133,518	203,041	144,000	120,190	136,788	205,280	151,005
Entry spaces	4.6%	9.2%	4.5%	3.7%	3.1%	4.6%	5.0%
Retail spaces	3.1%	11.0%	7.8%	6.3%	6.4%	5.2%	7.4%
Exhibit spaces	45.5%	38.8%	50.2%	51.4%	52.4%	52.3%	49.0%
Theater space	16.8%	10.0%	13.8%	15.6%	13.6%	14.4%	13.5%
Program spaces	5.3%	16.1%	8.4%	8.2%	5.6%	8.6%	9.4%
Administrative spaces	23.7%	7.0%	7.2%	5.5%	6.6%	7.6%	6.8%.
Facility support	1.0%	7.9%	8.1%	9.3%	12.3%	7.3%	8.9%

Table 84.14   Sample Comparison of Entrance Areas, Lobbies, and Retail Spaces

	Main Lobby	Lobby Support Spaces	Store and Support	Café and Support	Function and Support	Total
Museum	3.3%	1.3%	2.0%	1.1%	0.0%	7.7%
Peer A	10.2%	1.0%	2.3%	6.5%	2.2%	22.2%
Peer B	2.9%	1.6%	2.7%	4.0%	3.1%	14.3%
Peer C	3.2%	1.5%	2.4%	3.9%	0.0%	11.0%
Peer D	3.2%	1.0%	2.8%	3.7%	0.9%	11.5%
Peer E	2.9%	0.3%	0.8%	1.7%	1.0%	6.5%
Average of peers	4.5%	1.1%	2.5%	4.0%	1.4%	13.1%

Table 84.15 Sample Comparison of Exhibit Spaces

	Exhibit Hub	Core Exhibit Galleries	Travel Exhibit Gallery	Exhibit Support	Total
Museum	0.0%	35.7%	7.4	2.4	45.5%
Peer A	0.0%	28.6%	5.2%	4.9%	38.7%
Peer B	2.5%	32.5%	8.3%	9.5%	52.8%
Peer C	8.0%	35.1%	5.0%	5.2%	53.3%
Peer D	3.9%	34.5%	8.9%	7.4%	54.7%
Peer E	0.0%	31.0	5.5%	8.7%	45.2%
Average of peers	2.9%	32.3%	6.8%	7.1%	48.9%

An additional factor to explore is that, unlike the relative ease of turning a theater space to program use, for example, the transition of administrative space into a part of the visitor experience can often be difficult. Architects and planners often make a conscious effort to isolate the offices and their support spaces from the exhibit, theater, and program spaces, often making it difficult to integrate office space into the visitor experience.

- Review of the museum's facility support space, as seen in table 84.13, would be helpful in determining why the museum can operate sufficiently with less than one-third of the average space allotted by the peers group. One possible answer to this is the use of off-site exhibit shops, storage areas, or collections areas.

Delta and Learning Styles

- The proportion of space in table 84.9 that has rigidly permanent exhibits—the Oil Platform Gallery and the Formation Galley in particular—is too high. While there is some clear value to these permanent features as icons in the museum's experience, the overall impression that "nothing changes" is an important limit on developing repeat visitors.
- In table 84.11, space providing theater experiences appears to be the predominant type of space in the museum's experience, but that perception is skewed by the very large commitment of space (almost 14 percent of the entire facility) to the Dark Ride. The other theater-like experiences are limited in visitor capacity and—especially in the case of the Simulation Theater—have a limited variety of possible uses.
- In table 84.11, there appears to be too little workshop and studio space in the overall mix of spaces. This may be an inevitable result of the focus on the Dark Ride, but its potentially negative impact on the visitor experience may be important to ameliorate.
- In table 84.11, the lack of space shown that is dedicated to the concepts of discovery worlds and early childhood education for young visitors clearly affects the nature and effectiveness of their experience at the museum. There may be good reasons not to expand programming for what is a growing focus of many museums, but a cost–benefit study of this expansion would be beneficial.

Specific Spaces and Uses

- The lack of an exhibit hub in table 84.15 is significant. A hub could provide an organizing principle to the exhibit spaces and offer the visitor a way-finding icon, an orientation to the exhibits, and a place to simply stop for a breather.
- Table 84.15 also suggests that the amount of exhibit support space is significantly less than all the peer institutions.

Again, a careful review may illustrate that there are good reasons for this, but insufficient support space (e.g., the absence of an exhibit maintenance shop) can often lead to an increase in visitors assessing the exhibits as "out of order," "tired," or "all the same."

- On the other hand, the actual commitment of space to the museum's exhibit experiences, as shown in table 84.15, is in line with the comparison group. This suggests that the space for new or enhanced experiences at the museum could be repurposed from current exhibit space without risking a noticeable degradation of the visitor experience.
- The low commitment of space to theater lobbies, shown in table 84.16, may account for reported confusion in which queued theater audiences "back up" and interfere with other visitor circulation requirements.
- The high-level focus on the Dark Ride experience (feature theater #1) in table 84.16 invites a very careful review of the costs and benefits of this iconic feature of the museum.
- Setting the Dark Ride experience (feature theater #1) aside in table 84.16 as a feature unique to this museum, the commitment to true theater-like spaces and activities is by far the lowest of the group: about one-third the commitment of the next largest comparable and one-fifth of the largest. This suggests an exploration of the value that could be added to the visitor experience by a multipurpose theater or demonstration stage.
- The proportion of space for education and programs in table 84.17 is among the lowest of the group. This suggests that more classrooms, labs, and other teaching spaces that allow more flexibility in purpose and options for separate spaces for the different key visitor segments would be beneficial.
- Space devoted to administration—especially open office landscapes—seems extremely high in comparison to other institutions: nearly three times that of both the average and the next highest facility. Coupled with the facility support spaces, they occupy almost one-fourth of the entire facility. In the planning of new facilities, a good rule of thumb is that administrative space be held between 6 and 10 percent of the available on-site space; this advice could be applied to existing space. Part of the reason for the current scale of commitment to administrative space may be the very large size of the paid and volunteer staff that is required by the museum's current visitor experience. Another possible reason for this large commitment may be the scale of staff required to operate the outreach programs. In any case, it would be valuable to review this aspect of the museum's operations.
- The café—the major component in the "Café and Support" column in table 84.14—is by far the smallest café of the comparison group despite the fact that the attendance at the museum is significantly higher than several of the group. Increased size and an enhanced menu should be

Table 84.16 Sample Comparison of Theater Spaces

	Theater Lobbies	Feature Theater #1	Feature Theater #2	Multipurpose Theater	Other Theaters	Total
Museum	0.8%	13.6%	1.5%	0.0%	0.9%	16.8%
Peer A	1.3%	4.8%	0.0%	3.6%	0.3%	10.0%
Peer B	1.5%	8.3%	0.0%	5.0%	0.0%	14.8%
Peer C	4.2%	9.1%	0.0%	4.6%	0.0%	17.9%
Peer D	1.1%	7.5%	0.0%	2.4%	2.6%	13.6%
Peer E	2.9%	3.8%	0.0%	1.1%	0.4%	8.2%
Average of peers	2.2%	6.7%	0.0%	3.3%	0,7%	12.9%

Table 84.17 Sample Comparison of Education/Program Spaces

	Group Entry and Orientation	Labs and Classrooms	Early Childhood	Education Support	Total
Museum	0.0%	4.3%	0.0%	0.9%	5.2%
Peer A	3.8%	8.6%	3.6%	2.1%	18.1%
Peer B	2.1%	5.2%	0.0%	2.1%	9.4%
Peer C	2.1%	3.8%	3.0%	0.3%	9.2%
Peer D	1.2%	3.5%	0.0%	2.0%	6.7%
Peer E	0.0%	6.2%	0.0%	4.9%	11.0%
Average of peers	1.8%	5.5%	1.3%	2.3%	10.9%

Table 84.18 Sample Comparison of Administrative Spaces

	Open Office	Enclosed Offices	General Service	Office Support	Facility Support	Total
Museum	15.3%	3.3%	1.5%	3.6%	0.9%	24.6%
Peer A	2.4%	3.5%	1.5%	0.6%	2.9%	10.9%
Peer B	2.8%	2.5%	1.5%	1.4%	0.5%	8.7%
Peer C	1.6%	3.3%	0.9%	0.8%	6.9%	13.5%
Peer D	2.9%	0.7%	1.2%	0.7%	3.1	8.6%
Peer E	0.0%	4.1%	2.5%	1.1%	7.6%	15.3%
Average of peers	1.9%	2.8%	1.5%	0.9%	4.2%	11.3%

explored both to provide respite to guests mid-visit and to enhance the café as a revenue center for the operating budget.

- The lack of any dedicated function/rental space, as seen in table 84.14, is one of the principal reasons contributing to the museum's ranking low in the comparison group in retail spaces. While any space in the museum's facility is a potential candidate for occasional function rental activity, it is common for an institution with the size and the attractive location similar to the museum's to operate more than one function/rental facilities within their facility. Often, there is a large space for sizable gatherings (e.g., fund-raising events, science fairs, and camp-ins) and a smaller space suitable for more intimate meetings (e.g., nonprofit board meetings and weddings). Some factors are the following:
  - A prime reason for such function/rental spaces (besides supplementing income) is producing opportunities for people who might never otherwise be aware of the museum to get a firsthand sense of what it is about. For this reason, these function spaces are often placed firmly within the museum environment to advertise the brand and to differentiate it from neutral commercial facilities.
  - Scheduling is an important limitation on the use of exhibit or program spaces for function/rentals. The need to keep the museum experience fully open to the public makes it difficult to use "interior" spaces without significant disruption to operations.
  - Function facilities come with significant physical requirements. In addition to storage space for tables and chairs, they require comfortable access both for the guests and the service people operating the event. They also require a reasonably clear way-finding path and often a dedicated circulation path that allows the museum to operate simultaneously. Many of these requirements can be met in theory, but they may be difficult or impossible for the physical layout of existing museum space to accommodate.
- The traveling exhibit gallery, as seen in table 84.15, appears to be an appropriate size when compared with the group. The flexibility of that space to meet the extremely varied requirements of traveling exhibits is, however, reduced by its complex physical plan. Other potential

locations that might prove more flexibility for the future should be examined.

- The absence of a group entry or a group orientation area, as seen in table 84.17, could be part of the difficulties reported in the lobby areas. A cost–benefit review of reallocation space to these two uses would be valuable.

Sample Summary of Space Objectives

The sample observations, comments, and recommendations contained in the previous section have been distilled into the following sample "wish list" for renovated and/or new spaces and systems to be developed.

This wish list can inform the work of architects or in-house museum planners in what is inevitably the complex challenge of space renovation. The next step would be a prioritization of these objectives that would guide the thinking and designing processes and sort out the inevitable conflicts that will arise in any renovation of space.

Desired Space Modifications

- Provide visitors with greater flexibility in the length of time required by the experience.
- Provide visitors with greater choice in selecting which galleries or activities to engage in.
- Provide visitors with greater freedom to enter and exit the experience at will.
- Provide more effective signs and way finding for new and existing visitor circulation.
- Facilitate higher visitor throughput.
- Provide a more effective and efficient entrance.
- Create better lobby circulation, including the separation of inquiries from sales.
- Create greater visual connection between visitors and the cityscape.
- Provide a greater degree of universal access.
- Increase the museum store capture rate.
- Create better circulation route(s) bypassing the Dark Ride.
- Provide closer proximity between accounting, tickets, and gift shop cashier.

- Provide better support of camp-ins.
- Provide a bigger, better, and more accessible café.
- Increase the size of the staff pantry.
- Create a more flexible traveling exhibit gallery.
- Decrease the likelihood of congestion in the lobby and in the experience.
- Facilitate the ability of areas to be closed off when needed.

Desired New Spaces

- A central "gathering place" or "commons"
- Showers for camp-ins for both sexes
- Additional baby-changing/nursing rooms
- A multipurpose auditorium for 40 to 50 students
- More classrooms, themed labs, and other flexible teaching spaces
- Dedicated function/rental spaces
- One or more exhibit hubs
- A group entry and a group orientation area
- An early childhood area
- Additional restrooms
- A sick bay
- Dedicated studio/workshop area
- Additional storage, especially for props
- Staff recreation room
- Dedicated meeting rooms
- Locker room for volunteers
- Volunteer meeting room
- Donor wall

Desired Infrastructure Improvements

- E-ticketing and increased information online
- Integrated public address system throughout the facility
- Integrated wireless system throughout the facility
- Local control over heating, ventilation, and air-conditioning (e.g., to allow smoke from a cooking demonstration)
- Centralized media control of advertising and information
- Access to closed-circuit television to allow parents to find their children

Section 85

Stakeholders

Definitions

1. A museum's community, audiences, and supporters are the direct beneficiaries of its activities, receiving benefits of value to them from their engagements with the museum's activities.
   a. *Nonusers* and future generations can also benefit from a museum's activities as *indirect beneficiaries*.
2. The intended individual recipients of our impacts and benefits are a museum's *audiences* or, less frequently, its *users*. The core idea is that engaging with a museum activity will impact and/or benefit an audience member for the better.
   a. Audiences are segmented by their primary admission or registration transaction type into *visitors* and *program participants*.
3. The intended collected recipients of broader societal impacts or those groups of stakeholders the museum is trying to impact or serve, are a museum's *communities* or, less frequently, its *society*, *constituents*, and *authorizing environment*. This book defines *community* as broadly as possible: the external world. However, each museum must get specific about what communities it serves. The National Museum of the Marine Corps (Triangle, Virginia) serves at least three communities: the nearby residents, tourists, and the community of people around the globe affiliated with the U.S. Marine Corps.
   a. When using such terms as *contributing to social good* and *adding public value* to talk about a museum's potential impact on its community, the term *community* refers to the general public and society at large.
   b. When an urban museum thinks of its city and region as its community, it can use population and market data to quantify its resident community.
   c. If a museum receives substantial annual support from a government entity, such as History San Jose from the City of San Jose and the State Historical Museum of Iowa from the State of Iowa, then the museum is wise to think of its community as equal to the city or state, thereby serving the constituencies who support them with tax dollars.
   d. *Community* is also used with modifiers to reference specific affinity groups, such as the Hmong community, the science and technology community, the donor community, the abutting neighbors, underserved communities, the Churchillians, the home schoolers, and so on.
4. The organizations and people who support the museum financially are the museum's *private* and *public supporters*. Ideally and often, these supporters share the museum's intentional purposes and aspire to kindred impacts on the same audiences. Social investing reflects a recent trend to equate support funds to quantifiable social outcomes (Raymond, 2010), and support funds can be tied to outcomes, such as a foundation grant for a program with learning outcomes expected to have a desired impact on its audiences.
   a. Supporters benefit from the museum by advancing their philanthropic goals, along with other benefits from their museum partnerships and engagements, such as visibility and network building.

See "15. Bibliography for Museums" for citation references.

Section 86

Stakeholders

Categories

INTRODUCTION

Community is the big-picture, inclusive term, used broadly in many ways and often pluralized; it is roughly synonymous to the museum's markets, cultural context, authorizing environment, city, neighborhood, and so on. *Audiences* are those who attend the museum's exhibits and programs and are also known as visitors, users, learners, guests, program participants, and so on. *Supporters* provide the museum with its support revenues and in-kind services and are distinguished by source of funds into public and private and by kind of support into volunteer, partner, collector, and funder. The framework also recognizes *nonusers*.

This section provides the overview framework for researching, thinking about, and making decisions about the museum's community and its audiences and supporters. Many of these categories have separate sections.

Stakeholders: Community, Audiences, and Supporters

The museum's external environment—its communities, audiences, and supporters—is diagrammed in Table 86.1.

Table 86.1 The Community and Its Audiences and Supporters

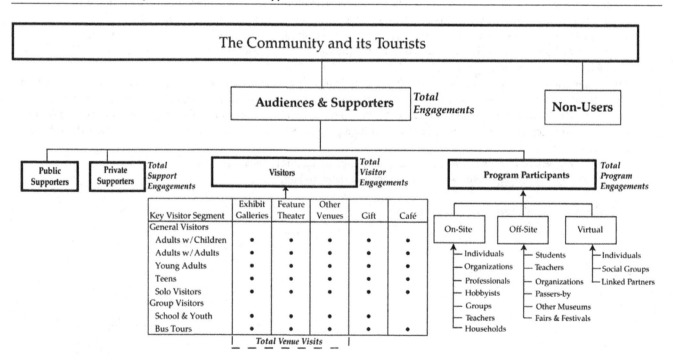

Audiences

Audiences are divided into three categories: visitors, program participants and nonusers. Visitors have been usefully categorized by their contexts, residence geography, motivation, admissions, and developmental levels—these are described in other sections.

Supporters: Funders, Partners, Volunteers, and Collectors

Museums typically receive support in addition to their earned revenues from the following:

- Funders and donors
- Partners
- Volunteers
- Collectors

Each of these is described in a section of its own.

Section 87

Support Facilities

INTRODUCTION

This section is a menu of possible support facilities (spaces) that a museum might consider incorporating into its facility. The support spaces outlined can be inserted into scopes of work for concept designs and cost estimating.

You can select and adapt these spaces from the menu to fit your museum's needs and future plans. You are likely to have some spaces already in some degree. The menu contains spaces and facilities requested by museums in the past; there are bound to be additional facilities desired.

POTENTIAL MUSEUM SUPPORT FACILITIES

Behind-the-scenes operating support facilities will be needed to run the museum efficiently. These will be programmed in broad categories:

Offices and Clean Spaces

- Staff offices and other clean support facilities
- Boardroom/conference room
- Staff lounge
- Volunteer lounge

Program Production and Maintenance

- Planning room
- Digital visualization studio
- Theater technology center
- Theater green room
- Theater prop storage
- Theater lighting and equipment storage
- Graphic design studio
- Information technology equipment workshop and headend
- Live animal room
- Aquarium support
- Conservation lab
- Collection storage
- Collection workrooms
- Exhibit maintenance/production workshop

Building Operations

- Maintenance shops and other workrooms
- Building and grounds maintenance and operations areas
- Loading dock/storage
- Security
- Walk-in chilled food storage
- Garbage handling
- Chilled garbage handling

Nonpublic Facilities and Support Spaces

- Research facilities
- Charter or other school (on-site)
- Collections storage (off-site)
- Greenhouse/conservatory
- Space(s) occupied by other tenants

Section 88

Support Systems

INTRODUCTION

This section is a menu of possible support systems that a museum might consider incorporating into its facility. The more than 25 systems outlined can be inserted into scopes of work for concept designs and cost estimating. The specification for an idealized e-concierge system can be adapted for use in a request for proposal (RFP).

You can select and adapt systems from the menu to fit your museum's needs and future plans. You are likely to have some systems already in some degree. The menu contains systems requested by museums in the past; there are bound to be additional systems invented as technologies and fashion develop and as the Internet of things matures.

POTENTIAL MUSEUM SUPPORT SYSTEMS

In addition to the conventional, building-oriented systems within any substantial facility, the museum will require a large inventory of specialized systems and equipment to support its objectives and methodologies. The following inventory is an overview of the types of systems that typically require integration into a successfully functioning facility. Some of these systems and equipment will have their own independent budgets, while some will be enhancements of the base building and will therefore draw on multiple budgets.

The list is intended to provide suggestions for board and staff discussions with architects, exhibit designers, and vendors to determine the appropriate systems to incorporate in each phase of development.

Acoustic and Ambient Light Control

- Acoustic absorption and/or diffusion materials
- Sound- and light-locked entrances to most theaters and some specialized exhibit areas
- Glare reduction materials and devices

Café, Vending, and Function Equipment

- Café equipment and furnishings
- Vending machines
- Function catering equipment
- Function furniture: tables and chairs
- Function audiovisual: portable sound and projection systems
- Environment and lighting
- Food carts for interior and/or exterior use

Cash-Handling and Security Systems

- Surveillance system
- Cash room equipment
- Cash registers (often integrated into the ticketing system)
- Safe/drop box

Computer Systems

- Office support (word processing, database, and spreadsheets)
- Finance system
- Membership/development system
- Ticketing and admissions system
- Facility use scheduling
- Electronic messaging

Data and Information Systems

- Information technology backbone: the primary delivery systems for all data and information between all departments
- Computer networks: servers, routers, firewalls, Internet access, electronic messaging, and so on
- Communication local area networks as required within departments, between staff and exhibits, and between visitor amenities and tracking systems
- Control local area networks as required for building, administrative, theater, and exhibit operation
- Connection to the external world: phone, Internet, cable, satellite, wireless, and so on

Distance Learning Systems

- Network connection and maintenance
- Video recording, editing, and reproduction system
- Broadcast and reception system(s)
- Audio/video archiving system
- Distance learning broadcast studio
- Broadband access to the Internet

Electrical Systems

- Buildingwide, programmable electrical control system
- Local dimmable room lighting: to independently control selected rooms of the building, especially in theater-like spaces, which typically are not integrated into the building lighting system
- UPS (uninterrupted power supply): to maintain operation of systems long enough to power down data and control systems; may be applied to specific equipment and/or entire systems
- Power conditioning: to guarantee electrical voltage at ±5 percent of nominal voltage to ensure the health of computer and data systems
- Higher-voltage/multiple-phase power: as required to service systems in the exhibit and theater areas
- Emergency power system for sustained power outages

Emergency Systems

- No-light emergency exit signs: to prevent light leakage from exit signs in conventional theaters, giant-screen theaters, specialty presentation spaces, and, particularly, in planetariums
- Magnetic-release doors for fire emergencies in areas where open corridors are desired

Exhibit and Demonstration Support Systems

- Water supply: hot and/or cold water may be required in many established exhibit locations as well as in any demonstration areas
- Drainage: for all sinks, water supply locations, and exhibit support
- Compressed air: required in the exhibit maintenance shop(s), the theaters, and throughout the exhibit galleries
- Natural gas: may be required in some theaters and demonstration areas
- Lighting: exhibit lighting infrastructure for positioning, powering, and controlling all aspects of the exhibit lighting system
- Exhibit "Out of Order" signage system

Furniture Systems

- Outdoor casual seating
- Indoor casual seating
- Theater seating
- Movable exhibit seating
- Movable office furniture
- Special event tables and chairs

Graphics and Signs

- Corporate identity system
- Institution logo and style sheet
- Exterior signs
- Interior signs
  - Directional signs
  - Location signs
  - Donor recognition
  - Code signs
- LED signs and systems
- Sign-generating system
- Imagery acquisition protocol and equipment
- Integrated visual reference system (graphic)

Heating, Ventilation, and Air-Conditioning Systems

- Local control of heating, ventilation, and air conditioning may be desired in some areas.
- Relative humidity: some projectors and computer equipment may require environments with very specific levels within narrow tolerances in especially wet or dry seasons
- Collections require very strict ranges of temperature and humidity

Lighting Systems: Special

- Exhibit lighting infrastructure: a standardized system of hanging positions and power availability throughout all dedicated and potential exhibit areas (e.g., an exhibit hub or lobby)
- Exhibit lighting dimming system(s): functionality added in particular exhibit areas to augment the base building exhibit lighting infrastructure
- DMX system(s): a network of control signals that can operate specialty lighting equipment: dimmers, intelligent light fixtures, control devices, and so on
- Task lighting: some areas will require very specific task lighting to achieve an effective ambiance within a space
- Work/maintenance lighting: separate work lights will be required in some spaces for flexible setup procedures and maintenance of specialized equipment

Maintenance Systems

- Janitor closets
- Floor-cleaning systems
- Personnel and equipment lifts
- Management systems
- Office support and data access (word processing, database, and spreadsheets)
- Telephone system
- Ticketing and admissions
- Finance system
- Membership/development support systems
- Facility use scheduling system

Media Systems Independent of Exhibit and Theater Programs

- Multimode media systems
- Digital media interfaces and conversion systems
- Audio announcement and music system (analog and digital)
- Video monitor network
- Integrated visual reference system (electronic)
- Audiovisual support equipment
- Wall clocks

Office Systems

- Office landscape systems
- Acoustic privacy systems ("white noise" and similar technologies)
- Telephone systems
- Printing system
- Fax system
- Duplicating systems
- Image manipulation systems
- Teleconferencing systems

Outreach Systems

- Teacher resource system
- Kit distribution system
- Outreach transportation system

Presentation Systems: Special

- Fog-generating equipment: sometimes to create a realistic effect of fog, sometimes to "thicken" the air so that beams of light are more visible
- Laser equipment: sometimes requires specific voltages, water supply, and drainage

Retail Shop Equipment

- Cash register units
- Other shop equipment
- Retail fixtures and environment
- Cart for outdoor sales

Signal Systems

- Raceways, cable trays, trenches, and so on: open and accessible routes for frequent additions and changes in the signal lines that control exhibit and theater systems
- Power separation: special precautions will be required to keep power and signal lines separate; this is particularly important for audio and data cables

Ticketing System

- Visitor experience design and mapping center software
- Point-of-sale ticketing system
- Telemarketing sales and reservations

Visitor and Program Participant Service Equipment

- Information booth equipment
- Membership booth equipment
- Box office equipment
- Cash room equipment
- Crowd-handling equipment and turnstiles
- First-aid room equipment
- Coatroom equipment
- Staff communications systems
- Public telephone system
- Audio announcement and music system
- Audiovisual support equipment

Web Systems

- Remote information access
- Remote ticketing
- Remote scheduling and reservations

- Remote teacher resource system
- On-site information access
- On-site visitor tracking system
- On-site visitor way-finding system
- On-site scheduling system

E-CONCIERGE SYSTEM

The following description is idealized. At this writing, no e-concierge system is on the market. The description is useful as a reminder of possible services to the visitor that could be offered by an intelligent museum that responds to the visitor's interests.

The description is written as a draft scope of work that the museum could send to qualified bidders.

The e-concierge system and website integrate a number of related functions designed to be the museum's electronic interface with the public. While many of its functions will also be covered by floor staff, telephone message systems, and print collateral, the e-concierge system should be able to orient visitors to the museum, promote its offerings, sell tickets via credit card, provide directions and routes within the building, link to related regional and subject sites, provide more in-depth information on topics in the galleries and theaters, and sell merchandise online. All these functions should be able to happen on-site at specially designed kiosks and online through the website. While the interface should appear seamless to visitors, a clear firewall will protect business software and data from program software.

The scope involves both the development of the digital information system (e.g., website, ticket-selling software, and information databases) and the physical delivery systems on-site (e.g., visitor kiosks, cashier terminals and ticket printers, and admissions gateways). The system should be based on an existing ticketing system designed to serve museums with multiple venues, and the system should be open to the addition of functions, terminals, and future upgrades and expansions. Development of the e-concierge system should be done in parallel with the museum's administrative system, which will cover the staff computer network and the museum's broadband service and its backbone. Design of the public kiosks should amplify the museum's brand identity and be coordinated with other high-quality cabinetry in the area.

The e-concierge system will include at least the following functions:

- Displaying museum marketing information
  - Products and services (marketing)
  - Schedule and calendar
  - Hours, prices, and maps
  - Membership
- Collecting (not retaining without permission) visitor/participant profiles
  - Transaction number
  - Membership
  - Date stamp
  - Party size
  - Interests
  - Visit itinerary and ticket suggestions
  - Credit card/billing information
  - Name and contact information
  - Personal query e-mail response to visitor's e-mail
- Admissions package
  - Reservations and sales software and hardware—"cashier stations"
  - Ticket printers credit card swipe and connections/accounts
  - Ticket reader gateways—"turnstiles"
  - Group sales and reservations
- Content depth
  - Museum's background Information on exhibits and programs
  - Links related to websites
  - Map of related exhibits and programs at the museum
  - Bibliography and resources (some in the museum store)
  - Sources and acknowledgments for exhibits and programs
- Opinion polling
- Management reports and maintenance access
- Attract loops and screen savers
  - Web: "Welcome to the Museum"
  - Open zone: "What Do You Want to Do Today?"
  - Program areas: "Want to Know More?"
  - Staff terminals: "Log-In and Customize"

Authoring System

The authoring system is made up of software tools that will be used to create the e-concierge program and websites and will be turned over to the museum's staff to maintain and expand the offerings. All software is to be registered to the museum for the purposes of obtaining upgrades and modifications.

Ticketing System

The e-concierge system and website should incorporate an established multivenue admissions ticketing system with firewall protection and features such as online credit card purchases, inventory control of timed tickets, membership tracking, discount and promotional codes, management reports, ticket and itinerary printing, postal code capture, party size, and numerous other features typically used by museums in similar settings.

Section 89

Support

Technology and Networks

INTRODUCTION

Technology will be embedded in the building operation. To maximize flexibility during the day, some spaces will be conceived of as multimode spaces, capable of being operated for different kinds of functions and different kinds of audiences at different parts of the day or week through the use of automated presets for lighting, window shades, audiovisual ambience, and access to the equipment in that space.

This section has a menu of networks serving various purposes and audiences for you to choose from. See also "88. Support Systems."

This section on technology hardware resources covers the most rapidly evolving museum practice. Thus, you should seek current counsel on systems and adapt the principles in this section.

SUPPORT: INFORMATION TECHNOLOGY INFRASTRUCTURE, TECHNOLOGY, AND ON-SITE NETWORKS

To be written at a later point in planning, the *information technology (IT) and technology plan* will lay out the information systems with schematic diagrams that illustrate the flow of information, kinds of access, and degrees of security. Functional standards for computers, media, and other technologies will be outlined. Particular attention will be paid to language access technologies and radio-frequency identification, mobile, and bar code technologies so that exhibit designers can understand how to incorporate them. Conceptual development of the program network will show how computer-based exhibits and media equipment can be linked centrally. Chapters on the use of Internet and social media will outline principal objectives and content, such as teacher support resources, marketing information, e-commerce, and advanced ticket sales.

There are several principal on-site networks:

- Administrative System: This intranet links staff, workstations, maintenance controls, institutional databases, filing, office e-mail, and so on. Staff and certified volunteers and contractors are the only ones allowed to use it, which they do through a password system. Certain branches of the network will be heavily secured, such as general ledger and payroll, donor databases, and so on.
- Program Network: This will link exhibits, theaters, and other public areas. Visitors will have access to information on this network, but it will be limited to selected pages of information and activities intended to focus and deepen their experience at particular exhibits or programs. Staff will be able to use the program network to monitor the status of computer-driven exhibits and theaters, upload new information, change operating mode, and send out coordinated signals in case of an emergency or a special event. A program network will link any exhibit with chips in it in order to monitor use and maintain units locally or centrally. The program network can pipe programs and information from central locations to individual screens or throughout the building. During a corporate rental, for example, it will be possible to put that company's presentation on all screens and media throughout the facility for its invited guests.
- Digital Asset Management System: This includes collection-quality archival storage of digital intellectual property, including collection items that are digital in their original state, such as music mixes and digital photos.
- Live Data Visualization Systems: These include screens, light tables, and projected spheres that can show live data feeds—cloud cover, airplane traffic, global exchange rates, oil markets, and so on—using visualization software and graphics to help audiences understand trends and explore for patterns. The museum maintains licenses, permissions, and other documentation supporting the museum's right to publicly display such data for educational purposes to paying audiences.

- Citizen Data Input Ports: These are stations where citizens (visitors and program participants) can enter their data on public research projects and see how their data align with overall patterns.
- Shared Technology Specifications: In order to simplify operations and increase flexibility, the museum will establish shared standards for all software and hardware in the IT system. The *Standardized Information Technology Specifications Manual* will be a constantly evolving but always integrated with and linked to a family of equipment and software in such areas as office workstations, building maintenance, computers, media systems in the exhibit areas, and other areas where information technologies are used. The standards will be broad enough to recognize different kinds of needs—for example, a print studio may need different computers than the finance office. This manual will be developed as part of the scope for the original designer of the IT system, and it will be updated and maintained by staff as new products and capabilities arise. Any purchase involving IT equipment should conform to the standards, yet there should also be an appeal process for exceptions, which should be granted on a reasonable basis.

Section 90

Supporters

Collectors

INTRODUCTION

Collectors support the museum as the source of objects, expertise, and, often, support funding.

Relationships with collectors are personal, varied, and idiosyncratic. There are no widely accepted categories for defining collector types.

There are potential issues with ethics and conflict of interest in a museum's dealings with a collector. You are encouraged to consult with peers and join professional associations such as the American Institute for Conservation and the curator and registrar professional interest groups of the American Alliance of Museums.

Tier 3 members of American Alliance of Museums can access sample documents covering collector agreements, conflict-of-interest disclosure forms, ethics statements, and other collector-related documents.

SUPPORTERS: COLLECTORS

Museums are expected to follow ethical principles with regard to their dealings with collectors and their possible conflicts of interest and opportunities for personal gain. The museum will be watchful about provenance, authenticity, price inflation, tax concerns, value accounting, condition, documentation, and other aspects of a collector's collection and the possible use or acquisition of objects from that collector by the museum.

Within this ethical framework, collectors are important relationships for collecting museums. Collectors are the museum's conduit for objects, as they act as either amateur or professional curators and are often the first to bring an object from the field into a documented collection. Collectors can also be the museum's source of expertise in the collector's specialty, and some collectors, such as Steve Martin, act as exhibition curators. Collectors are also candidates for fund-raising.

Section 91

Supporters

Public and Private Funders

INTRODUCTION

Funders, also called donors and social investors, support the museum by giving money. There are both public and private funders. The shift in wording from the traditional donors to the term social investors symbolizes a fundamental shift in thinking about relationships with partners in the business, government, and philanthropic communities. The museum is looking for social investors with whom we can partner to address significant long-term challenges facing our community (see tables 91.1 to 91.5).

SUPPORTERS: PUBLIC AND PRIVATE FUNDERS

Table 91.1   Public Funders: Public Support–Based Revenues

City
County
State
Federal (including the military)
Public foundation and agency grants
Tribal
Public university

Table 91.2   Private Funders: Private Support–Based Revenues

Donor bequests and gifts
Annual campaign
Memberships (higher levels)
Fund-raising events
Private foundation grants
Corporate membership
Corporate sponsorships
Private university

PLANNING WORKSHEETS

Table 91.3   Sources of Public Funding: Public Support–Based Revenues

	Current	Future
City		
County		
State		
Federal (including the military)		
Public foundation and agency grants		
Tribal		
Public university		

Table 91.4   Sources of Private Funding: Private Support–Based Revenues

	Current	Future
Donor bequests and gifts		
Annual campaign		
Memberships (higher levels)		
Fund-raising events		
Private foundation grants		
Corporate membership		
Corporate sponsorships		
Private university		

Table 91.5   Social Investor Benefit Categories

Philanthropic Cases	Museum Indicators of Impact and Performance (MIIP 1.0) Category	Current Museum Portfolio	Community Needs	Funding Availability	Future Museum Portfolio
Broadening participation	A				
Archival preservation	B				
Collection stewardship	B				
Heritage preservation	B				
Quality of life	C				
Social capital	C				
The region's future	C				
Community building	C				
Research	D				
Education	E				
Environmental stewardship	F				
Advancing social change	F				
Public identity and image	G				
Economic development	H				
Visibility to select markets	I				
Delivering community services	I				
Popular learning experiences	J				
Personal growth opportunities	J				
Recognitions and memorials	K				
Sanctuary and contemplation	K				
Public recreation	L				
Museum operations and activities	M				
Museum capital and infrastructure	N				

Section 92

Supporters

Partners

INTRODUCTION

Museums are becoming more partnership oriented. Partners are defined as other individuals and organizations that agree to work with the museum for mutual benefit. While partnerships may involve an exchange of money, once the sums become substantial, they become either funders or vendors, depending on which way the money is flowing.

Partnerships are also relatively new to museums, and terms and frameworks are still evolving. These frameworks look at potential partners by sector, type of collaboration, and depth of the partnership (see tables 92.1 to 92.4).

Table 92.1   Potential Collaboration Partners

Educational system (pre-K through postgraduate school)
Tourism developers
Corporate community
Social agencies and nongovernmental organizations
Media (advertising, public relations, and promotions)
Libraries
Neighborhood civic and religious organizations
Retail stores, banks, and service providers
Other museums and cultural organizations
Membership organizations (e.g., Girl Scouts and the American Association of Retired Persons)
Military and service organizations
Professional associations and chambers of commerce

Table 92.2   Categories of Partnerships

1. Program
2. Project
3. Marketing
4. Audience
5. Peer (other museums and cultural organizations)
6. Supporting

Table 92.3   Levels of Partnership by Commitment

1. Member
2. Advocate
3. Sustainer
4. Partner
5. Supporter

PLANNING WORKSHEET

Table 92.4   Potential Collaboration Partners

	No. of Current Partnerships	Department Liaison	No. of Future Partnerships
Educational system (pre-K through postgraduate school)			
Tourism developers			
Corporate community			
Social agencies and nongovernmental organizations			
Media (advertising, public relations, and promotions)			
Libraries			
Neighborhood civic and religious organizations			
Retail stores, banks, and service providers			
Other museums and cultural organizations			
Membership organizations (e.g., Girl Scouts and the American Association of Retired Persons)			
Military and service organizations			
Professional associations and chambers of commerce			

Section 93

Advice on Partnerships from the Institute of Museum Library Services

INTRODUCTION

The following advice on partnerships is from *Partnership for a Nation of Learners: Joining Forces, Creating Value* (Institute of Museum and Library Services and Corporation for Public Broadcasting, 2009).

ADVICE ON PARTNERSHIPS FROM THE INSTITUTE OF MUSEUM LIBRARY SERVICES

The goal in partnership for a Nation of Learners was to cultivate the art of partnering. Lessons Learned sections detail many tips and best practices the grantees have provided to illuminate their experiences. Partnerships are neither easy nor instantaneous, but they can be quite rewarding. If your organization is considering a partnership, we hope this publication will help to make your efforts more effective and fulfilling.

During their partnership, IMLS and CPB worked with their communities to identify five predictive characteristics that might indicate the likely success of a partnership and five outcome characteristics that can be expected as a collaboration matures.

Predictive Characteristics

- The collaboration grows out of shared experience and prior familiarity.
- The collaboration is strongly supported by the partnering leadership.
- The collaborators accept different forms of stakeholder equity.
- The collaborators understand the importance of mission alignment and mission overlap.
- The joint initiative has a meaningful place in the budgets of the collaborating organization.
- Outcome Characteristics
- The collaboration results in specific benefits to the public as well as to the collaborators that can be identified and, under the right circumstances, replicated.
- The collaboration produces institutional and cultural change over time, affecting how the partners set priorities; how they value and use their assets, how they think about and relate to their constituents, and how they are perceived.
- The collaborators take advantage of various assessment tools to create feedback loops that allow the collaborative activities to be further refined as they unfold.
- The collaboration stays grounded in the real needs, abilities, and circumstances that gave rise to it; the partners grow more secure in their roles; the responsibility for success is shared; and momentum is sustained by staying focused on the agreed-upon goals of the partnership.
- Credit for the collaboration, and for the outcomes it produces, is shared equally among the collaborators.
- Align Project Purpose with Institutional Mission and Community Need
- How can we best serve the community? Community need first, partnership second.
- Take the Time to Plan
- Time spent planning paid dividends throughout the life of the project and beyond and enabled the group to define early on the roles and responsibilities of each partner and to integrate each partner's activities.
- Choose Partners Carefully and Get to Know Them Well
- Capitalize on the strengths of partner institutions, ensuring that each partner will be contributing what it does best as an organization.
- Get to Know Your Partners and Their Different Cultures
- Hurdles include decision-making processes and standards of professionalism.

291

- Learn each other's language and practices.
- Building Relationships and Communicate
- Flexibility and adaptability are two important characteristics for successful partnerships.
- The time required and level of coordination needed to manage a large complex partnership.
- Partnerships impact every aspect of the institution, from finance and IT to governance.
- Continued regular communication among partners is essential.

- A Collaborative Whole Is Stronger Than the Sum of Its Parts

The "act of partnership" brought benefits on a whole host of levels—including insights into their own organizations' into the needs of communities and new strategies for public service: New skills, new capacity for communication and relationship building, and new understanding about what it means to engage communities.

See "15. Bibliography for Museums" for citation reference.

Section 94

Supporters

Volunteers

INTRODUCTION

In order to operate successfully, the museum will have a very active volunteer program with a unique focus on engaging members of the community as volunteers in projects, interpretation, mentoring, and other aspects that put faces to the museum's role as the gateway between the public and the region's leadership and professional communities.

Many volunteer activities will be in the delivery of educational services, and volunteers will also be active in the store, as entrance greeters, as market researchers, and in several other areas of the museum's operation. Volunteers will receive training in their areas that will amount to a continuing education program during their involvement with the museum. Volunteers will be made up of college and high school students, professionals, and retirees who are interested in passing their accumulated experience onto future generations.

In general, all of the museum's volunteer programs have the potential to grow in membership and to include other categories of volunteers. Among the programs is a ladder of involvement and responsibility. Conceptually, a visitor might be intrigued by the activities in one of the galleries and want to join in the effort, at which point he or she might get training to be certified in the operation of some of the equipment and then advanced to be part of a production team on an exhibition or program, graduate to lead such teams, and then become involved in the museum and its operation, possibly even at the governance level.

This continuum of volunteer opportunity from very casual to deeply responsible will be an attractive aspect of a growing cohort of skilled individuals. In a very real way, it transforms the museum into a participatory museum, where the public is engaging the public directly, curated and facilitated by museum staff in its facilities.

The following text may be selected and adapted to suit your museum.

SUPPORTERS: VOLUNTEERS

Volunteer program is built on the following assumptions:

- Volunteers are not recruited to fill essential positions that by definition should be held by paid staff members.
- People become volunteers for a variety of reasons—social exchange, activity after retirement or during a period of unemployment, dedication to a cause, part of an ethic of community giving and participation, or desire for continuing education. The museum's program recognizes that the volunteer commitment must be met with an institutional commitment to enrich the lives of those individuals who join in the museum's mission.
- In addition to service within the institution, volunteers serve a critical visibility role in the community at large. Creative volunteer opportunities can serve to engage a breadth of community sectors with the museum's mission.
- Not all volunteers have similar abilities; volunteers will be placed and trained or educated for activities that will be fulfilling to them and to the museum's mission.

Objectives

- To help serve the museum's missions.
- To welcome and guide visitors while providing a comfortable environment for learning.
- To learn about their culture, science, history, and technology.
- To contribute directly to the enrichment of visitor experiences.
- To expand visitors' knowledge of science and technology.
- To serve as program presenters.

- To serve as interpreters (a link between the museum's exhibits and its visitors). Interpretation is an information service, a guide service, an educational service, an entertainment service, a propaganda service, and an inspirational service. Interpretation aims at giving people insights, new enthusiasm, and new interests. A good interpreter leads people easily into new and fascinating worlds. The three basic elements needed are knowledge, enthusiasm, and good interpersonal skills.
- Interpretive staff responsibilities include the following:
  - To maintain a professional attitude not revealing personal opinions or personal problems.
  - To understand how different people learn.
  - To know appropriate subject matter and have interpretive strategies that will enable them to get the point across.
  - To be gracious, friendly, and warm to all visitors.
- Volunteers will be in the following areas:
  - Exhibit halls—as docents, explainers, presenters, and operators
  - Feature theater—as presenters
  - Library—as librarians
  - Gift shop—as sales staff and shopping assistants
  - Lobby—as greeters and membership salespeople
  - Discovery rooms—as interpreters and explainers
  - Membership—as additional sales staff, contacting individuals and families to become members or to renew memberships

Training Programs

The volunteer coordinator will supervise the recruitment, placement, training, and evaluation of volunteers. The number of sessions and length of time for training will depend on the volunteer's responsibilities. A volunteer "certificate" will be awarded, at each level of achievement, showing completion of the training program before volunteers can perform certain tasks.

VOLUNTEER BENEFITS

- Free admission to the museum galleries
- Educational training programs
- Discounts on workshops
- Opportunity to meet and work with others sharing similar interests
- Chance to help others explore and discover
- The first half hour of a three-and-a-half-hour shift is devoted training and development
- Free parking
- 35 percent discount in the café
- 25 percent discount in the museum shop
- Volunteer annual meeting and appreciation dinner, a champagne reception, and a sit-down dinner
- Volunteer Appreciation Week
- Volunteer Welcome Back Week
- Complimentary membership after one year of active service and at least 75 hours of volunteer service
- Bronze pin with 150 hours of services
- Silver pin with 500 hours of service
- Gold pin with 1,000 hours of service
- Gem pin with 2,000 hours of service
- Gift of appreciation with 3,000 hours of service
- Name on museum lobby volunteer plaque with 4,000 hours of service
- Special awards with 5,000 or more hours of service
- Free admission to participating cultural institutions

Governance and Advisory Roles

Individuals who serve as trustees, board members, advisers, committee members, event hosts, and other leadership roles in the museum are also volunteers. Each meeting is a shift and a museum engagement.

Section 95

Ticket Prices

Calculating Average Ticket Price

INTRODUCTION

Ticket prices for general admission are relatively simple compared to a museum offering two or more separately charged venues, as combination tickets add yet another option to confuse visitors at the admissions desk.

This section can help you mathematically test different price strategies: Will a deeper discount on the combination ticket drive more sales? What will the impact be if more children and fewer adults visit than expected? Who are our main sources of admissions revenue? How do our prices compare with our peers?

This section also presents different ways of analyzing the average ticket price (ATP) based on actual attendance and revenue.

This section is written by contributing author Jeanie Stahl.

Table 95.1 Recommended Price List: 20XX$

Ticket Categories			20XX (20XX$)
Solo Tickets			
Exhibit Halls	Adult	18 to 59	$7.50
	Child	3 to 17	$5.50
	Senior/Military	60+	$6.50
	School and Youth Groups		$5.00
Planetarium/Dome Thtr	Adult		free
	Child		free
	Senior/Military		free
	Family of 2 adult/2child		free
	Member-Adult		free
	Member-Child		free
	Member-Senior/Military		free
	School and Youth Groups		free
Feature Theater	Adult	18 to 59	$7.50
	Child	3 to 17	$5.50
	Senior/Military	60+	$6.50
	School and Youth Groups		$5.00
Combination Tickets			
Exhibit & Theater	Adult	18 to 59	$12.00
	Child	3 to 17	$9.00
	Senior/Military	60+	$11.00
	School and Youth Groups		$8.00
Non-school Groups	15 or more 10% discount if booked in advance		

Table 95.2 Sample Average Ticket Price (ATP) Calculations (20XX$): Two Venues

	20XX
On-Site Attendance	200,000
Ticketed Attendance	150,000
Exhibit Hall Attendance	138,000
Feature Theater Attendance	75,000
Total Venue Attendance	213,000
Feature Theater % of On-Site Attd	38%
Exhibit Hall Solo Ticket	75,000
Combination Ticket	63,000
Theater Solo Ticket	12,000
Total Ticketed Attendance	150,000

Venue Attendance	
Exhibits	138,000
Feature Theater	75,000
Exhibits	65%
Feature Theater	35%
Revenue	
Exhibits w. 1/2 of Combo Tx	$564,750
Theater w. 1/2 of Combo Tx	$346,500
Total Admissions Revenue	**$911,250**
Overall ATP	**$6.08**

Overall Solo	58%
Overall Combo	42%
Exhibit Solo	54%
Exhibit Combo	46%
Theater Solo	16%
Theater Combo	84%

Overall ATP	$6.08
Adult Combo Ticket	$12.00
Discount off Adult Combo	49%
Venue Visits/Visitor	1.42
Exhibit ATP	$4.09
Theater ATP	$4.62

Exhibit Solo	
Revenue	$281,250
Exh solo Attend	75,000
Exhibit Hall Adult Solo Tx	$7.50
Exhibit ATP	$3.75
Discount	50%

Feature Theater Solo	
Revenue	$63,000
Theater solo Attend	12,000
Theater Adult Solo Tx	$7.50
Theater ATP	$5.25
Discount	30%

Combination Tx	
Revenue	$567,000
Combo Attendance	63,000
Adult Combo Tx	$12.00
Combo ATP	$9.00
Discount	25%

TICKET PRICES

Museum Galleries Ticket Prices

In addition to the ticket categories of adult (ages XX and up), child (ages XX to XX), and senior (ages XX and up), the museum will offer group discounts and reduced-rate tickets for students attending as part of a school group. Members will be admitted free to the museum galleries but will [have to pay $XX for visitor venue 2]. [Get a discount of XX percent on all other purchases.]

Visitor Venue 2 Prices

Visitors will be permitted to buy a [visitor venue 2]-only ticket as well as in combination with the museum galleries ticket.

Combination Tickets

Combination tickets will be available for the museum galleries and visitor venue 2. The combination tickets have been discounted enough from the combined solo ticket prices to make them look attractive to visitors: $XX off for adults and $XX off for children. It is anticipated that XX percent of visitors will buy a combination ticket.

A ticket price schedule is presented in table 95.1. The ticket categories are adult (ages 18 and up), child (ages 3 to 17), senior (ages 60 and up) [and military], and youth group (e.g., school groups).

ATP and Revenue Calculations

The following demonstrates different approaches for calculating ATP. Both methods can be developed either based on actual attendance and revenue numbers (such as in table 95.1, which is in two parts) or as a template for projecting the ATP and revenue based on varying assumptions (such as in table 95.2).

The gross revenue from total ticket sales divided by the total admissions/ticketed attendance (including free) arrives at the ATP. The ATP (in 20XX$) is calculated to be $XX.

Table 95.3 demonstrates a method for projecting the revenue and revenue per ticket category based on "what if" scenarios. For example, you could change the percentage of attendance by ticket category to see what the impact would be if a higher percentage of children and a lower percentage of adults visited, and/or you could change the assumption for the percentage of visitors buying a solo ticket versus a combination ticket.

Table 95.3 Sample Projected Average Ticket Price and Revenue Calculations (20XX$): Two Venues

		Solo Tx	Combo Tx	Revenue from Exh Solo Tx 20%	Revenue from Thtr Solo Tx 40%	Revenue from Combo Tx 40%	Total Revenue
Adult	28%	$7.50	$12.00	$42	$84	$134	$260
Child	17%	$5.50	$9.00	$19	$37	$61	$117
Senior	5%	$6.50	$11.00	$7	$13	$22	$42
School Groups	22%	$5.00	$8.00	$22	$44	$70	$136
Other Groups	2%	$6.00	$9.00	$2	$5	$7	$14
Member (Thtr pd avg)	7%	$0.00	$6.50	$0	$0	$18	$18
Member Free	9%	$0.00	$0.00	$0	$0	$0	$0
Free	5%	$0.00	$0.00	$0	$0	$0	$0
Discount 80%	5%	$5.20	$8.80	$5	$10	$18	$33
TOTAL	100%			$96.80	$194	$331	$621
Average Ticket Price One Person= $Rev/100				$0.97	$1.94	$3.31	$6.21

PLANNING WORKSHEET

Table 95.4 Comparative Pricing Template

Peer and Relevant Museums	Adult	Child	Age	Senior	Age	Comments
The Museum						
Local Museums and Attractions						
Peer Museums						

Section 96

Value Exchanges

Definitions

1. The question of *value* starts with "of value to whom?" For example, a visitor's experience in a museum exhibition has a value to that visitor, and exposing that visitor to the content of that exhibition has a value to some supporters and possibly to the greater community. Museum activities result in impacts and benefits that have value to others.

2. *Value* is in the eye of the beholder, not in the mind of the owner. A museum cannot set its own value, but it can measure indicators of its value to its community, audiences, and supporters.

3. A museum's *value* lies in its impacts, says Weil (2005). However, the museum's value is actually expressed in terms of the value of the benefits. Since value is in the eye of the beholder, any valuation must first track the value that the community and its audiences and supporters place on their perceived benefits and then see if those findings relate to measuring the museum's desired impacts. When the desired impact is the same as the perceived benefit, such as the children's museum example where both the museum and the visitor want child development, the impact and the benefit are *aligned*. When they are different, such as the aquarium example, they are *unaligned*. Some degree of unalignment may be desirable for strategic or advocacy reasons.

4. Museums are free-choice marketplace organizations. No one has to go to, pay admissions to, or fund a museum. People and organizations choose to spend *time, effort*, and *money* on their museum engagements in exchange for perceived benefits.

5. The analysis of Museum Indicators of Impact and Performance (MIIP 1.0) found four main categories of impacts: *public impacts* benefit the community and society as a whole; *private impacts* benefit businesses, donors, and private foundations who are often also pursuing public impacts; and *personal impacts* benefit individuals, families, and households. A museum's activities can also benefit the museum institutionally, such as increasing its resources or improving its performance, resulting in *institutional impacts*.

6. A museum's *perceived value* is a judgment of the value of the benefits and impacts from engaging with the museum's activities by its community, audiences, and supporters and is usually a qualitative expression of what they received. *Exchanged value* is a quantification of the amount of time, effort, and/or money that the community, audiences, and supporters actually exchanged for the benefits they received. Exchanged value can be an indicator of perceived value.

7. Changes in the amounts of time, effort, and money that a museum's community and its audiences and supporters exchange for their museum benefits are indicators of changes in their perceived value of the benefits.

8. The museum's *key service markets* are its main sources of engagements and external operating revenue. There are three umbrella external service markets: the community as a whole, audiences, and supporters. These do not have to align with the museum's key community, audience, and supporter segments, but they could, and significant misalignments may be difficult to sustain. The museum itself is an internal market.

9. When the benefits to a key service market are the same as the desired impacts, then the value of the impact might be indicated by the exchanged value of the benefit. To the degree they are unaligned, the value of the impact would have to be discounted.

10. *Effort* is measured by the number of person-trips to a museum-sponsored location to engage in one or more museum activities. Like a physical museum engagement, a *person-trip* is defined as one physical (nonvirtual) trip to a museum or to a museum-sponsored program off-site by a person not employed or contracted by the museum to be there.
    a. The number of *person-trips* is equal to the number of *physical museum engagements*.

11. *Dwell time* can be measured by recording the length in minutes for each museum engagement from site arrival to site departure. Dwell time is not yet routinely measured or reported.

12. *Money* paid to the museum for its operational activities is measured as *external operating revenues*. The amounts are the monetary value of the museum's engagements to its direct beneficiaries, according to the subjective theory of economics (Menger, 1976). Revenues are indicators of the money the museum's community, audiences and supporters are willing to pay in return for the personal, private, and public benefits they receive.

13. A museum's *business model* is the mixture of activities and benefits provided to its community, audiences, and supporters in return for their money.

14. Revenue sectors are classified as *earned revenue, support revenue,* and *capital asset net income* (e.g., endowment, intellectual property, or lease income).

    a. Accounting practices distinguish between government and nongovernment support as public and private support revenues. Revenues for personal benefits tend to be categorized as earned revenues.

15. *Endowment income* and other capital asset net income can be added to the museum's external operating revenues to result in *total operating revenues*. Museums with substantial endowments can cover a higher percentage of their operating costs internally, making them less dependent on external, competitive marketplace funding from the community, audiences, and supporters. Conversely, museums with no endowment must be very responsive to their community, audiences, and supporters.

16. Money paid to the museum for *capital projects* is investing in the museum's resources and is not considered operating revenues related to the museum's operating activities.

17. For evaluation consistency and sample size, *annual totals,* typically aligned with the museum's *fiscal year,* are preferred. Some museum associations report annual totals as submitted by some of their museum members.

18. *Return on social investment* (ROSI) is a common nonprofit key performance indicator that divides the value of the impact by the cost. In many cases, this is a conceptual rather than mathematical fraction, as the value and cost can be intangible (e.g., treating Ebola at the risk of lives), but some ROSI calculations can be quantitative, such as the potential annual increase in museum engagements and revenue divided by the capital cost of a larger temporary exhibition gallery.

19. The dollar amount or tangible value of a museum's *capital assets* is most consistently drawn from the financial statements. However, these figures are mostly tallies of depreciated capital investments (e.g., the last expansion or gallery overhaul less its assumed wear and tear), the endowment, and, if the museum is fortunate, additional capitalization in the form of reserve funds, working capital, capital for facility replacement needs, and risk capital. The original building, if fully depreciated, is often no longer on the books, nor is the real estate value of the land nor the value of the collection and the museum's nonprofit tax status. There are valid arguments for using a higher capital evaluation than only the balance sheet listing; however, objectivity and consistency are important in how your museum calculates the denominator when comparing ROSI from one year to another, and balance sheet numbers may be your most stable indicators of your museum's total assets.

See "15. Bibliography for Museums" for citation references.""

Section 97

Venue Capture Rates

INTRODUCTION

In museum terms, a *venue* is a public space where the museum offers experiences inside a space or series of spaces with controlled admission. Museum galleries are a venue if they have an admissions control point; the impressionist gallery within is not a venue but rather a *component* of the museum galleries venue. A separately charged butterfly pavilion is a venue even if it is only an add-on charge and accessible from within the museum galleries; if there is no charge for admission, the butterfly pavilion is just a component.

Many museums have just one venue—their galleries. In such museums, "visiting the museum" is synonymous with visiting the museum galleries. Once there is a second venue, however, each venue needs its distinct name, as "the museum" must now be the sum of its parts, not the name of one of its parts. In multiple-venue museums, "the museum" is the umbrella term and the brand identity; in consequence, each venue needs its distinct identity.

A visitor who arranges admissions to more than one visitor venue during a visit is buying a *combination ticket*. An individual who makes a person-trip to the museum and then buys a combination ticket to two venues—say, to both the exhibit galleries and the historic house tour—is counted as one *site visit* and *two venue visits*.

Capture ratio is a venue's total number of venue visits divided by the museum's total site visits. If 100 people came to a museum and 20 bought solo admissions to the galleries, 30 bought solo admissions to the tour, and 50 bought combination tickets to both, then the galleries have a capture ratio of 70 percent, and the tour has a capture ratio of 80 percent. This example has 100 site visits and 150 venue visits.

If the costs of all admissions are equal, then this example generates 50 percent more revenue than a museum with only one venue. Herein lies the appeal of multiple venues: adding venues can add revenue, often from customers already on-site. Some venues, such as a feature exhibition hall or an IMAX theater, can act as *destination venues* that have enough appeal to motivate site visits; other venues, such as a planetarium or a miniature train ride, act as *secondary venues*, capturing visitors already on-site, drawn by one of the museum's destination venues.

The addition of new visitor venues has potential benefits beyond admissions revenue as listed in table 97.1. By offering more dwell time (more to do during a visit), the museum can expand its market reach, just as people will drive farther to reach a larger shopping mall as shown in table 97.2. Longer dwell time also correlates with more spending on-site in the store and café. An additional venue can also appeal to different audience segments, such as adding a children's discovery center. Too many venues, on the other hand, can cannibalize attendance from each other, complicate transaction time, and confuse the visitor. The pros and cons of adding venues are listed in tables 97.3 and 97.4.

You can use this section to analyze how your venues are faring in their relative capture ratios of site visitors. Used together with ticket prices, these tables also help you weigh the factors and potential impacts of adding a venue to your museum's current offerings.

VENUE CAPTURE RATES

As a museum's number of venues increases and as its size of public offerings and the degree and length of audience involvement increase, so do the museum's market radius, dwell time (maximum driving time is proportional to dwell time), and on-site spending per capita, as shown in Table 97.2.

Table 97.1   Impact of Adding Venues

Add to dwell time
Justify a longer trip (increase market size)
Add a meal
Enhance shopping opportunities
Add overnight stay
Broaden audience appeal
Appeal to specific audiences
Expand learning methodologies
Stimulate crossover traffic
Marketable change
Justify repeat use
Venue competition and potential erosion

Figure 97.2   Dwell Time Factors

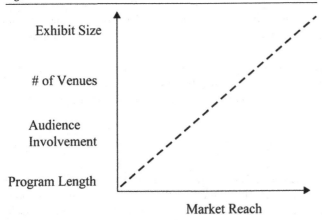

Table 97.3   Reasons for Higher Venue Capture Ratios

Heavily discounted combination ticket
Very small or very inexpensive exhibit halls
Only two ticketed venues
Good marketing campaign
Good on-site marketing
Exceptionally good programming

Table 97.4   Reasons for Lower Venue Capture Ratios

Small capacity versus very large museum attendance
More than two ticketed venues
Very large exhibit halls
Poor venue location
Underfunded marketing campaign
Poor preticketing and/or on-site marketing
Declining or absent appeal of the programming
Declining or absent appeal of the venue

PLANNING WORKSHEET

Table 97.5   Impact of Adding Venues

	Principal Impact	Strategy	Cost	Return on Investment
Add to dwell time				
Justify a longer trip				
Add a meal				
Enhance shopping opportunities				
Add overnight stay				
Broaden audience appeal				
Appeal to specific audiences				
Expand learning methodologies				
Stimulate crossover traffic				
Marketable change				
Justify repeat use				
Venue competition and potential erosion				

Section 98

Visitor Experience

Concepts

INTRODUCTION

This section offers a menu of concepts related to the visitor experience. The term is defined widely, applying to the whole museum site visit, including its anticipation and extension (see the discussion of compelling experiences below). Many of the applications, however, are specific to the exhibit halls and museum galleries.

This section is intended to complement the sections on public spaces and programs. Those sections address the spatial, architectural distinctions and what to do in those spaces. This section is about what to put in those spaces, such as exhibits.

You can use this section to identity concepts that your museum is already using and ones that you could adopt in the future.

VISITOR EXPERIENCE CONCEPTS

- Delta Museum Tactics: A museum with built-in infrastructure to facilitate change—the term is borrowed from the scientific symbol for change. Conceptually, the approach thinks of a museum much like a theater, with its stage, lights, grid, and other built-in systems that allow for a relatively economic changeover from play to play. In a community service museum, the Delta museum approach would seem logical. While it costs slightly more to implement Delta infrastructure at the start, subsequent program changes will be more economically manageable to allow the museum to stay in touch with its community to responding more quickly to new interests, stories, and opportunities. The Delta museum has implications for architecture, infrastructure, exhibit design, staff culture, and operating budget as well as for the institution's relationship with the community it serves.
- Universal Design: Cultural relevance, broader participation, multiple languages, American with Disabilities Act codes, respect, cultural competence, and guidelines issued by interest groups are factors to be considered in developing museum exhibits and programs. Jeff Kennedy's early work on universal design (Kennedy, 1997) has been augmented by Dr. Christine Reich's work on access, giving us well-researched guidelines for barrier-free designs (CAISE [http://www.informalscience.org]). Following universal design guidelines tends to make the experience better for everyone.
- Engagement in the Galleries: "'Engagement' as it is used in this report and in Public Engagement with Science literature and practice has a specific meaning that is characterized by mutual learning by publics and scientists—and, in some cases, policy makers. PES thus is framed as a multi-directional dialogue among people that allows all the participants to learn" (McCallie et al., 2009).
- Participation in the Museum: As explored in Nina Simon's book *The Participatory Museum*, "A participatory cultural institution is a place where visitors can create, share and connect with each other around content" (Simon, 2010, p. ii). Participation has since then taken many forms, including maker spaces, communal sculptures, talking circles, storytelling oral history kiosks, opinion polls, crowdsourcing information, theme weekends, citizen science and history, affinity group meet-ups, and so on.
- Use of Big Data: The potential of branded digital intellectual property and live big data will be included. Content and data developers as diverse as NASA, Getty Images, TED, Disney, YouTube, the BBC, the Star Wars franchise, the Centers for Disease Control, the Museum of Television and Radio, NOVA, and the Howard Hughes Medical Institute have intellectual property that they could provide show developers under some arrangement.
- Maker Spaces: The maker movement in science centers is learning about what different kinds of visitors will and will not do and what kinds of materials, tools, and challenges work in what kinds of visit contexts. The early work by the Ontario Science Centre with its Agents of Change had successes and failures that have evolved to the recently opened #Design Lab at the New York Hall of Science. Both the Exploratorium and the Tech are interesting places to watch for new ideas and operational policies for maker spaces.

- Visitor Activities: Within the museum galleries, most spaces will have places where visitor/participants can "do history" as well as "ask history." Punctuating these visitor-driven exhibits will be examples drawn from critical moments of regional history that are presented as examples of how others are doing history and recording and conserving the region's turning points and its cultural traditions. For example, in the family album gallery, visitors will be able to (1) do history by analyzing the paper, size, and chemistry of one of their own vintage photographs at a lab bench and (2) ask history at an image data bank display to look at other photographs from the same period of similar subjects while (3) studying a case with a historic photograph, with its curatorial registration, an object from the time, supporting documents, and a historian's label about the historical significance and (4) record history by entering your old photo into the museum database.
- Thematic Context: To help organize both the subject matter and the visitors' experience, the exhibit halls will be divided into theme areas. Reflecting trends in learning styles and in response to community interest, the exhibit halls should be organized according to applications or "microworlds" rather than the traditional organization according to topics or subject matter. Learning about science and technology in the context of real-world applications allows the visitor to understand simultaneously both the scientific principles involved and their social implications. This approach is interdisciplinary, and it means that certain topics, such as health, can be addressed in several contexts. The approach has two other strengths that will help attract visitors: the contexts lend themselves to the creation of interesting visual and audio environments, and these microworlds allow students to see what roles they might play in each of these applications. The theme areas have in common the following general approaches that should help orient the visitors. All will have some dominant architectural image, such as a town hall or a factory tower, that will be carried out in the visual environment that defines the area. We will feel as though we are "inside" a specific environment that

happens to include many hands-on interactive exhibits and presentations.
- Levels of Challenge and Involvement: The theme areas will also be organized in concentric circles of increasing levels of sophistication. The center will be a higher-level educational resource, such as a working laboratory, usable by those who are familiar with the subject and are prepared to spend some time pursuing personal information quests; at the outside circles, there will be attractive and entertaining exhibits designed to lure casual visitors into an interest in the theme.
- Compelling Experiences: Ultimately, a museum visit should be about positive transformation: in some dimension, visitors should leave the facility incrementally better than they entered them. If the core business is to inspire lifelong learning, then exiting visitors should feel just a little bit more capable, interested, and confident about their own learning abilities. Work has been done by a think tank in Chicago (The Doblin Group) on the nature of transforming experiences. They find there are five steps and six attributes to successful compelling experiences (see table 98.2).
- Visitor Focused: Keep the visitors' interests and values in mind. Everyone comes because they want to. Why? Research asking visitors why they come to a science museum tend to find three prioritized factors:
  - To spend quality time with friends or family
  - To experience something new
  - To learn something new
- Avoid Lecturing: Museum visitors do not want to pay today's high admission prices to be lectured at; rather, they want to pursue their own interests. Sometimes, those interests are in lectures, but the interest comes from the learners' needs for clarity and direction on a relevant topic. Museums are trusted sources of information, and the community looks to us as impartial authorities in our subject domains. However, we should not abuse this trust by becoming a boring uncle.
  - Yet we are used to being lecturers with points to get across. We start exhibit processes with "What is this exhibit trying to communicate? What is its main message?" We should start with "What can we do for the visitor this time?"
  - There is a strong temptation to think of a museum as a public soapbox. People with messages to communicate look to museums as platforms for their messages, as in "you ought to be telling this story." This sense of message obligation can result in deadly boring and empty exhibit galleries.
- Hands-On Interactives: Participation and active engagement promote learning and fulfillment for the visitor. From a pedagogical perspective, hands-on/minds-on exhibits provide complementary learning gateways to classroom learning by offering spatial, kinesthetic, experiential, visual, and other intelligences to add reality to

Table 98.1   Options for Thematic Exhibit Organization

	Example	Our Equivalent
By subject	Geology Hall	
By process of [science] [art]	Observe It!	
By chronology	Place over Time	
By era and cultures	Age of Steam	
Smorgasbord	Minnesota A–Z	
By specific to general	Where's Boston?	
By collection type	Tapestries and Tables	
By visitor type	Kids' Spot	
By visitor interest	Harry Potter Exhibition	

Table 98.2   Compelling Experiences

Part 1: Basic anatomy—Five stages: Great experiences seem to flow alike, consisting of three major stages and two transitions:
Attraction
   It calls to you. You want to try it, watch it, play it.
Entry
   As you enter the experience, you are removed from your everyday world.
Engagement
   You are doing it, feeling it, listening to it, smelling it, forgetting time.
Exit
   As the actual doing of it ends, you rejoin your everyday life.
Extension
   You want to share it, relive it. You collect programs, call a fellow traveler, search out similar experiences.
Part 2: Distinguishing characteristics—Six attributes: Likewise, there emerged some patterns in the ways people described these experiences:
Defined
   Do you know it? Can you describe it? Do the pieces hang together?
Fresh
   Is it novel? A twist on something familiar? Can you make it your own? Does it startle, amaze, amuse?
Accessible
   Can you try it? Work it? Get better at it? Get it to do what you want?
Immersive
   Can you feel it? Does it engage you? Can you lose yourself in it?
Significant
   Does it make sense? Does it make you remember?
Transformative
   Do you feel different? Might others think you've changed? Do you want to tell someone about it? Do you have something to show
      for it?

Source: The Doblin Group (https://doblin.com; go to "What's New," then to "Compelling Experiences").

textbook principles. Museum experiences can provide participants with resources for enhancing existing skills, developing new skills, and learning how to define and solve problems. It can encourage imagination, ingenuity, and creativity. A base of interactive, staff-driven activities, in combination with modest but highly attractive features, can make the museum an attraction to local and regional audiences.

- Skill Building: There will be some didactic information presented in the galleries, but the emphasis will be on introducing visitors to hands-on ways of exploring that they can use themselves. This emphasis on skill development over content transfer also leads to more open-ended exhibit resources that can serve visitors on a repeat basis as they get better and better at developing their own skills or need to come back in order to continue or report on their explorations outside the museum.

- Gateway to Partners: The museum will partner with other regional cultural institutions with kindred educational and community missions. One goal is to increase attendance and use of the partners' resources by promoting what the partners have to offer near exhibits that lead to the partners' specialties. In this way, the museum will be a gateway to other area museums.

- Interactive Dioramas: These will encourage visitors to investigate, identify, and observe by letting visitors interact with a diorama through interactive technologies that focus lighting and produce audio according to visitor

interests. For example, a child might make a rattlesnake rattle, or an adult may choose to identify a rare migratory bird or seldom-seen nocturnal mammal.

- Experience Dioramas: These will mix high-quality realistic dioramas with theater and media. Using techniques drawn from theme parks and the stage, visitors will look into dioramas from darkened passageways and into scenes that are amazingly lifelike. For example, by using a "pepper's ghost" technique (an illusion that is built on a 45-degree, half-mirrored glass panel between the audience and the diorama), we can create a snowstorm swirling around a trapped mountain goat on the edge of a cliff; some of the snow billows out to land on the railing and boulders that separate the audience from the scene.

- Immersion and Immersive Environments: The popularity of giant-screen and fulldome theaters, butterfly pavilions, and aquarium tunnels are due, in part, to their surrounding the visitor with rich, full environments, either real, scenic, or digitally projected. Immersive 3-D environments allow visitors to study data sets and to travel through data. Digital gigapixel imagery and red digital cameras can capture scenes in such great detail and project them back large enough to embrace the viewer. The following kinds of learning spaces are capable of immersive experiences:

  ○ Theater
  ○ Magic box (flexible black box with theatrical lighting and catwalks)

○ Tunnel of wonder
○ Discovery world
○ Icon and symbolic object spaces

- Exhibit Clusters: Exhibits that are adjacent and thematically connected can work together to influence a deeper level of learning and longer dwell times. The idea of clusters of exhibits rather than individual units is a way of both strengthening learning and addressing the different learning styles and developmental stages of multigenerational social groups of visitors. Exhibit clusters using different means and viewpoints can engage the whole family and social group (see figure 98.3).
- Exhibition Transformers: An exhibition transformer (working title) is an envisioned flexible sequence of reprogrammable and collapsible exhibit galleries and environments that offer visitors compelling changing experiences. While most large-scale exhibitions depend on unique artifacts and are therefore rare and difficult to organize, this innovation relies on visually changeable galleries, media interactives, immersive experiences, and locally sourced objects. This approach is easily reproduced simultaneously in multiple cities, and shows can be launched and run when the operator wants to. The physical aspect, including the equipment and its operating system, remains in place while new experiences are installed by downloading new software and installing new objects and graphics. A critical number of venues are a prerequisite for success with a platform that depends on an evergreen library of new shows. For this reason, the launch of the exhibition transformer must establish that critical mass by making a very attractive, risk and benefit–sharing offer to the founding members of the exhibition transformer network.
- The Growing Use of Digital Interactives: Digital media and information technologies have matured and stabilized in many areas, and the visiting public has developed interface skills and comfort with mobile phones, website navigation, game controls, and numerous other human–computer interfaces. In museum exhibits, stable media interactives tend to require less maintenance over their life span than many mechanical hands-on interactives. Whole-body gesture-based media have matured, with great potential for merging immersion and interactivity in memorable engagements. Live data from exclusive sources

Table 98.3   Exhibit Unit Clustering Tactic

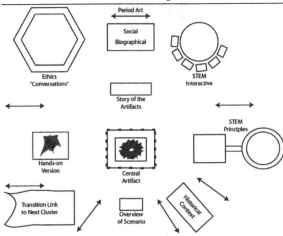

are available to view on large-scale walls, interactive tabletops, dome screens, or science-on-a-spheres. Fully exploiting the power and stability of new forms of digital interaction to convey content and deliver immersive learning experiences should be part of the new format.

PLANNING WORKSHEET

Table 98.4   Excellent Visitor Experiences

	Current	Future
Good times with family and friends		
New experiences; unique activities		
Learn something new; acquire a new skill		
Good value		
Great customer service		
Attractive ambiance		
Appealing programs		
Emotional and sensory engagement		
Strong word of mouth		

Source: Mark B. Peterson.

Theater analyst and planner Mark B. Peterson developed the dimensions of an excellent visitor experience, as listed in table 98.4.

See "15. Bibliography for Museums" for citation references.

Section 99

Visitor Experience

Factors

INTRODUCTION

Visitors who come to the museum on their own bring expectations and behave in similar ways across all disciplines. Museums that design their visitor experience with the factors listed in this section in mind are likely to provide their visitors with a more satisfying experience, as well as forewarn sponsors and managers against undue expectations or ambitions.

Some define *visitor experience* as what happens to the visitor while they are in the museum galleries. This book defines it as the whole museum engagement that day, from approach to the museum site to departure and follow-up.

Visitors will bring to their museum experience their personal frameworks of understanding and interests. Through front-end research, planners should identify visitors' interests, and those findings should inform the content of the exhibits and programs. By starting with what the visitor already knows and is interested in, the educator can engage the visitor at his or her level and interests and go on to develop skills and understanding from this more informed foundation.

In a family museum, it is often the experiences and social exchanges, more than the content, that people value, such as the immersion in a dome theater, creating a laser sculpture, and driving a canal boat simulator. For example, learning about electricity is low on the list of popular content, yet the experience of having your hair stand on end when you touch a static-electricity generator is one of the most popular science museum exhibits. For this reason, every gallery and program needs to be thought through from experience and content perspectives.

It is also important to understand some basics common to all museums and engrained in public expectations. Museums are social and physical, and these characteristics distinguish us from public television, textbook learning, online experiences, and many other media in the educational infrastructure. Most museum visitors come in small social groups, such as a family or a group of friends. The interaction of this group should be encouraged by the exhibit and theater programs rather than isolated to individual experiences. The physicality is evident with hands-on activities and physical collections but is equally a factor in an immersive planetarium experience and in outdoor environments as well as in architecturally distinct spaces and landscapes.

A central approach is to think of each of the museum's learning spaces from an experiential perspective: What does it feel like to be in the space? What kinds of public activities does the space suggest and support? What kinds of learning might happen best? And what can we add to the space to increase its natural strengths as a particular kind of learning experience? Some galleries may be naturally contemplative, while others are messy or interactive.

You can use this section as a checklist for qualities in your current and future visitor experience.

FACTORS OF THE VISITORS' EXPERIENCE OF THE MUSEUM

This section is based on writing by Dr. Robert "Mac" West. See table 99.1 for a summary.

- People Come to Museums for "Real" Experiences: Visitors come to see real objects (e.g., cultural or historic artifacts and living things) that aren't typically encountered in everyday life or to experience real phenomena or processes (e.g., light, color, and sound effects and to try out new technology). These experiences, by their very nature, are memorable.
- The Typical Exhibit Visit Averages between One and Two Hours: The duration of exhibit visits will vary widely, from less than an hour to half a day or more, and the median visit will average about one and a half to two hours.
- Visits Are Educational, Social, and Recreational: While frequent museumgoers seek educational experiences as a high priority in their visits, infrequent museumgoers may place a higher priority on the recreational and social aspects of visits to museums.

- Visitors Shop, Go to the Restroom, and Talk: A significant proportion of visitor time is spent in activities not directly associated with exhibits, such as going to the restroom or gift shop, getting oriented, or talking about subjects unrelated to the visit.
- Visitors Choose How to Spend Their Time: Many visitors sample exhibits and activities, spending a few seconds at some exhibits and a lot of time with a few exhibits that they find particularly interesting.
- Visitors' Knowledge and Interests Influence What They Do during a Visit: Visitors come to an informal educational setting with individual interests, preconceptions (sometimes erroneous), and individual learning styles.
- Most Visitors Develop Awareness, Not Knowledge, during a Visit: In most cases, visitors leave with attitude-influencing experiences and not with a large body of new knowledge or information.
- Icon Exhibits Can Make a Visit Memorable: "Icon" experiences (e.g., the Franklin Institute walk-through heart or the dinosaurs at the Field Museum in Chicago) are often the most memorable aspects of a museum visit.
- Volunteers and Staff Can Make a Visit More Significant: Visitor interactions with staff and volunteers can also make a lasting impression on visitors.
- Customer Service Is Important: Visitors like clean restrooms, easy way finding, courteous and helpful staff, visi-

tor amenities (e.g., a good place to eat, enough restrooms, coat check, and availability of strollers), and interactive exhibits that work.

PLANNING WORKSHEET

Table 99.1 Factors of the Visitors' Experience of the Museum

	Current	*Future*
People come to museums for "real" experiences		
The typical exhibit visit averages between one and two hours		
Visits are educational, social, and recreational		
Visitors shop, go to the restroom, and talk		
Visitors choose how to spend their time		
Visitors' knowledge and interests influence what they do		
Most visitors develop awareness, not knowledge, during a visit		
Icon exhibits can make a visit memorable		
Volunteers and staff can make a visit more significant		
Customer service is important		

Section 100

Visitor Services

Capacity Calculations

INTRODUCTION

Assumptions of attendance, seasonality, dwell time, and other areas of operation can be used to calculate the design day capacity and to size the functional architectural program. Once the dwell time in each of the public spaces is assumed, the museum can calculate the peak flow and throughput and derive the number of people expected to be in each space during peak conditions. These capacity assumptions bear further analysis in later stages of planning. These figures should be used as broad starting points rather than firm numbers.

This section looks at visitor services with regard to design day and peak capacity. It provides you with templates and formulas that you can adapt to your museum.

CAPACITY CALCULATIONS

Design Day, Dwell Time, and Peak Flow Calculations
Design Day

Is assumed to be a typical [peak day of week] in [peak month]. While the *master plan* assumes XX as the projected attendance, the building should be oversized for greater crowds and future expansions, and the museum has boosted the attendance potential estimate by XX percent to XX visitors.

During [peak month], XX percent of the yearly attendance is expected to be in the building, or XX percent during each of its four and one-third weeks. [Day of week]s are expected to attract XX percent of the peak week's attendance. Therefore, given the highest audience estimate, the design day and other planning figures can be calculated as shown in table 100.1.

This approach will result in a building reaching its maximum crowds on summer weekends but being emptier on other days. If capital costs become tighter, the building could be made smaller but with the consequence of crowding on summer weekends.

Dwell Time

How the design day's crowd is paced during the day is a factor of the following:

- The design and layout of the visitor's experience
- Natural patterns of visitation
- Building or traffic flow constrictions
- Program and exhibit capacity constrictions
- Dwell time in the building
- Marketing incentives
- On-site program timing
- Greeters and visitor assistance programs

Peter Anderson, in his book on start-up museums, states that in midsize to large science museums, peak capacity is often 50 percent of design day (Anderson, 1991) or that half the day's attendance is in the building at one time. Smaller museums with less to see have shorter dwell times, meaning that peak capacity will be a smaller share of the design day.

Table 100.1   Sample Capacity and Design Day Calculations: 20XX

Assumptions		
Typical year attendance	240,000	Site visits per year
Extraordinary loading factor	20%	In addition to typical year
Maximum building demand will be	288,000	Facility visits per year
Highest month capture ratio	13%	Peak month share of the yearly total
Highest day-of-week capture ratio	18%	Peak day's share of a summer week
Number of weeks in a month	4.33	52 weeks divided by 12 months
Average dwell time	3.00	Hours for the average visit
Peak dwell time capture ratio	50%	Of design day during heaviest hours
Visitors arriving by car	95%	During summer weekends
Visitors per car	2.7	During summer weekends
Volunteer and staff size	40	On-site at one time during weekends
Staff per car	1.1	Accounts for car pools, bikes, etc.
Calculations		
Design day capacity	1,556	Visitors on a typical August weekend day
Peak momentary capacity	778	Design capacity (code capacity should be higher)
Hourly peak flow	259	Visitors-per-hour processing speed
Peak flow	4	Visitors-per-minute processing speed
Peak car parking	274	Cars (weekends, principally)
Staff and volunteer parking	36	
Total parking	310	

Peak Flow Calculations

With a dwell time of XX minutes (XX hours), each component of the museum should be sized to handle a flow of XX visitors per minute (peak capacity/dwell time). Ticket-selling and ticket-taking operations and all other potential constrictions should be sized to handle peak capacity at XX seconds per visitor.

Dwell time has two natural limits: how long it takes to "do" the museum and the visitor's stamina. In larger museums, the visitor limit prevails as museum fatigue sets in around 90 minutes if no theater or café and around three hours if these chances to take a break and sit down exist. Of course, some museums are full-day experiences, and some visitors take all day to visit a small museum, while some visitors simply use the bathrooms and leave. All these dwell figures are averages.

Naturally, many rough assumptions have gone into this seemingly exact figure, which is best used as an approximation.

PLANNING WORKSHEET

Given the current program, the average individual dwell times are likely to be as shown in table 100.2.

See "15. Bibliography for Museums" for citation reference.

Table 100.2   Estimated per Capita Average Dwell Time: Stable Year; Summer Weekend (Assuming Peak Capacity: XX Visitors in the Building at Once)

Spaces Source/Formula	A Dwell Time (Minutes) Assume	B Capture Percentage of Visitors Assume	C Per Capita Dwell (Minutes) (A) × (B)	D Per Capita Share of Dwell (C)/ Total Dwell Time	E Peak Demand (Peak Capacity) × (D)
Parking	05	95%			
Entrance	15	100%			
Orientation theater	15	50%			
Exhibit gallery I	10	50%			
Exhibit gallery II	20	70%			
Exhibit gallery III	20	70%			
Exhibit gallery IV	30	70%			
Temporary exhibition	40	80%			
Feature theater	50	60%			
Kids' space	60	20%			
Gift shop	10	80%			
Café	20	45%			
Amenities	5	50%			
Totals				100%	XX visitors

Section 101

Visitor Services

Seasonality and Utilization

INTRODUCTION

This section looks at visitor services with regard to seasonality, public hours of operation, and utilization by mode. It provides you with templates and formulas that you can adapt to your museum.

VISITOR SERVICES: SEASONALITY AND UTILIZATION

Seasonal Variation for Attendance and Staffing

Table 101.1   Sample Seasonal Variation (U.S. Family Museum)

Season	Average Monthly Share	Months	Weeks	Weekly Operating Hours	Dates
Low	5.6%	5	22	47	September–January
Medium	9%	4	18	47	February—May
Peak	12%	3	12	68	June–August

Table 101.2   School-Based Seasonality

	Weeks	The Museum
School weeks available for tours	30	
School weeks not available for tours	7	
Summer weeks	11	
Miscellaneous and holidays	4	
Total	52	52

Note: Number of school weeks may vary by district, school, and weather.

Table 101.3   Attendance Share by Month: Seven Sample Museums

	CM #1	CM #2	Zoo #1	Zoo #2	Planetarium	Natural History	Living History
January	4.0%	8.4%	0.8%	0.0%	8.9%	6.7%	0.6%
February	10.7%	8.7%	1.7%	0.0%	8.6%	8.0%	1.2%
March	11.2%	9.1%	6.8%	2.3%	11.7%	8.6%	2.0%
April	12.5%	10.2%	11.0%	5.8%	12.3%	9.4%	5.8%
May	4.1%	9.8%	21.6%	8.7%	10.2%	9.0%	12.7%
June	6.4%	8.6%	16.5%	25.6%	6.1%	11.0%	14.2%
July	17.3%	9.9%	14.1%	25.2%	5.3%	11.2%	16.8%
August	18.1%	8.9%	12.6%	22.2%	7.5%	11.8%	19.5%
September	5.4%	3.2%	6.1%	5.2%	3.8%	8.2%	10.8%
October	3.0%	6.4%	6.0%	2.9%	9.1%	5.6%	10.2%
November	3.2%	7.8%	1.2%	1.0%	8.7%	6.4%	2.5%
December	4.2%	9.1%	1.4%	0.9%	7.7%	4.1%	3.7%
Total	100.1%	100.0%	100.0%	100.0%	100.0%	100.0%	100.0%

Note: CM = children's museums.

UTILIZATION BY MODE

Table 101.4   [Public Space XX]: Utilization per Operating Mode

Mode	A No. of Annual Engagements	B Turnover Time (Hours)	C Annual Hours (Hours)	D Design Capacity (People)	E Utilization Rate (%)
Source	Data	Data	Minutes/60	Choice (No. of Square FeetSF)	(A/(C/B))/D
Public mode	Visitors				
School/youth mode	Visitors				
Program mode	Participants				
Camp-in mode	Participants				
Sponsored event mode	Participants				
Function rental mode	Participants				
Utility modes	Engagements			0	N/A
Dark/closed mode	Engagements			0	N/A
Annual engagements			8,760 hours		

HOURS OF OPERATION

Table 101.5   Sample Public Opening Hours: Museum Galleries

Museum Galleries: Sample A	
Winter Schedule (Tuesday after Labor Day to February 28)	
Tuesday–Saturday	10:00 a.m.–5:00 p.m. (school groups at 9:00 a.m. by reservation)
Sunday	12:00 or 1:00–5:00 p.m.
Monday	Closed
Night	One night per week until 8:00 p.m.
Extended Schedule (March 1 to Labor Day)	
Monday–Saturday	10:00 a.m.–5:00 p.m.
Sunday	12:00 or 1:00–5:00 p.m.
Night	One night per week until 8:00 p.m.
Museum Galleries: Sample B	
Winter	
Tuesday–Saturday	9:30 a.m.–5:30 p.m.
Sunday	10:30 a.m.–5:30 p.m.
Monday	Closed
Summer (Memorial Day to Labor Day)	
Sunday–Thursday	9:30 a.m.–5:30 p.m.
Friday and Saturday	9:30 a.m.–9:30 p.m.

Table 101.6   Sample Public Opening Hours: Other Visitor Venues

Feature Theater (Scheduled Shows Only)	
Winter	
Tuesday and Wednesday	11:00 a.m., 1:00 p.m., 2:00 p.m., 3:00 p.m.
Thursday and Friday	11:00 a.m., 1, 2, 3:00 p.m., 7:00 p.m., 8:00 p.m.
Saturday	10:00 a.m., 11:00 a.m., 1:00 p.m., 2:00 p.m., 3:00 p.m., 4:00 p.m., 7:00 p.m., 8:00 p.m.
Sunday	11:00 a.m., 1:00 p.m., 2:00 p.m., 3:00 p.m., 4:00 p.m.
School shows:	
Monday–Friday	10:00 a.m. and 12 noon
Summer	
Monday	11:00 a.m., 1:00 p.m., 2:00 p.m., 3:00 p.m., 4:00 p.m. (evening functions)
Tuesday–Thursday	11:00 a.m., 1:00 p.m., 2:00 p.m., 3:00 p.m., 4:00 p.m., 7:00 p.m., 8:00 p.m.
Friday	11:00 a.m., 1, 2, 3:00 p.m., 4:00 p.m., 7:00 p.m., 8:00 p.m., 9:00 p.m.
Saturday	10:00 a.m., 11:00 a.m., 12 noon, 1:00 p.m., 2:00 p.m., 3:00 p.m., 4:00 p.m., 7:00 p.m., 8:00 p.m., 9:00 p.m.
Sunday	11:00 a.m., 12 noon, 1:00 p.m., 2:00 p.m., 3:00 p.m., 4:00 p.m., 7:00 p.m., 8:00 p.m.

PLANNING WORKSHEETS

Table 101.7   Typical Attendance Share by Day of Week: Family and School Museum

Day	Sample		The Museum		
	September–February	March–August	Low	Medium	Peak
Sunday	21%	18%			
Monday	Closed	10%			
Tuesday	13%	12%			
Wednesday	14%	13%			
Thursday	14%	14%			
Friday	17%	16%			
Saturday	21%	17%			
Total	100%	100%	100%	100%	100%

Table 101.8   Summary Share by Month: Family and School Museum

Month	5 Year Avg for 25 ASTC Museums	The Museum	Goal
January	7%		
February	8%		
March	10%		
April	10%		
May	9%		
June	9%		
July	10%		
August	10%		
September	5%		
October	6%		
November	7%		
December	8%		
Total	**100%**	**100%**	**100%**

Table 101.9   Daily Opening Hours: XX Season

	Grounds	*Free Zone*	*Gift Shop*	*Café*	*Museum Galleries*	*Theater*	*Learning Center*
6:00							
7.00							
8:00							
9:00							
10:00							
11:00							
12:00							
13:00							
14:00							
15:00							
16:00							
17:00							
18:00							
19:00							
20:00							
21:00							
22:00							
23:00							
24:00							
Hours							

Day of Week _____

Index

About the Authors

John W. Jacobsen, president of White Oak Associates, Inc., has over four decades of international experience as a museum analyst, planner, and producer. He was also associate director of the Museum of Science in Boston. During that time, the Museum served 2.2 million visitors during a 12-month period, an unsurpassed record. Before that management position and since then, Jacobsen and White Oak have led strategic planning and marketing initiatives for over 100 museums through hundreds of commissions. Recent projects represent over a billion dollars of actual and anticipated investment in new and expanding museums internationally. All White Oak's museum analysis and planning projects integrate economic and attendance indicators with conceptual and creative planning.

Mr. Jacobsen is the founding manager of the Museum Film Network (1985), the Planetarium Show Network (1988), the Ocean Film Network (1992), the American Alliance of Museums' (AAM) Professional Committee on Green Museums (PIC Green 2008), and the Digital Immersive Giant Screen Specifications (DIGSS 1.0, 2011). With Ms. Jeanie Stahl, Mr. Jacobsen formed the White Oak Institute in 2007, a nonprofit dedicated to research-based museum innovation, with completed awards and contracts with the National Science Foundation, the Institute of Museums and Library Services, the AAM, and the Association of Children's Museums (ACM) to develop fieldwide standards and data collection fields. Mr. Jacobsen's extensive writings on museum topics have appeared in *Curator*, the *Journal of Museum Management and Curatorship, Informal Learning Review*, and *Museum*, and he has presented at AAM, ASTC, GSCA, MMA, NEMA, ACM, and other museum conferences. Mr. Jacobsen's BA and MFA are from Yale University.

Victor A. Becker, director of program development for White Oak Associates, Inc., is a designer with particular expertise at the interface between museum functions and architecture. Mr. Becker has developed the architectural program and articulated the qualities and conditions that the owner should expect from the architect and the general contractor for all of White Oak's new and expanding museum clients. He has developed Delta gallery concepts and specializes in the geometries of theaters and other presentation spaces, particularly the complex spatial relationships inherent in large-format theaters—both flat screens and domes. Mr. Becker has served as guest architectural critic for Columbia, Yale, and Cornell schools of architecture.

Duane Kocik, chief financial officer and vice president of administration and finance (retired) at the Science Museum of Minnesota, has provided outside perspectives on budgeting, looking at the ratios among different types of expenses and revenues and keeping the entire process both realistic and in tune with current museum practices for all of White Oak's economic models for White Oak's museum clients.

Jeanie Stahl, vice president of White Oak Associates, Inc., has been with the firm for three decades, bringing her expertise in research, finance, and project management. She developed and maintains an extensive database on museums and their communities. She works closely with White Oak's clients to develop business plans that are sustainable and realistic. She has been a pioneer in developing key performance indicators (KPIs) for the museum industry and models for comparing museum performance among groups of peer institutions. Ms. Stahl was instrumental in developing the KPIs, performance indicators, and reports for the Association of Children's Museum Online Benchmark Calculator and was on the Association of Science-Technology Center's Trends and Analysis Committee, which oversaw the annual survey of its members. Contributions to this *Compendium* focused on market analysis, museum attendance, and financial operations.